# Political Socialization,
# Citizenship Education,
# and Democracy

# Political Socialization, Citizenship Education, and Democracy

Edited by
**ORIT ICHILOV**

Teachers College, Columbia University
New York and London

Published by Teachers College Press, 1234 Amsterdam Avenue
New York, NY 10027

*Library of Congress Cataloging-in-Publication Data*

Political socialization, citizenship education, and democracy / edited
    by Orit Ichilov.
        p.   cm.
    Based on papers presented at the International Symposium on
Political Socialization and Citizenship Education for Democracy,
held at Tel Aviv University, March 1987.
    Includes bibliographical references.
    ISBN 0-8077-2974-4 (alk. paper). — ISBN 0-8077-2973-6 (pbk. :
alk. paper)
    1. Political socialization — Congresses.   2. Civics — Study and
teaching — Congresses.   3. Democracy — Congresses.        I. Ichilov, Orit.
II. International Symposium on Political Socialization and
Citizenship Education for Democracy (1987 : Tel Aviv University)
JA 76.P5929   1989                                                89-5177
306.2 — dc20                                                          CIP

ISBN 0-8077-2974-4
ISBN 0-8077-2973-6 (pbk.)

Printed on acid-free paper

Manufactured in the United States of America

96  95  94  93  92  91  90  89      8  7  6  5  4  3  2  1

# Contents

# Acknowledgments

This volume has its roots in the International Symposium on Political Socialization and Citizenship Education for Democracy, held at Tel Aviv University in March of 1987; indeed, all of the chapters in this book, with the exception of Chapter 5, have their origin as papers prepared for that conference.

I am most grateful to Tel Aviv University, its School of Education, and the Sociology of Education and the Community Unit for taking the symposium under their academic auspices and providing financial support.

Both the symposium and the publication of the present volume were made possible through the generous support and assistance of Raphael Recanati, Stanley Stern, Meir Ezra & Son (1980) Company, Ltd., the American Jewish Committee, the P.E.F. Israel Endowment Fund, and the Israel Foundation Trustees.

A word of thanks is due to Roberta Sigel, Stanley Renshon, and Richard Merelman for their great help and good advice in the preparation of this volume. I would like to extend my sincere appreciation to Andre Mazawi, my teaching and research assistant, for his dedicated help throughout all stages of this project.

# Political Socialization, Citizenship Education, and Democracy

# Introduction

There is a growing awareness that democracy's vitality and continuity greatly depend upon transmitting to each young generation the visions of the democratic way of life and the commitment to it. This book is based on the premise that political socialization may stimulate the development of ideas and practices that may help to enhance the democratic way of life. Our major concern is to elaborate on the linkage between political socialization and democracy.

Political socialization has been dedicated traditionally to the exploration of the universal processes of induction into *any type* of regime. Such a broad understanding of how citizenship orientations emerge and change over time provides important insights into the ways by which the meanings of democracy can best be transmitted and reinforced, and by which the political democratic culture can be reproduced and enriched. The unique characteristics of democracy and democratic citizenship, however, must also be given careful consideration. From both philosophical and practical vantage points, the viability of democracy greatly depends on the voluntary acceptance of the democratic way of life by citizens.

Yet growing up in a democracy does not by itself guarantee the reproduction of the democratic political culture from generation to generation. Democracy is a most complex concept, from philosophical, historical, and institutional-structural viewpoints. It combines, for example, ideas and practices that can be conflicting, such as majority rule and minority rights. Democratic citizenship requires more than passive compliance: Citizens are also required to make choices, decisions, and judgments, to criticize and to object. Decision-making processes in democracy may seem cumbersome, projecting indecisiveness. Thus, there always exists a possibility that citizens would wish to replace democracy by installing a rigorous and uncompromising leader, thereby opting for a nondemocratic regime.

The difficulties that youngsters have in comprehending democracy have been reported in studies that were carried out within a variety of Western democracies (Abramson & Hennessey, 1970; Dennis, Lindberg, McCrone, & Stiefbold, 1968; Ichilov, Bar-Tal, & Mazawi, 1987; Sigel, 1979). Adults within modern, industrial, large-scale democracies have also

1

been reported to express often a low sense of political efficacy and political trust, and to be apathetic or alienated. There is a need to bring new perspectives into political socialization which will enable us to deal specifically with issues related to socialization for democracy. This is the major concern of this volume.

Political socialization and citizenship education have been dominated by a narrow perception of democracy as singularly political. This view has its roots in liberal philosophy, which advocates the separation of the "political" from the "social," of the "public" from the "private." Accordingly, democratic citizenship takes place in the political and public arenas, while personal fulfillment is to be sought in the social and private spheres (Levine, 1981; Macpherson, 1977; Pateman, 1979). This view is also based upon system theory within political science, which considers citizenship to consist primarily of expressing support for and making demands of a political system (Easton & Dennis, 1973). This narrow conception has directed scholarly attention primarily to the acquisition of behaviors and attitudes that are related to the political system, such as voting, party identification, political trust, and political efficacy. Citizenship involvement in causes, movements, organizations, and groups, such as the Parent-Teacher Association, Girl Scouts, or a church, have been neglected as nonpolitical. Not until the work of Verba and Nie (1972) were some of these activities clearly labeled as political. Furthermore, civic education has focused primarily on the legal and structural aspects of government, exposing youngsters mainly to a narrow role model of democratic citizenship (Ichilov, 1988; Oliner, 1983).

The premise on which we have based this volume is that the narrow view represents only one facet of democracy and democratic citizenship. It overlooks an important philosophical tradition, that of participatory democracy, which advocates the extension of democracy into all social spheres. The latter approach allows for additional arenas for democratic citizenship, such as sex-role egalitarianism, workplace democracy, and environmental concerns.

Both the narrow and broad conceptions of democratic citizenship represent equally legitimate democratic philosophies, which call for diverse patterns of citizenship. Preferring the one over the other remains a value judgment that each individual and society should freely confront. Our argument is that the narrow view of democracy does not capture the full range of ideas and practices concerning the democratic way of life. What this book attempts to do is to illuminate these neglected aspects of democratic citizenship.

Political socialization theories and studies have emphasized the importance of early experiences for the formation of citizenship orientations.

By the end of high school, one's "political character" is considered by some to have almost fully and permanently emerged (Easton & Dennis, 1965, 1967; Hess & Torney, 1967; Merelman, 1969, 1971). Our approach is that political socialization should be viewed as a lifelong process. The dynamics of modern living, including marriage and parenthood, the legitimation of a multicareer life, and social and geographical mobility represent some adult-life experiences that may reshape political attitudes and behaviors.

This book is also unique in bringing under one cover the works of an interdisciplinary team representing the areas of political science, psychology, sociology, economics, and communication, and in attempting to draw the educational implications from each of the works.

The five major divisions of this volume represent topics that have had enduring relevance for political socialization. Most of the works, however, address these topics using fresh approaches.

In Part I, "Political Socialization and Democracy," are three works that relate political socialization to the understanding of the functioning of democracy. In Chapter 1, Ichilov sets the agenda for the volume and lays out its central themes. Drawing on democratic theory, she provides a broad definition of democracy, which makes it possible to incorporate new dimensions into democratic citizenship. She identifies the dimensions that are used as building blocks of citizenship in democracy and suggests how these may be clustered to form a great variety of citizenship role patterns. From these may be derived a taxonomy of democratic citizenship orientations, as well as guidelines for a variety of research and educational pursuits.

DiRenzo presents in Chapter 2 a model of socialization that links two intellectual traditions, the "human needs" approach and the "societal requisites" tradition of functional analysis. He argues that, ideally, the kinds of personality structures that develop in the process of socialization should be congruent with the sociopolitical nature of society. At the same time, societies should be responsive to basic human needs. His model takes into account the limitations imposed both by human needs and by social systems and then delineates the psychosocial linkages between the two in modern democratic political systems. He argues that democracies, being responsive to their constituencies, provide the optimal conditions for simultaneously satisfying human needs and societal requisites.

In Chapter 3, Merelman addresses an overlooked aspect of political learning: the psychological mechanisms whereby children conceptualize political conflict in varying political regimes, and how they internalize it. He makes a distinction between contested regimes, described as regimes with no single legitimate political authority; and uncontested regimes, especially democratic ones, in which the majority of the population ac-

cepts a single authority. Merelman concludes that, in both types of regimes, childhood learning reproduces the fundamental mode of conflict
peculiar to the regime.

In Part II, "Patterns of Political Socialization in Democracies: Models
and Controversies," three different models conceptualizing processes of
acquisition of political attitudes and behavior are presented.

Sears addresses in Chapter 4 the issue of persistence of preadult political socialization residues through adulthood. The author provides a critical
overview of the literature and concludes that the issue has not been adequately treated from theoretical and research viewpoints. Sears argues that
attitudinal stability could reflect either strong resistance to change or simply a lack of pressure to change. Neither change nor the lack of it, therefore, necessarily reflects the strength of the underlying disposition. He
suggests that the genesis of political socialization research has been largely
in normative concerns driven by the perceived need to socialize youngsters
into those political orientations that parents and society applaud. This
approach does not take into account development and change through the
life-span. A more plausible approach, in his view, would be to ask what the
conditions are for training people to be open and responsive to new realities, as opposed to training them to be loyal to the reigning norms of their
childhood.

In the next chapter, Torney-Purta provides a new link between political socialization research and psychological theory about cognitive development, by applying the notion of schemata to the study of political socialization. Her work deals with the schemata of the political system, both
domestic and international, which young people are continually formulating and reformulating. Torney-Purta also illustrates a method for measuring and presenting these schemata.

Bar-Tal and Saxe's work (Chapter 6) interweaves generic principles of
social cognition with a specific focus on problems of political knowledge
acquisition and socialization for democracy. The authors develop a general
model of the process of political socialization which is intended to complement other sociological and psychological approaches. This is done by
incorporating elements of each in an analysis of how individuals come to
understand the political world.

In Part III, "Institutional Context of Political Socialization in Democracy," five works are included. The first part of Chaffee and Yang's work
(Chapter 7) summarizes some generalizations from two decades of empirical studies on mass-media effects on young people's political behavior.
They then go on to offer alternative conceptions to the traditional perception of the media as agents of socialization. These ideas are based on new
assumptions about both communication processes and the nature of politi-

cal socialization. Chaffee and Young consider the individual to be active in the task of becoming a political person, and they discuss the role of TV and the written media in this process. Their new approach is applicable not only to initial socialization into a political culture, but also to processes of resocialization, as indicated by their data on Korean immigrants living in the San Francisco Bay Area.

Levin argues in Chapter 8 that the schools in democratic and capitalist societies are expected to contribute to the formation of two types of personalities in the same person. On the one hand, it is necessary to shape the democratic personalities necessary for individuals to participate as expected in the governance of public institutions. On the other hand, the schools are asked to create workers who can operate under hierarchical and authoritarian workplace regimes. The question that Levin addresses is whether a movement toward workplace democracy would more nearly integrate the personalities that we wish to socialize by setting a more nearly uniform set of principles for adult competencies and the school experience. Levin addresses some specific workplace changes that are consistent with the economic imperative, as well as the educational practices needed to bring them about.

Westholm, Lindquist, and Niemi address in Chapter 9 the issue of the apparent paradox concerning school effects upon the political growth of children and adolescents. More precisely, among adults a clear relationship was demonstrated between level of education and a variety of citizenship orientations. In contrast, however, a host of school-related factors has shown weak or nonexistent effects upon youngsters. The authors go some distance toward resolving the paradox implied by these conflicting results, as well adding new evidence to the empirical foundation on which the controversy rests. Their study of the ability of a representative Swedish sample of 16- to 18-year-olds to identify major international organizations and events suggests genuine curricular effects.

In Chapter 10, Yogev and Shapira discuss the socializing effects of youth organizations in different types of societies and political regimes. Drawing on data from Costa Rica, Israel, Malawi, and the Ivory Coast, they demonstrate that youth organizations are instrumental for inculcating three sets of orientations in the younger generation: diffuse regime support, support of partisan ideologies, and support of modernity and higher career aspirations. The authors discuss the social conditions that account for the effectiveness of such groups as agents of citizenship socialization.

Kahane and Rapoport's point of departure in the next chapter is that people who participate in voluntary associations that are relatively free of compulsion and external constraints are likely to become more committed to democracy than those who have not been exposed to similar experiences. Kahane and Rapoport identify four organizational codes — formal, informal, professional, and primary — which can be found to various degrees in different types of bodies. They argue that the predominance of the informal code accounts for the effectiveness of voluntary organizations in developing commitment to democracy. These arguments are demonstrated through the analysis of the structural codes of youth movements in Israel.

Part IV, "Social Movements and Political Socialization in Democracy," focuses on the role new movements play as socializers. Sigel's Chapter 12 and Sapiro's Chapter 13 deal with the women's movement, while Milbrath's Chapter 14 addresses the environmentalist movement.

Sigel suggests that the study of adult women's experiences may have important implications for the political socialization of the younger generation. She asserts that, notwithstanding women's growing consciousness of their disadvantaged status, their gender-role orientations reflect a good deal of ambivalence. Women tend to incorporate into their gender perspective their construction of the male perspective. To the extent that the latter conflicts with their own ideal, women experience confusion and tension in their gender perspectives. She suggests public school education could do much to dispel this ambivalence. Both males and females should be socialized from an early age to accept women's active political role as an intrinsic part of their democratic citizenship, as both genders do in the case of men.

Sapiro regards the contemporary women's movement as an agent of democratic socialization, with effects on both participants and the wider culture. She focuses primarily on one outcome: the development of gender consciousness as a politicized form of social identity. Sapiro argues that expanding the range of public and private roles women play and encouraging women to exert greater influence over their own destinies will advance the cause of democracy.

In the final chapter of Part IV, Milbrath argues that environmentalism is a product of democracy, at the same time that it promotes the democratic way of life. He believes that knowledge of ecosystems and technological influences is a requisite for understanding social systems, and that environmental and technical considerations will be the predominant influences on the politics of the twenty-first century. Environmental education should thus become part of political socialization in democracies.

Part V, "Socialization for Democracy: A Lifelong Process," includes two works that extend the concerns of this volume beyond childhood political socialization. In Chapter 15, Conway examines the implications of public-choice theory for political participation. She examines the role of groups in the political process and the rationality of a group-based approach to political participation. She concludes that education for democratic citizenship would promote higher levels of effective participation if ways of promoting involvement through group activity received more emphasis.

Renshon discusses in Chapter 16 the numerous political, pedagogical, ethical, and practical issues that the idea of specialized education and preparation for political leaders may raise in a democracy. Among these are whether such education is not elitist and inherently antidemocratic; whether successful political experience is not a sufficient form of education; and what forms the education of leaders might take. Renshon addresses these and other issues in the context of a discussion of adult political socialization theory, especially as it focuses on the nature of political work and of personal and professional development in adulthood.

## REFERENCES

Abramson, P. R., & Hennessey, T. M. (1970). Beliefs about democracy among British adolescents. *Political Studies, 18*, 239–242.

Dennis, J., Lindberg, L., McCrone, D., & Stiefbold, R. (1968). Political socialization to democratic orientations in four Western systems. *Comparative Political Studies, 1*, 71–101.

Easton, D., & Dennis, J. (1965). The child's image of government. *Annals of the American Academy of Political and Social Science, 361*, 40–57.

Easton, D., & Dennis, J. (1967). The child's acquisition of regime norms: Political efficacy. *American Political Science Review, 6*(1), 25–38.

Easton, D., & Dennis, J. (1973). A political theory of political socialization. In J. Dennis (Ed.), *Socialization to politics* (pp. 32–55). New York: John Wiley.

Hess, R. D., & Torney, J. V. (1967). *The development of political attitudes in childhood*. Chicago: Aldine.

Ichilov, O. (1988). *Education for citizenship in democracy: Policy and contents* [in Hebrew]. (Position paper no. 5.88). Tel Aviv University, School of Education, Sociology of Education and the Community Unit.

Ichilov, O., Bar-Tal, D., & Mazawi, A. (1987). *The perception of democracy and its evaluation among Israeli youth* [in Hebrew]. (Research report 1-87). Tel Aviv University, School of Education, Sociology of Education and the Community Unit.

Levine, A. (1981). *Liberal democracy: A critique of its theory*. New York: Columbia University Press.

Macpherson, C. B. (1977). *The life and times of liberal democracy*. New York: Oxford University Press.

Merelman, R. M. (1969). The development of political ideology: A framework for the analysis of political socialization. *American Political Science Review, 63,* 750–767.

Merelman, R. M. (1971). The development of policy thinking in adolescence. *American Political Science Review, 65,* 1033–1047.

Oliner, P. (1983). Putting "community" into citizenship education: The need for prosociality. *Theory and Research in Social Education, 11,* 65–81.

Pateman, C. B. (1979). *Participation and democratic theory.* New York: Cambridge University Press.

Sigel, R. S. (1979). Students' comprehension of democracy and its application to conflict situations. *International Journal of Political Education, 2,* 47–65.

Verba, S., & Nie, N. (1972). *Participation in America.* New York: Harper & Row.

# PART I

# Political Socialization and Democracy

# 1

# Dimensions and Role Patterns of Citizenship in Democracy

## ORIT ICHILOV

The clarification of key concepts is an indispensable part of theory construction. As Merton (1964) has observed, "concepts, then, constitute the definitions (or prescriptions) of what is to be observed; they are the variables between which empirical relationships are to be sought" (p. 89).

Measurable outcomes are a central component of any socialization theory, yet traditional definitions of the anticipated outcomes of the political socialization process have been vague. These include, for example, acquisition of political orientations (Easton & Dennis, 1969); learning of values, attitudes, and other behaviors (Hess & Torney, 1967); acquisition of political norms and behaviors acceptable to an ongoing political system (Sigel, 1965); and political maturation of citizens (Dawson & Prewitt, 1969). The common denominator of these definitions is that they are content free and may apply equally to any kind of regime. They provide no clues concerning the norms, behaviors, and orientations appropriate for democratic societies. Furthermore, they have directed scholarly attention primarily to the study of isolated orientations rather than to those that are grouped into clusters and patterns.

Such perceptions of political socialization are rooted in the system theory of political socialization, whose most prominent exponents are probably Easton and Dennis (1973). They interpret the political system as "a vast conversion process through which the input of demands and supports [of citizens] are transformed by various structures and processes into outputs [of political authorities], that is, into authoritative decisions and actions" (p. 33). This is a highly mechanistic view of the interrelationships between citizens and the political system, where socialization to politics is narrowly seen as an instrumental process of "enabling some kind of political system to persist" (p. 36).

In the study presented in this chapter, the preparation of a society's members for the assumption of citizenship is considered to be the major objective and outcome of the political socialization process within democratic societies. I will thus attempt primarily to conceptualize and clarify the content and structure of the citizenship role in a democracy, drawing mainly on democratic theory and role theory. My point of departure is the assumption that, in order to capture adequately the essence of citizenship in a democracy, its characteristics must be outlined and the corresponding citizenship orientations explicitly stated. Unless scholars thoroughly conceptualize the dimensions of citizenship, they will be limited in their ability to identify antecedent conditions for their emergence. Democratic theory enables us to define citizenship more broadly, so that it includes different notions of (1) the relationships between individuals and their communities and (2) the quality of social life.

## CONCEPTUALIZING THE CITIZEN ROLE IN A DEMOCRACY

Democracy has had so many incarnations over various periods and in different societies, and it elicits such a variety of meanings for individuals and groups, that one really should speak of *democracies* rather than *democracy*. The corresponding citizenship patterns are just as varied and consequently cannot be summed up by any single model. Using democratic-theory literature, my concern is to identify the dimensions that are used as building blocks for numerous role models of citizenship in a democracy. Unlike many democratic theorists, I will not attempt to construct a single coherent and consistent model of citizenship out of the wide array of democratic ideas. I shall also avoid the issues and problems that are brought up in the vast literature pertaining to each dimension of citizenship. Instead, I will sum up these dimensions in a model suggesting how they may be clustered to form a variety of citizenship patterns, any of which the members of society may adopt. Citizenship role models may vary with regard to their selected scope and intensity and the degree to which they represent an integrated whole with internal consistency. Furthermore, my aim is not to advocate or justify a specific model of democracy and citizenship. I maintain that a variety of citizenship patterns is a legitimate manifestation of democratic pluralism.

An examination of socialization outcomes inevitably leads to consideration of the concept of *role*, in our case, *citizen role*. Based on role theory, both structural and interactionist perspectives are useful for examining the nature of the citizen role. From a structural perspective, citizenship may be regarded as a formal role that is legally defined; however, this outlines only the minimum standards of adequate performance. Many models of democracy—for example, representational versus participatory democracy—project different role expectations beyond the formal, legal definition of citizenship. Furthermore, empirical studies of the perceptions of the "good citizen" have captured a great variety of patterns, depending upon regional, socioeconomic, and ethnic differences, among others (Almond & Verba, 1963). From an interactionist perspective, this may suggest that citizenship consists of an informal component that is being shaped, rather than intentionally transmitted and learned, within interpersonal contexts, through a more fluid process of negotiation (George, 1983). Many aspects of citizenship are thus voluntary and based on self-selection, rather than being rigidly structured and defined.

## BEHAVIORAL AND ATTITUDINAL DIMENSIONS OF CITIZENSHIP

The various models of democracy share the notion that it essentially involves participation and a wide range of public choices. After all, totalitarian regimes often stimulate high levels of participation, but the absence of real political choice renders such participation meaningless, except in an emotional or symbolic sense. Differences exist, however, regarding the scope, spheres, objectives, and means of citizen participation. In this section, several questions concerning participation will be examined. First, what are the spheres in which citizens are expected to participate as citizens? Second, what are the basic orientations that should underlie citizen participation? Third, what are the legitimate objectives that citizens may wish to achieve through participation, and what are the legitimate means for pursuing these objectives in democracy?

### Spheres of Citizenship

The liberal and participatory models of democracy represent two ends of a continuum with regard to the spheres of citizenship. Liberalism supposes a radical separation of the political from the civic, of politics from society. The political domain is the realm of the state, the government, and of certain organizations such as political parties and pressure groups, which attempt to affect government decisions and actions (Dahl, 1963; Levine, 1981; Milbrath, 1965). Citizens operate in the political domain, while persons' self-realization and fulfillment take place in the social/civic domain. Milbrath puts it this way:

> The politics of non-governmental organizations are excluded from this definition [of politics]. Behavior which affects the decisional outcomes of a church or a corporation, for example, even if it were typically political in form and content, would not be considered political behavior by this definition. Politics

now can be defined as the process by which decisions about governmental outcomes are made. [pp. 1–2]

Participatory democracy, on the other hand, advocates citizens' participation in all social-political domains. Theorists embracing this view often start out by pointing to the shortcomings of both representational and liberal democracy, bringing up several arguments in support of participation (Macpherson, 1977; Pateman, 1979). First, it has been argued that democracy is a form of authority that accommodates individuals' interests better than other types. It should, therefore, be applied to all social concerns. Furthermore, Pateman (1979) regards smaller associations, which are run based on the participation and deep involvement of their members, as the means for promoting the development of desirable character traits. Second, it has been argued that the liberal idea of the separation of the political from the civic or the public from the private is false. In reality, much of people's world is shaped by government and politics, including such intimate areas as sexuality, reproduction, and the education of one's children. The principles of participation and democracy should, therefore, be extended beyond the political domain — in the liberal sense — and into the civil area. Participatory society, rather than participatory democracy, becomes the ideal. Accordingly, citizens are expected to operate as citizens in the various social domains — for example, the family, the school, and the church — as well as in politics.

Not until the work of Verba and Nie (1972), however, were some common nongovernmental activities clearly labeled as political, and a broad definition of citizenship has entered political socialization only recently. Sigel and Hoskin (1981) have extended the narrow definition of citizenship to include "citizen involvement in causes, movements, organizations, or groups — be they PTA or Boy Scouts, suicide prevention centers or the Sierra Club, antivivisection league or dog-curbing crusaders" (p. 40).

The overflow of democratic participatory principles from the "political" into the "social" domain has not remained a theoretical issue. There are numerous examples of citizens' demands to participate in decisions concerning their fate. Physicians' authority, for example, has been assumed to be complete and uncontestable. This has resulted in a highly asymmetrical doctor/patient relationship where the completely dependent patient has been excluded from decisions that concern her or his body, soul, and well-being. The legal doctrine of informed consent can be viewed as a turning point in the ethos of the medical profession, extending citizens' rights for self-determination into the realm of health care. Greater patient participation in the medical decision-making process is based on the realization that the quality of human life is measured not merely by improvements in physical custody, but also by advancement of liberty (Katz, 1984).

In the field of education, attempts have been made to enable the wider participation of those who have traditionally been underrepresented in the various levels of the educational system. Notable examples include ethnic and racial minorities. The struggle for egalitarian gender roles in the family and society and attempts to democratize the school and workplace are additional examples of a growing struggle to apply democratic principles and procedures to diverse social issues.

Another significant distinction among citizenship spheres concerns *national* and *transnational* categories. According to the legal definition, citizenship entails rights and duties within the boundaries of a nation-state. This may be changing with the introduction of transnational organizations such as the European Community, NATO, and the United Nations. The establishment of such organizations marks the recognition that economic well-being, preservation of the environment, and security from nuclear war can only be promoted through international cooperation. Even though channels for broad citizen participation in international organizations have not been established, groups of citizens often organize to make their voices heard concerning international issues. Citizens increasingly want their opinion to count when global decisions are made which affect their lives physically and morally. Citizens' participation thus may not be limited to the national arena, but may extend into the international realm as well (Brzezinski, 1970; Dahl, 1982).

Based on the foregoing distinctions, the role of citizen may be narrowly defined as related exclusively to the local and national political spheres, or broadly defined as also related to a wide array of social concerns, which may be international in scope.

## Participatory Orientation

In this section, the perspectives that participants may adopt toward objects in the various social spheres are discussed. Several important distinctions are made, the first between an *instrumental* versus a *diffuse* orientation, and the second between a *particularistic* versus a *universalistic* orientation. Participants may adopt an instrumental perspective, limiting the citizen role to task-oriented relations with other members of society. Democracy, however, more broadly conceived as a theory of society, suggests that persons are not just means for the satisfaction of needs, but ends in themselves. The diffuse relations that characterize intimate primary groups could be extended to the societal level as well. This would result in the overlapping of the concepts of the "good citizen" and the "good person." Such a diffuse orientation relates to human beings in their entirety, rather than to their specific qualities (Macpherson, 1977; Levine, 1981).

A particularistic orientation is specific to a given society and reflects its unique history, culture, national values, symbols, and institutions. A universalistic orientation represents values such as freedom and equality, which are shared by democratic societies regardless of their particular heritage. These two sets of orientations may often be inconsistent and even in conflict with one another.

Yet another distinction is made among three modes of activity, namely, the *active, passive,* and *inactive* postures toward citizenship objectives. The active/passive dimension discriminates activity of a productive nature—that is, activity directed toward the manipulation of the environment—from activity of a passive or consuming nature, or that has results mainly for the individual. For example, the characterization of a citizen as one who is readily active in public affairs expresses an active orientation, whereas the view of a citizen as one who regularly reads newspapers is a passive orientation. Inactivity, or the absence of action, can represent either resentment or apathy. Resentment corresponds to what Milbrath (1965) has labeled "avoidance," namely, a negative valence between actor and object; apathy expresses indifference toward the object.

A differentiation is also made between *verbal adherence to principles* and *actual behavior*, for example, verbally supporting voting versus actually participating in the elections.

Attitudinal dimensions are considered, too, distinguishing among the *affective, cognitive,* and *evaluative* responses of an actor toward a particular object. From a developmental point of view, an affective response characterizes early stages of development, whereas the cognitive and evaluative dimensions express advanced stages and a more sophisticated understanding of the political and social world. Similarly, according to democratic theory, rational processes are considered superior to affective ones, as they concern citizens' capacity to act responsibly, to evaluate their actions, and to make choices (Pateman, 1979).

Finally, reference is made to the source of motivation, with a distinction being drawn between *external requirement* and *inner* or *voluntary preference*. Acting in response to external requirement reflects a weaker internalization of democratic values and norms and less personal commitment than does voluntary behavior. Furthermore, the concept of self-assumed obligation is a necessary corollary of the liberal idea of individual freedom and equality. It is argued that, if individuals are naturally free and equal, then any restriction of their freedom and equality can only be justified if they voluntarily place themselves in that relationship (Pateman, 1979).

## Participatory Objectives and Means

Consent and dissent are twin aspects of participation in a democracy. Both stem from the ancient philosophical problem of political obligation: Why, or under what conditions and circumstances, are people obliged to obey the law? In democratic theory, obligation to, consent to, and support of the regime have drawn greater attention than dissent and disobedience. Two special reasons for obedience that are unique to democracy are often put forth. First, the vision of democracy as a society based on justice, freedom, and equality for all citizens alike obliges citizens to comply. Second, it is argued that citizens' participation in decision making (via elections, for example) gives rise to an obligation to act as if they had consented to be bound by the results of this procedure.

The justification of civil disobedience has been attempted from a variety of philosophical premises, notably the Socratic view of individuals' freedom of conscience, and the existentialist idea of alienation (Camus, 1951). Democratic theory realizes the legitimacy of dissent under specific circumstances. According to Locke (1964), for example, people are entitled to resist the incursions of the state if their independence, way of life, or fundamental rights are threatened by it. The articulation of the idea and methods of civil disobedience, however, is fairly recent. The Nuremberg verdicts and the Eichmann trial have advanced the acceptance of the view that the autonomy of the individual conscience is a vital resource in our highly technological and bureaucratized modern civilization. It is sometimes the obligation and not merely the right of individuals to disobey the law. There have been a number of examples of civil disobedience campaigns in recent history, notably those led by Mahatma Gandhi and Martin Luther King. In the 1960s, demonstrations and other manifestations of civil disobedience became daily occurrences in which large and varied segments of the public participated (Etzioni, 1970).

These developments revitalized scholarly interest in the dissent facet of individuals' political obligation. Recent justifications of disobedience relate to both the inherent inconsistencies within democratic models and the imperfections of liberal, representational modern democratic societies (Arrow, 1951; Etzioni, 1970; Levine, 1981; Macpherson, 1977; Pateman, 1979; Singer, 1973; Zashin, 1972). Civil disobedience is considered an attempt to produce change through unconventional methods when conventional methods are unlikely to produce the necessary or desirable outcomes. Etzioni (1970) argues, for example, that "demonstrations help to reduce the inequality among the member groupings of society in terms of their access to political tools; they add to the tools particularly appropriate to the middle and upper classes, one which is particularly suited to the under-privileged and young" (p. 20). Macpherson (1977) maintains that the movement of liberal democracy within large nation-states in the direction of fuller participation may require mechanisms other than the standard party system.

Civil disobedience, therefore, while mostly latent, must always be a possibility within a democracy. This idea may be accessible to relatively few and acceptable to fewer still. However, as Dahl (1966) has noted concerning opposition parties, "That there might legitimately exist an organized group within the political system to oppose, criticize, and if possible oust the leading officials of government was until recently an unfamiliar and generally unacceptable notion" (p. xvii). Consent and dissent, via conventional and unconventional methods, may become equally legitimate dimensions of citizenship in a democracy.

## CITIZENSHIP ROLE PATTERNS: A STRUCTURAL MODEL

Having outlined the major dimensions out of which role patterns are structured, I will apply Guttman's (1950, 1959, 1964) facet theory to suggest how these factors may be clustered to form numerous profiles of citizenship in a democracy.

As discussed in the previous section, the concept of citizenship may be analyzed by means of 10 dimensions that differentiate among the various aspects of this role. These dimensions have been further divided and discussed in terms of eight dichotomous facets and two three-dimensional facets, all of which are shown in Table 1.1. The ordering of the facets within each dimension represents a hierarchy, with the lower-order items coming first. These facets may range, for example, from "less" to "more" on a particular dimension, or from "easy" to "difficult," or from "simple" to "complex," and so forth. I will now discuss each facet once again, in order to clarify these hierarchical values.

To illustrate, consider the first dimension, which is theoretical versus practical orientation. It differentiates between verbal support of a principle and actual behavior. As noted earlier, it is assumed that verbal commitment alone is less valuable to a democracy than the willingness to engage in actual behavior. There is, however, some interaction between the two, since behavior may not only result from support of a principle but lead to support of one as well.

The second dimension, attitudinal orientation, is broken down into the affective, cognitive, and evaluative facets of response toward a particular object. It is assumed that affection represents a less sophisticated approach than cognition and evaluation. Here, too, the hierarchy is not

**Table 1.1**  The 10 dimensions of citizenship, broken into facets

| | |
|---|---|
| 1. Theoretical vs. Practical<br>  1a. Verbal adherence to<br>      principle<br>  1b. Actual behavior | 6. Value Orientation<br>  6a. Particularistic<br>  6b. Universalistic |
| 2. Attitudinal Orientation<br>  2a. Affective<br>  2b. Cognitive<br>  2c. Evaluative | 7. Participatory Objective<br>  7a. Expression of consent<br>  7b. Expression of dissent |
| 3. Motivational Orientation<br>  3a. External/obligatory<br>  3b. Internal/voluntary | 8. Participatory Means<br>  8a. Conventional<br>  8b. Unconventional |
| 4. Action Orientation<br>  4a. Inactive<br>  4b. Passive<br>  4c. Active | 9. Domains of Citizenship<br>  9a. Political<br>  9b. Civic/social |
| 5. Means/Ends Orientation<br>  5a. Instrumental<br>  5b. Diffuse | 10. Arenas of Citizenship<br>  10a. National<br>  10b. Transnational |

necessarily fixed, since there may be interactions among facets. Evaluation, for example, can reflect emotions and cognition simultaneously.

The third dimension refers to the source of motivation, as seen by the individual, and distinguishes between external/obligatory stimuli and internal/voluntary preference. As noted earlier, acting upon external pressure reflects a weaker internalization of and commitment to social values and norms than does voluntary compliance.

The fourth dimension, action orientation, is comprised of three facets: inactivity, passivity, and activity. It is assumed that inactivity is generally the less desirable response, reflecting apathy and indifference. When inactivity signifies passive resistance, however, or withdrawal due to resentment, it may overlap with either the active or passive facet, depending on the circumstances.

The fifth dimension, means/ends orientation, differentiates between instrumental and diffuse consideration of others. It is assumed that the diffuse perspective is more desirable, as it represents a more total consideration of others, compared to the instrumental view of people merely as the means for furthering personal or societal ends.

Value orientation, the sixth dimension, differentiates between the particularistic and universalistic orientations of actors. In this case, the salience and valence assigned to each perspective depend on the history and heritage of particular societies. In new democracies, for example, it can be assumed that particularistic considerations will take precedence over universalistic ones, whereas in veteran democracies these two facets may be more equally balanced.

In the seventh dimension, participatory objective, a distinction is made between expressions of consent and dissent. While both facets are important, expressions of dissent are considered more difficult, since they usually take more courage than do expressions of consent. Similarly, concerning the eighth dimension, the means of participation, it is assumed that the use of unconventional means usually reveals greater daring and imagination than conventional approaches.

The ninth and tenth dimensions refer to the scope or sphere of citizenship. In both cases, the broader, more inclusive view is considered to be the better. This means relating citizenship to a plurality of civic/social domains, rather than restricting it to the political sphere; it means extending the arena beyond the boundaries of the nation-state. Such an approach reflects a deep sense of civic awareness and involvement.

Based on these 10 dimensions and their facets, it is possible to draw individual and group profiles of citizenship perceptions. These may reflect prescribed orientations; for example, based on the constitution, or on expressions of leaders, it is possible to draw profiles of the desirable citizenship orientations in a democracy. On the aggregate level, it is possible to show which are the most prevalent individual profiles within a group.

The classification of various objects (actions, attitudes, symbols, institutions) is done by positing a mapping sentence (Guttman, 1950, 1959, 1964), which shows the perception of these items by the individual citizen. An item's classification may vary from one dimension to the next, depending on the social setting to which it is related. To illustrate, Figure 1.1 shows a mapping sentence that is based on the structural model of citizenship dimensions presented earlier.[1]

## CONCLUSION

In this chapter, I have attempted to clarify the concept of citizenship in a democracy, relating to both its contents and structure. The dimensions that have been outlined were derived from democratic and role theories, not merely from the study of political systems. Based on the analysis, citizenship orientations can be arranged along a continuum from a narrow

**Figure 1.1** Mapping sentence for various facets of citizenship, as presented in Table 1.1

Individual $X$ perceives citizenship in a democracy as comprised of

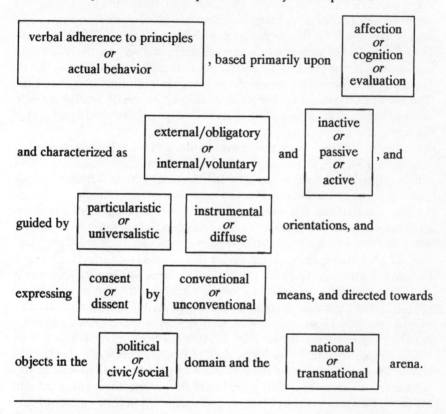

to a broad definition of the citizen role. The narrowest extreme involves verbal support of principles, based primarily on affection, and is characterized as obligatory and passive and is guided by particularistic and instrumental orientations. It expresses consent by conventional means and perceives citizenship as related to objects exclusively in the political domain and within the national arena. The broadest profile consists of actual behavior, based upon cognition and evaluation, and is characterized as voluntary and active and is guided by a diffuse orientation. It reflects a more equal balance between universalistic and particularistic orientations and may include the expression of dissent via unconventional methods.

Citizenship is perceived as related to a plurality of civic/social domains, including the national and the transnational arenas.

These two extremes and the numerous possible profiles ranging between them represent legitimate concepts of citizenship in a democracy, according to a variety of democratic theories. These profiles enable one to capture the richness of the political culture which, according to Almond and Verba (1963), "is the particular distribution of patterns of orientations toward political objects among members of the nation" (p. 13). Following this approach, the citizen role is seen, on the one hand, as determined by the political culture and, on the other hand, as one of its manifestations. The meanings attached to democracy and its components depend not only upon individual differences, but upon the social/cultural settings of which the actors are a part.

The "taxonomy" of citizenship dimensions that has been developed in this chapter has important implications for both political socialization and citizenship education. Scholars may use the categories as a framework for viewing the political socialization process in democracy. The reconceptualization of the citizen role calls for a new definition of the outcomes of the political socialization process, focusing scholarly attention upon role patterns and their variability within various subgroups, their durability and change, and their specific meanings for individuals.

As for existing citizenship education, it seems fair to conclude that it directs youngsters primarily to a rather narrow definition of the citizen role. Citizenship is perceived as exclusively related to the political sphere, emphasizing the legalistic and structural aspects of government, and often avoiding controversial issues. This is reflected both in textbooks and in teacher practice (Ichilov & Nave, 1981, 1984, 1986; Oliner, 1983). The dimensions outlined in this chapter should help educators to expand this definition considerably. For policy makers, curriculum builders, and teachers, this taxonomy may be suggestive of the kinds of objectives that should be pursued through diverse educational activities and materials. It can also be instrumental in reevaluating existing textbooks, teacher-training programs, and classroom and school practices.

I do not consider it my task to decide which is the most desirable model of citizenship — the narrow, the broad, or some sort of intermediate pattern. Instead, as stated at the outset of this chapter, I regard the ability of individuals to choose among patterns of citizenship as a manifestation of democratic pluralism, which is an essential guarantee of freedom. The educational system in a democracy is expected to afford individuals with choices concerning their futures. My view is that the schools should expose youngsters to the full range of citizenship patterns, enabling them to adopt the one that suits them best.

## NOTE

1. It is also possible to map citizenship orientations using Guttman's (1964) method of smallest space analysis. An example of the use of this technique can be found in Ichilov & Nave, 1981.

## REFERENCES

Almond, G., & Verba, S. (1963). *The civic culture*. Princeton, NJ: Princeton University Press.

Arrow, K. (1951). *Social choice and individual values*. New York: John Wiley.

Brzezinski, Z. (1970). *Between two ages*. New York: Viking.

Camus, A. (1951). *The rebel*. New York: Alfred A. Knopf.

Dahl, R. A. (Ed.). (1963). *A preface to democratic theory*. Chicago: University of Chicago Press.

Dahl, R. A. (1966). *Opposition in Western democracies*. New Haven, CT: Yale University Press.

Dahl, R. A. (1982). *Dilemmas of pluralist democracy*. New Haven, CT: Yale University Press.

Dawson, R. E., & Prewitt, K. (1969). *Political socialization*. Boston: Little, Brown.

Easton, D., & Dennis, J. (1969). *Children in the political system*. New York: McGraw-Hill.

Easton, D., & Dennis, J. (1973). A political theory of political socialization. In J. Dennis (Ed.), *Socialization to politics* (pp. 32–55). New York: John Wiley.

Etzioni, A. (1970). *Demonstration democracy*. New York: Gordon & Breach.

George, L. K. (1983). Socialization, roles and identity in later life. *Research in Sociology of Education and Socialization, 4*, 235–264.

Guttman, L. (1950). The problem of attitude and opinion measurement. In S. A. Stauffer (Ed.), *Measurement and prediction*. Princeton, NJ: Princeton University Press.

Guttman, L. (1959). Structural theory for intergroup beliefs and action. *American Sociological Review, 24*, 318–328.

Guttman, L. (1964). A general nonmetric technique for finding the smallest coordinate space for a configuration of points. *Psychometrica, 3*, 469–506.

Hess, R. D., & Torney, J. V. (1967). *The development of political attitudes in children*. Chicago: Aldine.

Ichilov, O. (1984). *The political world of children and adolescents* [in Hebrew]. Tel Aviv: Yachdav.

Ichilov, O. (1986). *Attitudes of civic education and social sciences teachers in the Israeli high schools concerning citizenship education in democracy* [in Hebrew]. (Report No. 2.86). Tel Aviv: Tel Aviv University, School of Education, Sociology of Education and Community Unit.

Ichilov, O., & Nave, N. (1981). "The good citizen" as viewed by Israeli adolescents. *Comparative Politics, 13*, 361–376.

Katz, J. (1984). *The silent world of doctor and patient.* New York: Free Press.

Levine, A. (1981). *Liberal democracy: A critique of its theory.* New York: Columbia University Press.

Locke, J. (1964). *Two treatises of government.* New York: Cambridge University Press.

Macpherson, C. B. (1977). *The life and times of liberal democracy.* New York: Oxford University Press.

Merton, R. K. (1964). *Social theory and social structure.* New York: Free Press.

Milbrath, L. W. (1965). *Political participation.* Chicago: Rand McNally.

Oliner, P. (1983). Putting "community" into citizenship education: The need for prosociality. *Theory and Research in Social Education, 11,* 65–81.

Pateman, C. (1979). *The problem of political obligation.* New York: John Wiley.

Sigel, R. S. (1965). Assumptions about the learning of political values. *Annals of the American Academy of Social and Political Science, 361,* 1–9.

Sigel, R. S., & Hoskin, M. B. (Eds.). (1981). *The political involvement of adolescents.* New Brunswick, NJ: Rutgers University Press.

Singer, P. (1973). *Democracy and disobedience.* New York: Oxford University Press.

Verba, S., & Nie, N. (1972). *Participation in America.* New York: Harper & Row.

Zashin, E. M. (1972). *Civil disobedience and democracy.* New York: Free Press.

# 2

# Socialization for Citizenship
# in Modern Democratic Society

## GORDON J. DIRENZO

Traditional concerns with socialization have focused almost exclusively on its objective functions, that is, those which serve society and its institutions. Equal emphasis needs to be placed on subjective functions in terms of the sociological and psychological development of the individual. It is only in this dual perspective that we can expect to fully comprehend the dynamics and consequences of social learning, whether in terms of its relevance for society or for the individual member.

Elsewhere (DiRenzo, 1977a) I have proposed a comprehensive model of socialization, one that focuses on a reciprocal linkage between the human system and the sociopolitical system. There I placed my emphasis on conceptual specifications and on the delineation of the distinctive subprocesses involved in social learning. Here I focus my concern on the interfaces of these processes and an elaboration of the dynamics within them.

### KEY CONCEPTS

My model incorporates four subprocesses of social learning: maturation, socialization, culturation, and personality development. Only two of these processes are central to my discussion here, socialization and personality development, and I shall begin by briefly defining them.

*Socialization*, considered as a distinctive subprocess of social learning, refers more properly to the purely processual and/or structural dimensions of human development. The concerns of socialization in this respect include such elements as the issues, objectives, mechanisms, structures, agents, and stages of human development. Socialization, then, is not concerned so much with the specific contents and societal differences of social learning (i.e., culturation) as much as it is with the universal elements of the process which pertain to the development or actualization of distinctively human attributes (e.g., rational thought, conscience, self-conceptions, values, free will, morality, language). Socialization thus deals essentially with the relatively universal fundamentals in the process of humanization—the process by which biologically human organisms are transformed into functionally human beings. Accordingly, one must speak of human nature as emergent—as socially emergent—rather than as a genetically or biologically given attribute.

*Personality development* consists of the psychological formation of the individual in terms of uniquely personal or individuating attributes. Personality may be defined as one's acquired, unique, dynamic, yet relatively enduring, system of internal predispositions to behavior.

The formation of personality, by and large, is a latent and unintended process and, as such, a by-product of socialization and culturation. The conscious intent and effort of the agents of social learning are normally focused on culturation—the transmission of the "way of life" of the respective society. The psychological results or residue of this experience—the unique experience of a specific set of social interactions—constitute personality. (For an elaboration of the definition of personality, see DiRenzo, 1974, 1987.)

Personality development thus is a nonconscious affair for both the individual and the agents of socialization. It need not be, and, indeed, I propose that it not be, but in practice such is the case for the overwhelming number of people in the world at large. Only in a relatively small number of cases is there a conscious effort, however unsuccessful in many instances, to develop personality or a particular type of personality.


## SOCIALIZATION AND THE DEVELOPMENT OF BASIC HUMAN NEEDS

One of the major and widely neglected products of the socialization process is the development of basic needs, which consist of a set of sociogenic motivations that are *inherent* in human nature, as opposed to biogenic needs, which are *innate* in the human organism.

Basic human needs refer to a universal set of motivations that have attributes of their own and which, as such, are not determined by particular cultural experiences or social structures. It is important, however, to stress that the sociogenic motivations of which we speak here are in the nature of functional requirements of the *human* system, much as we speak of the functional requirements or needs of the *biological* system (e.g., food, air, sleep, temperature, excretion). Basic human needs refer to what in structural-functional language could be called functional prerequisites. Their gratification, at least to a minimal degree, is considered imperative for the psychological homeostasis and human functioning of the individual. They cannot be ignored except at the risk of doing substantial functional harm to the individual.

Some sociologists and psychologists have long recognized the existence of human needs (e.g., Thomas & Znaniecki, 1918), and, although the search for their discovery and/or classification remains ongoing, we can point to several of the more basic and important of these functional requisites. Chief among them are the needs for social response, social recognition, new experience (freedom from boredom), security (physical and social), self-esteem (a satisfying self-concept), cognitive clarity, and freedom from alienation. This brief list is meant to be more suggestive than comprehensive.[1] Indeed, considerable research effort is needed to determine not only the explicit nature of these needs, but also their occurrence and relative strength. Although basic human needs are by definition universal, it is important to understand that individuals may vary in their appetite for them as they do in the case of biological needs. Moreover, while basic human needs are lifelong, they may not be equally salient at all stages of the life cycle.

The phenomenon of basic needs is important for socialization in a number of specific and significant respects. Chief among these are (1) the matter of societal response, that is, the fulfillment of basic human needs considered imperative for the healthy functioning of both the individual and the society; (2) the matter of human malleability, or the social-learning limits of the individual; and (3) the matter of the personal and social consequences of the nonfulfillment of basic human needs. Let us discuss each of these questions in more detail.

## Responsive and Unresponsive Societies

Since basic human needs are universal, and because societies differ in their cultural patterns, it is plausible to assume that societies, and more specifically their social institutions, might differ as well in the extent to which they are able to satisfy the basic human needs of their members.

One can ask, then, which kinds of societies and social institutions are most effective in gratifying the basic human needs of their members? To use a few simple examples, in terms of structural size and social complexity, one could ask, What is the optimal size of a family, a college class, a university, or a political organization, in order to permit each member to experience the optimal fulfillment of his or her basic needs? How big or small should political and governmental systems be for this purpose? Such a question seems especially appropriate in this context, as we hear of more and more speculation about regional governments within societies, and of international governments, such as the European Parliament, on the world scale. What about different kinds of societies, politically speaking, or different kinds of political systems and institutions? Are democratic structures as responsive as authoritarian structures? Are socialistic systems as responsive as capitalistic systems? Are ideologically pluralistic systems as responsive as those that are ideologically monolithic? In more sociological terms, are communal societies (*Gemeinschaft*) as responsive as associational societies (*Gesellschaft*)?

An inauthentic or unresponsive society is one that, by its very structure and content, is unable to respond effectively to the basic human needs of its members (Etzioni, 1968b, 1977; Israel, 1971). Of course, it is important to keep in mind that there can probably be no fully responsive society, nor one that is totally unresponsive. The question is the degree to which a society and its institutions are capable of meeting the needs of its members — or, in other words, the extent to which it is capable of functioning at an optimal level. This issue is complicated by societal evolution over the past decades and even centuries, as societies have moved from hunting and gathering types to industrial and even postindustrial types.

Many sociologists have expressed grave concern about the infinite or unlimited movement of human society toward an ever-expanding *Gesellschaft*-type social structure. Is such a society infinitely viable? The assumption in this doubt, one gaining more and more attention, is that it is not possible to build society on an absolutely, or even predominantly, associational or secondary-group structure. Such an attempt is considered to be dysfunctional, if not totally fatalistic, for society. Basic to this argument is the position that individuals are psychologically structured to need, as a functional requisite, the psychosocial experience that can be had only in and from communal or primary-group structures.[2] Assuming this position to be correct, what is not known is the point of no return, or that point on the *Gemeinschaft* to *Gesellschaft* (primary-group to secondary-group) continuum beyond which societal disaster or serious social and personal disorganization would become inevitable.

Some social scientists have argued in similar terms that there has arisen in modern *Gesellschaft*-type societies a myriad of "quasi-primary" groups, or "surrogate primary groups," particularly in the nature of voluntary associations, which, while devoted to specific goals on the level of manifest function, are primarily intended on the latent level to provide the psychological essentials of primary-group experience, however limited their success may be. For example, the formation of neighborhood organizations or block associations devoted to such things as leisure-time and recreational activities, and even the extensive development of encounter groups and other forms of group therapy, are seen in large part as stemming from the pursuit of primary-group experience and the gratification of basic human needs.

It is not difficult, moreover, to find social scientists who argue that in many respects modern society has reached, and in some instances even has gone beyond, a point of no return (e.g., Berger, Berger, & Kellner, 1973; Hsu, 1977; Zijderveld, 1971). They decry the rampant alienation and dehumanization that they perceive to be the omnipresent consequence of technological modernization. These observers argue that it is in the "modern technocracy" that people suffer the most profound loss of meaning and identity: While many people in modern societies long to belong more desperately than ever, they belong nowhere anymore — they are homeless (Berger et al., 1973). The essential argument of these scholars is that, more than ever, we need to develop a keen recognition of the basic human needs of individuals and to design our social systems such that they are capable of being responsive to these personal requirements. One of the fundamental problems facing all contemporary societies in this regard, as they evolve from more traditional and authoritarian structures into those of a more modern and democratic variety, is that of the need of personal freedom versus institutional authority.

## Human Malleability

Another dimension of the phenomena of basic human needs in modern societies, and even in more traditional societies that seek to become modern, is the increasingly strong emphasis on, and greater expectations for, the possibilities of social engineering. If it is the case that societies and social systems can be actively constructed, rather than being merely the naturally passive product of social evolution, then we need to raise the question of whether there are limits to social engineering in the light of basic human needs. What may be possible or sociologically functional on the societal level may not be psychologically functional on the human level and that of socialization. Here we speak of the malleability of the human person.

The dominant belief that has persisted for ages is that all kinds of societies can be developed through social engineering, and that all one needs to do is to mold people — to socialize them — for whichever society or whichever kind of society or social systems one might construct. If people prove to be incapable of learning and performing adequately and/or as required, then the problem is seen invariably as one of inadequate or faulty socialization. Such a situation is thought to require remedies in the form of "resocialization." (Note that such a process, by definition, would be impossible in our model.) The approach to the resolution of social problems in this perspective is the application of measures that adapt people to social roles, rather than the modification of society (e.g., passing new laws or making changes in social institutions).

One thing that seems to be grossly overlooked, especially in social engineering, is whether the individual is psychologically capable of adapting to and functioning within whichever forms of social systems and cultural technology we might be able to develop, or even whichever ones might emerge spontaneously in the evolutionary process. The implicit belief that is prevalent in these efforts is that human beings are infinitely malleable or plastic in terms of their psychological and/or human nature.

Yet, just as plausible, it would seem, is the contrary thesis that there is a fixed human nature that cannot be ignored or transgressed except at the cost of extensive social dysfunction as well as serious personal harm to the people involved. It seems more logical, given our knowledge of many other entities, and more empirically justified, given the results of social and behavioral research, to assume that there might be, at any given point in the evolutionary process, a fixed and delimited nature for the human psychological system, one with its own inherent structure, functional requisites, laws, and dynamism. The issue here is that human society and its technology have undergone radical transformation over the centuries; human nature, however, has not necessarily changed in recent history.

The available data in support of the thesis of a specific and limited human nature, as opposed to a highly malleable one, are not conclusive. The thesis, nonetheless, has gained in plausibility as a result of numerous studies that show, contrary to popularly held beliefs, that attempts to remold people via such techniques as psychotherapy, brainwashing, and criminal rehabilitation have little success (Etzioni, 1977).

That people can adapt and are adapting to a large variety of societal structures and cultural patterns is not sufficient evidence that they are infinitely or even highly malleable, because one can argue that adaptation might have a higher price in one society than another, as manifested by differences in rates of personal and societal dysfunction. The fact, moreover, that human beings in many instances do not adapt effectively to social change and different social structures is itself compelling evidence that they might not be automatically and infinitely malleable. Otherwise, the frustration and anxiety, as well as other personal and social problems, that allegedly stem from such situations should not occur.

## Consequences of Non-Gratification

What happens when basic human needs are not satisfied, or, more likely, not adequately satisfied? Some social scientists (e.g., Etzioni, 1968b) have argued that unresponsive social systems are a major source of social and personal deviance. The implication of this argument is that society itself may be the cause, or at least partly to blame, for its problems, rather than their resulting from merely personal deviation and/or inadequate socialization.

For the individual, the basic consequence is the development of a state of alienation, of total emotional withdrawal and separation from society. The alienated person is an individual who is said to be *in* society but not *of* it; one who feels powerless and insignificant; one who, in other words, cannot be expected to manifest any significant degree of citizenship.

Related to this situation is what Fromm (1944) called "moral aloneness" or lack of relatedness to values, symbols, and social patterns. Large segments of people throughout the world feel increasingly excluded from, and powerless and insignificant in the face of, the evolutionary and structural dynamics of contemporary society. Various countercultural and cultist manifestations that have appeared in the past several years are considered to be manifestations of this situation. Religious movements, communes, and many other alternative lifestyles are seen in great part as the demonstrable consequences of unresponsive social systems and as defenses against their alienation and dehumanization.

Alienation can be manifested in various forms of personal and/or social deviance. Examples of this deviance might be mental illness, crime and delinquency, drug and alcohol addiction, marital and family dissolution, and even suicide. Such negative coping on a massive scale can result in significant social problems, which society usually attempts to resolve through a multitude of programs of individual treatment and rehabilitation, or through what often is called "resocialization."

The inadequate gratification of basic human needs may also lead to social unrest that often is manifested in such forms as political dissent and revolution. That such might have been much of the basis for the civil rights movement and the student revolution during the 1960s and 1970s, and even for the political revolts around the world in the 1980s, is perhaps an easily accepted position. Indeed, how much governmental unrest of any type, including the instability of governments, is due primarily to inadequate gratification of basic *human* needs, rather than to physical needs?

## SOCIALIZATION AND PERSONALITY

Personality, as indicated already, is an inextricable product of the socialization/culturation process. Once formed, however, personality represents a system that has its own needs, both as a universal phenomenon as well as a uniquely personal entity. In certain respects, then, personality and basic human needs both have a common development and a common nature in their dependent relationship to socialization. Moreover, like basic human needs, personality has functional consequences for both the individual and society.

One issue of direct relevance to our considerations here involves the differential influence of variations in patterns and structures of socialization on the emergence of various personality structures and psychological dynamics, especially those related to political participation. Considerable research (see DiRenzo, 1974) shows that politically active people exhibit personality profiles that differ significantly from those of the general population, and that people are differentially attracted to political structures on the basis of personality. There is a good body of empirical data, for example, which shows significant correlation (positive and negative) of certain personality variables with political participation. It is of interest to point out, in this regard, that self-esteem shows the highest level of positive correlation with political activity, while authoritarianism shows a negative correlation (Milbrath & Klein, 1962).

Personality is more generally instrumental in political behavior in that it facilitates the acceptance and/or creation of political options that are personally meaningful and the rejection of those that are similarly incompatible (Levinson, 1959). When, however, a personally congenial mode of political activity is not readily available and the individual cannot create one, he or she may nominally accept an uncongenial form of political action, without strong commitment or involvement.

An incompatibility between personality and sociopolitical systems can result in a number of different consequences. One of these that is particularly significant, and quite likely, in terms of citizenship roles is the emergence of what Goffman (1961) has termed "role-distancing behavior," which indicates to the individual and to others that one does not take one's role seriously, that one does not embrace it wholeheartedly, and that there exists a psychological "distance" between one's personality and the particular role. Individuals in these types of circumstances manifest an apathetic conformity and usually meet only the minimal requirements of role performance. Such commitment, or lack thereof, is a functional threat to any sociopolitical system.

A continually interesting question is, Are the institutions of government related to the kinds of personality that are recruited into the political systems, or to those types that are potential recruits? Certain types of personality tend to be attracted and/or recruited to particular political systems and political roles in a differential rather than in a random or unsystematic fashion, and seemingly so disproportionately as to constitute modal types of personality for these positions. I have argued (DiRenzo, 1974) that these findings reflect the principle of congruency, which maintains that a functional dependency, or simply a congenial fit in some cases, exists between sociopolitical systems and personality systems, which is mutually beneficial for the effective and harmonious operation of both systems. A lack of substantial congruence between personality and sociopolitical roles and organizations produces a state of conflict that has dysfunctional consequences for both the individual and social/political order.

Much of the functional problem of congruity, it seems to me, can be met by a mutually compatible socialization that recognizes the nature and requirements, including the scope and limits, of both the personal system and the sociopolitical system.

## The "Right Kind" of Personality

A related and most important issue concerns the question of whether particular types of society and social institutions require certain types of personality. In other words, are there strategic necessities between personality and political systems? If so, does political socialization (culturation), at least in its objective dimension, require the development of particular types, "the right kind" of personality? Many scholars of politics have answered this question in the affirmative.

Berelson (1952), for example, states the following in regard to democracy:

> There appear to be two requirements in democratic society which refer primarily to characteristics demanded of the electorate as it initially comes to make a political decision. These are the preconditions for electorate decisions. The first is the possession of a suitable *personality structure:* within a range of variations, the electorate is required to possess the types of character which can operate effectively, if not efficiently, in a free society. Certain kinds of personality structures are not congenial to a democratic society, could not operate successfully within it, and would be destructive of democratic values. Others are more compatible with or even disposed toward the effective performance of the various roles which make up the democratic political system. . . . The second requirement . . . is the factor of *interest and participation;* the electorate is required to possess a certain degree of involvement in the process of political decision, to take an appropriate share of responsibility. [pp. 315–316]

Such a notion, however new or modern it might seem, is, like much of our knowledge, really quite ancient, at least in its barest outlines. Similar thoughts can be found in the classic writings of the early Greek thinkers. Plato, for example, in his *Republic* dealt with the issue of developing in young people the qualities of character thought to be necessary for effective citizenship; and Aristotle in his *Politics* commented on the necessity of fitting the constitution of a city-state to the character of its people. In much more recent history, de Tocqueville (1835/1969) remarked in his classic analysis of *Democracy in America* that "the manners [character] of the Americans of the United States are, then, the *real* cause which renders that people the only one of the American nations that is able to support a democratic government. . . . The physical circumstances are less important than the laws, and the laws very subordinate to the manners [character] of the American people" (p. 334).

In order for any political or social system to function well, and as intended, its members must possess the kind of personality that makes them want to act in the way that they have to act as members of that system. The individual, as Fromm (1944) maintained, must *want* to do what *needs* to be done.

Without denying the basic tenets of these arguments, it seems unlikely that any given character type will be associated invariably with a single form of political system, such as democracy. Certain roles (e.g., soldier, police officer, parent) within democratic systems might need authoritarian or other types of personality, and, correspondingly, the converse would be true of authoritarian systems. What is important is the fundamental principle that the relationship between personality and social systems is symbiotic. Fromm (1941) argued in this regard that the personality systems of a given society serve either as a cement holding the system together or as an explosive tearing it apart, depending on the degree to which a given personality type fits the demands of the system and finds satisfaction within it. (For further discussion of the "right kind" of personality, see DiRenzo, 1974.)

## Emergence of Political Character

What kinds of social and political character are modern democratic societies producing? Attempts to document changes in social character in modern societies during the past few decades have been many. Much of the evidence, however, may not be strongly manifest, since modifications in social character do not appear to experience the dramatic changes in terms of magnitude and rate that are true of society and its institutions. Many of the answers to relevant questions, therefore, are quite speculative and tentative.

Among the more pertinent studies may be mentioned those of Marcuse (1964), who has formulated the conception of "one-dimensional man" as the product of a culturally homogeneous and mass society; Lifton (1976), who with his concept of "protean man," and Toffler (1970), who with that of "modular man," discuss the multiple identities of the modern person; Yablonsky (1972), who describes the "robopath"; Kando (1975), who discusses the emerging leisure consciousness; Lasch (1979, 1984), who speaks of the super-narcissistic individual; Sennett (1977), who assesses the emergence of "privatized man," whom he describes as one moving out of the public domain into his own private world; Etzioni (1982), who speaks of an "ego-centered mentality" that is damaging modern social institutions; and, most recently, Bellah, Madsen, Sullivan, Swidler, & Tipton (1985), who speak of both materialism and narcissism.

These many observers have concerned themselves with different aspects and dimensions of personality (e.g., values, self-images, beliefs, attitudes, motives). One of the chief themes of several of these various assessments, however, is that dehumanization and alienation are emerging as distinctive marks of people in Western societies. Such individuals are perceived to have become less individualistic, less autonomous, less inner-oriented, and less innovative. They are correspondingly more other-directed, conforming, sheepish, and essentially chameleonlike, changing appearances at will and taking on the coloring of a variety of social atmospheres as needed. Such tendencies are not only recognized but especially deplored by their many observers. Essentially, these various scholars would maintain that the ethic of individualism and self-sufficiency is vulnerable to large-scale social change over which the individual has little, if any, control. Such characterological consequences, in short, are viewed as detrimental to the viability of modern, democratic political systems. Democracies, it is argued, need a modal social character that is altruistic, not narcissistic.

Not all social scientists, of course, would view many of these alleged developments in social character as totally negative. Fromm (1947), for example, argues that some of these traits (e.g., other-directedness and sensitivity to others) may be functional in that rapid social change in modern and highly technological societies requires a great degree of flexibility. He sees sensitivity to others as permitting or facilitating necessary social change. Others would argue that the complexities of social life today do not permit the degree of independence and freedom that may have been true in earlier times. It is incumbent on us, therefore, to look to the futuristic society and the nature of socialization within it.

## SOCIALIZATION AND SOCIAL CHANGE

The final topic for this chapter involves the consideration of socialization and social change. There are several dimensions to this question. Some involve substantive issues; others are more methodological in nature. The various points discussed here will focus on only two aspects of these questions. One concerns simply the phenomenon of social change itself and the implications that it has for socialization. The other involves the nature that socialization for societies of the future, especially democratic ones, should assume. This latter question is particularly crucial in light of the fact that social change and modernization throughout much of the world is tantamount to the democratization of societies.

## Human Responses to Social Change

An unmistakable change occurring in the world is the movement from structurally and culturally simple forms of social organization to highly complex ones. Whatever benefits this movement may have in terms of social engineering and technological development, we need to ask, with respect to the principle of basic human needs, just how gargantuan — how complex and bureaucratic — society can become without it and its members paying the price of dysfunction. Given the visions of the postindustrial and ultramodern models, is it conceivable that we might develop, or at least try to develop, societies and a technological potential whose structure and content would render them incapable of being responsive to and gratifying the basic human needs of their members?

Among the fundamental issues, as I see them, is that social learning (I refer primarily but not exclusively to culturation) is invariably undertaken, even in highly advanced and rapidly changing societies, in terms of the present. That is to say, socializing agents (chiefly familial, educational, and religious) transmit to children their own culture and that of their here-and-now society. Socialization of this type is invariably out of date in many respects by the time the socializee enters early adulthood, as a consequence of the many significant modifications that usually have taken place in society and its basic institutions. Indeed, it is this very type of cultural lag that is basic to the generation gaps we have acknowledged as the source of so much social turmoil and personal stress during the past few decades.

The simple fact here is that the constant encounter of new socio-cultural phenomena renders obsolete the learned and ingrained patterns of social behavior. Accordingly, one's socialization is always, to a certain extent, inadequate or inappropriate; hence, one persistently finds oneself in a situation of being "unsocialized."

One might argue that the generation gap is not a new phenomenon. If such be the case, it merely reinforces our argument. On the other hand, while social change (and generation gaps) may not be new, what is novel about social change today is its magnitude, rate, force, and direction, which have taken on geometric proportions. It is these characteristics of contemporary social change that are of particular significance for socialization in the modern democracy. Three or four decades ago, there was very little demand on people to adapt to social change. Such a situation is no longer true today; on the contrary, the demand for both personal and social change is very strong and very extensive. What, then, does such a situation mean in terms of the nature and structure of socialization in the modern and future society?

One of the fundamental elements in all of these dynamics is the degree of cognitive ambiguity that the current modes of social change invariably produce for the individual. Cognitive ambiguity represents a psychological state of confusion about the status of social reality, which in a relatively extreme degree people find quite intolerable. The inability to cope with cognitive ambiguity can lead to personality dysfunction and social paralysis, characterized by an absence of appropriate and relevant behavior and/or deviation from one's expected obligations and socially relevant norms. One example of such a situation might be reflected, as many argue, in the phenomenon of "information overload" resulting from the current emergence of what, among other things, has been called the "information society."

Cognitive ambiguity, in this perspective, produces anomie, which consists of a state of relative normlessness and/or social instability, accompanied by a low degree of social cohesion. Anomie has its psychological counterpart in anomia, a subjective state in which the individual experiences a distressing lack of purpose, direction, and social integration (see Srole, 1956). Not only does anomie result in the nongratification of basic human needs, it also makes an effective and enduring socialization quite difficult. Even more basic is the fact that the tolerance of ambiguity is a function of personality structure which, as we have argued, is a product of socialization.

## Institutional Inconsistency

Another persistent problem of socialization in the context of social change relates to the long-standing issue of consistency. One of the frequent experiences of adult socialization, often beginning in late adolescence, is that of "reality shock." People come to learn, usually at the cost of considerable psychological pain, that their conceptions and expectations of the world do not conform to reality, and that there are numerous inaccuracies in this respect in terms of the earlier socialization that was provided for them. Such a situation often is manifested in the discontinuities of status transition — the movement from one social position to another within a sequence of statuses. Here we have the confusing and dysfunctional syndrome of learning-unlearning-relearning that not only continues to characterize socialization in modern society, but also has far more significant consequences today for both the individual and society.

Is consistency in socialization as impossible or ineffective in modern societies as some would argue? If so, then, is it at least reducible to a certain degree? Such a consideration is all the more relevant when one considers that, with the extension of the life-span, one's primary socialization must serve one for many more years than was the case two or three generations ago — nearly one-quarter to one-third of a century longer nowadays! It may well be that the inevitability of consistency in socialization is apparent as such only in terms of the particular objectives, structures, and context that one may predicate for socialization.

We have in our midst one mechanism that is capable of revealing, at least for certain segments of society, the implication of the future-oriented type of socialization to which we allude. This mechanism can be found in the development and expansion of computer technology and information processing. The ever-expanding technology of the electronic computer continuously outpaces the capacity of society to absorb the consequences of its seemingly endless applications (see Turkle, 1984). One cannot deny that increasingly larger segments of modern societies have come to perceive, and to anticipate, even eagerly, the endless application of computer technology. Yet many of the other astounding advances of science and engineering in recent years (e.g., cloning, test-tube fertilization, in-utero surgery, organ transplants) have not prepared the vast majority of people for potential and highly probable developments (e.g., genetic implants of the brain) that speak to the very essence of the human being. Such profoundly iconoclastic changes are likely to require a highly specific and heretofore unknown kind of socialization in all of its processual components.

One of the much-neglected methodological questions of socialization research, particularly as concerns the future, is the consideration that at the present time in many of the more advanced societies more and more socialization is being performed by secondary institutions. This situation is due, in part, to the sharp increase in the scale of the problem of the socialization of children and youth in modern and highly technological society. One consequence of this situation, argues Almond (1977), is that the social institutions (familial, educational, religious) normally performing these functions have lost some of their authority and indoctrinative capacity. The abandonment and/or transfer of many socialization functions from the primary institutions is reflected also in the expanding role of the mass media, especially the electronic and visual forms.

Under particular challenge by other and newer agencies of socialization, some competitive and others substitutive in nature, is the dominance and priority of the family. Day-care centers and nurseries, for example, fulfill many socialization functions for the children of the ever-increasing number of working mothers and two-career families. The decline in the domestic responsibilities of the family, as well as the expanding rates of family instability and dissolution, have been seen by some social scientists as constituting a deterioration of the appropriate social context for the sociological and psychological development of children, with the eventual consequence of increased alienation and psychological dysfunction.

Both the quality and quantity of the socialization involved in this institutional change and/or agency shift need to be vigorously assessed, particularly since one rather common belief is that, as socialization becomes more and more specialized, it is *ipso facto* better. Whether performed by secondary and/or more specialized institutions, the basic question emerges again: Are these new forms of socialization more or less effective in meeting the basic human needs of the socializee?

## Social Change and Social Character

Last, and just as fundamental, is the issue of the future of social character in modern democratic societies. The question from a socialization point of view concerns the kind of political and social character that is needed, as well as the development and implementation of mechanisms for their attainment.

One of the chief themes that we find in several assessments of the effects of social change on social character, as discussed earlier, is that dehumanization and alienation (i.e., the lack of fulfillment of basic human needs) are becoming more and more prevalent among people in Western societies. This thesis, not unexpectedly, has been strongly challenged (e.g., Inkeles, 1983; Suzman, 1977). The primary consideration, nonetheless, is not who or which argument is correct at the present, but rather that we recognize the potential effects of social change on social character and vice-versa, particularly with regard to our concern for producing an effective citizenship.

A decade ago, Almond (1977) maintained that, given the rapid diffusion of a new political culture among young people, the characterological expectation is for a more open, change-oriented, and complex personality, with a greater analytical and problem-solving capacity than the more closed, rigid, and parochial type that had been (and still is) prevalent. Similar views have been expressed by Marcuse (1964), Keniston (1968), and Reich (1979).

Rothman and Lichter (1978a, 1978b; Lichter & Rothman, 1982), however, marshal quantities of empirical data to challenge the thesis that the radical students of the 1960s were the vanguard of a "liberated" generation and a new type of "protean man" or multifaceted individual—one characterized by warmth, openness, humanitarianism, social motivation, advanced morality, and psychological health. Quite to the contrary, they view the radical movement and its protagonists as authoritarian, self-interested, and pragmatic. Given the seeming reversals in the political culture (values and motivations) of youth in many modern societies during the past decade, this question of characterological trends is a much more complicated one and its outcome is far less certain.

Another focal dimension of this question of characterological change, one that seems to have some endurance for the time being at least, is the alleged changes in the self-system. Gergen (1977), among others, has spoken in this regard of "multiple identities" to describe the structure of the kind of self that is associated in his view with highly pluralistic, heterogeneous, and complex modern societies. He argues that the lack of strong and consistent experiences in contemporary childhood is producing a modal type of individual who is marked by a multiplicity of self-conceptions, rather than the unitary and well-integrated self-image that Gergen believes may have characterized a bygone era. Individuals in modern societies, he states, must play an increasing number of roles each day, and most demand a performance that is convincing, both to others and to ourselves.

This conception of the multifaceted and complex self is consistent with the formulation of "protean man" by Lifton (1976), as well as that of the "modular man" proposed by Toffler (1970). Gergen (1977), however, unlike these other social scientists, contends that the new psychosocial development of what he calls a "repertory culture" and its "multiple-identity personality" is a positive one, since it will create a more flexible and more adaptive individual who will be able to respond effectively to the problems of contemporary society.

One might argue in more global terms that the basic characterological need in the modern democracy is that of individuals who possess what Inkeles (1983) has labeled the "individual modernity syndrome." This psychic structure may be described in part as consisting of the following elements as its principal components: belief in the efficacy of science and technology, control over nature, assertion of increasing independence from traditional authority figures, orientation to the future, aspirations for self and family, planning ahead, active citizenship in community affairs and local politics, secularism, tolerance for diversity, and an openness to new experience and social change. This syndrome thus does not refer to a merely contemporary profile, but, more significantly, describes a type of personality that is thought to be indispensable to the function of industrialized society. Such a thesis has not been without criticism (Armer & Isaac,

1978), yet it is one that empirical evidence has neither substantially refuted nor confirmed. This undertaking can only be accomplished by longitudinal data from substantial studies of a cross-national nature.

## Personality and Social Change

Social change, as with all social behavior, is in a number of ways dependent upon those individuals who are its agents. Thus, while research shows that all kinds of personalities may be involved in social change, individuals participate in significantly different ways and in substantially different proportions (DiRenzo, 1978). Only some types of personalities are receptive to social change; others are resistant to and relatively intolerant of innovation in the social order. Similarly, some types of personalities are receptive to only certain kinds of social change, or to only certain techniques for its achievement. Change-oriented individuals tend to be innovators who not only are for change but actively seek it, often comprising the avant-garde of movements for social and political reform.

Empirical data (DiRenzo, 1978) show that individuals can be distinguished in terms of modal patterns of personality structure in regard to (1) differential orientations to social change, (2) differential participation in movements of social reform, (3) the utilization and/or advocation of different modes of social protest and social reform, and (4) differential activity in specific forms of social protest and social reform. It is situations such as these that perhaps account, at least in part, for the fact that the occurrence of social change is not uniform in the various segments of society, nor even in all societies.

Successful attempts at social change require both the right kind of social structures and social processes, as well as the right kind and the right number of individuals. Whether movements of political protest and social reform, for example, can become viable forces of social change is contingent upon the extent to which there exists among the ranks a sufficient number of individuals with the necessary personality structures. These personalities must be both change oriented and appropriately change congruent for the particular modes of social change that are involved or are advocated for ideological and/or practical purposes.

Citizenship in a modern democracy, for some observers, implies a commitment to social change. Some social scientists have foreseen, and in the company of many laypeople even have promoted, the "active society" (Etzioni, 1968a), one in which the members are actively in control of their social destiny. Even without this activist approach, social change appears to be not only ubiquitous but inevitable in modern society. Accordingly, it would seem to be incumbent upon any authentic and responsive society to socialize its members for this social phenomenon, no less than it socializes them for social stability.

What type of socialization might this situation require? Socialization needs to be undertaken, both in content and structure, such that it incorporates the expectation of social change. People need to be socialized in such a sociological and psychological fashion as to be change oriented — to look forward to innovation, not necessarily in order to value the future, but more especially to be capable of adapting to it.

Rapid and extensive social change, moreover, requires other psychological qualities that permit and/or facilitate it. Among these attributes are flexibility, other-directedness, tolerance of ambiguity, sensitivity to others, and a respect for the lack of permanency. We need, moreover, to develop individuals who not only are socialized for "future shock" but who also possess those qualities, such as achievement orientation and creativity, that future societies will demand, if only for the sake of personal survival. Futuristic socialization of this kind must be carried out by authentic and responsive societies in a way that guarantees the basic human rights of their members for the fulfillment of their basic human needs and thereby generates the effective citizenship required for the viability of any modern society.

## CONCLUSION

In this chapter I have offered a broad outline of a model of the psychosocial linkages between authentic and responsive democracies in modern society and their members. My message, in summary, is that effective socialization for citizenship in the modern democracy requires social structures and institutions that (1) are responsive to the basic human needs of its members and (2) produce those styles of personality systems that share a functionally congruent relationship with its political systems. What is required to achieve these objectives is a socialization that is a more conscious and intentional process. Citizenship in a modern democracy requires nothing less than these fundamentals.

One issue that needs to be explored by those scholars interested more specifically in political socialization is the relationship of basic human needs to basic human rights. Can basic human needs be combined in an intrinsic and complementary way with one's basic human rights as a citizen in democracy? If one has basic human rights in a democracy, does one also have a right to the fulfillment of basic human needs? For example, one fundamental question is whether citizenship in a democracy confers the basic human right to be fundamentally free of alienation. Such a consideration would extend the conception of an authentic and responsive society—certainly an authentical and responsive democratic society—from one that fulfills the basic human needs of its members because of functional requirements, to one that also has a moral and legal obligation to do so.

The link between basic human needs and democracy, however, is much more fundamental. A democracy is a political structure that exists not only by and of the people, but also *for* the people. Hence, by definition, a democracy is ideally a responsive society. More significantly, it is the case that there can be no conflict between personal needs (basic human needs) and social needs, because the latter, in the responsive society, exist only in order to fulfill the former.

One might ask whether it is undemocratic for democratic societies to develop democratic people. Pushing such a position to its maximum, is it undemocratic to produce people who are capable of adequately functioning in the reality in which they exist? Is it undemocratic to make people functional for their contemporary and/or futuristic society? These questions are moot in my conceptual scheme.

My argument is not intended to be ideological in any way. Rather, the theoretical position is a purely functional one, since it applies to any society, regardless of the nature of its belief or value systems, that pretends to be both authentic and responsive. Every authentic society has the obligation to develop human nature and to fulfill the basic human needs of its members. Indeed, to socialize individuals in any other fashion is to be not only unresponsive, but also ideologically imposing.

My position implies an assumption of what human nature is—not a value-judgment of what it ought to be. It is not the case, as critics might allege, that to fulfill basic human needs and/or to produce change-oriented types of personalities is to subject the individual to a particular ideological mold. Rather, I propose a type of socialization that involves the development of a psychological and cognitive structure capable of permitting the individual to make ideological choices. Such a socialization, in other words, is designed to prepare people how to believe—not what to believe.

The sociological and psychological processes that are described here comprise, in my judgment, the functional requisites for maximizing the role of political participation and effective citizenship in the modern democracy. I recognize all too well, of course, that the formulation of these requirements is a far more simple undertaking than the development of the social structures and mechanisms that will guarantee their realization. The task is challenging. Its promise merits our committed response.

## NOTES

1. For one list of basic human needs, and for a discussion of them with particular relevance to political behavior, see Davies (1963). Other lists can be found in Etzioni (1968b) and DiRenzo (1987).

2. A communal society, defined in ideal-typical terms, is one that tends to be relatively small in size, primary-group based, informal, and generally simple and homogeneous in social organization, with a minimal division of labor and role specialization. Correspondingly, a primary group is characterized by an expressive orientation, face-to-face interaction, the emergence of emotional bonds, totality of personality involvement, and enduring interaction. Antithetical characteristics are found in associational societies and secondary groups. For further elaboration of these concepts, see DiRenzo (1987).

## REFERENCES

Almond, G. A. (1977). Youth character and changing political culture. In G. J. DiRenzo, (Ed.), *We, the people: American character and social change* (pp. 115–146). Westport, CT: Greenwood Press.

Armer, M., & Isaac, L. (1978). Determinants of behavioral consequences of psychological modernity: Empirical evidence from Costa Rica. *American Sociological Review, 43*, 316–334.

Bellah, R. N., Madsen, R., Sullivan, W. M., Swidler, A., & Tipton, S. M. (1985). *Habits of the heart: Individualism and commitment in American life.* Berkeley: University of California Press.

Berelson, B. (1952). Democratic theory and public opinion. *Public Opinion Quarterly, 16*, 313–330.

Berger, P., Berger, B., & Kellner, H. (1973). *The homeless mind.* New York: Vintage Press.

Davies, J. C. (1963). *Human nature in politics.* New York: John Wiley.

de Tocqueville, A. (1973). *Democracy in America* (Vol. 1). New York: Knopf. (Original work published 1835)

DiRenzo, G. J. (1974). *Personality and politics.* New York: Doubleday.

DiRenzo, G. J. (1977a). Socialization, personality, and social systems. *Annual Review of Sociology, 3*, 261–295.

DiRenzo, G. J. (Ed.). (1977b). *We, the people: American character and social change.* Westport, CT: Greenwood Press.

DiRenzo, G. J. (1978). Personality typologies and modes of social change. *Social Behavior and Personality, 6*, 11–16.

DiRenzo, G. J. (1987). *Sociological perspectives.* Lexington, MA: Ginn Press.

Etzioni, A. (1968a). *The active society.* New York: Macmillan.

Etzioni, A. (1968b). Basic human needs, alienation, and inauthenticity. *American Sociological Review, 32*, 870–885.

Etzioni, A. (1977). Basic characterological needs and changing social systems. In

G. J. DiRenzo, (Ed.), *We, the people: American character and social change* (pp. 273–284). Westport, CT: Greenwood Press.

Etzioni, A. (1982). *An immodest agenda: Rebuilding America before the twenty-first century.* New York: McGraw-Hill.

Fromm, E. (1941). *Escape from freedom.* New York: Rinehart.

Fromm, E. (1944). The individual and social origins of neurosis. *American Sociological Review, 9,* 380–384.

Fromm, E. (1947). *Man for himself: An inquiry into the psychology of ethics.* New York: Rinehart.

Gergen, K. J. (1977). The decline of character: Socialization and self-consistency. In G. J. DiRenzo (Ed.), *We, the people: American character and social change* (pp. 252–272). Westport, CT: Greenwood Press.

Goffman, E. (1961). *Asylums.* Chicago: Aldine.

Hsu, F. L. K. (1977). Individual fulfillment, social stability, and cultural progress. In G. J. DiRenzo (Ed.), *We, the people: American character and social change* (pp. 95–114). Westport, CT: Greenwood Press.

Inkeles, A. (1983). *Exploring individual modernity.* New York: Columbia University Press.

Israel, J. (1971). *Alienation: From Marx to modern society.* Boston: Allyn and Bacon.

Kando, T. M. (1975). *Leisure and popular culture in transition.* St. Louis: C. V. Mosby.

Keniston, K. (1968). *Young radicals.* New York: Harcourt Brace Jovanovich.

Lasch, C. (1979). *The culture of narcissism.* New York: Warner Books.

Lasch, C. (1984). *The minimal self.* New York: W. W. Norton.

Levinson, D. C. (1959). Role, personality, and social structure in the organizational setting. *Journal of Abnormal and Social Psychology, 58,* 170–180.

Lichter, R. S., & Rothman, S. (1982). The radical personality: Social psychological correlates of new left ideology. *Political Behavior, 4,* 207–235.

Lifton, R. (1976). *The life of the self.* New York: Simon & Schuster.

Marcuse, H. (1964). *One-dimensional man: Studies in the ideology of advanced industrial society.* Boston: Beacon Press.

Milbrath, L. W., & Klein, W. W. (1962). Personality correlates of political participation. *Acta Sociologica, 6,* 52–66.

Reich, C. A. (1979). *The greening of America.* New York: Random House.

Rothman, S., & Lichter, R. S. (1978a). The case of the student left. *Social Research, 45,* 535–609.

Rothman, S., & Lichter, R. S. (1978b). Power, politics, and personality in post-industrial society. *Journal of Politics, 40,* 675–707.

Sennett, R. (1977). *The fall of public man.* New York: Alfred A. Knopf.

Srole, L. (1956). Social integration and certain correlates: An exploratory study. *American Sociological Review, 21,* 709–716.

Suzman, R. (1977). The modernization of personality. In G. J. DiRenzo (Ed.), *We, the people: American character and social change* (pp. 40–77). Westport, CT: Greenwood Press.

Thomas, W. I., & Znaniecki, F. (1918). *The Polish peasant in Europe and America*. Boston: Gorham Press.

Toffler, A. (1970). *Future Shock*. New York: William Morrow.

Turkle, S. (1984). *The second self: Computers and the human spirit*. New York: Simon & Schuster.

Yablonsky, L. (1972). *Robopaths: People as machines*. Indianapolis: Bobbs-Merrill.

Zijderveld, A. C. (1971). *A cultural analysis of our time*. New York: Anchor Books.

# 3

# The Role of Conflict in Children's Political Learning

RICHARD M. MERELMAN

The role of conflict in the socialization of children is important to the stability of political systems. Every political system is shaped fatefully by the particular conflicts within it, and to these conflicts socialization heavily contributes. Consider democracy, for example. The relationship of democracy to the socialization of conflict is ambivalent and complex. In giving ordinary people the principal role in governance, democracies must allow popular conflicts to invade political institutions. Indeed, the democratic principle of majority rule actually institutionalizes conflict between majorities and minorities.

*Unmanageable* conflicts, however, ultimately destroy democracy. History records vivid instances in which democratic institutions — parliaments, elected executives, representative bureaucracies, competing political parties, voluntary associations — simply could not survive intense social conflicts. Thus, democracies use the socialization process to restrain conflict as well as to promote it. A full understanding of democracy requires us to understand how conflict emerges within the socialization process, for it is partly through this process that political conflict reproduces itself from generation to generation.

My purpose in this chapter is to describe some ways in which children learn about conflict in varying political regimes. In particular, I wish to examine socialization in polities where legitimacy is *uncontested*, in that the overwhelming majority of the population consents to a single political authority within a single defined territory, and compare these to regimes where authority is *contested*, in that no such majority consent exists, but instead competing pretenders to authority struggle against each other within a territorially divided political unit. In short, I compare socialization in regimes where there exist widely accepted norms by which a single group effectively claims a "right to rule," to socialization in regimes where no such norms exist. The truest examples of the latter regimes include Lebanon and Northern Ireland; less extreme cases include Afghanistan, Sri

47

Lanka, the Philippines, and perhaps Spain. In all these countries hostile factions violently contest power. In Northern Ireland and Lebanon no single group possesses secure control over its opponents. In Afghanistan, the Philippines, Sri Lanka, and Spain, sizable and powerful minorities struggle against a vulnerable central government. South Africa represents a special case; the white South African government, though currently in full control of its territory, nevertheless faces a massive black opposition which occasionally contests its power directly and which, even when quiescent, causes anxiety among the white minority.

Of course, political conflict has many dimensions, from which I could generate a quite complex conflict typology. This would not further my present purpose, which is to comprehend how the conflict norms of a regime enter the socialization process so as to advance or retard regime legitimacy. Such norms subsume particular configurations of conflict. For my purposes, the simply defined distinction between contested and uncontested regimes suffices, although it should be kept in mind that within these two basic categories there exist variations. Contested regimes always contain at least a few elements of harmony; uncontested regimes always exhibit some fractiousness. But these are muted themes.

I confine myself here to but a subset of uncontested regimes, those in which democratic institutions provide the general public with an opportunity to choose its own leaders. Such regimes present an interesting psychological phenomenon: Although in theory the people rule, in practice the people do not rule directly. Instead, power resides day by day in the hands of public officials. From a perceptual standpoint, therefore, it is easy for the general public to think of its leaders, rather than itself, as the source of legitimate power. This psychological anomaly has important consequences for the persistence of uncontested democratic regimes.

## LEARNING ABOUT CONFLICT IN UNCONTESTED DEMOCRACIES

In uncontested democracies severe political conflict generally appears to young children as a morally dubious aberration. This is so because the socialization process in such societies marginalizes severe conflict (Gitlin, 1980). Indeed, this begins in the peer group, where youngsters learn to label aggressive peers as "troublemakers," a characterization which the latter themselves quickly internalize (Dodge & Richard, 1985). The eventual result of this labeling process is that aggressive children first recoil from their peers; then launch a series of clumsy, self-defeating, aggressive attempts at friendship; then experience further rejection. In the course of this vicious cycle, conflict as an accepted mode of social interaction quickly becomes suspect.

Although the marginalization of severe conflict among peers is probably endemic to all regimes, it receives strong reinforcement in uncontested democracies. Since parents rarely engage in aggressive political conflict, cultivating aggressiveness among their children provides little political payoff. Indeed, parents afflicted with aggressive children will experience pain as they watch their children become troubled, stigmatized, and rejected. They will therefore discourage aggression. By contrast, because aggressiveness and the willingness to inflict suffering are necessary to group conflict in contested regimes, parents in such regimes may well permit and even encourage their youngsters to develop a taste for peer-group aggression. The point is that conflict patterns in society condition parental socialization techniques.

For its part, the political socialization literature describes several psychological mechanisms that assist children in accepting an image of an uncontested democratic order, and in marginalizing severe conflict. Initially, of course, there is the "benevolent leader" phenomenon. Although political tribulations such as the Watergate affair may impede the child's tendency to accept authority, most children apparently prefer to seek out single authorities and to consider them benevolent (Greenstein, 1975). In uncontested democratic regimes, such authorities are readily visible and apparently accessible. Even in democratic regimes that have suffered challenges to legitimacy (such as India), young people apparently use their image of a benevolent leader (in this case, Mrs. Gandhi) to allay their doubts about the regime's worth (Iyengar, 1979).

This process sometimes reaches unexpected proportions. Moore, Lare, and Wagner (1985), in a study of children's political views, report that a substantial proportion of their youngest respondents made no substantial distinction between religious and political authority. "For example, 30% of the kindergartners answered 'God' or 'Jesus' when responding to the question 'Who does the most to run the country?'" (p. 44). This comes from children in "hedonistic" Los Angeles, not in the fundamentalist South!

Young children also prefer to situate authority in a single territorial unit. The disposition to nestle early concepts of local units within a later-cognized larger unified territory emerges clearly in Jahoda's (1963a, b) work. The concept of "federalism"—of some autonomy for different governmental units within the same territory—therefore seems developmentally problematic for children. Indeed, federalism is a difficult concept for older people as well. We need only consult our experiences in teaching American government to provide anecdotal support for this assertion.

It is not cognitive simplicity alone that accounts for this phenomenon. There appears to be a distinctive emotional security that young people experience from feeling themselves bonded to a single united territory.

Robert Coles (1986) notes that children in contested regimes are especially anxious in this regard, and so they claim that "their" group really controls things, even when the facts are clearly otherwise. According to Coles, the emotive hold of a single united territory springs from the child's feeling that land itself is a source of personal strength. This anthropomorphic connection between territory and power is something children in uncontested democracies take for granted; in contested regimes, however, children must seek it out by creating in fantasy an amalgamation of territorial and political authority where none presently exists in fact. The history of Zionism in the Jewish Diaspora amply demonstrates that such a creative act is possible as, indeed, do the political aspirations of contemporary Palestinians.

Finally, to the twin appeals of a single benevolent leader and a single integrated territorial entity we can add the psychological attractions of a unified chain of command. A fine depiction of how such a perceived chain of command develops in childhood appears in Connell's *The Child's Construction of Politics* (1970). At first, young people array vaguely conceived political tasks like jigsaw puzzle pieces on a table. From this "task pool" they gradually assemble a single task/office hierarchy. Significantly, they do not generally perceive that those at the bottom of their constructed hierarchies — "the people" — are the putative rulers of democratic regimes, a lapse which will occupy us later.

We cannot be certain of the extent to which territorial unity, benevolent leadership, and a single chain of command are developmentally natural for children. There is experimental evidence, however, that shows that people force spatial orderings into single dimensions, even when objective information does not support the existence of only one dimension. This proclivity, it has been argued by Holyoak and Gordon (1984), helps account "for the well-known 'halo effect' obtained when people are asked to evaluate others along multiple dimensions. The obtained judgments tend to correlate too highly across dimensions; for example, rated voice quality is likely to correlate with rated intelligence, even though the two attributes are actually independent" (p. 59).

In addition, though on a more modest level, there is Singer and Singer's finding (1985) that in New Zealand individuals wearing a police uniform receive more social approval than do those same persons otherwise attired. In uncontested democratic regimes like New Zealand, the uniform of authority perceptually validates the individual who wears it. People apparently use dress and perhaps even bodily build (Stewart, Powell, & Chetwynd, 1979) to make judgments about each other. In uncontested democratic regimes, these details of appearance work to the perceptual advantage of authorities.

Despite these processes, young children in uncontested democracies do become exposed to severe political conflict, but it is usually second-hand and principally by anecdote or through the mass media. For example, the socialization effect in this country of the Vietnam conflict was almost solely the consequence of children's viewing television reports of the war. The child's reliance upon television has an important consequence, in that television exaggerates the intensity of all forms of political conflict. Cohen, Adoni, and Drori (1983), in reporting their own study of Israel and in summarizing studies from a number of societies, support this contention. Gerbner and Gross (1976a, 1976b) report corroborative findings for adults who are dependent upon the media; their "cultivation hypothesis" is supported by their studies indicating that heavy television viewers overestimate the amount of danger and conflict in their communities. Because television reporters select vignettes that are heavily biased toward intense political conflict, and because most children in uncontested regimes have no personal political experience with which to counteract these vignettes, these children may well overestimate the danger that political conflict poses within their societies. They may then shrink from conflict.

A reasonable, if paradoxical, conclusion to be drawn from this research is that anxiety about and resistance to political conflict, even among children, may actually be widespread in uncontested democratic regimes. For example, according to Connell (1970), Australian children employed a "fear schema" as they interpreted televised scenes of conflict in the Vietnam War. Not only did they perceive their country's involvement in Vietnam to be a necessary defense against imagined Communist encirclement, they also believed Australian policy to be in the tradition of earlier heroic defenses of the national interest. They therefore distrusted internal dissent to the war. Similar conclusions can be drawn from research by Sears and his colleagues, which suggests that fearful reactions to group conflict often have little to do with self-interest and much more to do with schema that label some groups as inherently dangerous, aggressive, and potent (Sears, Lau, Tyler, & Allen, 1980; Sears & Citrin, 1982).

I would go even further. I suspect that in uncontested democratic regimes many people come to believe that the few among them who do question the regime are morally and psychologically untrustworthy. If so, this bias itself has socialization consequences; it forces potential opponents of the regime to risk stigmatization should they act on their beliefs. Equally interesting are the consequences for regime supporters, who are tempted to believe that children in *contested* regimes must be harmed psychologically by their experience of conflict. An example of this psychological projection is the American perception of children in Northern Ireland; a spate of mass-media reports has spotlighted the alleged psychological harm that the "troubles" have created in the children of Belfast. The question here is not about the *accuracy* of these perceptions, but rather about their *consequences*. The belief that political conflict inflicts harm upon children in contested regimes discourages serious political conflict in uncontested democracies. The symbol of the "damaged child" is one further subtlety in the socialized reproduction of uncontested democratic regimes, and in the marginalization of severe conflict.

## LEARNING ABOUT CONFLICT IN CONTESTED REGIMES

I have argued that most children are psychologically disposed to construct single hierarchies of legitimate authorities within a unified territory. How, then, do children come to embrace serious political conflict in contested regimes, where their own group identifications are subjected to constant attack? Let me turn to political socialization research and to other work in cognitive development, cognitive psychology, and social psychology, in order to sketch out some possible answers to this question. I will first discuss childhood phenomena, then phenomena pertaining also to adults, and, finally, phenomena that characterize the structure of contested regimes themselves.

### Childhood Phenomena

To begin with, even children in contested regimes are able to discover benevolent political leaders, these being the ones who represent their own group loyalties. For example, Palestinian children regularly name Yasir Arafat as their hero; they attribute to Arafat the same potent combination of compassion and power that children in uncontested democratic regimes attribute to duly elected national leaders (Farah, 1980).

An aspect of childhood reasoning that may help form an image of group-based benevolent leadership in contested regimes is *pictorial rehearsal*, which involves the imaginative visualization of conflict as a heroic undertaking. Here is an example of pictorial rehearsal from a Catholic girl's account in Northern Ireland:

> One of the hunger strikers had just died, you know? Francis Hughes, I think it was. Yah, it was. And Julie and her friend had just come out of a shop. And there was the bangin' of the lids. Suddenly people started running. And the army Saracens came down the road, you know? Six-wheeler Saracens? And Julie dove. But when her friend tried to pick her up she couldn't move. She was still conscious on the way to the hospital. But she wasn't all there, like, when we left her. Mommy kept ringing the doctors all night to see how she

was. The thing they were afraid of was the blood leakin' into her brain. [Rosenblatt, 1983, p. 31]

Such accounts, as seen here, often contain vivid images of conflict, suffering, and heroism and provide rich material for elaboration and extension, becoming quite refined, concrete, and emotionally evocative.

Another feature of childhood reasoning that contributes to the reproduction of conflict in contested regimes is the child's inability to attribute apparently opposing characteristics to the same person. Children cannot imagine that a person whom they believe to be acting badly might also possess certain good qualities not currently on show (Cooney & Selman, 1978; Harter, 1982). To children, people are either "all good" or "all bad." In contested regimes, of course, children often observe or at least hear about many instances of "bad" behavior on the part of members of other groups. They also observe or hear mainly about instances of heroic and "good" behavior among their own group's members. It is easy to imagine them generalizing from these particular instances to full-blown, dichotomized group stereotypes.

In turn, bifurcated and dichotomized group stereotypes hasten the process of political *deindividuation*, by which I mean the perception of people primarily as members of groups rather than as unique individuals. To perpetuate serious conflict requires groups to picture their opponents as "all the same," thereby eliminating demoralizing compassion for deserving individual opponents. Group leaders have a strong interest in deindividuating their opponents. In adults, of course, ideologies of nationalism, racism, and sexism assist in this endeavor; the beginnings of such ideologies may lie in the child's incapacity to sustain nondichotomous attributions.

Childhood reasoning also features the early emergence of *affective group evaluations*. Tajfel (1981) notes several studies that have shown that by the age of three, "evaluations precede understanding, whether the relevant groups are or are not in direct contact, and whether clear-cut physical or behavioral cues do or do not exist to facilitate discrimination" (p. 187). Once early affect-laden group classifications stabilize, later analytical learning may be powerless to interfere. In any case, in contested regimes, socialization agents rarely dispense analytic knowledge that might substantially dispute the child's affect-laden group classifications; by contrast, in uncontested democratic regimes, socialization agents often provide enough mature causal and analytic reasoning at least to challenge previously learned group evaluations.

So far the psychological phenomena we have surveyed have been fragmentary. How might the child integrate them into a single learning process? One possible answer lies in the works of Nelson and her colleagues, who have investigated *general event representations* among young children. Nelson (1986) demonstrates that children not only possess complete renderings of the event sequences that typically occur in their surroundings, but also that they apply causal principles to these sequences. In contested regimes, instances of conflict may become important components of the child's general event representations, for such regimes make political conflict a regular constituent of the child's world. Once incorporated within the child's general event representation, conflict may lose its aberrant and morally reprehensible quality and instead become conventional, acceptable, and even necessary.

Three features of event representations may assist this process. First, as Nelson et al. (1986) report, children generalize from singular experiences to an interpretation of the world as a whole. For example, the child's particular school experience slips over imperceptibly into an account of how *all* schools operate. The same process may apply to the child's perception of conflict in contested regimes, so that each child's own experience with conflict exemplifies a *generally* conflictual world, a world so conflictual, in fact, that one cannot escape it and therefore must simply accept it.

Second, children impart to temporally bounded sequences of events a timeless character slipping quickly from "This happened, and then this . . ." to "This is the way things *always* happen." A sense of timelessness reduces the possibility of ameliorating conflict in general. Each occurrence of conflict becomes the most recent instantiation of a historically fated, repetitive, and unalterable struggle, rather than a contingent event open to manipulation.

Finally, the principle of contiguity ties the child's event representations together (Kassin & Pryor, 1985). To the child, proximate events appear to be causally related, which means that children will be captives of many situations they observe. For example, they will find it difficult to introduce extrasituational phenomena to help explain what happens in circumstances they perceive. Concepts such as repression by absent third parties will be difficult for children to grasp as explanations of observed conflicts between two parties. Instead, children search for visible provocations, situational peculiarities, or trait qualities of participants. As a result, external sources of conflict may escape detection and children may remain mired in repetitive sequences of strike and counterstrike.

All of these childhood phenomena, taken together, mean that in contested regimes young children may develop event representations and social scripts in which groups constitute basic units in a scheme of morally sanctioned severe political conflicts. In such cases the very definition of *group* entails legitimate struggle from the outset, setting the stage for later combat. What remains for us now is to pursue the consequences of such classi-fications into adulthood.

## Adulthood Phenomena

The firmest theoretical grounding for our endeavor resides in social identity theory as propounded by Henri Tajfel (see Merelman, 1986). Tajfel proposes that personal identity depends crucially upon group identifica-tions. This dependence allows Tajfel's "minimal group" experimental para-digm often to simulate group antagonisms under the slightest provocations and pretexts. Tajfel summarizes his experimental design in the following way:

> In our experiments, there was no externally defined conflict; if there was competition, . . . it was fully and actively brought into the situation by the subjects themselves as soon as the notion of group was introduced by the experimenters. The subjects were never together as a "group"; they neither interacted nor did they know who was in their group and who in the other; there were no explicit social pressures on them to act in favour of their own group; and in no way was their own individual interest engaged in awarding more money to a member of their own group. [Tajfel, 1981, p. 273]

If group conflict emerges out of ambiguous and unpromising experi-mental circumstances such as these, how much easier it must be for con-flict to surface in regimes where, because of political and historical events, there already exist opposed groups who dispute each other for control. In contested regimes, political conditions reinforce cognitive tendencies for people to depend upon group alignment to anchor their own social identity.

Once a person's social identity incorporates membership in one of several conflicting groups, related cognitive dynamics fan the flames of conflict. Four processes in particular bear discussion: contagion, misplaced determinism, exaggeration, and the illusion of unanimity. *Contagion* re-fers to the belief that contact with a hostile group causes contamination, pollution, and decay. Here the causal principle of contiguity plays an especially pernicious role. Consider the following observations by a Protes-tant child in Northern Ireland:

> Mummy believes daddy "caught" his drinking troubles from the Irish, the Papists here. They all drink as though beer and whisky are pure water or the milk from the cow in a pasture nearby. If you live near people, too close, you'll catch all their bad habits and diseases, even if you start out good and strong. [Coles, 1986, pp. 136-137]

The crystallization of opposing group classifications may also create *misplaced determinism*. Research indicates that people are uncomfortable about attributing events to chance, even when they have been told beforehand that the odds favor chance. For example, even when people have been told that two groups have an equal probability of producing a certain outcome, they discount this fact for one group and respect it for the other. Thus, if an outcome is favorable, people attribute it to the "competence" of well-dressed, neat participants. But if the outcome for the same group is unfavorable, it will be attributed to chance (Jones, 1982). In short, people assume that objectively irrelevant qualities — in this case, dress — bias the odds either for or against a particular group. In so doing people replace the psychological discomfort of unexplained outcomes with misplaced determinism.

Misplaced determinism increases group conflict, because it transforms contingent, unpredictable, complex clashes between opposed groups into fated, predictable, and unidimensional struggles. In consequence, a group may feel that it has been charged with creating conflicts for which it is not responsible. Soon a secondary conflict, over which group bears the blame for the original conflict, exacerbates tensions.

Group classifications also cause *exaggeration* of the perception of individuals. Tajfel and Wilkes discovered that experimental subjects judged lines of different lengths, which were otherwise identical, to be more unequal when the lines were labeled "A" and "B" than when they appeared without labels (Tajfel, 1981). The obverse consequence also applies: People minimize differences among individuals within the same group classification, perceiving members as more alike than they really are.

Perceptual exaggeration provides the foundation for an *illusion of group unanimity*. Noelle-Neumann (1984) demonstrates that, once people perceive public opinion to be tending in a particular direction, they imagine the tendency to be irreversible and therefore seek to join the trend. The result is the well-known "bandwagon effect." Similarly, Janis (1972) examines several political decisions in which decision makers assumed wrongly that their reservations about a course of action were solely their own. Not surprisingly, they held their peace. The result, ironically, is that real group unanimity does emerge, but only as a species of pluralistic ignorance.

Such forces would be less reinforcing of group conflict were it not that individuals tend to identify themselves by reference to their most distinctive features (Jones, 1982), rather than by features which they share with others. But group conflict artificially restricts the range of individual features that members of opposed groups perceive in each other. It therefore is quite easy for members of opposed groups to distinguish themselves from their opponents. By contrast, in uncontested democratic regimes, people may perceive a wider spectrum of individual characteristics, so they will have to search longer to find group characteristics that distinguish them from their putative opponents. As a result they may become aware mainly of things they share with others, a perception that retards the emergence of serious group conflict.

## Structural Phenomena

The psychological forces by which children in contested regimes internalize conflict are opposed by previously discussed tendencies for children to prefer peaceful hierarchies of territorially unified authorities headed by benevolent leaders. In contested regimes several societal-level socialization processes tip the balance in this struggle, toward the reproduction of conflict. Three such processes bear discussion.

First, the *awareness of history* aids the socialization of conflict. A striking aspect of Coles's (1986) and Rosenblatt's (1983) interviews with children in contested regimes is the children's alertness to history. Time and again they came upon children who could recount in detail the salient events, personages, and grievances that have shaped the group conflicts to which they have fallen heir. In this respect, such children contrast sharply with youngsters in uncontested regimes. How shall we explain this phenomenon?

Because they face constant political opposition to their group identity, children in contested regimes may feel a special need to validate themselves. Lacking validation in the present, they turn to the past. Indeed, given their tendencies to see all events as part of a single temporal stream, these children may construe the past as the key to the present, and therefore as something to be embraced, rather than, as is so often the case in uncontested regimes, something to be ignored. Put differently, the historical circumstances that produced the original conflict live on to legitimate the struggles of succeeding generations.

This awareness of history leads in turn to the second process, the *mythologizing of history*, for the version of the past that remains is a moralized, sanitized, heroic one. The hardships children experience in contested regimes demand more than impartial analysis. These children want relief and redemption, not social science. They wish to know that their suffering is not in vain; history as myth provides the necessary reassurance. The myths of a golden past and a utopian future transform present tribulations into bearable discomforts along the road to ultimate vindication. History as teleology becomes the child's talisman.

Finally, myth and history merge to produce *interpretive frameworks* (Landsman, 1985), which situate particular instances of conflict within a reassuring symbolic context. For example, when local whites disputed the rights of Native Americans to live in a residential area of Upstate New York, the whites interpreted the event not as a response the actions of the Native Americans, but to the actions of urban liberals whose misplaced "do-goodism" had long encouraged the Native Americans to "cause trouble." This interpretive framework turned an otherwise ugly instance of white prejudice toward Native Americans into justified opposition to urban exploitation, a conflict in which indigenous people play only a supporting role. The example illustrates how interpretive frameworks pyramid symbols, so that episodes of conflict become necessary parts of an increasingly dramatic and powerful group history. The socialization of group conflict in contested regimes thus develops a momentum all its own.

## POLITICAL EDUCATION AND POLITICAL CONFLICT

I have attempted to describe the way that the conflict configurations of political regimes enter the stream of political learning. One implication of my argument is that schools face formidable obstacles should they attempt to reduce the human cost of severe conflict in contested regimes, or to foster an appreciation for conflict sufficient to minimize the process of marginalization in uncontested democratic regimes.

Nevertheless, in most regimes there exists a minority, including some educators, who favor altering the conflict configurations of their particular regimes. In contested regimes, humane minorities regret the suffering caused by seemingly interminable severe conflict and therefore hope to turn socialization processes to more peaceful ends. In uncontested democracies, dissident minorities dispute existing distributions of power and authority and therefore hope to expand political debate and dispel the distracting forces of marginalization. Can the analysis we have undertaken assist these minorities in designing new strategies of political education? Let us examine this question for each type of regime.

### Reducing Conflict in Contested Regimes

For peace-seeking minorities in contested regimes, the first step is winning student trust. As Ehman (1980) points out, major student gains in political tolerance begin with and depend upon students trusting tolerant teachers. The factors that promote trust between teachers and students are undoubtedly variable and idiosyncratic, but some basic suggestions seem possible. The initial step in any such program must be entirely nonpolitical; that is, teachers should concentrate on transmitting to young people educational skills that are universally valuable and politically noncontroversial. The effective teaching of reading, of artistic endeavor, and of mathematics not only helps students develop a sense of competence but also fosters a belief that the teachers responsible for transmitting such skills are helpful persons worthy of trust.

An important element of such noncontroversial teaching is receptiveness to student suggestions and discussion. Attempting too early to debate group *political* aims would destroy trust, alienate students, and bring parental reprisals. Encouraging a *general* feeling of openness can assure students that the teacher respects them, so that, at a later point, when the teacher evinces skepticism about the claim that student political aims can only be accomplished by a declaration of war, students will not immediately dismiss the assertion. Openness to student suggestions will pay political dividends later.

Once trust exists between teacher and students, it will become possible for teachers to introduce subjects of immediate political relevance. Again, however, subtlety and imagination are requisites in the design of effective teaching materials.

One educational procedure that promises to reduce group conflict is role playing and role exchange. Role-playing skills, as Selman (1980) points out, allow students to place themselves in the positions of others. Initially, such role-playing exercises need not and should not touch on political issues. Instead, teachers may attempt to develop nonpolitical role-playing abilities through discussions about the feelings of, say, abused children or the physically handicapped. Only later should the feelings of opposition-group members emerge as a topic of discussion or role playing.

Another educational strategy builds upon the child's desire for territorial roots. Demonstrations of the roles that property and land play in the child's search for security may be a useful prologue for discussions of how children in other groups feel when their property and land are threatened. The point of such an exercise is to show that instances of hostility involving other groups may be a result of fear, rather than unprovoked malice.

A related procedure plays upon the child's preference for a single line of authority. Exercises involving such issues as the class's use of free time can demonstrate how the absence of an agreed-upon decision-making mechanism paralyzes action, and how, with sufficient peaceful debate, some such mechanism might emerge. From such demonstrations the teacher might later forge subtle connections to the question of divided sovereignty in contested regimes, connections that suggest that all groups might be better off if they could agree upon a single legitimate decision-making mechanism.

Finally, teachers might use instances of misbehavior among students as opportunities to demonstrate that single misdemeanors do not necessarily tell the whole story about a person's character. Teachers could endeavor to rehabilitate the reputations of classroom transgressors by immediately assigning them to undertake worthwhile, feasible tasks. This would teach the class that even vivid cases of bad behavior may not reveal the "real" person; the moral of such demonstrations for later political analysis is obvious.

Once the teacher has constructed a secure, cognitive foundation for the reinterpretation of group conflict, explicit political discussion should ensue. The teacher must assure students that proposed methods for resolving political conflict will not betray parents' and students' legitimate group aspirations. Instead, the teacher must demonstrate to students that, while parental desires and aspirations are legitimate and praiseworthy, alternative political arrangements are necessary to their realization. This is necessary because students who believe the teacher to be undermining the values of parents will immediately reject the teacher's efforts, and the movement toward political reeducation will collapse.

One method for allaying the fears of students is to demonstrate that their opponents are similar to them in many ways, and that the groups share the same hopes and fears. Such an interpretation paints the political actions of opponents as understandable reactions to fear, rather than as aggressive forays in the pursuit of immoral ends. The role-playing skills developed through previous teaching should assist students in reaching this more benign judgment.

At some point in their explicit consideration of group conflict, teachers must arrange for their students to meet with students in the opposing group. In so doing, teachers must proceed delicately and sensitively. One alternative is to avoid political discussions initially, instead arranging for integrated classes on nonpolitical subjects. Another possibility is to engage the combatants in games or in collaborative tasks, such as constructing buildings, cleaning up slum areas, and so forth. Avoiding outright competitive situations is a *sine qua non* if trust is to emerge between opposed groups; research from Sherif (1967) to Tajfel (1978) suggests how rapidly conflict groups become reestablished under competitive circumstances.

In no way do I suggest that an educational sequence of this sort will inevitably succeed in reducing severe group conflict. In contested regimes, the odds always favor conflict, no matter how subtle the teacher. But my suggestions rely upon already rehearsed evidence about the socialization dynamics that support group conflict. As such, they hold promise for advancing "do-goodism" a little distance from sentiment to science.

## Legitimizing Conflict in Uncontested Democratic Regimes

When we turn to uncontested democracies, the prospects brighten. The task for political education in uncontested democracies is to reduce the student's susceptibility to the marginalization of conflict. Marginalization restricts the range of discourse in democratic regimes, disparages the claims of powerless groups who turn to protest out of despair, and reinforces unwarrantedly the power of entrenched elites. The aim of political education under these conditions is to subject the claims of leaders to close and realistic scrutiny, to widen democratic discourse, and to admit presently powerless groups into the circle of legitimate power.

The teacher interested in reducing marginalization may choose among several approaches. One possibility is to use the classroom itself as a model of conflictual debate. Torney-Purta (1981) demonstrates that teachers who encourage discussion, eschew lectures, and are receptive to diverse student viewpoints produce students who are more tolerant of conflict. Moreover, such students reject patriotic appeals by leaders interested primarily in protecting their power.

Before we dismiss this open teaching strategy as inevitably rare in uncontested democracies, we should remember that in such systems periodic waves of educational reform call for precisely these methods. Respected educational thinkers, not "wild-eyed radicals," have recently argued for such procedures as a way of improving American schools. An example is Theodore Sizer (1984), who recommends that American public schools jettison lecture-based "coverage" of subjects, in favor of classroom dialogue. Sizer is interested in teaching fundamental cognitive skills, but if marginalization would be undercut by his methods, so much the better.

Another course teachers might pursue is to introduce classroom material that disputes the building blocks of marginalization, namely, the triumverate of the benevolent leader heading a single line of authority in a unified territory. Teachers may gently question each of these phenomena. For example, the teacher might point out that not all American presidents have been benevolent leaders, utilizing Richard Nixon and Lyndon Johnson as illustrations. Or, the teacher might stress that, during the tenure of certain leaders, their contemporaries often disagreed sharply about their qualities, even though many historians later pronounced them benevolent. Here a brief historical excursion into newspaper attacks on Andrew Jackson or Abraham Lincoln might prove instructive.

Teachers might also point out to students that uncontested democracies include several different modes of authority. The differences between hierarchical bureaucratic authority in large corporations and elected dem-

ocratic leadership in local governments might be simply but effectively
highlighted. Similarly, instances of popular resistance to legislative acts
might be discussed, to illustrate the limits a single line of authority occasionally confronts. In the United States, popular resistance to Prohibition
comes to mind as a case in point.

The concept of federalism might be used by teachers to dispute the
necessity for territorial unity under a single authority. The federal system
(where it exists, as in the United States) is an example of multiple authorities within the same territory. Though difficult to teach, federalism demonstrates that social order and democratic government do not require a
single chain of command. Teachers might also point out that some ideas
and values are widely accepted, even in the absence of any territorial
authority. American Catholics do not live under Vatican political control,
but many nevertheless view themselves as bound by Church doctrine. The
United Nations lacks territorial jurisdiction, but the idea of human rights
embodied in its charter is now strong enough to challenge established
regimes.

Finally, teachers might confront instances of marginalization in contemporary politics. For example, analysis of the way television covers political events might describe the way news programs marginalize conflict
(Bennett, 1983; Broh, 1987). The teacher need not attempt to debunk
media coverage entirely (which would be politically foolish, empirically
unwarranted, and educationally counterproductive), but could instead develop students' analytic skills. Certainly if there is one subject that fasci-
nates young people these days, it is the use and abuse of television. All
teachers need to do, then, is to focus this interest on the process by which
mass media shapes opinion, including our perceptions of conflict. The rest
will follow naturally enough.

## CONCLUSION

In this chapter I have attempted to sketch some modes of socialization
toward conflict in uncontested democracies and in contested regimes. Understanding the socialization of conflict is a necessary preliminary to furthering the prospects of democracy. I have also suggested some pedagogical
techniques that might be used to apply our knowledge about the socialization of conflict to the development of democratic citizens. In uncontested
democracies, the principal pedagogical task is to widen democratic dialogue and to prevent the unwarranted concentration of power in elected
leaders. In contested regimes, the task is to reduce the severity of conflict so
as to enable conflict groups to envisage a viable democratic future togeth-

er. Somewhere between the lacerating struggles of contested regimes and the truncated dialogue of uncontested democracies lies my goal for political education: the pursuit of a richer democracy for all citizens.

## REFERENCES

Bennett, L. (1983). *News: The politics of illusion*. New York: Longman.

Broh, A. (1987). *A horse of a different color: Television's treatment of Jesse Jackson's 1984 presidential campaign*. Washington, DC: Joint Center for Political Studies.

Cohen, A., Adoni, H., & Drori, G. (1983). Adolescents' perceptions of social conflicts in television news and social reality. *Human Communication Research, 10*, 203–225.

Coles, R. (1986). *The political life of children*. Boston: Atlantic Monthly Press.

Connell, R. W. (1970). *The child's construction of politics*. Melbourne, Australia: Melbourne University Press.

Cooney, E. W., & Selman, R. (1978). Children's use of social conceptions: Towards a dynamic model of social cognition. In W. Damon (Ed.), *Social cognition* (pp. 23–45). San Francisco: Jossey-Bass.

Dodge, K., & Richard, B. A. (1985). Peer perceptions, aggression, and the development of peer relations. In J. B. Pryor & J. D. Day (Eds.), *The development of social cognition* (pp. 35–59). New York: Springer-Verlag.

Ehman, L. (1980). The American school in the political socialization process. *Review of Educational Research, 50*, 99–119.

Farah, T. (1980). Learning to support the PLO: Political socialization of Palestinian children in Kuwait. *Comparative Political Studies, 12*, 470–484.

Gerbner, G., & Gross, L. (1976a). Living with television: The violence profile. *Journal of Communication, 26*, 172–199.

Gerbner, G., & Gross, L. (1976b, April). The scary world of TV's heavy viewer. *Psychology Today*, pp. 41–45.

Gitlin, T. (1980). *The whole world is watching*. Berkeley: University of California Press.

Greenstein, F. (1975). The benevolent leader revisited: Children's images of political leaders in three democracies. *American Political Science Review, 69*, 1371–1398.

Harter, S. (1982). A cognitive-developmental approach to children's understanding of affect and trait labels. In F. Serafica (Ed.), *Social-cognitive development in context* (pp. 27–62). New York: Guilford Press.

Holyoak, K. J., & Gordon, P. C. (1984). Information processing and social cognition. In R. S. Wyer, Jr., & T. K. Srull (Eds.), *Handbook of social cognition* (Vol. 1, pp. 39–71). Hillsdale, NJ: Lawrence Erlbaum.

Iyengar, S. (1979). Childhood political learning in a new nation. *Comparative Politics, 11*, 205–225.

Jahoda, G. (1963a). The development of children's ideas about country and nationality. Part I: The conceptual framework. *British Journal of Educational Psychology, 33*, 47–60.

Jahoda, G. (1963b). The development of children's ideas about country and nationality. Part II: National symbols and themes. *British Journal of Educational Psychology, 33*, 143–153.

Janis, I. (1972). *Victims of groupthink.* Boston: Houghton-Mifflin.

Jones, R. A. (1982). Perceiving other people: Stereotyping as a process of social cognition. In A. G. Miller (Ed.), *In the eye of the beholder: Contemporary issues in stereotyping* (pp. 41–92). New York: Praeger.

Kassin, S. M., & Pryor, J. B. (1985). The development of attribution processes. In J. B. Pryor & J. D. Day (Eds.), *The development of social cognition* (pp. 3–35). New York: Springer-Verlag.

Landsman, G. (1985). Ganienkeh: Symbol and politics in an Indian/white conflict. *American Anthropologist, 85*, 826–840.

Merelman, R. (1986). Domination, self-justification, and self-doubt: Some social-psychological considerations. *Journal of Politics, 48*, 276–300.

Miller, A. G. (1982). Historical and contemporary perspectives on stereotyping. In A. G. Miller (Ed.), *In the eye of the beholder: Contemporary issues in stereotyping* (pp. 1–41). New York: Praeger.

Moore, S. W., Lare, J., & Wagner, K. A. (1985). *The child's political worlds: A longitudinal perspective.* New York: Praeger.

Nelson, K. (Ed.). (1986). *Event knowledge: Structure and function in development.* Hillsdale, NJ: Lawrence Erlbaum.

Noelle-Neumann, E. (1984). *The spiral of silence.* Chicago: University of Chicago Press.

Rosenblatt, R. (1983). *Children of war.* Garden City, NY: Anchor/Doubleday.

Sears, D., & Citrin, J. (1982). *Tax revolt: Something for nothing in California.* Cambridge, MA: Harvard University Press.

Sears, D., Lau, R. R., Tyler, T. R., & Allen, H. M., Jr. (1980). Self-interest vs. symbolic politics in policy attitudes and 1976 presidential voting. *American Political Science Review, 74*, 670–684.

Selman, R. (1980). *The growth of interpersonal understanding.* New York: Academic Press.

Sherif, M. (1967). *Group conflict and cooperation: Their social psychology.* London: Routledge & Kegan Paul.

Singer, M. S., & Singer, A. (1985). Self and other perceptions of the police and university students in New Zealand. *Journal of Social Psychology, 125*, 729–733.

Sizer, T. (1984). *Horace's compromise.* Boston: Houghton-Mifflin.

Stewart, R., Powell, G., & Chetwynd, S. J. (1979). *Person perception and stereotyping.* Farmsborough, England: Saxon House.

Tajfel, H. (Ed.). (1978). *Differentiation between social groups.* London: Academic Press.

Tajfel, H. (1981). *Human groups and social categories.* New York: Cambridge University Press.

Torney-Purta, J. (1981). Recent psychological research relating to children's social cognition and its implications for social and political education. In I. Morrissett & A. M. Williams (Eds.), *Social/political education in three countries* (pp. 91–111). Boulder, CO: Social Sciences Education Consortium.

# PART II

# Patterns of
# Political Socialization
# in Democracies:
# Models and Controversies

# 4

## Whither Political Socialization Research?
## The Question of Persistence

DAVID O. SEARS

This chapter begins with a very brief look at the history of political socialization research and an assessment of current activity in the field. The great burst of activity of the 1960s and early 1970s appears to have subsided and in some respects has nearly disappeared altogether. My feeling is that this is due mainly to a loss of faith in the strength and persistence of preadult socialization. The remainder of the chapter considers how persistence has been conceptualized and assessed empirically, and provides an overview of the main findings.

### HISTORICAL OVERVIEW

#### The Early Years

The late 1950s and early 1960s were a time of burgeoning research interest in political socialization. Some "classic" books were produced, such as those by Hyman (1959), Greenstein (1965), Hess and Torney (1967), and Easton and Dennis (1969); as were textbooks, books of readings, and many journal articles. The topic warranted a chapter in the *Handbook of Political Science* (Sears, 1975), and then an entire handbook in its own right (Renshon, 1977).

Why was interest in the topic so great? There are many familiar answers. Partly, it picked up on a tradition of practical interest in civic education (or call it early political indoctrination) that went back to the Greeks and was well-represented in the field of education. Moreover, the principal psychological theories of the day—behavioristic and psychoanalytic—both emphasized the lasting effects of early experience and the irrational and anachronistic quality of adult decision making. A "psychological" approach to politics usually involved personality or such childhood roots of adult behavior, probably because of the dominance of learning and psychoanalytic models, which indeed were the primary models at the most prestigious universities, such as Yale, Harvard, and Stanford. It was natural, therefore, to analyze the roots of political behavior in early experience.

In the area of race relations, the conventional wisdom was that racial prejudice was implanted in childhood; indeed, the hope for improved racial tolerance was a combination of greater education (Stember, 1961) and interracial contact in childhood (Proshansky, 1966). The optimism and hopefulness of postwar America had it that the worst of human problems, such as anti–Semitism, racism, poverty, and the like, could be solved through education and proper child rearing. If these were the solutions, then surely early experience was the problem.

The interest in political socialization was also partly driven by developments in political science as a discipline. The end of colonialism in the Third World, at least in the familiar nineteenth-century Western European mode, had given rise to an intense interest in how democratic systems might be developed in these new postcolonial nations. Development theorists thought democratic orientations might follow from broader educational experience, which would be an inevitable consequence of freedom and growing affluence (Almond & Verba, 1963). Moreover, the dominant theories of political behavior viewed party identification as a central determinant of adult voting behavior, and this in turn seemed to be a highly stable product of preadult, family socialization (Campbell, Converse, Miller, & Stokes, 1960). Similarly, the notion of "political generations" was popular in political sociology, and at least implicitly invoked the lasting effects of preadult socialization (Lipset, Lazarsfeld, Barton, & Linz, 1954).

### Current Status

Following Hyman's pioneering literature review in 1959, research on political socialization burgeoned for a decade and a half. Greenstein (1970, p. 969) felt that "political socialization is a growth stock," and I concurred, noting that "research output has increased at a geometric rate, resulting recently in the publication of several texts and readers" (Sears, 1975, p. 94). Yet only a decade later, Cook (1985) concluded, probably accurately, that "not so long ago, political scientists were enthusiastically proclaiming that political socialization was a growth stock. But interest in the subfield has slackened, and the bull market has turned bearish" (p. 1079). Similarly, Merelman (1986), in his review essay, described the field as having an image of "stagnation." The topic itself seemed to remain as important as ever; in fact, Lindblom (1982, p. 17), in his American Political Science Association presidential address, said that it was "as important a question for political science as can be examined." Nevertheless, Cook (1985) noted the gradual disappearance of articles on political socialization, particularly on preadolescents, from the political science journals.

In order to confirm for myself a sense of how active the field is in political science today, I reviewed all articles published in the last six years (1982–1987) in six major journals that publish work on political behavior: *The American Political Science Review, American Journal of Political Science, Public Opinion Quarterly, Political Behavior, Political Psychology,* and *American Politics Quarterly.*

To summarize the results briefly, in the 125 issues thus reviewed, offering well over 1,000 articles, there were but 14 articles on what might be called the "traditional" topic of political socialization research. Not only that, but only three contained empirical data on preadolescents: Minns (1984), on children's perceptions of the role of voting; Williams and Minns (1986), on children's perceptions of the agents of their socialization; and Owen and Dennis (1987), on the development of political tolerance in both preadolescents and adolescents. Several others looked exclusively at adolescents' attitudes. One investigated the meaning of patriotism among adolescents (Kelly & Ronan, 1987); three others, the intrapsychic determinants of adolescents' attitudes in terms of gender, personality, and religious attitudes (Furnham, 1985; Sidanius, 1985; Smidt, 1982); and one (Ekehammar, Nilsson, & Sidanius, 1987), the effects of different educational experiences on their political ideology. Three articles dealt with intergenerational attitude transmission: Dalton (1982), using the Jennings-Niemi (1981) panel; Rapoport (1985), using the Barnes-Kaase multination study; and Ward (1985), conducting a follow-up of Lane's (1962) *Political Ideology* sample. The remaining three were nonempirical theoretical pieces: Lindblom (1982), on the nature of political socialization, and two on the value of cognitive development theory (Cook, 1985; Peterson, 1983). This indeed is a bear market.

For the record, I should also note a small set of articles on psychobiography that focus particularly on childhood (McIntyre, 1983; Kearney, 1983; Rintala, 1984), though this genre never was treated as part of the political socialization literature.

The other substantial body of recent work I will loosely categorize as addressing "the question of persistence." This work has in common the goal of assessing the impact of preadult experience on later adult attitudes and behavior. Here I counted another 16 articles. Some of this work is very loosely categorized here, such as studies of the short-term effects of such possibly formative experiences as the unemployment of late adolescents (Breakwell, 1986) or adolescents' responses to the threat of nuclear war

(Goodman, Mack, Beardslee, & Snow, 1983). The remainder are explicitly concerned with persistence.

Some assess persistence from individuals' own memories about their earlier experiences. Roberts and Lang (1985) consider the political memories of former Woodrow Wilson Fellows, and Markus (1986) focuses on the distortions in memories of partisan attitudes among members of the Jennings-Niemi (1981) panel study. In both cases the concern is with such memories as indicators of early, formative experiences that might have had persisting effects. In the latter case, the conclusion is that retrospective judgments overestimate persistence. The three waves of the Jennings-Niemi panel of adolescents and their parents allow for a longitudinal assessment of persistence in its own right. Thus, a most important assessment of persistence is provided by Jennings and Markus's (1984) study of the stability of individuals' partisanship over time. The results contribute to a "revisionist" view: Partisanship is not particularly stable until the mid-twenties but is quite stable thereafter. A subsequent paper (Jennings, 1987), based on the same three-wave panel, found substantial continuity in Vietnam-era protestors' attitudes, as did another longitudinal study of 1960s civil rights protestors (Marwell, Aiken, & Demerath, 1987).

Three other studies tackle the problem of persistence by comparing the effects of earlier and later experiences. Franklin's (1984) study used the Jennings-Niemi (1981) panel, again to justify a "revisionist" view of persistence. He found significant revisions of their party identification from late adolescence to young adulthood to accommodate it to their later policy views. Franklin and Jackson (1983) also attempted to assess the responsiveness of party identification to political influences in adult life. Miller and Sears (1986) followed a similar strategy, comparing the effects of preadult, early-adult, and later-adult social environments upon adults' social tolerance, using the General Social Surveys. They found support for both the original persistence theory and a revisionist view. Both preadult and early-adult environments had substantial effects, while later-adult environments tended mainly to reinforce those earlier effects, because they usually provided continuity of environmental tolerance norms.

Finally, a series of cohort analyses assessed persistence by determining whether or not early cohort differences persist through later life. Markus's study (1983) of partisanship in the entire National Election Studies (NES) series and Rowland and Carp's (1983) study of U.S. trial judges' voting behavior are good examples. An analysis of cross-sectional data produced some inferences about generational effects on party identification (Billingsley & Tucker, 1987). There is, in addition, a substantial literature that has followed from Inglehart's provocative (1971) theorizing on "post-materialist values," such as environmentalism and support for civil liberties, by using cohort analyses to compare the formative power of early economic experiences with the power of later-life experiences. European and American data (Abramson & Inglehart, 1986; Inglehart, 1985) and Japanese data (Jagodzinski, 1983) were used to provide such analyses.

In short, in current political science journals in the United States, there is relatively little research on the "classic" problems of preadult political socialization. There is almost none on preadolescents: only three empirical studies in over 1,000 articles in the past six years. There is, however, a continuing interest in the general problem of persistence vs. change in the later life cycle.

## The Question of Persistence

My interpretation of these trends is that the absence of interest in preadult socialization today is related quite directly to a change in the conventional wisdom about the importance of preadult political socialization. Most researchers have simply concluded that children's political attitudes are not very strong or very persistent and therefore have little impact in adulthood. If they do not have much impact on adult attitudes or behavior, why study them?

It was once said that the Jesuits could control people's thinking for life if they controlled their education up to the age of five. Similarly, it was said that "a man is born into his political party just as he is born into probable future membership in the church of his parents" (West, 1945, p. 85). Early researchers on political socialization felt quite confident that the bulk of an individual's most important political dispositions were set by early adolescence (Davies, 1965; Easton & Dennis, 1969; Hess & Torney, 1967). Racial prejudices, too, have long been thought to be formed by preadult learning (Harding, Proshansky, Kutner, & Chein, 1969; Katz, 1976). Such observations have been echoed many times over by shrewd social observers as well as by empirical researchers: Major religious, social, and political attitudes, they contend, tend to be highly stable through the life-span and therefore highly resistant to change at any given point in it.

Early researchers on political socialization regarded persistence as at least partially demonstrated by available data, such as adults' retrospective accounts of their own attitudes (Butler & Stokes, 1974; Campbell et al., 1960); or by longitudinal studies (Bloom, 1964; Feldman & Newcomb, 1969). Others simply assumed persistence (Davies, 1965; Dawson & Prewitt, 1969) or were willing to accept it provisionally in the absence of hard evidence (Easton & Dennis, 1969); still others raised it as a research question (Jennings & Niemi, 1968; Langton, 1969).

It often happens in academia that one school of thought attracts great attention and enthusiasm and becomes the vehicle by which younger scholars rise to the top of the profession, ultimately to shape the conventional wisdom of the mainstream and of the great men and women of the field. Yet one can be certain that, right behind them, will be a school of even younger, ambitious, academic piranha, nastily complaining and attacking, publishing embarrassing data, and ultimately in turn making their own reputations by reducing the previous conventional wisdom to a pile of abandoned bones.

So it was that the early enthusiasm for the persistence viewpoint was succeeded by an equally impressive backlash against it. Some resoundingly critical reviews appeared (see especially Conover & Searing, 1987; Marsh, 1971; Peterson & Somit, 1982). They suggested that the assertion had simply been an article of faith, or that at best the evidence for it had been quite indirect. Indeed, a close look revealed that the evidence was not overwhelmingly solid. Hess and Torney (1967) had inferred the persistence of socialization from a lack of change in marginal frequencies over the years of adolescence, and similarities in marginal frequencies between adolescents and adults; Hyman (1959) from the existence of persisting generational differences in adulthood; Proshansky (1966) and Greenstein (1965) from the existence in childhood of adultlike racial or partisan attitudes; and Campbell et al. (1960) from voters' claims of stable partisan attitudes over the years. A priori faith in the persistence postulate, along with these hints of empirical evidence, sustained the collective belief in persistence, at least for a time.

Then embarrassing data began to emerge. Research by Searing and colleagues (Searing, Schwartz, & Lind, 1973; Searing, Wright, & Rabinowitz, 1976) put forward the argument that "the primacy principle" had been overstated. Long-term longitudinal studies appeared, implying that partisan tendencies change more after the preadult years than the persistence view would allow (Himmelweit, Humphreys, & Jaeger, 1985; Jennings & Niemi, 1981). Empirical demonstrations were published that showed that voters' recall underestimated the extent to which they had changed their minds over the years (Markus, 1986; Niemi, Katz, & Newman, 1980).

The early socialization of support for a regime, which was thought to be the foundation of later citizen support for it, ran into trouble from several quarters. In the aggregate, partisan socialization proved to be very unstable among adults (Miller, 1974) and in specific cases did not have the force on adult compliance to authority that it had been presumed to have (Sears, Tyler, Citrin, & Kinder, 1978). It seemed hopelessly enmeshed with much more transitory attitudes about current incumbents and their policies (Citrin, 1974; Sears, 1975). Watergate, Vietnam, and other related troubles in the United States produced both more cynicism in the seemingly trusting generation initially studied and more cynical subsequent generations of children (Sears, 1975; Sigel & Brookes, 1974). Indeed, some members of the generation of American children that seemed so wedded to political authority in early political socialization studies wound up rioting in the streets of Chicago or smoking dope in Vietnam or working as carpenters under assumed names in Toronto. Further, a look at more culturally diverse populations suggested less ubiquitously supportive attitudes to begin with (Greenberg, 1970; Sears, 1975; Sigel & Hoskin, 1981).

Even the preadult origins of party identification drew skeptical reports. Europeans' party identification seemed much less enmeshed in preadult socialization than Americans' (Budge, Crewe, & Farlie, 1976). Children's partisan attitudes seemed to be weak and inconsistent (Vaillancourt, 1973). Finally, and worst of all, young American adults became less likely to adopt clear partisan preferences. The socialization process seemed not to be working anymore (Miller & Shanks, 1982; Wattenberg, 1984), which started to make the earlier period look less typical than had once been assumed.

These doubts about the persistence of early socialization residues have been swept up in a more general zeal for altering psychologists' traditional belief in the enduring power of early experiences. As Brim and Kagan (1980) wrote, regarding their book, *Constancy and Change in Human Development,* "The view that emerges from this book is that humans have the capacity for change across the entire life span" (p. 1). Others have felt that adults' attitudes were actually rather susceptible to change, given appropriate technology or conditions. Throughout the twentieth century, the electronic media have been thought potent propagandistic instruments for promoting vast changes, whether those promoted by the modern-day White House (e.g., Minow, Martin, & Mitchell, 1973) or by the networks (Robinson, 1976). Rational-choice theorists argue that voting behavior, and even standing partisan preferences, are highly responsive to the voters' current calculations of their own and the national interest (e.g., Downs, 1957; Fiorina, 1981).

The revolution had bred a counterrevolution; "revisionism" came to be the mode of the day. Not only was early socialization not so terribly important, but perhaps people were constantly revising their thinking, in some quite reality-based, sensible, data-oriented manner. Even some of the pioneers in political socialization came to see a more limited role for the effects of preadult experiences in dictating adult behavior (e.g., Greenstein, 1974).

But counterrevolutions in academia rarely have things their own way without dispute. The data on which these challenges were based were not themselves unassailable. The major longitudinal study of the day, the Jennings-Niemi panel study (e.g., Jennings & Markus, 1984; Jennings & Niemi, 1981) made its case for lack of persistence primarily on the instability of youth's attitudes in one particular cohort during their 17-to-24-year-old period. But that cohort was highly unusual, living its formative years through the decade of the most tumultuous social and political change since the Revolutionary and Civil Wars. Much of the evidence of lack of impact or constraint of socialization residues (Searing et al., 1973; Sears et al., 1978) rested on a small and possibly quite flawed set of trust and efficacy measures in the National Election Studies (NES) series. And the weakness of such residues, and their instability, was usually demonstrated with rather insensitive statistical techniques, principally bivariate correlations of often rather insubstantial single items.

In the same era, other research gave some considerable reason to believe that persistence might be fairly substantial, after all. Other researchers continued to emphasize the striking stability of certain attitudes throughout the life-cycle, particularly party identification and racial prejudice (Converse, 1975, 1976; Converse & Markus, 1979; Kinder & Rhodebeck, 1982).

Moreover, the phenomena that began the political socialization movement, if it may be called that, remain with us. It is clear that racial attitudes and party identification continue to have major impact on the political choices of Americans (Carmines & Stimson, 1984; Kinder & Sears, 1981; Sears, 1988; Wattenberg, 1984). They are quite startlingly stable over time, whatever their adjustments in the context of political campaigns (Converse & Markus, 1979). Political ideology, whatever its cognitive ambiguities or idiosyncracies to the individual voter, remains a highly stable and powerful affective disposition (Converse & Markus, 1979; Converse & Pierce, 1986; Levitin & Miller, 1979).

Finally, who can read the daily news from Lebanon or Afghanistan or South Africa without feeling that nationalism, religious fundamentalism, and ethnic identity represent enduring and powerful affective commitments, which surely are not invented in sober and rationally economic decisions by middle-aged women and men? So, in our enthusiasm for the current rediscovery of sensible, rational, flexible thinking in the human being, perhaps it would be well not to forget the phenomena that gave original impetus to investigations of the political socialization process.

The debate bracketed by these conflicting viewpoints concerns the persistence of early religious, social, and political attitudes throughout the life-span. This debate raises fundamental questions about the extent to which adult humans form opinions based upon their current informational environments, as opposed to applying long-standing (and often anachronistic) predispositions. Put another way, to what extent do they engage in "data-driven" as opposed to "theory-driven" information processing (Nisbett & Ross, 1980)?

The rest of this chapter is concerned with how this question of persistence is best conceptualized and assessed and what the current literature on the subject looks like.

## CONCEPTUALIZING PERSISTENCE

### Models of Persistence

Many hypotheses describe how the potential for change in political dispositions might vary with age or life stage. Oversimplifying only a little, such hypotheses reflect one or another of four basic ideas (Sears, 1975, 1981, 1983). The *persistence* viewpoint suggests that the residues of early (preadult) socialization are relatively immune to change in later years. This asserts a simple main effect of age, with dispositions acquired primarily in the preadult years. At the other extreme, the *lifelong openness* notion suggests that dispositions have an approximately uniform potential for change at all ages; it essentially asserts that age is irrelevant for attitude change.

Two other views express intermediate possibilities. The *life cycle* view suggests that people are particularly susceptible to adopting particular dispositions at certain life stages; it essentially asserts that interactions between age and content determine readiness to accept an attitude position. Familiar examples would be the alleged radicalism of youth and conservatism of the aged (hence the old French saying, "He who is not a radical at 20 has no heart; he who is at 40 has no head"). A final view could be termed the *impressionable years* viewpoint, which suggests that *any* dispositions are unusually vulnerable in late adolescence and early adulthood, given strong enough pressure to change. In other stages of life, people are resistant to change, and even in the most vulnerable life stage, they would not change in the absence of substantial pressure to change. At all ages, the content of the disposition is irrelevant. A special, and particularly interesting, instance of the impressionable years hypothesis is the *generational* effect. This occurs when a sizable number of those in the supposedly impressionable life stage (late adolescence and early adulthood) are subjected to a common massive pressure to change on some particular issue; for example, when the nation is engaged in an unpopular war. It presumably yields interactions of birth cohort and dispositional content.

The "revisionist" view of persistence alluded to earlier takes different forms in different hands; usually all are agreed that adult attitudes are a joint function of preadult socialization and later attitude change, but they vary in the relative weights given to each, and in whether later-life change is concentrated in early adulthood (as in the "impressionable years" view) or distributed more evenly across the adult years.

## Pressure to Change Versus Resistance to Change

The question of persistence can be addressed at either the phenotypic or the genotypic level. We can phenotypically describe attitude stability empirically across some segment of the life-span or, alternatively, attempt to assess genotypically the strength of the underlying attitude. In the one case, we measure stability and ignore degree of challenge to the attitude; in the second case, we ask how sturdily the attitude resists challenge.

This requires considering both pressure to change and resistance to change. Attitude change results when the pressure outweighs resistance. Sometimes very strong pressure is required to overcome great resistance to change, as when the American public gradually but reluctantly became persuaded that Richard Nixon was involved in criminal activity in the Watergate affair. On other occasions only modest pressure is required because of low levels of resistance to change; hence, very modest marketing devices can influence consumer choices when all competing products are essentially the same.

Observed levels of stability can be difficult to interpret, then. Stability could reflect either strong resistance to change or simply a lack of pressure to change. So change, or the lack of it, must not be used as the sole index of the strength of the underlying disposition.

## Symbolic Predispositions and Non-Attitudes

Early definitions of "attitudes" emphasized their enduring quality. They were portrayed as stable dispositions to make a particular response to a wide variety of objects and situations (see Calder & Ross, 1973). Converse (1964, 1970) challenged the generality of this proposition by demonstrating the very considerable instability of some policy attitudes. On the other hand, numerous other attitudes are highly stable through adulthood (Converse, 1975; Converse & Markus, 1979). Such research suggests that further distinction needs to be made before we proceed.

Attitudes vary a good deal in their stability over time, and presumably also in their intrinsic resistance to change. People can be highly committed to or ego-involved in some of their attitudes but not others (e.g., Sherif & Cantril, 1947). Individual attitudes can therefore be thought of as falling somewhere along a dimension of affective strength running from an enduring predisposition to a "non-attitude." In social psychological terms, they vary in commitment or ego-involvement. Such a distinction can be made in public opinion data using three criteria: short-term stability, consistency over variations in item wording, and influence over attitudes toward new objects (Sears & Whitney, 1973).

The question of persistence is largely moot for attitudes at the "non-attitude" or low ego-involvement end of this dimension, since such attitudes are plainly extremely malleable. The question becomes interesting only for attitudes at the high ego-involvement end of this continuum. My colleagues and I have used the term *symbolic predisposition* to describe such attitudes: strong affects that are conditioned to particular symbols, such as *blacks, America, Democrat, or communism*. In a number of studies we have tried first to define what attitudes fit into this category for most Americans. Among the most obvious are party identification, racial attitudes, and certain moral attitudes (Sears, 1975). This would vary considerably from one political system to another, of course, and among individuals within a particular system. Second, we have tried to determine the impact of these predispositions on policy attitudes and voting behavior (Kinder & Sears, 1981; Sears & Citrin, 1985; Sears, Hensler, & Speer, 1979; Sears, Lau, Tyler, & Allen, 1980). Third, we have tried to determine their cognitive characteristics (Sears & Citrin, 1985). This chapter follows other works (Sears, 1983, 1984) in examining a fourth question, that of the persistence of these attitudes through the life-span.

It might be noted in passing that these symbolic predispositions generally have more societal importance than do non-attitudes. They tend to focus on the issues that get the most attention from the media and in ordinary conversation. They tend to reflect the most recurrent and controversial issues. They also help people organize the ongoing flow of information concerning many different political and social issues. So an understanding of attitude change over the life cycle on these particular issues has some special priority.

Note also that symbolic predispositions are marked by the strength of affective responses to specific attitude objects. People also differ, of course, in how emotionally involved they are in politics in general. General political involvement is typically correlated with education, information level, political activity, and a variety of other indices. Whether or not it is correlated with persistence is less clear.

## ASSESSING PERSISTENCE

Five general research paradigms have been used to address the question of persistence. In the limited space available here, I cannot do justice to the wide variety of studies that have been done using each of these paradigms. Rather, let me hit the highlights of each, giving the flavor of some of the more reliable results.

### Retrospective Judgments

The earliest studies of persistence relied heavily upon the citizen's own retrospective judgment of his or her earlier attitudes. Such evidence often led them to assert that attitudes such as party identification were highly stable over time (e.g., Campbell et al., 1960). It will come as no surprise to learn that these retrospections overestimate stability. Systematic evidence on this point is now accumulating (e.g., Himmelweit et al., 1985; Markus, 1986; Niemi et al., 1980). Such recent research has indicated that retrospective judgments are not sufficiently accurate to serve as a reliable indicator of persistence. Evidently people either do not want to admit that they have changed their minds, because it is socially undesirable to do so, or they misremember their own histories as having been more stable than they were in fact. Nevertheless, memories of formative political experiences are of interest in their own right and have some value in predicting attitudes later in adulthood (Roberts & Lang, 1985).

### The "Structuring Principle"

A second approach involves determining whether the presumed residues of early socialization influence adults' attitudes toward new political events, candidates, and issues. The argument is that truly long-standing predispositions must perforce be strong enough to control attitudes toward attitude objects appearing later in life. Searing et al. (1973) have called this the "structuring principle." Such research is certainly relevant to the persistence hypothesis, since its most important implication is that predispositions acquired early are potent in later life. But it is not exactly on the point: Such data test the potency of particular attitudes, rather than their long-standingness.

Much cross-sectional evidence does exist on the association between basic predispositions and responses to contemporary political persons, issues, and events. In their attempt to assess systematically the strength of these relationships, Searing et al. (1973) correlated a long series of seemingly basic political orientations (falling into the general categories of partisanship and system support) with a series of policy attitudes. This shotgun effort, not surprisingly, yielded generally weak correlations, and they concluded that the structuring principle did not hold very powerfully.

This has been succeeded by efforts focused more specifically on a shorter list of symbolic predispositions for which there is better reason to expect persistence, such as party identification, liberal/conservative ideology, and racial prejudice. These have had demonstrably strong effects on policy and voting preferences and on evaluations of political candidates and events (e.g., Kinder & Rhodebeck, 1982; Kinder & Sears, 1981; Levitin & Miller, 1979; Mann & Wolfinger, 1980; Sears & Citrin, 1985; Sears et al., 1979; Sears & McConahay, 1973; Sears et al., 1980). Research using this paradigm has yielded impressive evidence for persistence, as long as it is limited to predictors that are plausible candidates for long-standing persistence, and it steers clear of system support.

## Cohort Analyses

Another method of assessing persistence is cohort analysis. If the attitudes of two samples taken from a common birth cohort are roughly comparable at the two measurement points, the inference is that the *individuals'* attitudes have not changed very much, or at least not in a uniform direction. Since such analysis, at best, tracks the aggregated attitudes of an entire birth cohort, inferences about the stability of individuals' attitudes are, of course, chancy. Cohort analyses also, by their nature, are never free of the confounding effects of period, aging, and cohort (Glenn, 1977; Mason, Mason, Winsborough, & Poole, 1973), since only two independent variables (birthdate and time of interview) are available to assess these three effects.

Cohort analysis has been the primary analytic technique used to test the "life-cycle" hypothesis that stage-specific needs result in the adoption of particular political attitudes. Such studies have found no diminution with age in the number of self-professed Independents nor any rush to the Republicans or to conservatism more generally (Glenn, 1980), as life-cycle theories of adolescent rebellion and the conservatism of the elderly would suggest. The devotion of today's late adolescents to political independence is probably due more to their inexperience with the political system and to weakening party loyalties more generally, than to their legendary life-cycle proclivity for youthful rebellion. It usually does not reflect great opposition to their parents' politics and shows few of the expected links to antagonism toward parents (Jennings & Niemi, 1974; Tedin 1974).

Such cohort analyses usually yield better evidence for generational than life-cycle effects. Postmaterialist values also have been fairly stable in

European, American, and Japanese cohorts, though there is somewhat more evidence of their responsiveness to fluctuating economic conditions (Inglehart, 1985; Jagodzinski, 1983). The cohort of U.S. trial judges appointed by a particular president has fairly stable voting preferences in controversial cases (Rowland & Carp, 1983). Commitment to party does appear to strengthen somewhat over the life cycle, though (Converse, 1976; 1979).

Cohort analyses have also generally shown greater shifts by younger than older cohorts in response to such "period" forces as increasing liberalism on civil liberties issues in the post–McCarthy era or the decline in partisanship in the late 1960s and 1970s. In fact, shifts among the older groups have usually been negligible (Glenn, 1980; Sears, 1983). The overall burden of evidence is surprisingly uniform in leaning toward an "impressionable-years" viewpoint, although in any given case other explanations are possible, of course.

It is possible also that some eras generate more change than others. Our own era, with its pattern of weakening party loyalties in particular, and perhaps less forceful early partisan socialization (Beck, 1974) may be a case in point, though that empirical case remains to be made in detail.

## Longitudinal Studies

The seemingly most appealing alternative is the longitudinal study, in which the preadult child is tested and then interviewed again as an adult. Longitudinal designs have many advantages, of which the most obvious is that they yield the best single estimate of the stability of a particular individual's attitude over a given period of time. Such evidence is hard to come by, however. The best data on political attitudes are furnished by some relatively recent studies, especially the panel study conducted by Jennings, Niemi, and Markus of high school students and parents initially interviewed in 1965; several reinterviews by Himmelweit and her colleagues (1985) of adolescent boys originally contacted in 1951; and the Newcomb, Koenig, Flacks, and Warwick (1967) 20-year follow-up of Bennington College graduates. A related technique is the use of shorter panels, such as the 4-year studies of the general public initiated by NES in 1956 and 1972 (e.g., Converse & Markus, 1979).

Despite their obvious attractions, longitudinal studies have their limitations. First of all, the effects of aging are confounded with cohort and period effects in any longitudinal study. The cohort that is tracked was born at one historical time and experiences just one unique historical period. Hence those interviewed by Jennings and Niemi were members of the famed postwar "baby boom" and spent their late adolescence and early adulthood in the midst of the Vietnam and Watergate eras. One cannot isolate the effects of life stage from these external influences. For example, Jennings and Niemi (1981) report substantial attitude changes between two interviews done in 1965 and 1973, including a substantial decline in political trust. Whether youthful trust is generally not very persistent, or declines with age in general, or just did so during that historical period because of the many unusual shocks to the political system in those years (Vietnam, Johnson's withdrawal from his campaign for reelection, the storm over desegregation, Watergate, and so forth), is indeterminate.

There are minor irritants with any longitudinal study as well. Sample attrition may produce important biases; for example, Jennings and Niemi successfully reinterviewed 83 percent of the whites in their sample but only 59 percent of the nonwhites. Inevitably, some questions that later turn out to be important were not anticipated in early waves; for example, Vietnam was skipped in Jennings and Niemi's first interview, conducted in 1965.

Moreover, in order to evaluate the persistence of attitudes across the time-spans contained in these studies, a number of methodological problems must be surmounted. Most important, measurement error contributes to instability, as well as genuine attitude change. There has been considerable controversy about how to allocate obtained levels of instability between these two sources (see Achen, 1975; Converse & Markus, 1979; for a summary of this literature, see Kinder & Sears, 1985). The unreliability problem is compounded by the fact that all the major longitudinal studies depend heavily on attitude items generated in (and in many cases unmodified since) the 1950s and early 1960s — the very earliest days of electoral research and a different era in many respects. Even demonstrably stable items, such as that measuring party identification, have turned out to have measurement shortcomings (Dennis, 1981; Weisberg, 1980). The length of time between measurements normally influences stability, but not unreliability, presumably. So comparisons across different time-spans must be adjusted for the former (presumably by some geometric function; see Converse & Markus, 1979) but not the latter. For all these reasons, stability estimates improve considerably as one progresses from single items through additive scales to structural equations that index unmeasured latent variables. For example, consider analyses of attitudes about racial desegregation in the NES 1972–1976 panel study. The test-retest coefficient for a single item was .41; for a five-item scale, .62; and for a LISREL model, .83. Comparable data for attitudes toward gender equality were .52, .59, and .77, respectively (Converse & Markus, 1979; Sears & Gahart, 1980).

All this is simply preface. What do longitudinal data show? The best-known data come from the Jennings and Niemi panel study, based on a national sample of high school seniors and their parents, interviewed in 1965 and again in 1973 and 1981. Their report gives substantial evidence of the incompleteness of political socialization at age 17, in that most political attitudes showed considerable instability during the eight years following.

Equally impressive, however, are those attitudes that show a high level of stability. Party identification is a clear example. Only 9 percent of all 1965 Democrats and Republicans in the youth sample had switched to the opposite party by 1973 (Jennings & Niemi, 1981). The second reinterview of the panel revealed considerably greater "hardening" of party identification in the youth sample, no longer so youthful, of course (Jennings & Markus, 1984). Similarly, the Newcomb et al. (1967) 20-year follow-up of Bennington College alumnae discovered impressive stability: Their senior-year conservatism during the 1930s correlated +.47 with their 1960 conservatism and +.48 with the number of Republican presidential candidates supported in the interim.

In general, these longitudinal studies have demonstrated considerable stability over time for attitudes toward certain specific classes of attitude objects. One such category is comprised of the two major partisan attitudes. Converse and Markus (1979) estimate two-year stability of the single party identification item at .81 during the 1972–1976 period, and at .97 when it is corrected for unreliability. Liberal-conservative self-designation similarly is quite stable. Other categories yielding high levels of stability include basic values such as individualism, egalitarianism, and postmaterialism (Feldman, 1983; Inglehart, 1985); racial attitudes (Converse & Markus, 1979; Kinder & Rhodebeck, 1982; Sears & Gahart, 1980); political-moral attitudes, such as abortion, marijuana, and women's status; and attitudes toward prominent public persons. On the other hand, substantially lower stability estimates are obtained concerning most policy issues, as well as diffuse subjective orientations, such as political trust, political efficacy, political interest, and citizen duty (Converse & Markus, 1979; Jennings & Niemi, 1981; see also Merelman & King, 1986, for an impressive demonstration of early socialization of political activism, using the Jennings/Niemi panel data).

High stability correlations simply indicate that people retain the same *relative* position over time, not that they retain exactly the same attitude. Ward (1985) has shown that fathers who were racist in the terms of the 1950s — being opponents of "miscegenation" — bred offspring who as adults were racially unsympathetic, at least, in the terms of *their* day — being opponents of busing and affirmative action. This suggests that a latent racism had been passed on and retained over the years, but was manifest in a different form.

## Natural Experiments

A final paradigm tests attitude change in response to systematic pressure to change. It asks whether basic political predispositions prove resistant to such pressures to change, as the persistence view would suggest, or
adjust and change, as the openness view would suggest. Such research
resembles a naturalistic, quasi-experimental version of simple attitude-
change experiments. Ideally, one would like randomly to assign respondents of different life stages to varying degrees of pressure to change; however, in practice that has rarely been done, even in laboratory experiments.
Hence one must rely on natural experiments and post hoc controls.

Several bodies of research provide relevant evidence on this point, by
assessing the effect of various possible influences upon adults' attitudes,
particularly those stemming from (1) direct personal experiences, (2)
changes in one's location in the social structure, and (3) political events and
communications about them. This is surely not an exhaustive list of possibilities, and there are shortcomings with each of these literatures. Nevertheless, by pooling the results from these several approaches, we may maximize the "heterogeneity of irrelevancies," in Campbell's terms (quoted in
Brewer & Collins, 1981).

Personal Experiences.   Direct personal experiences with political matters, according to most psychological theories, ought to have a special
potential for eroding the residues of preadult socialization. Unfortunately,
all too few studies have been conducted on this question. One exception is
the Jennings and Markus (1977) report on the 1965 high school seniors who
subsequently served in the armed services in and out of Vietnam. Indices of
initial political socialization, such as pre-Vietnam levels of political cynicism, faith in the government, civic tolerance, and measures of social
background such as race and educational level, all had powerful residual
effects upon post-Vietnam attitudes, independent of the effects of Vietnam
experiences (e.g., measures of military service and attitudes about the war
itself). However powerful the Vietnam experience upon these late adolescents and young adults, therefore, their prior attitudes had strong residual
effects. In fact, the Vietnam experience itself had only "modest" (in the
authors' words) effects upon these youths' political attitudes.

A wide variety of changes can occur in an adult's living situation that
are able to induce changes in his or her political self-interest. Such changes
can in turn create systematic pressures to change one's political predispositions. People's taxes go up, for example, or their children enter and then
leave school, and such changes could conceivably induce pressure to make
self-serving changes in political attitudes, supporting an openness view. On

the other hand, symbolic predispositions persisting from earlier socialization may overpower these later-life changes in self-interest, leaving the person's political attitudes more or less unaffected by them. To test this, we have conducted an extensive series of studies pitting private self-interest against long-standing predispositions (such as party identification, racial prejudice, or liberalism/conservatism) as determinants of policy attitudes and voting preferences in various realms of political life. These have assessed the effects on adults' political attitudes of (1) several kinds of personal racial threats (such as busing, neighborhood desegregation, crime, or economic competition), (2) economic self-interest (such as falling personal financial fortunes, unemployment, inadequate medical insurance, or property tax burdens), (3) crime victimization, (4) energy crises, and (5) close relatives' or friends' vulnerability to war.

In most of this work, self-interest turns out to have remarkably little effect on either policy attitudes or voting behavior. For example, self-interest in the busing issue (e.g., having children in public school in districts with busing or expecting busing into or out of one's own children's schools) has been essentially uncorrelated with whites' opposition to it (Kinder & Sears, 1981; Sears & Allen, 1984). Personal employment problems have little relationship to attitudes toward government job policies (Sears et al., 1980). The most notable exception is some fairly strong self-interest effects in the California tax revolt, particularly among homeowners and those feeling themselves to be especially burdened by taxes (Sears & Citrin, 1985). Even here, however, standing predispositions accounted for large shares of the variance; many types of self-interest had very little effect (e.g., being service recipients); and at most self-interest generally had narrow attitudinal effects. These studies suggest that adults' basic political attitudes are, most of the time, unresponsive to their self-interest, as the persistence view would suggest.

Changes in Social Location.    Whenever people are placed in an environment with social and political norms contrary to those of their original political socialization, there is pressure to change. The classic case study is Newcomb's (1943) analysis of Bennington College women. He showed that these largely conservative women, placed in a politically progressive college environment, moved substantially to the left. When these women were reinterviewed some 20 years later, Newcomb et al. (1967) found substantial continuity in their political attitudes. Moreover, the supportiveness or discrepancy of their postcollege social environments had a powerful effect upon the persistence (or "regression") of their college-originated attitude changes. Even such a powerful experience did not completely override the effects of initial political socialization, however: Adulthood attitudes were highly correlated with *both* pre-Bennington (freshman-year) and post-Bennington (senior-year) attitudes. The latter yielded higher correlations, indicating substantial, but far from complete, resocialization during the college years.

Both geographical and status mobility expose people to new environments whose social and political norms may differ from those dominating their original socialization. The most systematic quantitative analysis of the political effects of migration (Brown, 1981) finds some adaptation to new partisan environments on the part of migrants, contrary to the persistence viewpoint. However, two aspects of these data provide more support for the persistence hypothesis. Most respondents were not vulnerable to change, since most spent most of their lives in environments whose partisanship was congruent with that of their early adulthood environments. Even migrants tended to move to environments with the same partisan complexion as those they departed, so migration did not usually subject them to major pressure to change. Second, change toward the new partisan norms of a new environment was greatest for those who had spent relatively more time in the new environment. Hence young migrants were more likely to change than were older migrants. Since the highest rates of migration occur in late adolescence and early adulthood, such a finding gives more support to the impressionable-years model than to lifelong openness. Nevertheless, this literature gives evidence that basic partisan predispositions can change in later life, if the individuals are surrounded for a long period of time by environments attitudinally discrepant from those of their earlier socialization. It also gives evidence that such predispositions normally do *not* change because of migration, because normally an individual does not change from one partisan environment to another.

An analogous hypothesis is that status mobility might induce resocialization to the prevailing norms of the class of destination. There is an extensive literature on this problem, which can only be alluded to here. Many apparent mobility effects are almost certainly due to selective recruitment, that is, to the persistence of class-inappropriate early socialization. Some anticipatory resocialization also occurs prior to adulthood. Above and beyond these effects, mobile young adults do seem to adapt partially (though not completely) to the political norms of their destination social class (e.g., Abramson, 1972). The extent to which such mobility effects continue to occur through the rest of the life-span is unclear, but the best current guess is that the lion's share of mobility-instigated resocialization is accomplished in late adolescence and early adulthood (see Kinder & Sears, 1985, and Sears, 1975, for references to this literature).

The overall effects of various kinds of environmental change upon the persistence of early learned tolerance have been assessed by Miller and Sears (1986). They tested the relative impact, upon racial, gender, and sexual tolerance, of (1) preadult environments, in terms of parental status characteristics, early geographical location, and initial religious commitment; (2) early adult environment, in terms of educational background; and (3) adulthood environments, in terms of the respondents' adult status characteristics, geographical location, and religious commitment. They found that preadult environments had about twice as great an impact as did adult environments, and that most people lived throughout their lives in environments with tolerance norms that were consistent with their early ones. However, in that minority of instances where people did change environments, some attitude change evidently occurred.

Finally, either status mobility or adulthood status discrepancies (i.e., inconsistencies among different indices of social class) have often been hypothesized to induce tensions that produce greater ultraconservatism, racial prejudice, or radical egalitarianism. An extensive empirical literature has succeeded mainly in establishing that such inconsistencies rarely yield anything other than simple main effects of the constituent status dimensions. For example, rich Catholics' partisan preferences tend to fall halfway between those of the rich in general and those of Catholics in general. This would imply an averaging of the persisting residues of socialization associated with both characteristics; that is, the Republican-party tendencies of the rich and the Democratic-party sympathies of Catholics. The only two major exceptions to such an averaging process also seem to represent clear instances of the persistence model: Jews and blacks of high achieved status are more liberal than would be expected from their status. This is more likely to be due to the persistence of strong ethnic socialization than to any adulthood radicalization due to the shock of status tensions (Knoke, 1972; Sears, 1975).

Political Events and Communications.    Another relevant literature examines the effects of distal political events upon basic predispositions and particularly considers their possible greater impact upon younger citizens. An excellent example is Markus's (1979) analysis of the impact of Vietnam and racial conflict upon party identification and cynicism. Using the Jennings and Niemi panel data, he found a substantial level of persistence, especially for the older (parental) cohort; that reactions to those political events altered party identification; and that those events had a generally stronger impact upon the younger than the older cohort. Similarly, Franklin (1984) and Jackson (1975; Franklin & Jackson, 1983) have found that the party attachments of younger citizens are influenced by policy preference, and more than are the attachments of their elders. These results fit neatly with the mounting revisionist argument that party identification is in part an ongoing political choice, as the openness model would have it (e.g., Fiorina, 1981). But it also suggests such modification of partisan identification is easiest for those in the "impressionable" years.

The minimal-effects model of mass communication influence, so popular nearly 30 years ago (Klapper, 1960), argued that the media rarely produced major changes in adults' established attitudes. This view has come under considerable attack in recent years. The growth of massive exposure to television has been accompanied by equally widespread assumptions about its persuasive impact. Extensive and reliable revisionist reviews have been supplied by Comstock, Chaffee, Katzman, McCombs, and Roberts (1978) and Kraus and Davis (1976), but even they finally turn out not to argue that television generally changes attitudes very much. Instead, they find and emphasize the discernible media impacts they uncover on other dependent variables, especially information diffusion and "agenda-setting." In any case, it is hard to see any major shift in the nature of evidence on the media's persuasive impact on adults' attitudinal commitments. It still seems minimal, at least on the most important of their attitudes, even in today's much more refined and sophisticated research (see Kinder & Sears, 1985; Kraus & Perloff, 1985; McGuire, 1986).

So, at least at some very crude level, symbolic predispositions appear to show high levels of persistence after late adolescence and early adulthood. The data are, of course, in most cases not completely adequate, there are exceptions, there is at least some modest revision of such predispositions throughout life, there is a good bit of "error variance" (however unexplained variance is to be interpreted in this context), and this characterization could never be anything but crude. Nevertheless, I think it is possible to argue that some combination of the "persistence" and "impressionable-years" notions best describe the life course of that subset of political and social attitudes that are most important to ordinary people and most consequential for society.

It is less clear whether this obtained persistence is due to the intrinsic psychological strength of early learned attitudes or to a waning level of discrepant communication in one's proximal environments as one ages. In other words, it remains unclear whether high resistance to change or diminishing pressure to change is responsible for this observed persistence. The migration and mobility studies would suggest that people *can* change, but their adult environments normally provide them with much social support for their original attitudes, so they usually *do not* change very greatly.

## POLITICAL SOCIALIZATION:
## INDOCTRINATION VERSUS DEVELOPMENT

Some years ago, I suggested that political socialization could be defined in two quite different ways: as the inculcation of orientations that were valued by adults, or as the gradual development of the individual's own particular and idiosyncratic views of the political world (Sears, 1975). The stimulus for most of the interest in empirical research on political socialization came almost entirely from the former. Political scientists were much preoccupied with the value of a strong party system, and Hyman's (1959) early review suggested that party loyalties were born in the political socialization process. Research thus focused on discovering the details of that inculcation process.

Similarly, the trials and tribulations of newly postcolonial nations stimulated great interest in the fundamental loyalties of citizen to nation and to political rules of the game in democratic systems (Almond & Verba, 1963). These, too, were thought to be inculcated in the political socialization process (Easton & Dennis, 1969). Again, researchers sought to define the details of *that* inculcation process.

In other words, the genesis of political socialization research has been, I believe, largely in normative concerns driven by the perceived need to socialize—or indoctrinate, to use a more loaded word—children and adolescents into those political orientations that parents and society in general applaud.

But one could take the other definition of political socialization and see where it leads. It might indeed suggest research on a fuller appreciation of development and change throughout the life-span (Brim & Kagan, 1980). Even if one assumes that the potential for change slows down with advancing age, it is not removed altogether. What are the conditions under which it occurs? Instability may well be a function of meaningful learning and reorientation, rather than mere random movement. Indeed, another norm that is widely held is that people ought to be open to change throughout their lives; much of the political criticism directed at older people in the 1960s focused on their unwillingness to reexamine old premises about patriotism, morality, and other such political issues.

One might therefore ask what the conditions are for training people to be open and responsive to new realities, as opposed to training them to be loyal to the reigning norms of their childhood. Such questions go well beyond the scope of this particular chapter, but they are provocative and, to my mind, provide justification for continued attention to the field of political socialization, albeit oriented by a different concern and a different vision of how it might contribute to the individual's development.

## REFERENCES

Abramson, P. R. (1972). Intergenerational social mobility and partisan choice. *American Political Science Review, 66*, 1291-1294.

Abramson, P. R., & Inglehart, R. (1986). Generational replacement and value change in six West European societies. *American Journal of Political Science, 30*, 1-25.

Achen, C. H. (1975). Mass political attitudes and the survey response. *American Political Science Review, 69*, 1218-1231.

Almond, G. A., & Verba, S. (1963). *The civic culture*. Princeton, NJ: Princeton University Press.

Beck, P. A. (1974). A socialization theory of partisan realignment. In R. G. Niemi (Ed.), *The politics of future citizens* (pp. 119-219). San Francisco: Jossey-Bass.

Billingsley, K. R., & Tucker, C. (1987). Generations, status and party identification: A theory of operant conditioning. *Political Behavior, 9*, 305-322.

Bloom, B. S. (1964). *Stability and change in human characteristics*. New York: John Wiley.

Breakwell, G. M. (1986). Political and attributional responses of the young short-term unemployed. *Political Psychology, 7*, 575-586.

Brewer, M. B., & Collins, B. E. (Eds.). (1981). *Scientific inquiry and the social sciences: A volume in honor of Donald T. Campbell*. San Francisco: Jossey-Bass.

Brim, O. G. Jr., & Kagan, J. (1980). *Constancy and change in human development*. Cambridge, MA: Harvard University Press.

Brown, T. (1981). On contextual change and partisan attitudes. *British Journal of Political Science, 11*, 427-447.

Budge, I., Crewe, I., & Farlie, D. (1976). *Party identification and beyond: Representations of voting and party competition*. London: John Wiley.

Butler, D., & Stokes, D. (1974). *Political change in Britain* (2nd ed.). New York: St. Martin's Press.

Calder, B. J., & Ross, M. (1973). *Attitudes and behavior*. Morristown, NJ: General Learning Press.

Campbell, A., Converse, P. E., Miller, W. E., & Stokes, D. E. (1960). *The American voter*. New York: John Wiley.

Carmines, E. G., & Stimson, J. A. (1984). The dynamics of issue evolution: The United States. In R. J. Dalton, S. C. Flanagan, & P. A. Beck (Eds.), *Electoral change in advanced industrial democracies* (pp. 134-158). Princeton, NJ: Princeton University Press.

Citrin, J. (1974). Comment: The political relevance of trust in government. *American Political Science Review, 68*, 973-988.

Comstock, G., Chaffee, S., Katzman, N., McCombs, M., & Roberts, D. (1978). *Television and human behavior*. New York: Columbia University Press.

Conover, P. J., & Searing, D. D. (1987, September 4). *Citizenship regained: A new framework for the study of political socialization*. Paper presented at the annual meeting of the American Political Science Association, Chicago, IL.

Converse, P. E. (1964). The nature of belief systems in mass publics. In D. E. Apter (Ed.), *Ideology and discontent* (pp. 206–261). New York: Free Press of Glencoe.

Converse, P. E. (1970). Attitudes and non-attitudes: Continuation of a dialogue. In E. R. Tufte (Ed.), *The quantitative analysis of social problems* (pp. 168–189). Reading, MA: Addison-Wesley.

Converse, P. E. (1975). Public opinion and voting behavior. In F. I. Greenstein & N. W. Polsby (Eds.), *Handbook of political science* (Vol. 4) (pp. 75–170). Reading, MA: Addison-Wesley.

Converse, P. E. (1976). *The dynamics of party support: Cohort-analyzing party identification.* Beverly Hills, CA: Sage.

Converse, P. E. (1979). Rejoinder to Abramson. *American Journal of Political Science, 23,* 97–100.

Converse, P. E., & Markus, G. B. (1979). Plus ça change . . . : The new CPS election study panel. *American Political Science Review, 73,* 32–49.

Converse, P. E., & Pierce, R. (1986). *Political representation in France.* Cambridge, MA: Harvard University Press.

Cook, T. E. (1985). The bear market in political socialization and the costs of misunderstood psychological theories. *American Political Science Review, 79,* 1079–1093.

Dalton, R. J. (1982). The pathways of parental socialization. *American Politics Quarterly, 10,* 139–157.

Davies, J. C. (1965). The family's role in political socialization. *Annals of the American Academy of Political and Social Science, 361,* 10–19.

Dawson, R. E., & Prewitt, K. (1969). *Political socialization.* Boston: Little, Brown.

Dennis, J. (1981). *Some properties of measures of partisanship.* Paper presented at the annual meeting of the American Political Science Association, New York, New York.

Downs, A. (1957). *An economic theory of democracy.* New York: Harper & Row.

Easton, D., & Dennis, J. (1969). *Children in the political system: Origins of political legitimacy.* New York: McGraw-Hill.

Ekehammar, B., Nilsson, I., & Sidanius, J. (1987). Education and ideology: Basic aspects of education related to adolescents' sociopolitical attitudes. *Political Psychology, 8,* 395–410.

Feldman, K. A., & Newcomb, T. M. (1969). *The impact of college on students: Vol. 1. An analysis of four decades of research.* San Francisco: Jossey-Bass.

Feldman, S. (1983). Economic individualism and American public opinion. *American Politics Quarterly, 11,* 3–30.

Fiorina, M. P. (1981). *Retrospective voting in American national elections.* New Haven, CT: Yale University Press.

Franklin, C. H. (1984). Issue preferences, socialization, and the evolution of party identification. *American Journal of Political Science, 28,* 459–478.

Franklin, C. H., & Jackson, J. E. (1983). The dynamics of party identification. *American Political Science Review, 77,* 957–973.

Furnham, A. (1985). Adolescents' sociopolitical attitudes: A study of sex and national differences. *Political Psychology, 6,* 621–636.

Glenn, N. D. (1977). *Cohort analysis.* Beverly Hills, CA: Sage.

Glenn, N. D. (1980). Values, attitudes, and beliefs. In O. G. Brim, Jr., & J. Kagan (Eds.), *Constancy and change in human development* (pp. 596–640). Cambridge, MA: Harvard University Press.

Goodman, L. A., Mack, J. E., Beardslee, W. R., & Snow, R. M. (1983). The threat of nuclear war and the nuclear arms race: Adolescent experience and perceptions. *Political Psychology, 4,* 501–530.

Greenberg, E. S. (1970). *Political socialization.* New York: Atherton.

Greenstein, F. I. (1965). *Children and politics.* New Haven, CT: Yale University Press.

Greenstein, F. I. (1970). A note on the ambiguity of "political socialization": Definitions, criticisms, and strategies of inquiry. *Journal of Politics, 32,* 969–978.

Greenstein, F. I. (1974). Personality and politics. In F. I. Greenstein & N. W. Polsby (Eds.), *Handbook of political science: Vol. 2. Theoretical aspects of micropolitics* (pp. 1–92). Reading, MA: Addison-Wesley.

Harding, J., Proshansky, H., Kutner, B., & Chein, I. (1969). Prejudice and ethnic relations. In G. Lindzey & E. Aronson (Eds.), *The handbook of social psychology* (Vol. 5) (pp. 1–76). Reading, MA: Addison-Wesley.

Hess, R. D., & Torney, J. V. (1967). *The development of political attitudes in children.* Chicago: Aldine.

Himmelweit, H. T., Humphreys, P., & Jaeger, M. (1985). *How voters decide* (rev. ed.). Philadelphia: Open University Press.

Hyman, J. (1959). *Political socialization.* Glencoe, IL: Free Press.

Inglehart, R. (1971). The silent revolution in Europe: Intergenerational change in post-industrial societies. *American Political Science Review, 65,* 991–1017.

Inglehart, R. (1985). Aggregate stability and individual-level flux in mass belief systems: The level of analysis paradox. *American Political Science Review, 79,* 97–116.

Jackson, J. E. (1975). Issues, party choices, and presidential votes. *American Journal of Political Science, 19,* 161–185.

Jagodzinski, W. (1983). Materialism in Japan reconsidered: Toward a synthesis of generational and life-cycle explanations. *American Political Science Review, 4,* 887–894.

Jennings, M. K. (1987). Residues of a movement: The aging of the American protest generation. *American Political Science Review, 81,* 367–382.

Jennings, M. K., & Markus, G. B. (1977). The effect of military service on political attitudes: A panel study. *American Political Science Review, 71,* 131–147.

Jennings, M. K., & Markus, G. B. (1984). Partisan orientations over the long haul: Results from the three-wave political socialization panel study. *American Political Science Review, 78,* 1000–1018.

Jennings, M. K., & Niemi, R. G. (1968). The transmission of political values from parent to child. *American Political Science Review, 62,* 169–184.

Jennings, M. K., & Niemi, R. G. (1974). *The political character of adolescence.* Princeton, NJ: Princeton University Press.

Jennings, M. K., & Niemi, R. G. (1981). *Generations and politics.* Princeton, NJ: Princeton University Press.

Katz, P. A. (1976). The acquisition of racial attitudes in children. In P. A. Katz (Ed.), *Towards the elimination of racism* (pp. 125–156). Elmsford, NY: Pergamon Press.

Kearney, R. B. (1983). Identity, life mission, and the political career: Notes on the early life of Subhas Chandra Bose. *Political Psychology, 4,* 617–636.

Kelly, R. M., & Ronan, B. (1987). Subjective culture and patriotism: Gender, ethnic, and class differences among school students. *Political Psychology, 8,* 525–546.

Kinder, D. R., & Rhodebeck, L. A. (1982). Continuities in support for racial equality, 1972 to 1976. *Public Opinion Quarterly, 46,* 195–215.

Kinder, D. R., & Sears, D. O. (1981). Prejudice and politics: Symbolic racism versus racial threats to the good life. *Journal of Personality and Social Psychology, 40,* 414–431.

Kinder, D. R., & Sears, D. O. (1985). Public opinion and political action. In G. Lindzey & E. Aronson (Eds.), *Handbook of Social Psychology: Vol. 2* (3rd ed.) (pp. 659–741). New York: Random House.

Klapper, J. T. (1960). *The effects of mass communications.* Glencoe, IL: Free Press.

Knoke, D. (1972). Community and consistency: The ethnic factor in status inconsistency. *Social Forces, 51,* 23–33.

Kraus, S., & Davis, D. (1976). *The effects of mass communication on political behavior.* University Park, PA: Pennsylvania State University Press.

Kraus, S., & Perloff, R. M. (1985). *Mass media and political thought: An information-processing approach.* Beverly Hills, CA: Sage.

Lane, R. E. (1962). *Political ideology: Why the American common man believes what he does.* Glencoe, IL: Free Press.

Langton, K. P. (1969). *Political socialization.* Boston, MA: Little, Brown.

Levitin, T. E., & Miller, W. E. (1979). Ideological interpretations of presidential elections. *American Political Science Review, 73,* 751–771.

Lindblom, C. E. (1982). Another state of mind (APSA presidential address, 1981). *American Political Science Review, 76,* 9–21.

Lipset, S. M., Lazarsfeld, P. F., Barton, A. H., & Linz, J. (1954). The psychology of voting: An analysis of political behavior. In G. Lindzey (Ed.), *Handbook of social psychology* (Vol. 2) (pp. 1124–1175). Reading, MA: Addison-Wesley.

Mann, T. E., & Wolfinger, R. E. (1980). Candidates and parties in congressional elections. *American Political Science Review, 74,* 617–632.

Markus, G. B. (1979). The political environment and the dynamics of public attitudes: A panel study. *American Journal of Political Science, 23,* 338–359.

Markus, G. B. (1983). Dynamic modeling of cohort change: The case of political partisanship. *American Journal of Political Science, 27,* 717–739.

Markus, G. B. (1986). Stability and change in political attitudes: Observed, recalled, and "explained." *Political Behavior, 8*, 21–44.

Marsh, D. (1971). Political socialization: The implicit assumptions questioned. *British Journal of Political Science, 1*, 453–465.

Marwell, G., Aiken, M. T., & Demerath, N. J. III. (1987). The persistence of political attitudes among 1960s civil rights activists. *Public Opinion Quarterly, 51*, 359–375.

Mason, K. O., Mason, W. M., Winsborough, H. H., & Poole, W. K. (1973). Some methodological issues in cohort analysis of archival data. *American Sociological Review, 38*, 242–258.

McGuire, W. J. (1986). The myth of massive media impact: Savagings and salvagings. In G. Comstock (Ed.), *Public communication and behavior* (Vol. 1) (pp. 173–257). Orlando, FL: Academic Press.

McIntyre, A. (1983). The aging narcissistic leader: The case of Sir Oswald Mosley at mid-life. *Political Psychology, 4*, 483–500.

Merelman, R. M. (1986). Revitalizing political socialization. In R. Herrmann (Ed.), *Political Psychology* (pp. 279–319). San Francisco: Jossey-Bass.

Merelman, R. M., & King, G. (1986). The development of political activists: Toward a model of early learning. *Social Science Quarterly, 67*, 473–490.

Miller, A. H. (1974). Political issues and trust in government: 1964–1970. *American Political Science Review, 68*, 951–972.

Miller, S., & Sears, D. O. (1986). Stability and change in social tolerance: A test of the persistence hypothesis. *American Journal of Political Science, 30*, 214–236.

Miller, W. E., & Shanks, J. M. (1982). Policy directions and presidential leadership: Alternative interpretations of the 1980 presidential election. *British Journal of Political Science, 12*, 299–356.

Minns, D. R. (1984). Voting as an influential behavior: Child and adolescent beliefs. *American Politics Quarterly, 12*, 285–304.

Minow, N. N., Martin, J. B., & Mitchell, L. M. (1973). *Presidential television.* New York: Basic Books.

Newcomb, T. M. (1943). *Personality and social change.* New York: Dryden Press.

Newcomb, T. M., Koenig, K. E., Flacks, R., & Warwick, D. P. (1967). *Persistence and change: Bennington College and its students after 25 years.* New York: John Wiley.

Niemi, R. G., Katz, R. S., & Newman, D. (1980). Reconstructing past partisanship: The failure of the party identification recall questions. *American Journal of Political Science, 24*, 633–651.

Nisbett, R., & Ross, L. (1980). *Human inference: Strategies and shortcomings of social judgment.* Englewood Cliffs, NJ: Prentice-Hall.

Owen, D., & Dennis, J. (1987). Preadult development of political tolerance. *Political Psychology, 8*, 547–562.

Peterson, S. A. (1983). Biology and political socialization: A cognitive developmental link? *Political Psychology, 4*, 265–288.

Peterson, S. A., & Somit, A. (1982). Cognitive development and childhood political socialization: Questions about the primacy principle. *American Behavioral Scientist, 25*, 313–334.

Proshansky, H. M. (1966). The development of intergroup attitudes. In L. W. Hoffman & M. L. Hoffman (Eds.), *Review of child development research* (Vol. 2) (pp. 311–371). New York: Russell Sage Foundation.

Rapoport, A. (1985). Like mother, like daughter: Intergenerational transmission of DK response rates. *Public Opinion Quarterly, 49*, 198–208.

Renshon, S. A. (Ed.). (1977). *Handbook of political socialization: Theory and research*. New York: Free Press.

Rintala, M. (1984). The love of power and the power of love: Churchill's childhood. *Political Psychology, 5*, 375–390.

Roberts, C. W., & Lang, K. (1985). Generations and ideological change: Some observations. *Public Opinion Quarterly, 49*, 460–473.

Robinson, M. J. (1976). Public affairs television and the growth of political malaise: The case of "the selling of the Pentagon." *American Political Science Review, 70*, 409–432.

Rowland, C. K., & Carp, R. A. (1983). The relative effects of maturation, time period, and appointing president on district judges' policy choices: A cohort analysis. *Political Behavior, 5*, 109–134.

Searing, D. D., Schwartz, J. J., & Lind, A. E. (1973). The structuring principle: Political socialization and belief systems. *American Political Science Review, 67*, 415–432.

Searing, D. D., Wright, G., & Rabinowitz, G. (1976). The primacy principle: Attitude change and political socialization. *British Journal of Political Science, 6*, 83–113.

Sears, D. O. (1975). Political socialization. In F. I. Greenstein & N. W. Polsby (Eds.), *Handbook of political science* (Vol. 2) (pp. 93–153). Reading, MA: Addison-Wesley.

Sears, D. O. (1981). Life stage effects upon attitude change, especially among the elderly. In S. B. Kiesler, J. N. Morgan, & V. K. Oppenheimer (Eds.), *Aging: Social change* (pp. 183–204). New York: Academic Press.

Sears, D. O. (1983). The persistence of early political predispositions: The roles of attitude object and life stage. In L. Wheeler & P. Shaver (Eds.), *Review of personality and social psychology* (Vol. 4) (pp. 79–116). Beverly Hills, CA: Sage.

Sears, D. O. (1984, September). Attitude objects and political socialization through the life cycle. Paper presented at the annual convention of the American Political Science Association, Washington, DC.

Sears, D. O. (1988). Symbolic racism. In P. A. Katz & D. A. Taylor (Eds.), *Eliminating racism: Profiles in controversy* (pp. 53–84). New York: Plenum Press.

Sears, D. O., & Allen, H. M. Jr. (1984). The trajectory of local desegregation controversies and whites' opposition to busing. In N. Miller & M. B. Brewer (Eds.), *Groups in contact: The psychology of desegregation* (pp. 123–151). New York: Academic Press.

Sears, D. O., & Citrin, J. (1985). *Tax revolt: Something for nothing in California* (Enl. ed.). Cambridge, MA: Harvard University Press.

Sears, D. O., & Gahart, M. T. (1980, September). The stability of racial prejudice and other symbolic attitudes. Paper presented at the annual meeting of the American Psychological Association, Montreal, Canada.

Sears, D. O., Hensler, C. P., & Speer, L. K. (1979). Whites' opposition to "busing": Self-interest or symbolic politics? *American Political Science Review, 73,* 369–384.

Sears, D. O., Lau, R. R., Tyler, T. R., & Allen, H. M. Jr. (1980). Self-interest vs. symbolic politics in policy attitudes and presidential voting. *American Political Science Review, 74,* 670–684.

Sears, D. O., & McConahay, J. B. (1973). *The politics of violence: The new urban blacks and the Watts riot.* Boston, MA: Houghton-Mifflin.

Sears, D. O., Tyler, T. R., Citrin, J., & Kinder, D. R. (178). Political system support and public response to the 1974 energy crisis. *American Journal of Political Science, 22,* 56–82.

Sears, D. O., & Whitney, R. E. (1973). *Political persuasion.* Morristown, NJ: General Learning Press.

Sherif, M., & Cantril, H. (1947). *The psychology of ego-involvements.* New York: John Wiley.

Sidanius, J. (1985). Cognitive functioning and sociopolitical ideology revisited. *Political Psychology, 6,* 637–662.

Sigel, R. S., & Brookes, M. (1974). Being critical about politics: The impact of political events and individual development on young people. In R. Niemi (Ed.), *The politics of future citizens* (pp. 103–125). San Francisco: Jossey-Bass.

Sigel, R. S., & Hoskin, M. (1981). *The political involvement of adolescents.* New Brunswick, NJ: Rutgers University Press.

Smidt, C. (1982). Civil religious orientations and children's perceptions of political authority. *Political Behavior, 4,* 147–162.

Stember, C. H. (1961). *Education and attitude change.* New York: Institute of Human Relations Press.

Tedin, K. L. (1974). The influence of parents on the political attitudes of adolescents. *American Political Science Review, 68,* 1579–1592.

Vaillancourt, P. M. (1973). Stability of children's survey responses. *Public Opinion Quarterly, 37,* 373–387.

Ward, D. (1985). Generations and the expression of symbolic racism. *Political Psychology, 6,* 1–18.

Wattenberg, M. P. (1984). *The decline of American political parties, 1952-1980.* Cambridge, MA: Harvard University Press.

Weisberg, H. F. (1980). A multidimensional conceptualization of party identification. *Political Behavior, 2,* 33–60.

West, J. (1945). *Plainville, U.S.A.* New York: Columbia University Press.

Williams, C. B., & Minns, D. R. (1986). Agent credibility and receptivity influences on children's political learning. *Political Behavior, 8,* 175–200.

# 5

# From Attitudes and Knowledge to Schemata: Expanding the Outcomes of Political Socialization Research

JUDITH TORNEY-PURTA

An examination of the research on political socialization from the 1960s to the recent past shows that, while models for using independent variables as predictors have become increasingly sophisticated, the outcomes or dependent variables they have been used to predict have remained remarkably similar. These outcomes have usually included attitude measures (often the sense of political efficacy or partisanship) and, in some studies, measures of knowledge or awareness of issues (often obtained using some sort of multiple-choice test). Debates have raged over whether dependent variables have been appropriately measured, but not over whether anything important has been left out of the definition of these outcomes. Nor has there been attention to whether the research utilizing these outcome measures is well suited for drawing implications for citizenship education.

The purpose of this chapter is to argue that the notion of schema as used by cognitive psychologists would make a useful addition to the outcome measures employed in research in this field. The schemata of the political system, both domestic and international, which young people are continually formulating and reformulating, are important but unmeasured outcomes of political socialization. I illustrate a way of measur-

This chapter incorporates material originally presented at the meetings of the Association of American Publishers (Washington, DC, March 1988) and at the International Society for Political Psychology (Meadowlands, NJ, July 1988). The author is grateful for financial support from the Danforth Foundation and the Center for Educational Research and Development at the University of Maryland. The Maryland State Department of Education provides support for the summer centers where the interview data were collected; these centers are coordinated by Antoinette Favazza-Wiegand. The computer-assisted simulation is conducted by Jonathan Wilkenfeld and his associates at the University of Maryland, Department of Government and Politics. Warren Phillips and Victoria Goddard-Truitt served as research assistants for data collection and analysis.

ing these schemata, and I argue that research oriented around these schemata and the processes by which they change could provide a new link between political socialization research, on the one hand, and current psychological theory about cognitive development and recent research in education, on the other.

## PROBLEMS IN APPLYING RESEARCH FINDINGS
## TO IMPROVE CITIZENSHIP EDUCATION

Political socialization research using surveys of attitudes and knowledge have given many clues about what is important in the process, especially parts of that process relating to schooling. Jennings & Niemi (1971), for example, assessed the importance of a variety of factors ranging from the explicit curriculum (especially relevant for disadvantaged students) to extracurricular activities. Torney, Oppenheim, and Farnen (1975) showed in nine countries that a classroom climate that fostered free discussion and participation was associated with students becoming more knowledgeable and more supportive of democratic values, while a stress on patriotic ritual and rote memorization had the opposite impact. Subsequently, Torney-Purta and Landsdale (1986) showed that classrooms in which students reported that they were free to disagree with the teacher seemed to foster higher scores on multiple-choice tests of knowledge of international security and international economic issues, even when the educational background of the family was partialed out.

These studies, and a number of others, have suggested that schooling is important for citizenship and that a long-term goal of educational reform in this area should be to ensure that classrooms are places in which students are actively involved in the learning process, rather than passive recipients of information. The majority of these studies also are problematic, however, when it comes to making inferences about education.

The first problem is that serious questions continue to be raised about how attitudes are related to behavior, and the extent to which attitudes expressed by a 14- or 17-year-old predict attitudes held at 25 or 30 years of age. Further, the general public and educators express concern about the extent to which attitude change should be in the mandate of schools; many schools in the United States are stressing cognitive outcomes in all subject areas, leaving those interested in citizenship education wondering how research that is primarily focused on attitudes can be applied.

Looking at the cognitive side of political socialization, although there have been attempts to use research to tailor curricula to the particular concepts that seem to be understood by children of a given age level,

Piagetian theory has not provided much useful guidance for curriculum developers in civic education. Some argue that this is because there is too much spread in the cognitive stages of children of any given age or grade level. Others, including many developmental psychologists, have recently argued that there are very few inferential abilities that characterize cognitive functioning generally across subject areas or domains in the way that the stage concept would suggest. Some researchers are even questioning the existence of homogeneous and discrete stages within such limited domains as the child's understanding of number (Gelman & Baillargeon, 1983).

## ASSIMILATION, ACCOMMODATION, AND RESTRUCTURING: IMPLICATIONS FOR EDUCATION

The processes of development that Piaget identified — assimilation and accommodation — have become the basis of some new approaches to understanding cognitive development and education that do not rely on the delineation of stages. For example, to test assimilation, which is the process by which new information is incorporated into a schema without altering it, Vosniadou & Brewer (1987), questioned children about observational astronomy. They classified the children's answers as (1) reflecting a phenomenological or "naive scientist" view of the earth as being larger than the sun, flat, and motionless, while the sun's movement causes the night/day cycle, or (2) reflecting a Copernican view. A child with a naive schema who was told that there is day in Europe at the same time as night in America assimilated this information into the representation of a flat earth by viewing it as a sort of layer cake, in which a flat America was under a flat Europe; the sun dropped through the European layer to shine on America, and at nightfall went back again. The child, according to these authors, may *accumulate* knowledge, either by assimilating it into an existing conceptual framework or by storing it in a piecemeal fashion where it remains relatively unconnected to previously acquired concepts or knowledge.

Vosniadou and Brewer (1987) also delineate two processes related to the other Piagetian concept, accommodation. Accommodation is the process in which new information causes a change in a schema. Presenting knowledge to the child may result in *weak restructuring*, a kind of accommodation in which concepts become more complex or more closely connected to each other. Finally, new knowledge may result in *radical restructuring*, accommodation of a schema or concept resulting in a relatively complete reorganization. In the area of astronomy, this could mean a new view of the earth as spherical and in motion, as the child moves from a naive scientific model to one that matches more closely with the realities as scientists perceive them. Another term sometimes used for radical restructuring is *paradigm shift*.

How does education contribute to these restructuring processes? According to Vosniadou & Brewer (1987), children are prompted to restructure their views of the earth when they are shown physical analogies or models and when they are involved in Socratic dialogue. This focus on dialogue parallels the description by Furth (1980) of developmental experience as observed during interviews in which children expressed changed concepts of social institutions. It also is similar to the findings of Torney, Oppenheim, and Farnen (1975) concerning the role of a climate for open discussion of issues in the classroom.

There has been considerable interest among science educators in the implications of children's assimilation of facts and accommodation in the form of weak or more radical restructuring (Posner, Strike, Hewson, & Gertzog, 1982). Carey (1986) has concluded that science teaching has an impact when erroneous schemata based on naive, common-sense notions are replaced or restructured. These views of concept development as restructuring within a specific domain appear to have much more relevance for curriculum development than the notion of homogeneous stages that operate in a generalized way across content domains.

## SCHEMATA IN THE STUDY OF POLITICAL SOCIALIZATION

Basic to the new understanding of cognitive growth as it influences education is the idea of schema or representation. This is a cognitive structure that organizes previously acquired information and has an impact on remembering and retrieving information and using it for solving problems. It may also be related to attitudes. Glaser (1988) has defined schemata as "modifiable information structures that represent generic concepts stored in memory" (p. 25). A schema is constructed by an individual and is therefore not a faithful reflection or copy of a reality existing in the world. Cognitive psychologists usually study schemata by relatively indirect methods, for example, by asking subjects to think aloud about the linkages they see between elements of information, or by testing speed of reaction time to stimuli that relate in different ways to hypothesized schemata.

Looking at schemata from the point of view of cognitive development, Mandler (1983) makes a distinction between representations of space (e.g., images of scenes existing in space) and representations of events (e.g., scripts of action sequences that take place in certain places or under certain conditions). A spatial representation includes both general knowledge about objects and generalized images of the kind of objects one is likely to see in a particular place and their relation to each other. For example, the scene schema for a schoolroom will be larger than for a bedroom and will be more likely to have furniture arranged in rows. The analogy between a scene schema and a mental map of the world has interesting implications for political socialization (see Torney-Purta, 1989).

Event representations are organized temporally and linguistically, rather than spatially, and they describe sequences of actions rather than objects. The notion of "script" is used to describe an expected sequence of events, such as might occur during a visit to a restaurant. Political roles are often understood by young people as connected with the script for an event, so that the president is seen as someone who gives speeches, while the police officer's role is to arrest criminals.

Observation and some research indicate that young children have vague and poorly structured representations of many aspects of politics. Some of these ideas are idiosyncratic to an individual, and others are relatively common to groups of children (misconceptions held by many children in a given age group, for example). Experience, including class-room experience, presents an impetus to modify or restructure those representations, usually in a way that makes them more like the schemata of informed adults. Take the event schema in which a leader exerts power. Young children have vague ideas that political leaders exert power by tell-ing people what to do and often believe that this influence is exerted personally in a kind of infinite personal chain of command (e.g., the president tells someone who tells someone else, who tells someone else, and so on). They may even see a divine connection, as illustrated by the Moore, Lare, and Wagner (1985) report that many young children believe that God or Jesus appoints the president of the United States or tells him what to do.

Many other illustrations could be drawn from the literature on domes-tic political socialization, especially those studies that have used interviews (e.g., Connell, 1971; Furth, 1980; Hess & Torney, 1967; Stevens, 1982). For example, many young children believe that citizens as individuals can have a direct and immediate influence on government policy—such as calling up the president of the United States and telling him what they think (Hess and Torney, 1967). In the model discussed here, this would be interpreted as the child possessing a script for the citizen's efforts at exert-ing political influence which is personal and does not involve cooperation with groups. This event schema corresponds in some respects to the mis-conceptions about astronomy described earlier.

Recently political scientists have used the concept of schema to study adults' political cognitions and belief systems (see Conover & Feldman,

1984). Lau and Sears (1986) have illustrated schemata for political figures such as Ronald Reagan. Bennett (1981) has provided an extensive review of an information-processing framework for the study of politics, making some links with a framework for studying political socialization, although no research was reported on young people. Studies of political cognition have been limited to adults and have not concentrated on processes of schemata change. As a result, the existing research on political cognition has had only limited applicability for those concerned with citizenship education for young people.

## RECENT EDUCATIONAL RESEARCH RELATING TO SCHEMATA

Several recent studies by cognitive psychologists and by researchers specializing in cognitive processing in reading in the social studies content area suggest the importance of student-elaborated schemata in the process of learning.

Pressley, Symons, McDaniel, Snyder, and Turnure (1988) conducted an experimental study on children's memory for sentences such as, "Apples were first cultivated in Nova Scotia," or, "The worst tornado was in Alberta." Four experimental groups were given different instructions. The base group was simply told to remember the sentences; a second group was given the sentences together with elaborations provided by the experimenter; the third group, the elaborated-image group, was instructed to construct a visual image of the sentence (e.g., apples being grown in Nova Scotia); the fourth group was told to construct a verbal elaboration of the sentence, to think why it would make sense that apples would be cultivated in Nova Scotia. All three of the groups using elaborations remembered the sentences better than the base group; however, the most successful, especially after the age of about 10, were the students who constructed their own elaborated visual imagery. This illustrates the value in general of elaborated schemata and of students' being encouraged to contact their existing knowledge base in a domain by relating new information to existing knowledge and schemata.

A study by Davey and McBride (1986) also relates to the value of student-produced elaborations. Here, social studies textbook material concerning people performing different jobs was used. Students in one group were taught over the course of five sessions how to generate questions as they read, questions that would both tap the important information and link information across sentences in the text. In other words, they were asked to compose questions that could not be answered from only one text sentence. On a test of comprehension students instructed in this way outperformed not only students given no training at all, but also those who were told to generate questions but not instructed on how to link information across sentences, and those who were asked to generate other kinds of questions. The elaboration of schemata can be fostered in a number of ways and is a distinct aid to understanding and remembering.

In a study by Ohlhausen and Roller (1988) fifth, seventh, and ninth graders were asked to read one of three versions of a social studies passage about an unknown country, and to underline important information in it. One version (content and text structure passage) included an explicit hierarchical structure in which factual material about geography (location, landforms, and climate) was presented. Another (content-only passage) listed the same factual material, but with the sentences in random order, and without any "structuring" sentences, such as, We will first describe the physical geography of Melanesia. The third version (structure-only passage) included the expository text structure and signal sentences for structure but substituted nonsense words for content information. As expected, the best performance in identifying important information was by the group given both content and text structure. For the two youngest groups, however, the structure-only passage (with nonsense words) was easier than the content-only passage (with meaningful words but no guides as to how to incorporate material into structures or schemata). The authors refer to the importance of the use of schemata in interpreting information about other countries.

The final illustrative study regarding schemata is one in which Berkowitz (1986) trained students in the process of using the material in texts to generate "graphic maps of concepts" such as "nation." These were similar in many ways to the schemata described earlier. Groups trained in this way were compared to one group that studied maps for the same concept but produced by others, and to groups that either practiced rereading procedures or answering questions from the text. On the average, a student who generated her or his own graphic representation or schema, even if it was not complete or totally accurate, showed a clear and significant advantage in recall over a student who studied the concept maps produced by others or who studied the passage in other ways. This illustrates again the power of an individual's self-generated schemata and the importance of helping students to relate what is in a text actively to their existing schemata and to their knowledge base.

Adding schemata of the political and economic system to the outcomes studied by those interested in political socialization could initiate a fruitful set of relationships between current educational research, such as that just described, and studies of the basic processes by which political concepts are formed.

## VIEWING CLASSROOMS AS ARENAS FOR
## COGNITIVE RESTRUCTURING AND PROBLEM SOLVING

In a major review of research on social studies education, Armento (1986) described an emergent focus on studying classrooms as situations in which both the students and teachers are active constructors of meaning who cognitively organize incoming stimuli on the basis of prior knowledge and existing values, by employing active constructive processes. The implication of such a situation, as she sees it, is that "any instructional method that increases students' macroprocessing of the content of instruction is apt to improve achievement" (p. 946). She goes on to note that helpful instructional techniques include those that increase students' image making, their relation of prior knowledge to new information, or the hierarchical system of interrelationships that they see. This approach, however, often called the cognitive or constructivist approach, has not yet been tied effectively to constructs such as schema to provide an appropriate link between research and practice.

A major area of research on cognitive processing has been the construction of models of problem solving, but the bulk of this research has been conducted using problems in logic, geometry, or physics. Subjects are asked to think aloud while solving problems, thus allowing the researcher to trace the problem solver's approach to goals and subgoals and the use of rules and justifications for solutions. Models of these processes can then be built. Hayes and Simon (see Hayes, 1981) looked at the processes by which an individual encodes the written instructions for a complex logical problem. The elements included the actors and "legal" ways for them to operate.

There are, however, many contrasts between this research on science, mathematics, and logic, and research involving problem solving in the more vaguely defined area of the social sciences. Here, think-aloud protocols give only the most rudimentary notions about goals or subgoals; it is not at all clear to the subject or the experimenter when a solution has been reached; solutions cannot be characterized as correct or incorrect; and there are no widely agreed-upon constraints on operations, as there are in geometry.

Voss, Tyler, and Yengo (1983) have analyzed the cognitive processing associated with solving the more ambiguously structured social science problems by novices and experts. Their framework is domain specific and addresses some of the differences between these problems and problems in logic or mathematics. They have used problems such as the following:

Assume you are the head of the Soviet Ministry of Agriculture, and assume crop productivity has been low over the past several years. You now have the

responsibility of increasing crop productivity. How would you go about doing
this? [p. 211]

In analyzing the problem-solving strategies in these think-aloud protocols,
the sequence of different elements of the argument (e.g., stating a sub-
problem, stating a solution, evaluating a solution, stating a fact, elaborating) is of critical importance. Voss et al. note that experts (professors specializing in Soviet affairs) spend much more time defining a problem and
are more attentive to constraints upon specific solutions than are novices
(undergraduates). He argues that the structuring phase, in which an individual sets out goals and reaches into the knowledge base for relevant
information, is an important part of the representation of a social science
problem, its recomposition into subproblems, and its solution.

Although this type of problem analysis is of potential interest for
educators, the method is far easier to apply to relatively articulate adults
than to adolescents or preadolescents, whose problem-solving abilities are
relatively poorly developed and difficult to elicit with the standard think-
aloud instructions. Further, Voss et al.'s (1983) method of analysis gives a
relatively content-free picture of respondents' thinking, which is not maxi-
mally helpful to educators who must focus on the content as well as the
process of problem solving.

## USING THINK-ALOUD PROBLEM SOLVING
## TO DERIVE SCHEMATA OF THE POLITICAL SYSTEM

I have recently modified a think-aloud problem-solving technique in
order to collect data that can be represented in graphic models of schemata
for the social, political, and economic systems as seen by adolescents. The
major elements of these schemata are *actors* in the political system, *actions*
in which they can engage, and *constraints* upon their actions. A schema is
more complex when it involves a large number of potential actors, who are
each able to perform a varied set of actions. Another aspect of schema
complexity is the inclusion of relevant constraints upon actions and the
recognition of connections between the potential actions performed by
different actors. I have tested the feasibility of this methodology by conducting research on the effectiveness of an educational program whose
aims are to increase the accuracy, complexity, and connections present in
adolescents' social, political, and economic schemata.

The remainder of this section presents examples of how I have used
this think-aloud problem-solving technique to derive models of such sche-

mata. The data were gathered through interviews regarding hypothetical international problems conducted at the Maryland Summer Center for International Studies (MSCIS). This is a two-week program for gifted and talented students aged 13 through 17. Following two days of lectures and readings, students are divided into six teams (Brazil, Nigeria, Mexico, the USSR, France, and Japan). Each team meets in its own room, which includes an IBM computer linked to a central unit. Students on one team send messages to other teams over this computer system. The topics of these messages are international problems detailed in a scenario and presented in agendas for on-line conferences on topics such as North–South issues, human rights, and nuclear arms control. The aims of the program include enhancing the participants' knowledge of other countries and international problems, as well as helping them to understand the perspectives of different countries on global issues. Given special importance is the aim of enhancing critical thinking skills as the students discuss with each other the content of messages they plan to send, before the computer network is engaged to transmit them.

Observations of these team meetings in 1985 and 1986 suggested that participants' schemata of the international economic and political systems were being restructured. Questionnaires collected before and after the sessions also indicated changes in perceptions of foreign policy making, especially policies dealing with developing countries and international debt. A number of the on-line conferences dealt with North–South issues, and half of the students played on the teams of developing countries, a perspective that is new to most U.S. adolescents.

In order to test the feasibility of schemata and restructuring as explanatory concepts, in 1987 18 students (from teams of Brazil, Nigeria, and the USSR) were given pre- and postsession interviews and asked to think aloud in solving four problems. The illustrations of schemata presented in this chapter are taken from responses to the following problem that I constructed:

Imagine that you are the finance minister of a developing country. The interest payment on your debt to banks in the industrialized countries is due very soon. There is not enough money in your treasury to cover this interest payment. What would you do to solve this problem?

Three interviewers conducted the interviews, after a brief period of training. Following the presentation of the problem, the student was instructed, "Think aloud to solve this problem. Just say whatever comes to your mind until you can't think of anything else." After the student had paused for several seconds or otherwise indicated that he or she was finished with the solution, the interviewer asked, "Can you think of any problems with those solutions, any reasons they might not work?"

These presession interviews were conducted on the first full day of the MSCIS session. Those interviewed late in the day had already heard one or two lectures on international politics or economics. A set of postsession interviews was conducted 10 days later as the simulation was concluding.

As a preliminary analysis, transcripts of the participants' responses were scored on a number of dimensions by a trained scorer (after a reliability check), and $t$ tests for differences between pretest and posttest means were computed. There were a number of significant presession/postsession differences for the problem dealing with the finance minister of a developing country. For example, technical economic terms were more frequently mentioned (e.g., *moratorium on debt, interest cartel*) on posttest. Students after the simulation were more likely to mention the need to see others' point of view or to propose a tradeoff that recognized the need for reciprocity. They also were somewhat more likely to mention an elaborated version of negotiation or refer to a situation in the real world. One can interpret the findings about the use of technical terms and the mention of real-world situations as suggesting that the knowledge base of these students had been enhanced. There was also a significant increase in scores on a brief multiple-choice knowledge test.

The major analysis of the pre- and postsession think-aloud solutions offered by the six Maryland adolescents who were members of the Brazilian team was done by constructing graphic presentations of the schemata of the international economic system that they appeared to operate from in offering their solutions. Like the problem-solving analysis of Hayes and Simon (Hayes, 1981), these schema-maps focused on actors and actions. The schemata for two Maryland adolescents participating in the simulation are presented in Figures 5.1 and 5.2. Presession responses appear on the top of the page; postsession responses appear on the bottom. The basic elements, represented by triangles, are the actors mentioned who might be approached by the finance minister or involved to solve the problem. The most frequently mentioned actors are the banks who hold the loans and the governments or economies of the countries where the loans are held. It was sometimes difficult to distinguish one from the other. If interest payments or defaults were discussed, it was assumed that it was the banks that were being referred to. The governments or economies of other countries were included in the figure only if they were explicitly mentioned or if the proposed action was unlikely for a bank (e.g., exporting or importing goods or giving foreign aid).

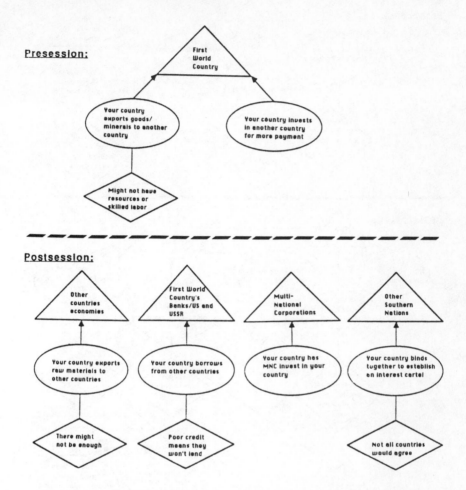

**Figure 5.1** Student A's presession and postsession schemata of actors, actions, and constraints in international debt crisis (Brazilian team)

On the average, more actors and more actions were mentioned after the MSCIS simulation. In particular, the students who were playing on the Brazilian team, where debt was a big issue, were more likely after the simulation to propose getting together with other Southern or debtor nations to form an interest cartel or in some way put pressure as a group on the developed countries to lighten the debt load. They were also much more likely after the simulation to refer to actions within their own economy, particularly the institution of austerity measures.

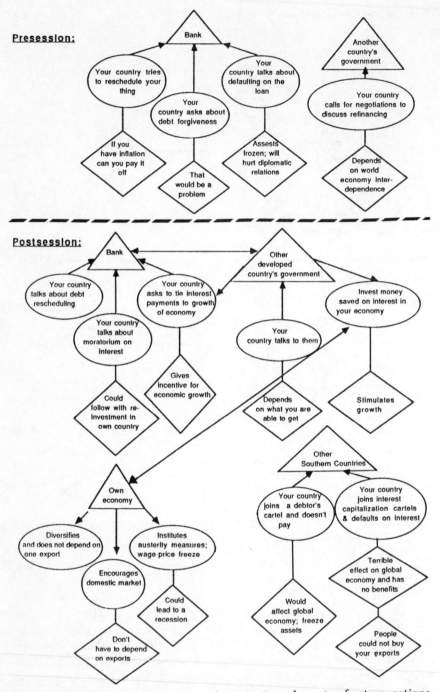

**Figure 5.2** Student B's presession and postsession schemata of actors, actions, and constraints in international debt crisis (Brazilian team)

110

The ovals in Figures 5.1 and 5.2 are used to represent particular actions and the elaborations on them which these actors might perform or be asked to perform; for example, the banks might be asked to reschedule the debt, or the Brazilian economy might encourage domestic markets for goods. Arrows are used to represent the direction of the requests. Below the ovals, enclosed in the diamonds, are the evaluations of or constraints on these actions. No sequence of discussion is indicated in these figures.

There was some consistency between the pre- and postsession interviews for any given individual with respect to which actors in the economic system were mentioned. The schemata of actors, actions, and constraints were much more complex after the simulation experience for three of the six Brazilian team members; in two cases the level of complexity was unchanged; and in one case the schema was slightly less complex. Figures 5.1 and 5.2 represent the problem-solving protocols of two of the team members whose postsession schemata were more complex. To illustrate the use of this technique as a political socialization measure, I will examine them in detail.

The schema of the international economic system in Figure 5.1 was very rudimentary at the presession interview. The only actions mentioned had to do with investment in and export to another country's economy. This was the only respondent of the six who did not mention acts particular to a bank or financial institution. After the simulation, in addition to other countries, multinational corporations, lending institutions in other countries, and other southern nations were mentioned. The constraints listed were relatively rudimentary.

Figure 5.2 depicts the ideas generated by the respondent who showed the greatest change in complexity of schema. As she herself admitted before the presession interview, "I don't know that much about economics." At the postsession interview, however, she said, "There are a lot of things I could say; I know about this because we are Brazil." There were only two actors mentioned in the presession interview — a bank and another country's government. Negotiation was mentioned, as were several constraints and the impact on the world economy; however, the language was somewhat vague ("reschedule your thing"). At the postsession interview, the banks and other developed countries' governments were given quite complex activities depending on negotiation, recognition of reciprocity ("depends on what you are able to get") and a sense of sequential activities ("tie interest payments to growth of economy"). Brazil's own economy, a new actor, was given three possible actions, ranging from diversification to austerity measures. Two of the three were seen with constraints, and those were linked in a much more complex way to the global economy. In addition, other developing countries were mentioned and linked to the global economy. This individual's responses showed so many linkings between actors, reactions, and elements in the answer that it seemed appropriate to include arrows on the figure to indicate them.

In summary, this model-making technique proved quite successful in representing the complexity of actors and potential interactions in the international economic system. Of note with regard to the two schemata just highlighted is that the actors engaged only in what most would agree were legitimate activities (e.g., banks were not asked to undertake austerity measures). Of the six Brazilian team members, only two connected the actions of one actor with those of other actors, or with the system as a whole. The other four respondents listed solutions in a relatively disconnected way.

The use of a problem-solving think-aloud interview technique to create such models shows considerable promise as a way to represent both individual differences in the schemata of actors and actions in the international economic system *and* changes in the complexity of those schemata. One way of defining what it means for someone to have a complex concept of the international system is to say that the individual has a schema for connecting a variety of relevant actors, their actions, and constraints in a particular domain. This represents the schema of the international system in a way that has interesting parallels to conceptualizations of systems of actors and actions involved in the solutions to logical problems. In those problems, of course, there are clearly understood limits, placed by the structure of the problem, on who can act and how. In these international problems, in contrast, these constraints are relatively elastic (although some seem to be consensually accepted).

The purpose of presenting in detail these students' schemata is to give a concrete example of the feasibility of eliciting from students information that can be represented in a graphic model, which itself illuminates how they actually see a political or economic system operating. It includes their assessment of the complexity of this system, for example, how many actors are envisioned, how many actions they engage in, what constraints exist on their actions, and how the actors/actions are connected to each other.

Envisioning a network of actors, actions, constraints, and connections as forming the individual's schema in a given domain is a way of linking the study of political socialization with both cognitive psychology and educational research. First, it gives a specific definition to the complexity of a schema of relatively abstract ideas, such as the economic or social system. Second, it provides a way of graphically describing cognitive restructuring as a movement from unconnected, unconstrained actions to connected, constrained ones. Third, it can be related to existing recent research on cognitive approaches to educational problems.

## CONCLUSIONS

This chapter has argued for an expansion of outcome measures in research on political socialization, to include young people's schemata of social, political, and economic systems. Such an expansion of outcomes would link political socialization more closely to current research in cognitive development conceived as domain-specific cognitive restructuring. It would also link political socialization work with recent research on the role of schemata in the learning that takes place as a student reads text or participates in classroom recitation or discussion. Such linkages could suggest particular methodologies for the classroom, such as making and discussing cognitive maps or engaging students in schema elaboration. Science education has already used findings based on similar approaches to improve its curricula; an examination of these efforts could provide further suggestions for innovations in social studies and citizenship education.

However, a number of questions still remain. First is whether the idea of schema is helpful in understanding young people's views across a wide range of subtopics within the domain of politics and citizenship education, and across a wide range of ages. The major illustrations given here were of adolescents' international schemata collected in the setting of a simulation, although some data from interview studies of children's views of the domestic political system were also discussed. Second, what prompts an individual to restructure schemata in the social and political domain? Previous research in science education and in social studies, as well as the observed restructuring prompted by the computer-assisted simulation reported in this chapter, suggest the importance of students' active involvement and exposure to alternative views of a situation. Third, how do existing schemata influence the way new information is processed and existing information is brought to bear from the knowledge base? A related question concerns the influence that ideas formed early in life may have on later schemata. Fourth, how are these structures related to attitudes, values, beliefs, and commitments?

The arena for research in political socialization would be expanded by including political schema in the outcomes addressed. Research that built models of these cognitive structures in the political domain and investigated the processes by which they are formed and change could provide valuable new directions for understanding effective citizenship education.

## REFERENCES

Armento, B. (1986). Research on teaching social studies. In M. Wittrock (Ed.), *Handbook of research on teaching* (pp. 942–951). New York: Macmillan.

Bennett, W. L. (1981). Perception and cognition: An information processing framework for politics. In S. L. Long (Ed.), *The handbook of political behavior* (pp. 69–176). New York: Plenum Press.

Berkowitz, S. (1986). *Reading Research Quarterly, 21,* 161–178.

Carey, S. (1986). Cognitive science and science education. *American Psychologist, 41,* 1123–1130.

Connell, R. (1971). *The child's construction of politics.* Carleton, Victoria, Australia: Melbourne University Press.

Conover, P. J., & Feldman, S. (1984). How people organize the political world: A schematic model. *American Journal of Political Science, 28,* 95–126.

Davey, B., & McBride, S. (1986). Effect of question-generation training on reading comprehension. *Journal of Educational Psychology, 78,* 256–262.

Furth, H. (1980). *The world of grown-ups.* New York: Elsevier-North Holland.

Gelman, R., & Baillargeon, R. (1983). A review of some Piagetian concepts. In J. Flavell & E. Markman (Eds.), *Handbook of child psychology* (Vol. 3) (pp. 167–230). New York: John Wiley.

Glaser, R. (1988). Cognitive science and education. *International Social Science Journal, 40,* 21–44.

Hayes, J. R. (1981). *The complete problem solver.* Philadelphia: Franklin Institute Press.

Hess, R. D., & Torney, J. V. (1967). *The development of political attitudes in children.* Chicago: Aldine.

Jennings, M. K., & Niemi, R. (1971). *The political character of adolescence.* Princeton, NJ: Princeton University Press.

Lau, R., & Sears, D. (Eds.). (1986). *Political cognition.* Hillsdale, NJ: Lawrence Erlbaum.

Mandler, J. (1983). Representation. In J. Flavell & E. Markman (Eds.), *Handbook of child psychology* (Vol. 3) (pp. 420–494). New York: John Wiley.

Moore, S., Lare, J., & Wagner, K. (1985). *The child's political world: A longitudinal perspective.* New York: Praeger.

Ohlhausen, M., & Roller, C. (1988). The operation of text structure and content schemata in isolation and in interaction. *Reading Research Quarterly, 23,* 70–88.

Posner, G. J., Strike, K., Hewson, P., & Gertzog, W. (1982). Accommodation of a scientific conception: Toward a theory of conceptual change. *Science Education, 66,* 211–227.

Pressley, M., Symons, S., McDaniel, M., Snyder, B., & Turnure, J. (1988). Elaborative interrogation facilitates acquisition of confusing facts. *Journal of Educational Psychology, 80,* 268–278.

Stevens, O. (1982). *Children talking politics.* Oxford: Martin Robertson.

Torney, J. V., Oppenheim, A. N., & Farnen, R. (1975). *Civic education in ten countries: An empirical study.* New York: John Wiley.

Torney-Purta, J. (1989). Political cognition and its restructuring in adolescents. *Human Development, 32,* 14–23.

Torney-Purta, J., & Landsdale, D. (1986, April). *Classroom climate and process in*

*international studies: Data from the American Schools and the World Project.*
Paper presented at the American Educational Research Association.

Vosniadou, S., & Brewer, W. (1987). Theories of knowledge restructuring in development. *Review of Educational Research, 57,* 51–68.

Voss, J. F., Tyler, S., & Yengo, L. (1983). Individual differences in the solving of social science problems. In R. Dillon & R. Schmeck (Eds.), *Individual differences in problem solving* (pp. 205–232). New York: Academic Press.

# 6

# Acquisition of Political Knowledge: A Social-Psychological Analysis

DANIEL BAR-TAL
LEONARD SAXE

Political socialization is a misnomer for what we study, because we study what children have learned . . . not how they have learned it. [Sigel, 1966, p. 3]

Political socialization studies . . . strain towards generalization and consistently suppress the immediacy and concreteness of the present situation; their ultimate search is for abstract cross-situational laws. [Connell & Goat, 1972–1973, p. 186]

Given that political socialization research has uncovered variations in who learns what, etc., based on such characteristics as sex, race, socioeconomic status, ethnic group affiliation, and political culture, the chances of discovering universal processes seem remote. [Renshon, 1977a, p. 8]

This chapter offers a cognitive social psychological framework for understanding the way in which children and others acquire political knowledge and become socialized for participation in democracy. The present approach suggests that knowledge about democracy is acquired via an epistemic process and that the necessary conditions for the acquisition of political knowledge are its availability and relevancy. This approach also posits that cognitive capacities and epistemic motivations greatly influence the acquisition of political knowledge and that an individual's epistemic authority exert a determinative influence on the acquisition of political knowledge.

Research on political socialization has focused principally on two major problems: (1) investigation of the content of political knowledge possessed by children and adolescents of different ages and from different social groups and (2) examination of the relative influence of the sources of knowledge (i.e., family, school, peers, and media) on the transmission of political knowledge (e.g., Dawson & Prewitt, 1969; Easton & Dennis, 1969; Greenstein, 1965a; Hess & Torney, 1967; Hyman, 1959; Jaros, 1973; Jennings & Niemi, 1974; Renshon, 1977b; Sears, 1975). The first type of research, focusing on content, has attempted to determine what different social groups of children and adolescents know in terms of their political knowledge and the origins of these differences. The second type of research has focused on the role of political socialization agents. Since family, school, peers, and media are considered the major sources of information for individuals, attempts have been made to determine the extent of influence of each source and to elucidate the ways through which each source provides political knowledge.

The sociological and psychological theories that have been the basis of much of this research provide useful guidance for research on political socialization. This chapter expands the application of these theories, by using social cognition principles to develop a general model of the process of political socialization. Sociological theories have focused on the institutions, mechanisms, and controls that society uses to transfer political knowledge to new generations. Psychological theories, as applied to political socialization, have emphasized the conditions under which individuals learn about political matters and their cognitive capacity for understanding new information. The theoretical orientation of the present chapter, in contrast, emphasizes a variety of intrapersonal cognitive processes as they are influenced by environmental, cognitive, and motivational factors. The conceptual model presented here is intended to account both for individual and group differences in the way in which children and adults acquire political knowledge. This approach should complement other sociological and psychological approaches by incorporating elements of each in an analysis of how individuals come to understand political knowledge.

A feature of our analysis here is to differentiate between what is possible to generalize universally and what can be described in terms of a particular case. Our proposed framework is intended to have universal use. It describes principles, factors, and processes that can be applied to any individual, across time and situation. It delineates a universal microprocess whereby individuals acquire knowledge and also points out the limiting factors, which are of general value and can be applied to the analysis of knowledge acquisition under any circumstances. In addition to describing universal elements, it also points out particularistic elements. Contents of knowledge, available information, sources of information, and specific cognitive capacities or motivations characterize individuals or a group in certain times and places. Individuals and groups differ with regard to these elements.

## SOCIAL COGNITION APPROACH

Much of the discussion in this chapter is derived from social psychological analyses of cognitive processes. Social psychology, as utilized here, provides an alternative perspective on the process whereby political socialization is accomplished. Recently, social psychologists have made the acquisition and change of social knowledge a central focus of research and theorizing. This work has emphasized topics such as cognitive structures (e.g., schemata, scripts, prototypes), cognitive contents (e.g., values, ideologies, concepts, attributions, attitudes), and cognitive processes (e.g., perception, inference, encoding, storage, organization, retrieval). Although various theorists use different terms to describe cognitive social phenomena, there is widespread agreement about the importance of understanding these processes (e.g., Bar-Tal & Kruglanski, 1988; Fiske & Taylor, 1984; Hastorf & Isen, 1982; Kruglanski, in press; Markus & Zajonc, 1985; Wyer & Srull, 1984).

Our premise, based on the results of research across a number of problem domains, is that the acquisition of political knowledge subscribes to the same principles as the acquisition of any other knowledge content. There is substantial research that documents the function of these processes, and there are no indications that the processes of political knowledge acquisition, or its structures, are any different (see Lau & Sears, 1986). The application of such cognitive social principles provides a new perspective on political socialization and suggests a number of research questions.

The chapter describes five research questions, which are derived from conceptions of cognitive social psychology in general and specifically from the theory of lay epistemology as proposed by Kruglanski (1980a, in press). The latter theory suggests general principles of knowledge acquisition that characterize children, as well as adults, and that underlie the detailed models elaborated by various social cognitivists, such as Bargh (1984), Trope (1986), and Wyer and Srull (1986). This theory will be described in detail first, after which its implications with regard to our five questions will be examined.

## LAY EPISTEMOLOGY

The fundamental assumption of lay epistemology, as developed by Kruglanski (1980a, in press), is that each individual comes to understand her or his world in a somewhat different way, via a complex process involving both rational and irrational elements. The theory focuses on the processes by which individual motivation and content interact to result in a person developing an understanding. Although the theory suggests that there is a virtually infinite number of ways in which individuals can come to understand the same situation (or, in the present context, to form a political knowledge on the basis of the same information), the process by which individuals acquire the knowledge is the same and can be identified.

## Epistemic Phases

Lay epistemology identifies two distinctive phases in the epistemic process of knowledge acquisition. The first phase begins with the epistemic questions, around which the person tries to form some type of knowledge. This phase is called the cognitive generation stage, and it is during this time that knowledge contents come into existence, as individuals generate contents and entertain them for possible adoption. The contents enter an individual's mind on the basis of information available from the environment and/or inferences from stored knowledge, that is, the ideas of individuals themselves (Markus & Zajonc, 1985). Thus, the determinants of entertained contents are their availability and their saliency (Fiske & Taylor, 1984; McArthur, 1981). Saliency refers to the degree to which the information "stands out." Individuals process information that is useful for the achievement of an epistemic objective (Kruglanski, 1979; Taylor & Crocker, 1981; Wyer & Srull, 1986). In other words, individuals continuously pose to themselves various epistemic questions which they try to answer. In order to answer some of the questions, they receive and/or search for relevant information.

In the second phase of the epistemic process, called the cognitive validation stage, the individual assesses the degree of validity of generated contents by attributing to them degrees of confidence. This phase involves some sort of deductive process of making implications about the generated contents and testing them against the evidence the individual possesses. If the implications are logically consistent with the evidence, then the individual's confidence in the generated content is high and it is likely to be accepted as firm knowledge. If, on the other hand, the evidence is inconsistent, then confidence may be low and the content therefore rejected.

A central proposition of lay epistemology is that the process does not have a natural point of termination. In principle, it is always possible to come up with a number of alternative contents that may be inconsistent with the same body of evidence and change the formed knowledge. In reality, though, individuals often terminate the epistemic process with regard to certain contents. They do so by bestowing on them a high degree of confidence without considering further alternatives. This cognitive phenomenon is known as epistemic freezing. In contrast, a phenomenon of entertaining alternative contents, validating them, and eventually substituting them instead of previously held beliefs, represents epistemic unfreezing. Freezing and unfreezing reflect the dynamic nature of human knowledge acquisition. Individuals continually add, change, and subtract beliefs (i.e., units of knowledge) from their repertoire of knowledge.

## Influencing Factors

The utility of the epistemic framework for the understanding of political knowledge acquisition comes from the identification of factors that influence the way in which the process unfolds and specific contents are integrated. There are two such principal factors, cognitive capacity and epistemic motivation (Markus & Zajonc, 1985; Ostrom, 1984). These influence the quantity and quality of individuals' absorbed information or created ideas, as well as their processing, comprehension, and storage.

Cognitive Capacity.   Two types of cognitive capacity can be identified. One is based on ontogenetic limitations or strengths of specific individuals, and the other is based on the phylogenetic limitations as expressed in human development.

The ontogenetic type is related to individuals' characteristics as reflected in their various cognitive skills and styles, which affect the contents of knowledge that they store and use (Holyoak & Gordon, 1984; Messick, 1976). The list of these skills and styles is a long one and not necessarily final. Carroll (1983), for example, outlined in his terms some of the cognitive abilities responsible for individual differences, as follows:

Abilities to perceive aspects of the physical and social environment; abilities to notice and remember specific events, sequences of stimuli, similarities and differences among stimuli, and relationships; abilities to produce and comprehend speech and writing; abilities to form concepts, reason, make inferences, and arrive at decisions to achieve specific goals; abilities to learn to perform tasks requiring higher levels of complex information processing; abilities to process information rapidly and to make quick and appropriate responses when such responses are required; knowledge of a wide range of information; competence in the use of information-processing procedures. [pp. 1–2]

The phylogenetic type of cognitive capacity is related to universal developmental qualities that characterize humans. Human beings develop their cognitive capacities as they age and go through various stages of cognitive development, which means that children and adolescents of different ages differ in their ability (Inhelder & Piaget, 1958; Piaget, 1950, 1970). Specifically, cognitive capacity is limited by general structures that underlie cognitive functions. With increasing age, these structures change into more complex, advanced systems and characterize distinct stages, which develop universally in an invariant order. These developmental changes influence the understanding of information coming from the environment and increase the amount of information a person absorbs. Also, the developmental changes of cognitive capacity affect the process of inference, which allows for the formation of knowledge beyond the collected information.

Epistemic Motivation.    Motivational tendencies tied to specific needs or desires influence the information that individuals collect and the inferences that they make. As a consequence, they affect the contents of knowledge that individuals store. The list of proposed specific motivations is a long one, a few of which have received special attention. For example, much research has been devoted to the effects of the motivation to enhance and protect the individual's ego.

Recently, Kruglanski and Ajzen (1983) have suggested that these motivations can be organized in terms of three categories: motivation for validity, motivation for structure, and motivation for specific content. The motivation for validity is the desire for valid knowledge and is characterized by an openness to considering various ideas before accepting any one as valid. Motivation for structure implies general closure on any new knowledge. Individuals commit themselves to a certain belief system and refrain from critically challenging it. This motivation implies cognitive freezing, since individuals neither generate alternative ideas nor collect substitute information. The motivation for specific content is the desire to hold specific knowledge as truth. Under this motivation, individuals seek support for the desired content and avoid any information or hypotheses that do not correspond with it. These three categories of motivation will be discussed in more detail later.

Epistemic Authority.    Since much of an individual's knowledge is acquired from external sources, of special importance for understanding the contents of knowledge that individuals acquire is to examine the epistemic authorities of these individuals. Epistemic authority is defined as a source from which an individual tends to accept information as true and factual and not to be disregarded. It exerts a determinative influence on the tendency to accept any information as valid, even information inconsistent with already held knowledge (Kruglanski, 1980b). An epistemic authority has no specific distinguishing characteristic; its identification is a matter of perception and is in the eyes of the beholder. Usually individuals attribute such authority to a source on the basis of expertness, power, attraction, credibility, or similarity (Bar-Tal, Raviv, Raviv, & Brosh, 1988). In principle, any characteristic may make a source an epistemic authority, and individuals may consider any source of information as such. They may use general sources, such as printed words, television, or leaders, or particular sources such as specific newspapers, specific journalists, or certain leaders.

## IMPLICATIONS: FIVE RESEARCH QUESTIONS

The epistemic framework just described delineates the principles that guide the acquisition of knowledge, including political knowledge, by identifying the processes and conditions that underlie knowledge formation and the factors that influence it. The way in which these principles enhance our understanding of political socialization will be described in this section. This discussion interweaves generic principles of social cognition with a specific focus on problems of political knowledge acquisition and socialization for democracy. The framework is intended not only to be descriptive, but also to suggest new research questions and a broad research agenda for the study of political socialization.

1. *What contents of political knowledge are available, and what contents are salient in the environment of the group?* Formation of political knowledge depends both on the availability of political information and its saliency. Therefore, the study of the contents of knowledge must be related to the investigation of its availability in the environment. When political information in specific content domains is unavailable, then individuals have difficulty forming knowledge about these contents. Likewise, the political knowledge that *is* available is more likely to be found in their repertoire. As suggested by Greenstein (1965a), in the context of children's knowledge acquisition, "One obvious reason why children learn first about the institutions which are best understood and considered most important by American adults, is that these are the institutions adults are likely to discuss in the presence of children and to be able to explain and answer questions about" (pp. 75–76).

The question of which contents are available and salient directs analyses of political socialization to assess available contents of political information across various groups, including contents related to political socialization for democracy. Differences in availability of information may partially explain group differences in political knowledge, such as those found by Greenstein (1965a) with regard to socioeconomic classes. Groups may reveal ignorance about certain topics of political knowledge, such as those related to democracy, just because these contents are unavailable. Certain kinds of political information may be unavailable in various groups for different reasons, which may be the subjects of investigation by themselves. Lack of interest, blocking of conflicting contents, or control of information are only a few determinants of political knowledge availability.

A related issue, of course, is saliency. Information may be available in the environment, but may not be salient. Information that stands out is given relatively more attentional processing (Bargh, 1984) and has disproportionate impact on knowledge formation. Saliency increases the likelihood of given information to be absorbed. It is therefore important to find out what kind of political information in a given group is salient, as reflected in its repetition or prominence. Even in groups open to absorbing new political knowledge, one kind of information may be more salient than another.

Within the framework of research on availability and salience, it is possible to examine the kind of political contents presented by different socialization agents. Such research may shed light on the relative role of the traditional agents of socialization with respect to knowledge acquisition. It is possible that the family, the school, the peer group, and the media differ with regard to available and salient political information. For example, in schools, children and adolescents acquire political knowledge formally through instruction in the curriculum and informally through experiences in the classroom and the school at large (Ehman, 1980). Of special importance are formal courses in subjects such as civics, social sciences, history, literature, foreign languages, and geography. Such training is explicitly designed to provide political knowledge. The analysis of available and salient contents in school books and school curricula allows an understanding of what pupils can possibly learn at school (*Citizenship Education*, 1963; Gillespie, 1975; Oppenheim, Torney & Farnen, 1975). A specific example is the research by Litt (1963), which analyzed textbook content used in civic education programs by three schools representing different socioeconomic status groups. The programs were found to be different and appeared to reflect the prevailing political climate of the community. As a result, they trained the students to play different political roles.

Also important is the study of political contents made available and salient by other agents of socialization: family, media, and peer groups. In this vein, Orren and Peterson (1967) looked at the effects of political contents' availability in the family. Using a sample of white, urban, middle-class families, they investigated children's knowledge about presidential assassination and found that children's knowledge was determined by the contents provided by their parents. Parents selected the contents that they transmitted as a function of children's age, their involvement in the event, and the extent of their political knowledge. Jaros and Kolson (1974) investigated Amish children whose parents' formal ideology was explicitly antipolitical, with the result that many political contents were unavailable to them. The results of the study showed that these Amish children were quite politically unsophisticated. They lacked many political contents altogether, and those that they had frequently reflected the political opinions of their parents.

2. *Is political knowledge relevant to children and adolescents? If so, what contents are relevant for them?* This issue is based on the assumption that individuals process information to the extent that it is relevant to their pursuit of an epistemic objective or question. Inquiries can be made either on the basis of previous knowledge or as a result of exposure to new information. It is therefore important for the study of political socialization to examine the extent of interest by particular groups about political knowledge, in general, and also about specific political contents such as those related to education for democracy.

The study of the acquisition of content knowledge can be related to the examination of the relevancy of that content. It may explain why individuals or groups know little or much about a political domain, and why they know about some specific political contents and not others. An example of investigation of the relevance of political content is a study of human concerns conducted by Cantril (1965). He found that 2 percent of Americans indicated that their concerns about political matters reflected their fondest hopes, while 5 percent said they reflected their worst fears. With respect to the international situation, 10 percent referred to fondest hopes and 5 percent to worst fears. This study shows that, in general, Americans have had little concern regarding political matters.

Another direction for research on political contents is found in studies that examine group differences. For example, several investigations have demonstrated that pupils in selective, higher-status schools more frequently express a high level of political interest than pupils in nonselective schools. In addition, such studies find that adolescent offspring of white-collar parents are more likely to report a high level of political interest than the children of blue-collar parents (e.g., Dowse & Hughes, 1971; Stolte-Heiskanen, 1971). There is also evidence that there is a decrease in political interest among women during the late teens and early twenties in the manual labor strata of society (e.g., Stolte-Heiskanen, 1971).

3. *What influence is exerted by cognitive capacity on the acquisition of political knowledge?* This question refers to individual and age differ-

ences regarding knowledge acquisition, resulting from different cognitive capacities. However, since the study of individual differences pertains more to idiographic research, our analysis will focus on age differences, these being the result of developmental abilities and limitations (Rosenau, 1975). Depending on their development, children of different cognitive developmental levels will form differing contents of political knowledge, even after being exposed to the same contents of political information. Also, children are limited in their skills for comprehending various contents of political knowledge, in comparison to adults.

Decisive changes occur in the comprehension of the political world and the development of political thought during childhood and adolescence. These changes are not only a function of continuously accumulated political information, but also a result of cognitive changes that enable a child to acquire and store political knowledge in a more mature way. With increasing age, a child's political knowledge becomes arranged in reasonably coherent structures. Complex modes of political thinking develop which enable the young person to use political information and concepts more effectively, analyze political problems from more than one viewpoint, and apply general principles in specific situations.

In addition, with normal cognitive development, children become increasingly able to confront their political environment in conceptual terms — specifically with regard to political positions, objects, figures, and institutions — and to process them abstractly and differentially. They begin to comprehend such concepts as authority, liberty, socialism, or civil rights. At the same time, their time perspective is extended, so that they can anticipate the short-run and remote consequences and weigh the probable effects of alternative courses of political action in the future. Another development that influences contents of political knowledge is the appearance of sociocentrism. Young adolescents, for example, begin to be able to appraise political events with regard to their consequences for groups of people, to understand social goals or communal needs, and to realize that collective actions are based on socially defined standards.

One of the first studies to examine explicitly the developmental limitations of children at different ages was done by Piaget and Weil (1951). They posited that young children are limited in their ability to make cognitive and affective integration and to broaden their focus of interest. They hypothesized that children at 4 to 5 years of age and 14 to 15 years of age differ in their knowledge about their homeland and other countries. The results confirmed the hypothesis: Such knowledge is dependent on the development from egocentricity to reciprocity. This process reflects gradual decentralization, together with increased ability to integrate and build large categories.

Students of political socialization have recognized the influence of cognitive development on political knowledge acquisition. Greenstein (1965a) pointed out that "the sequence of learning is also affected by what children are able to absorb at various ages" (p. 78). Thus, it is not surprising that the study of cognitive developmental effects on the acquisition of political knowledge has been one of the central concerns of political socialization research. Typical studies have compared different age groups of children and adolescents with regard to various contents of political knowledge (see Stacey, 1978). Greenstein (1965a), in a now classic study, compared political knowledge of children from fourth through eighth grades, in various contents. He found that children of different ages vary in their knowledge regarding political authority, political institutions, and partisan knowledge. For example, the main change in children's view of authority was a shift during the fourth through eighth grade period away from idealization of leaders to a more cynical and critical view. Also, he observed that only older children began to differentiate between the two major parties, although they lacked comprehension of ideological differences.

One series of studies that has investigated age-related changes of knowledge and has direct relevance to socialization for democracy was conducted by Adelson and his associates (Adelson, 1971; Adelson, Green & O'Neil, 1969; Gallatin & Adelson, 1971). They examined the knowledge of youngsters aged 11 to 18 years, about civic affairs, law and government, individual rights, and the public good, and found age differences. Children at 11 years of age had not typically achieved formal operational thinking; rather, it was concrete, egocentric, and tied to the present, and they were limited in ability to foresee long-range consequences and to reason from premises. As a result, their understanding of political concepts was limited and their political knowledge differed from older adolescents.

4. *What kind of epistemic motivation regulates the acquisition of political knowledge?* The formed contents of political knowledge are influenced by the type of epistemic motivation that guides the person in the process of their acquisition. Epistemic motivations can extend the scope of political contents that individuals acquire, or they can limit them, by directing the individuals only to specific contents while disregarding others. Motivations may not only affect individuals' or group members' processing of information and/or generation of ideas, but also the availability of political information in a given group. In this vein, it should be noted that, although epistemic motivation affects the acquisition of political knowledge on the individual level, it is possible to analyze how various needs or situations on the group level can influence what an individual knows (see, e.g., Bar-Tal, in press-a).

This brings us once again to the three categories of epistemic motivation discussed earlier. As noted, when individuals or groups are guided by motivation for validity, they are open to any political information. The wish to avoid mistakes leads individuals to search for alternative political information, to entertain rival hypotheses, and to accept various political ideas. In contrast, motivation for structure implies systemic cognitive freezing. Individuals under this motivation are closed to any new political information, preferring the structure to the uncertainty of considering alternative political ideas. This motivation may be aroused in situations of stress, pressure, or overload of information. The third motivation, for specific content, leads individuals to accept specific political information as valid (Bar-Tal, Klar & Kruglanski, in press). This, too, involves freezing, but in a particular area. Individuals usually reject political ideas and information that contradict their knowledge in that area, probably because of certain underlying needs, desires, or fears (Bar-Tal, in press-b). The needs to maintain a positive image, to feel superior, to belong, to be secure, to receive justice, and to be free of limitations are only several examples of psychological wishes and fears that individuals may have.

This motivational analysis indicates that the acquisition of political knowledge is not a wholly rational, untainted process, as it can often involve exposure to information that elicits considerable personal involvement. In such situations, it can be assumed that motivation for structure or for specific content mediates the acquisition process. It implies that there are individual differences with regard not only to how knowledge is attended to, but also to how it is integrated. In the case of motivation for specific content, individual's emotional needs underlie much of the formation of political knowledge by guiding the individuals to accept certain information that serves particular needs and reject other ideas that are inconsistent with the person's need. Thus, even the exposure to the same information results in formation of different knowledge by different individuals. Moreover, since previously stored knowledge plays an important role in assimilation of new information, and individuals differ in their stored knowledge, political information is always subjectively interpreted and understood.

Renshon (1975) pointed out the relationship between political knowledge acquisition and a motivation, noting that, "basic beliefs are acquired in the attempt to satisfy certain basic human needs" (p. 37). His analysis referred to the influence of psychological needs, as proposed by Maslow (1954), on the acquired contents of political knowledge. In a more specific analysis, Greenstein (1965b) proposed that the political knowledge of an authoritarian personality can be understood on the basis of an analysis of his or her ego-defense needs. Greenstein's analysis is based on the seminal work about authoritarian personality by Adorno, Frenkel-Brunswik, Levinson, and Sanford (1950), who delineated the relationship between individuals' psychological needs and their acquisition of political contents. In addition, several other examples demonstrate the effect of motivation for specific content. Partisans almost invariably overestimate their own candidate's chances of being elected (e.g., Bernham, 1965; Lazarsfeld, Berelson, & Gaudet, 1948) and seem to overestimate the support to their party by various social groups (e.g., Berelson, Lazarsfeld, & McPhee, 1954; Converse & Dupeux, 1962). They also exaggerate differences between candidates or parties and perceive their own ideas as more similar to the ideas of the preferred candidate than they really are (e.g., Berelson et al., 1954).

Children and adolescents acquire political knowledge under the influence of epistemic motivations. Psychological and social needs, as well as societal, political, or economic factors may influence the type of epistemic motivation aroused. The study of political socialization may elucidate these needs and factors, providing partial explanation for why certain contents of political knowledge are formed.

**5.** *What sources serve as epistemic authorities for the acquisition of political knowledge in a group?* This question directs the political socialization research to the investigation of the perceptions and beliefs of children and adolescents regarding various sources of political information. Epistemic authority exerts a determinative influence on the tendency to accept information, even when it is inconsistent with a person's held knowledge. Thus, epistemic authority has great influence on the formation of political knowledge.

The political socialization literature has traditionally been concerned with the relative influence of the four major agents of socialization: family, school, peers, and media (e.g., Beck, 1977; Chaffee, Jackson-Beeck, Duvall, & Wilson, 1977; Davies, 1965; Patrick, 1977; Silbiger, 1977). Our analysis, however, suggests that the focus on these agents is unnecessarily restrictive and that other sources may also be important. In a recent study, which directly investigated the perceptions of epistemic authorities by children and adolescents, important age differences were found (Raviv, Bar-Tal, Raviv, & Houminer, 1988; Raviv, Bar-Tal, Raviv, & Peleg, 1988). First, political knowledge was viewed as part of a factor that included general scientific knowledge and specific topics taken from school subject-matter instruction. With age, the epistemic authority of parents decreases, at least with respect to these contents. In spite of this, the father continues to be perceived as the most important source of political knowledge until the age of 18. Teachers' epistemic authority increases and becomes more important at the age of 18 than that of the mother. Peers are perceived as the least important epistemic authorities regarding political knowledge. Similar results were obtained in a study by Bar-Tal, Raviv, Raviv, and Brosh (1988) which directly assessed political knowledge among fourth, eighth, and twelfth graders. They found that, in general, across the grade levels, the father was perceived as the most important epistemic authority for political knowledge. Media were perceived differentially as a function of age and sex. Other sources such as teachers or the mother were not perceived by the majority of children and adolescents as important epistemic authorities for political knowledge.

## CONCLUSION

We have argued, both implicitly and explicitly, that the study of political socialization should consist of attempts to unravel both universal and particularistic elements. On the one hand, it is necessary to elucidate the underlying universal principles that provide an explanation for the political socialization process. On the other hand, only through the study of particularistic elements is it possible to comprehend and characterize the uniqueness of a specific group. This includes both delineating a group's cognitive repertoire and sources of knowledge and studying the relationships between political knowledge and political behavior, or between political knowledge and a political structure or system. In this respect, the cognitive social psychological approach described here provides both particularistic and universalistic approaches to political knowledge acquisition.

The importance of a joint emphasis on universalism and particularism is apparent when one considers how quickly political knowledge changes. Although individuals weigh and integrate information by using the same cognitive processes, the facts of political life constantly change. So, while the thrust of this chapter has been on understanding intrapersonal processes, we must remember that these processes are also affected by a host of changing factors external to the person. Our view is that the availability of information from various agents of socialization plays an important role in shaping individuals' political knowledge. In addition, so do those individual potentials, as reflected in differential cognitive capacity and motivation, that underlie the process of knowledge acquisition. These all result in individual differences in how people interpret and understand political knowledge.

As social scientists concerned with contributing our understanding of the process of political socialization to the betterment of society, we must come to appreciate both the content of political debate and the process by which individuals acquire such knowledge. There is an interesting and potentially very important parallel between the approach developed here and the nature of being a democratic citizen. The essence of democracy is participation in decision making. We need to understand how individuals use information across contents, and what factors affect its use, in order to strengthen our democratic systems. The knowledge of these processes will help us cope with the influence of demagogues, one-sided information, and rapidly changing social forces.

## REFERENCES

Adelson, J. (1971). The political imagination of the young adolescent. *Daedalus*, *100*, 1013–1050.

Adelson, J., Green, B., & O'Neil, R. (1969). Growth of the idea of law in adolescence. *Developmental Psychology, 1*, 327–332.

Adorno, T. W., Frenkel-Brunswik, E., Levinson, D. J., & Sanford, R. N. (1950). *The authoritarian personality*. New York: Harper & Row.

Bargh, J. A. (1984). Automatic and conscious processing of social information. In R. S. Wyer & T. K. Srull (Eds.), *Handbook of social cognition* (Vol. 3) (pp. 1–43). Hillsdale, NJ: Lawrence Erlbaum.

Bar-Tal, D. (in press-a). Israel-Palestinian conflict: A cognitive analysis. *International Journal of Intercultural Relations*.

Bar-Tal, D. (in press-b). *Group beliefs*. New York: Springer Verlag.

Bar-Tal, D., & Bar-Tal, Y. (1988). New perspective for social psychology. In D. Bar-Tal & A. W. Kruglanski (Eds.), *Social psychology of knowledge* (pp. 83–108). Cambridge, England: Cambridge University Press.

Bar-Tal, D., Klar, Y., & Kruglanski, A. W. (in press). Conflict termination: An epistemological analysis of international cases. *Political Psychology*.

Bar-Tal, D., & Kruglanski, A. W. (Eds.). (1988). *Social psychology of knowledge*. Cambridge, England: Cambridge University Press.

Bar-Tal, D., Raviv, A., Raviv, A., & Brosh, M. (1988). *Attribution of causality for a choice of epistemic authority as a function of domain, source, and age*. Unpublished manuscript. Tel Aviv: Tel Aviv University.

Beck, P. A. (1977). The role of agents in political socialization. In R. A. Renshon (Ed.), *Handbook of political socialization* (pp. 115–141). New York: Free Press.

Berelson, B. R., Lazarsfeld, P. F., & McPhee, W. N. (1954). *Voting: A study of opinion formation in a presidential election*. Chicago: University of Chicago Press.

Bernham, T. W. (1965). Polling for a presidential candidate: Some observations on the 1964 campaign. *Public Opinion Quarterly, 29*, 185–199.

Cantril, H. (1965). *The patterns of human concerns*. New Brunswick, NJ: Rutgers University Press.

Carroll, J. B. (1983). Studying individual differences in cognitive abilities: Through and beyond factor analysis. In R. F. Dillon & R. R. Schmeck (Eds.), *Individual differences in cognition* (Vol. 1) (pp. 1–33). New York: Academic Press.

Chaffee, S. H., Jackson-Beeck, M., Duvall, J., & Wilson, D. (1977). Mass communication. In R. A. Renshon (Ed.), *Handbook of political socialization* (pp. 223–258). New York: Free Press.

*Citizenship education: A survey of requirements for citizenship education among the 50 states*. (1963). New York: Robert A. Taft Institute of Government.

Connell, P. E., & Goat, M. (1972–1973). Science and ideology in American political socialization research. *Berkeley Journal of Sociology, 27*, 166–193.

Converse, P. E., & Dupeux, G. (1962). Politicization of the electorate in France and the United States. *Public Opinion Quarterly, 26*, 1–23.

Davies, J. C. (1965). The family's role in political socialization. *Annals of the American Academy of Political and Social Science, 361*, 11–19.

Dawson, R. E., & Prewitt, K. (1969). *Political socialization*. Boston: Little, Brown.

Dowse, R. E., & Hughes, J. A. (1971). The family, the school, and the political socialization process. *Sociology, 5*, 21–45.

Easton, D., & Dennis, J. (1969). *Children in the political system*. New York: McGraw-Hill.

Ehman, L. H. (1980). The American school in the political socialization process. *Review of Educational Research, 50*, 99–119.

Fiske, S. T., & Taylor, S. E. (1984). *Social cognition*. Reading, MA: Addison-Wesley.

Gallatin, J., & Adelson, J. (1971). Legal guarantees of individual freedom. A cross-national study of the development of political thought. *Journal of Social Issues, 27*, 93–108.

Gillespie, J. A. (1975). Relationships between high school and college instruction. *Teaching Political Science, 2*, 381–408.

Greenstein, F. I. (1965a). *Children and politics*. New Haven, CT: Yale University Press.

Greenstein, F. I. (1965b). Personality and political socialization: Theories of authoritarian and democratic character. *Annals of the American Academy of Political and Social Science, 361*, 81–95.

Hastorf, A. H., & Isen, A. M. (Eds.). (1982). *Cognitive social psychology*. New York: Elsevier.

Hess, R. D., & Torney, J. V. (1967). *The development of political attitudes in children*. Chicago: Aldine.

Holyoak, K. J., & Gordon, P. C. (1984). Information processing and social cognition. In R. S. Wyer & T. K. Srull (Eds.), *Handbook of social cognition* (Vol. 1) (pp. 39–70). Hillsdale, NJ: Lawrence Erlbaum.

Hyman, H. (1959). *Political socialization*. Glencoe, IL: Free Press.

Inhelder, B., & Piaget, J. (1958). *The growth of logical thinking: From childhood to adolescence*. New York: Basic Books.

Jaros, D. (1973). *Socialization to politics*. New York: Praeger.

Jaros, D., & Kolson, K. L. (1974). The multifarious leader: Political socialization of Amish "Yanks." In R. G. Niemi (Ed.), *The politics of future citizens*. San Francisco: Jossey-Bass.

Jennings, M. K., & Niemi, R. G. (1974). *The political character of adolescence: The influence of families and schools*. Princeton, NJ: Princeton University Press.

Kruglanski, A. W. (1979). Causal explanation, teleological explanation: On radical particularism in attribution theory. *Journal of Personality and Social Psychology, 37*, 1447–1457.

Kruglanski, A. W. (1980a). Lay epistemologic process and contents. *Psychological Review, 87*, 70–87.

Kruglanski, A. W. (1980b, July). *The field of cognitive social psychology: Cognitive pluralism and irrationalism re-considered*. Paper presented at the Symposium on New Developments in Attribution Theory, Oxford, England.

Kruglanski, A. W. (in press). *Basic processes in social cognition: A theory of lay epistemology*. New York: Plenum.

Kruglanski, A. W., & Ajzen, I. (1983). Bias and error in human judgment. *European Journal of Social Psychology, 13*, 1–44.

Lau, R., & Sears, D. O. (Eds.). (1986). *Political cognition*. Hillsdale, NJ: Lawrence Erlbaum.

Lazarsfeld, P. F., Berelson, B. R., & Gaudet, H. (1948). *The people's choice* (2nd ed.). New York: Columbia University Press.

Litt, E. (1963). Civic education, community norms, and political indoctrination. *The American Sociological Review, 28*, 69–75.

Markus, H., & Zajonc, R. B. (1985). The cognitive perspective in social psychology. In G. Lindzey & E. Aronson (Eds.), *Handbook of social psychology* (3rd ed., Vol. 1) (pp. 137–230). New York: Random House.

Maslow, A. (1954). *Motivation and personality*. New York: Harper & Row.

McArthur, L. Z. (1981). What grabs you? The role of attention in impression formation and causal attribution. In E. T. Higgins, C. P. Herman, & M. P. Zanna (Eds.), *Social cognition: The Ontario symposium* (Vol. 1) (pp. 201–246). Hillsdale, NJ: Lawrence Erlbaum.

Messick, S. (1976). *Individuality in learning: Implications of cognitive styles and creativity for human development*. San Francisco: Jossey-Bass.

Oppenheim, A. N., Torney, J., & Farnen, R. (1975). *Civic education in ten countries*. New York: Halstead Press.

Orren, K., & Peterson, P. (1967). Presidential assassination: A case study in the dynamics of political socialization. *Journal of Politics, 29*, 388–404.

Ostrom, T. M. (1984). The sovereignty of social cognition. In R. S. Wyer & T. K. Srull (Eds.), *Handbook of social cognition* (Vol. 1) (pp. 1–38). Hillsdale, NJ: Lawrence Erlbaum.

Patrick, J. J. (1977). Political socialization and political education in schools. In R. A. Renshon (Ed.), *Handbook of political socialization* (pp. 190–222). New York: Free Press.

Piaget, J. (1950). *Psychology of intelligence*. New York: Harcourt.

Piaget, J. (1970). Piaget's theory. In P. Mussen (Ed.), *Carmichael's manual of child psychology* (3rd ed., Vol. 1) (pp. 703–732). New York: John Wiley.

Piaget, J., & Weil, A. M. (1951). The development in children of the idea of the homeland and of relations with other countries. *International Social Science Bulletin, 3*, 561–578.

Raviv, A., Bar-Tal, D., Raviv, A., & Houminer, D. (1988). *Development in children's perceptions of epistemic authorities.* Unpublished manuscript. Tel Aviv: Tel Aviv University.

Raviv, A., Bar-Tal, D., Raviv, A., & Peleg, D. (1988). *Perception of epistemic authorities by children and adolescents.* Unpublished manuscript. Tel Aviv: Tel Aviv University.

Renshon, S. A. (1975). The role of personality development in political socialization. In D. C. Schwartz & S. K. Schwartz (Eds.), *New directions in political socialization* (pp. 29–68). New York: Free Press.

Renshon, S. A. (1977a). Assumptive frameworks in political socialization theory. In R. A. Renshon (Ed.), *Handbook of political socialization* (pp. 3–44). New York: Free Press.

Renshon, S. A. (1977b). *Handbook of political socialization.* New York: Free Press.

Rosenau, N. (1975). The sources of children's political concepts: An application of Piaget's theory. In D. C. Schwartz & S. K. Schwartz (Eds.), *New directions in political socialization* (pp. 163–187). New York: Free Press.

Sears, D. O. (1975). Political socialization. In F. I. Greenstein & N. W. Polsby (Eds.), *Handbook of political science* (Vol. 2) (pp. 93–153). Reading, MA: Addison-Wesley.

Sigel, R. S. (1966). *Political socialization: Some reactions to current approaches and conceptualizations.* Paper presented at the annual meeting of the American Political Science Association. New York, New York.

Silbiger, S. L. (1977). Peers and political socialization. In R. A. Rensohn (Ed.), *Handbook of political socialization* (pp. 172–189). New York: Free Press.

Stacey, B. (1978). *Political socialization in Western society.* London: Edward Arnold.

Stolte-Heiskanen, V. (1971). Sex roles, social class and political consciousness. *Acta Sociologica, 14*, 83–94.

Taylor, S. E., & Crocker, J. (1981). Schematic bases of social information processing. In E. T. Higgins, C. P. Herman, & M. P. Zanna (Eds.), *Social cognition: The Ontario symposium* (Vol. 1) (pp. 89–134). Hillsdale, NJ: Lawrence Erlbaum.

Trope, Y. (1986). Identification and inferential processes in dispositional attribution. *Psychological Review, 93*, 239–257.

Wyer, R. S., & Srull, T. K. (Eds.). (1984). *Handbook of social cognition* (Vols. 1–3). Hillsdale, NJ: Lawrence Erlbaum.

Wyer, R. S., & Srull, T. K. (1986). Human cognition in its social context. *Psychological Reveiw, 93*, 322–359.

# PART III

# Institutional Context
# of Political Socialization
# in Democracy

# 7

# Communication and Political Socialization

STEVEN H. CHAFFEE
SEUNG-MOCK YANG

The traditional approach to the role of communication in political socialization has consisted of attempts to document the importance of mass media as agents of socialization of young people (Atkin, 1977, 1981; Chaffee, Ward, & Tipton, 1970; Conway, Stevens, & Smith, 1975; Hawkins, Pingree, & Roberts, 1975; Kraus & Davis, 1976; Meyer, 1976; Rubin, 1976). This was originally a reaction to the tendency among political scientists to take for granted the communication process and the media, particularly television, which bring the world of politics to the citizen (e.g., Campbell, Converse, Miller, & Stokes, 1960), or to accept the outmoded "limited-effects" or "minimal-consequences" view of media influence (e.g., Dawson & Prewitt, 1969). We have repeatedly found that the news media play a central role in political socialization.

In this chapter, we will not abandon that socialization-agent tradition, but will seek to build upon it by offering some alternative conceptions that make different assumptions about both communication processes and the nature of political socialization. We will begin by summarizing some generalizations from two decades of empirical studies on mass-media effects on young people's political behavior, and then turn to alternative approaches.

## YOUTH, MEDIA, AND POLITICS

When Chaffee et al. published a large-sample panel survey study in 1970, it was not presumptuous to give it the broad title, "Mass Communi-

The authors thank Diana Mutz for her comments on an earlier version, and their colleagues Clifford Nass, Sung Gwan Park, and Juju Chang, who collaborated on the study of Korean immigrants partially reported here. The study was supported in part by a grant from Samsung Semiconductor, Inc.

cation and Political Socialization." At that time they found fewer than a half-dozen empirical papers relating the two areas. Their article helped stimulate a number of similar studies by mass-communication scholars, who were encouraged by the fairly strong indications of major media effects. Evidence has since accumulated to justify the following general account of the roles media play in young people's socialization to politics:

1. In Western democracies at least, young children's first contact with politics tends to come via mass-media television (Drew & Reeves, 1980). Open-ended responses by children to questions about the meaning of government are rife with references to things they have noted on TV (Connell, 1971).

2. Television continues to be a major bridge to politics throughout childhood, bringing to young people images of lively figures — dominated by the head of state — to flesh out the "textbook" concepts of government and national history they are learning at school. As children grow into adolescence, however, they become more aware of the distinction between reality and what they see on TV (Cohen, Adoni, & Drori, 1983).

3. Print media gradually supplant TV, from early adolescence on. Those who become readers of newspapers and newsmagazines rapidly outstrip their nonreading adolescent peers in knowledge both of current politics and of the more enduring structure and process of government (Chaffee & Tims, 1982).

4. Heavy consumption of television news also continues to be associated with high levels of political knowledge throughout adolescence (Atkin, 1981). Even though print media are becoming more important, those who follow the news in any medium are more knowledgeable than their peers who do not.

5. The association of news media use with public affairs knowledge is not a tautological matter of seeking and finding political information. It is the general habit of reading and watching media news that predicts learning of political information and orientations, even though this ranks relatively low as a motivation for news-media use by adolescents.

6. In adulthood, and perhaps young adulthood, reliance on TV for news comes to predict below-average knowledge levels in cross-sectional surveys. Adults who spend a lot of time watching TV not only know much less about politics, they also lack political orientations such as party identification or ideology (Gerbner, Gross, Morgan, & Signorielli, 1984).

7. When attention to television, rather than simple exposure to or reliance upon it is measured, attention specifically to news on TV predicts acquisition of political knowledge, even among adults (McLeod & McDonald, 1985). This is especially clear in panel studies, which permit

controls for prior information deficits that might result from other limitations in the person's background, such as low levels of education or intelligence. This holds for both adolescents and their parents (Chaffee & Schleuder, 1986).

8. Comparatively low knowledge levels and lack of political identity are part of a general syndrome of sociostructural deficiencies that characterize heavy viewers of U.S. television, young or older. This probably stems from the general motives for heavy use; TV is seen primarily as a medium for entertainment by most people. In the early years of diffusion of television in the United States, its audience was more elite and presumably more politically aware. A recent survey in China, where television reaches only about half the population, found that heavier viewers were younger and better educated than those who rarely saw TV (Rogers et al., 1985).

9. High media news and public affairs consumers, young and adult alike, exhibit many kinds of political autonomy (Choe, 1982; Dennis, 1986). They are independent of interpersonal influence (e.g., from parents; Wilson, 1984), responsive to current changes in the political picture (Kennamer & Chaffee, 1982), and resistant to persuasion from the media.

10. Media factors do not appear to account for political participation among young people, although the two are correlated. It is more likely that family factors, such as having politically active parents or older siblings, or perhaps peer or community structural influences, bring adolescents into active volunteer roles in political campaigns (Chaffee, Jackson-Beeck, Durall, & Wilson, 1977).

11. A critical time in the political evolution of an individual is the first election campaign the person follows closely. At one time this might have meant the first time the person votes, but, with television, in many cases this first experience is vicarious. Danowski and Ruchinskas (1983), in a secondary analysis of National Election Studies data from 1952 through 1980, show strong cohort effects (as contrasted with supposed aging effects) on socialization to following politics via TV. Adults who had entered the age of political awareness during times of heightened political activity in the United States apparently became — and, just as important, remained — devotees of television news.

12. When prevoting-age adolescents follow a campaign via the mass media, they often focus their attention on news and commercials concerning their favored candidate. This "selective exposure," which is much more marked than in parallel data for their parents, probably stems from the fact that the young person does not have much information to back up a partisan choice (Chaffee & Miyo, 1983).

13. Independence from parents' political preference begins to occur in adolescence. Parent-adolescent correlations in candidate preference

reach their peak around age 12 or 13, when the child is becoming interested enough to follow a campaign. For party identification, the peak correlation comes later, around age 14 to 15, perhaps because parents' "expertise" on abstract parties is seen by the adolescent as more enduring than is the case for the more concrete candidate in a specific election.

14. The popular fear that televised politics generates negative political affect, such as alienation or anomie (Ranney, 1983; Robinson, 1976) has not stood up well in empirical tests. Some forms of negative affect, such as skepticism or distrust of the system, are associated with greater political learning from media (Mutz, 1986).

The foregoing inferences map out an undeniably essential role for the media in political socialization. (One might wonder why it should seem necessary to do that, considering that in most Western countries young people have scant opportunity to experience politics directly.) This conclusion may seem analogous in a way to the notion that oxygen is necessary to human life. At one time, that was a powerful scientific finding, but it's not exactly news anymore. So it is with mass communication and political socialization. Media-effects studies are getting to the point of belaboring a proposition that few doubt. So what's new?

## THE PRIMACY OF READING

Many critical developmental events that help explain later political socialization in young people occur before there is any appreciable political content to their thinking. Paramount is acquisition of the habit of reading, specifically the regular reading of newspapers and newsmagazines.

It is, as we've noted, not necessary to read in order to keep abreast of politics. Radio and TV make it easy to follow current events without the daily newspaper or weekly newsmagazine. Young people in particular gain a good deal of political knowledge and competence, relative to their peers and indeed to their parents, if they follow politics on TV regularly.

But two facts stand out in the data that are accumulating in this area. First, those who follow politics most closely on TV also follow politics closely in print media. That is, TV is not pitted against the press in a zero-sum game; instead, it is a supplement for many citizens, emergent and otherwise. What happens during adolescence is that print media start out as an auxiliary to TV for news and gradually become the more important source, for those who use both. Those who rely solely on TV for news begin to slip behind in the political realm, and this has a cumulative effect so that the "knowledge gap" gradually widens between a well-informed stratum of consumers of both print and TV news, and an exclusively TV-dependent stratum that does not acquire or retain political cognitions very strongly.

The second key fact seems to be that the latter group does not care very much about this state of affairs. Television-dependent citizens, which is to say those who are content to get their news from TV, are not citizens in the strong, proactive sense of that term. They are less likely to vote, to have reasons for their voting decisions, to work on or otherwise contribute to political campaigns or movements, or even to understand how political processes affect their lives.

The point has to do much less with specifically political reading than with the general acquisition of reading as a habit. Despite the fact that reading seems integral to political socialization, the general division of a youth cohort into readers and nonreaders seems to occur around age 9 or 10, which is to say before there is much political content to the reading. Most children learn to read for reasons that have nothing to do with politics, but whether or not they become readers has enormously to do with their eventual political competence.

Roberts and his associates have perhaps the best recent data on the development of reading skills and their relation to mass media. In the course of testing the widely believed proposition that heavy television use retards reading skills — a proposition that they, by the way, find *not* consistent with their data — they note that variance in reading skills expands abruptly in the fourth grade, which is to say at about age 9 or 10. There is little variance at earlier grade levels (Ritchie, Price, & Roberts, 1987; Roberts, Bachen, Hornby, & Hernandez-Ramos, 1984). Then, from the fourth grade on, some children are good readers and others are not. Equally important, these individual differences become highly stable. In structural relations models, the autocorrelations for reading scores on standardized tests, when disattenuated for unreliability so that "true" correlations are being estimated, exceed $r = .95$ from both the sixth to seventh and the seventh to eighth grades. Similar estimates of stability for time spent reading are around $r = .85$ (Ritchie et al., 1987). Their disattenuation procedure might exaggerate these stability estimates somewhat, because when using different items reliability can be underestimated, resulting in overcorrection. But the conclusion that reading and television use habits stabilize during adolescence is supported by other research.

In particular, the extremely high Ritchie et al. (1987) stability estimates resemble findings of Chaffee and Tims (1982) with adolescent panel data. From their initial analysis of a cross-section of youngsters aged 10 to

17, they had concluded that media use followed a Guttman scale pattern. Radio use was the lowest level, followed by TV, then graduation on to the newspaper and finally the newsmagazine. This stairstep model had been suggested earlier, in passing, in a major electoral behavior analysis by Campbell, Converse, Miller, and Stokes (1966), as well as in other sources. But when Tims and Chaffee (1983) attempted to replicate their own findings one and two years later, using the same measures from the same young people, the Guttman scale pattern broke down. The children didn't move up the ladder; they generally stayed at the level where they had been in the first year of the study. Some even dropped back from newspapers to seeming dependence on TV, usually in cases where older adolescents left home and no longer had a daily paper provided for them.

Age, during adolescence, does not appear to be the important factor; media use is. Reading newspapers and newsmagazines predicts far more of the variance in indices of public affairs knowledge than age does, even though this sample spanned ages from late childhood (10 years) to early adulthood (19 years). The major break in the four-level Guttman scale was the middle—the division between the radio/TV levels and newspaper/magazine levels. That split, representing a simple division between nonreaders and readers, accounted for most of the variance in the many different kinds of political cognitions Chaffee and Tims (1982) examined.

Reading is of course not a simple, discrete behavior. It represents a number of cognitive skills, which it in turn may further stimulate developmentally. But its high stability even in late childhood, and its raw empirical power in separating the politically knowledgeable from everyone else—the latter group including both TV-dependent news followers and those utterly uninterested in politics and public affairs—suggest that it is a factor worth incorporating into typologies and other models of differentiation in political socialization.

This is in a way an ironic conclusion to arrive at. Television has been the phenomenon that attracts our attention to mass media, and it is indeed often the first channel to link the young person to politics. Many scholars who casually employ the term *mass media* will admit under questioning that all they were thinking about was television. To account for important differences in the way individuals eventually relate to politics in terms of workable knowledge, however, we turn to an older, less controversial medium, the printed page.

Newspapers and newsmagazines do not attract the nearly universal audiences of TV, nor do they command as much attention by behavioral researchers, but they are read regularly by some 75 and 25 percent, respectively, of adults in the United States. The newspaper's 75 percent includes nearly all of those who vote, and the newsmagazine's 25 percent quite probably represents more than half of those who vote regularly. The heavy political content of newsmagazines and metropolitan newspapers — about 40 percent of the "news hole" involves politics and government — is a clear, if rough, indicator of the interests of the audiences of major print media.

Young people are not being socialized to newspaper reading habits nearly so strongly as were earlier generations. In surveys, they mention competing media and other demands on their time as reasons for not using the newspaper much (Cobb, 1986). The decline in newspaper readership in the United States over the past 50 years, despite an increase of about 2 years in median education, is a good example of how misleading cross-sectional studies can be. Years of education is a very strong predictor of newspaper reading at the individual level, yet the two variables are moving in opposite directions at the aggregate level over time. Chaffee and Choe (1981) found that, with education and other structural factors controlled, it was transitional constraints (e.g., moving, changing occupational or marital status) that predicted changes in newspaper reading behavior. This was particularly the case with young adults.

Television is a worthy supplement to these print media, but reliance on TV alone may be associated with socialization away from politics. To say, "I get most of my news from television," as a majority of Americans today do, may be a socially acceptable way of admitting, "I don't care much about politics." Television dependence is probably more often an indicator than a cause of such an apolitical posture. Just before the widespread diffusion of television, Lazarsfeld and Merton (1948/1971) warned of a possible "narcotizing dysfunction" of attention to mass media. People who follow the news, they feared, might consider this a sufficient substitute for organized social or political action. Their functional analysis is more likely to apply to TV than to the print media, which were the dominant news sources at the time they wrote.

## PERCEPTIONS AND COGNITIONS AS CRITERION VARIABLES

The most important consequences of political socialization via mass communication may consist of perceptual cognitions about the political world, rather than the traditional indicators of knowledge, namely, participation, directional attitudes, or partisan allegiances. That, at least, is a conclusion one might draw from some recent studies. It is an assertion worth pondering, because it carries a certain plausibility.

Recent research has emphasized two novel themes regarding cognitive effects of media use that represent forms of political socialization. One has to do with perceptions of other nations. Socialization to adopt certain images of other, distant peoples is an old idea, a slight reworking of the "stereotypes" literature of a half-century ago. It is clear that the mass media play a central role in the shaping of these international perceptions (e.g., Perry, 1985). Chaffee and Lee (1987) found attention to international news media associated with changes in the factor structure of Americans' "liking" of other nations. Between 1978 and 1982, they found that China had moved from a factor representing Communist Bloc countries (Cuba, USSR) to a separate factor that included Poland. This shift only occurred among those who followed international news, though; among those who didn't follow the news, China was still perceived as part of the Communist Bloc.

This latter example points up the second, related theme—structure. Chaffee and Lee's study (1987) demonstrates that the media enable people to keep track of changes in the structure of international relations. This contrasts with stereotyping, which consists of a stable and unidimensional configuration of perceptions, and with simple learning effects where the sheer number of cognitions might serve as the criterion variable. The same approach shows up in Kennamer and Chaffee's (1982) finding of an increase in structuring of the 1980 presidential candidacies after the New Hampshire primary election, which had effectively eliminated all but the leading candidates. The reduction of uncertainty (i.e., increased structuring) about candidate preferences was limited to those who were high in news-media attention. Notably, this effect was found equally among adolescents and their parents, again underscoring the importance of mass-communication habits rather than simply age.

## FAMILY COMMUNICATION PATTERNS

Interpersonal communication, and particularly the structure of intra-familial interaction in the home, influences the direction of political socialization and interacts with media sources to produce highly varied individuals, despite what appears to be a common political culture.

This general assertion is the product of a long program of research (Chaffee, McLeod, & Wackman, 1973; McLeod & Chaffee, 1972) on family communication patterns. The empirical details are well summarized elsewhere, so only the general theory will be summarized here. The assumption is that the family provides a microcosm in which the child learns communication roles that can be carried into the large world beyond the home. These vary quite a bit, because family norms for children's communication behavior regarding politics vary as well.

Media use, which is acquired (and mostly occurs) in the home, varies according to the interpersonal roles a person carries out. A child who is asked for opinions on current events tends to seek opinions, and thus turns to the news media. A child who is discouraged from arguing with parents is thereby discouraged from following controversial events and, indirectly, from following the news. A child whose parents stress family unity (from the child's perspective, this is conformity) is implicitly being encouraged to learn enough about politics to create a façade of agreement within the home.

There is a circularity of effect in all of this. Family communication behavior norms shape the child's media use, which in turn influences the child's development as a nascent citizen. A pluralistic democratic society presumes a citizenry toleration of divergent viewpoints, but most people are not raised in homes where such tolerance is practiced, so they do not develop mass-communication habits that are appropriate to sustaining that pluralistic posture.

Meadowcroft (1986) shows that protective home communication environments are the rule for children, with pluralistic environments becoming more common in late adolescence. It is clear that the child contributes to the shaping of communication within the home. Tims and Masland (1985), applying structural relations modeling to a panel of parents and adolescents, found considerable measurement error in survey indicators of family communication. This included both unreliability and apparent invalidity, in that parent and child reports were not very strongly correlated with one another, even though the questions asked were presumably about the same parent-child communication events. Nonetheless, the measures introduced by McLeod and Chaffee (1972) continue to serve adequately in research on such themes as social values (Tims, 1986) and perceived reality of television (Messaris & Kerr, 1983).

It does not seem too large a leap to propose that cultures in which few families are pluralistic in their communication patterns are unlikely to develop and maintain democratic processes and institutions at the societal level. Use of mass media, which are the means of communication that link the primary home environment to the larger society, constitutes a sort of intervening variable in this model.

## THE PERSONAL TASK OF BECOMING A POLITICAL PERSON

System needs and demands are the focus of most accountings of political socialization research. What will serve democracy, or preserve the state in times of radical social change, are the kinds of questions that most often inform our studies. But a social process involves two entities, in this case the system and the individual. We could generate a very different view of political socialization if we began with the assumption that its primary impetus comes from within the individual. For the young person this might be construed as "the problem of growing up" or of "becoming a responsible citizen." For immigrants it might mean "the problem of becoming an Israeli," say, or "an American" (more on this later).

From this perspective, all system-level institutions, including mass media, would be of importance to the extent that they enabled the person to achieve self-development. Just as political scientists tend to see socialization from the political system's viewpoint, communication scientists tend to view it in terms of effects of communication systems and structures on the person.

Research on political socialization generally views the process as unidirectional, but, from a self-development perspective, several lines of conceptual alternation might be suggested. Two that we will pursue here are desocialization and resocialization. By *desocialization* we mean the abandonment of political orientations and ties to which one was originally socialized. This may occur, for example, in older citizens, for whom the political scene no longer seems especially relevant, or at least not worth the effort it requires. By *resocialization* we refer loosely to the ongoing problem everyone faces, of continually maintaining or reasserting their acquired political orientations.

We turn in this section to an arena quite different from that of young people—the topic of political socialization of immigrants who have moved in adulthood to a new political culture. For them, resocialization to the political system of their origin is a constant challenge; desocialization from that system of origin is an alternative. It may or may not be accompanied by a new socialization process, to the political system of the host country to which they have come. In all events, communication and especially the mass media play a key role.

## Political Socialization of Immigrants

Immigrants to a new political system have a dual problem of self-development. Not only do they face the challenge of socializing to their host country, they must deal separately with the question of whether to maintain their orientation to their country of origin (i.e., to engage continually in resocialization) or instead to desocialize themselves from it. These are not parts of a single process. Some immigrants might become socialized to the host political system and yet continue their ethnic resocialization, too. This pattern might be described as "plural socialization" or even "oversocialization."

Communication demands are considerably greater if the person is both socializing to the host country and resocializing to the country of origin, than if socialization to the host country is accompanied by the more passive desocialization process. A mass-media system is central in both socialization and resocialization, but they require different media. There are news media available for fostering socialization of immigrants in the host country, and we might imagine that this process works about the same way for immigrants as it does for young people born in the host country and becoming socialized to its political system via those media. Then there may also be at least a minor media system emanating from the country of origin, in either the language of origin or (in the case of large, long-standing immigrant groups) in the host language. The desocializing immigrant need not pay much attention to the second, ethnic media system; by the same token, the immigrant who does not become socialized to the host country can ignore the host media. But those who are combining resocializing and socializing (oversocialization) must follow news in both kinds of media.

This accounting makes matters sound more purposeful than they might be in most cases. If we think of communication, rather than individual motivation, as the causal agent, it can be said that (1) one who does not adopt host media will not become very strongly socialized to the host country and (2) one who loses contact via ethnic media will become desocialized from the country of origin, rather than maintaining a resocialized relationship with it.

The more popular unidirectional model of assimilation of immigrant populations over time is not an adequate accounting of their political socialization. Current literature (Subervi-Velez, 1986) emphasizes a "pluralistic" model, in which the questions of socialization to one's host country and of what we are calling resocialization to the ethnic country are separated. The passage of time itself is not counted on to accomplish either task; rather, the central factor is what one does with that time, particularly what kinds of communication linkages one establishes with each system. While education, status, and linguistic competency enter in, and while psychological identification and interpersonal social contact play their part, it is our working contention that mass media occupy a major role in each socialization process.

**The Bay Area Korean Study**

We have recently been examining these ideas in a survey of Korean immigrants living in the San Francisco Bay Area. We will summarize here some preliminary results from this study, taken from the second author's

Ph.D. dissertation (Yang, 1988). Approximately 1,000 households were randomly selected from a directory of some 7,000 Korean households provided by the Multi-Service Center for Koreans in San Francisco. Each household was sent questionnaires (in both Korean and English) by mail in the fall of 1987, with the request that one adult member of the household complete either questionnaire. The final sample ($N=239$) was rather high in socioeconomic status (a majority had completed college) but also in ethnicity (two-thirds chose to complete the questionnaire in Korean rather than English). Given that many of the addresses were out of date, the mailed return represents a response rate between 35 and 40 percent; we will concentrate here on relationships between variables rather than on marginal descriptions of this somewhat unrepresentative sample.

Background.   Immigrants to a democracy who come from a nation with nondemocratic institutions constitute an underrecognized problem for the country assimilating them. One reason these people are "a problem" is that they often do not desocialize, because they view their new polity in terms appropriate to that of their origin. Korea, while it is industrializing and otherwise modernizing at a considerable pace, was at the time of our survey an autocracy centrally controlled by a government that had little patience with democratic institutions, including a free press. Korean immigrants would thus have a long history of experience with television news and newspapers that are subject to censorship and suppression, media that in practice simply go along with the government's wishes. Some students in universities may dissent and demonstrate and risk state reprisals for their actions, as do students and editors alike in Latin America. But in Korea editors are unlike these students; the media have not strayed far from the official line.

In Korea news media are, as in most nondemocratic countries, seen as mouthpieces of those in power rather than as a politically independent entity from which one might gain valid information. In our study we hypothesized that this orientation to media that are closely associated with the government carries over when people immigrate from Korea to the United States. Theoretically this should be the case for immigrants from any nondemocratic system to one where the press is free and its citizens control their governance through the vote. Experience with the more critical "free press" of the democratic host country should serve to counteract this image, socializing the new citizen to a clearer understanding of the independence of the news media in one's adopted land.

The Bay Area provides enough media opportunities to support ethnic resocialization as well as host socialization. There are several Korean-language daily newspapers published in California, plus some weeklies in English. Most of their political content comes from their sister newspapers in Seoul and so is similar to the government-controlled information readers would be getting had they not immigrated to the United States. There is also a UHF television station that broadcasts some Korean programming, including at least a minor amount of daily news from Seoul.

Findings: Systemic Perceptions.  Clear evidence on behalf of our reasoning emerged in the strength of correlations between measures of trust in the news media and trust in the government, separately for the media and governments of the Republic of Korea and the United States. Table 7.1 shows both the raw correlations and partial correlations that are controlled for 11 related factors, including age and length of time in the United States, English competency, education, citizenship, cultural identification, and interpersonal contacts with other Koreans and Americans.

A fourfold typology based on use of Korean and American news media is presented in the table. This typology is constructed from two indices, each built from questions regarding frequency of reading newspapers or watching television news programs. The index for exposure to American news media was divided at the median, as was the analogous Korean media index. Thus our total sample was subdivided into four groups:

1. Korean media users (high on the Korean index, low on the American)

**Table 7.1** Correlations between media trust and government trust of Korea and the United States, by immigrants' news media use

|  | Media-government trust correlation (Pearson $r$)[a] | |
|---|---|---|
| Media use group | Korean | American |
| Low media users ($n=32$) | .67 (.79) | .75 (.79) |
| Korean media users ($n=71$) | .61 (.62) | .59 (.61) |
| American media users ($n=72$) | .61 (.61) | .53 (.43) |
| Plural media users ($n=61$) | .74 (.69) | .39 (.25)[b] |

[a]Entries are Pearson product-moment correlation coefficients. Entries in parentheses are partial coefficients, controlling for age at immigration, length of stay in U.S., intention to stay, socioeconomic status, education, English competency, citizenship, identification with Korean and American cultures, and frequency of social contact with Koreans and Americans. All entries are significant at the $p < .001$ level, unless otherwise noted.

[b]Significant at the $p < .05$ level.

2. American media users (high on the American index, low on the Korean)
3. Plural media users (high on both indexes)
4. Low media users (low on both indexes)

The positive connection we expected Korean-Americans to make between government and media is shown throughout Table 7.1, although these generally positive correlations could be due to response set as well. Those who say they have more trust in each government display correlatively more trust in its media system as well. More to our point are the differences among the four groups in the table. All four evaluate the government and media of Korea quite similarly. The lowest correlation, though, is found among the American media users, which suggests that they are indeed becoming desocialized. By not following the Korean news, they may be losing the perception of a close media-government identity there. The resocialization hypothesis is borne out by the fact that the highest correlations representing Korean media-government associations are found in the two groups that continue to read news from Seoul (Korean media users and plural media users).

There is much more variance across the four groups in perceptions of American government-media associations. The two groups that follow the American media (American media users and plural media users) exhibit reduced correlations. This is particularly the case among the plural media users, who have recurrent opportunity to compare the two sources of news. The plural users, whose heavy communication activities predict both socialization and resocialization, appear most clearly to understand the contrast. In other words, they recognize that, in the United States, unlike Korea, the news media are independent of government and that to place trust in the one would not necessarily imply a corresponding degree of trust in the other. By contrast, the low media users, lacking communication on which to base any judgment, see U.S. media-government relations as, if anything, closer than those in Korea! In a sense, they have not even achieved desocialization, much less socialization to the American political system. They are viewing the American system as if it operates the same way as in Korea. The low media users contrast most vividly with the plural media users, who are able to achieve both socialization and resocialization so that they recognize the difference between the Korean and American systems of government-press relations.

This analysis of trust in broader societal institutions takes its place alongside some of the other studies we noted earlier, where the indicator of political socialization has to do with the structure of people's perceptions of the political sphere. It makes clear that the effects of mass media on socialization to politics and on an understanding of macrosystems do not depend simply upon the sheer amount of exposure to news media. It also matters a great deal which media are involved. Those Korean immigrants who continue to get their news from Korean sources appear to continue also with the erroneous assumption that the U.S. press is as closely tied to the purposes of the government as is the case in Korea.

Findings: Political Learning and Stimulation. The Korean-American study also gives us an opportunity to compare the principal American news media — television and newspapers — in terms of their contributions to political socialization. Recall that U.S. surveys have shown that television makes an important contribution early on, when the child is first becoming aware of politics, but that TV is supplanted by print media in later adolescence, and that eventually in adulthood heavy reliance on television for news is associated with comparative deficits in public affairs knowledge. A nice empirical question, then, is whether adult immigrants experience political socialization via television along the same lines as young Americans growing up, or whether the process is more dependent on print, as is the case with American adults.

The answer seems to be that American television and newspapers make approximately equal and significant contributions to the socialization of Korean immigrants to American politics. The second author's dissertation (Yang, 1988), examined four criteria of American political socialization as dependent variables: knowledge of American politicians, knowledge of American political issues, interest in American politics, and discussion of American politics. He first controlled, in a hierarchical regression analysis, for 11 other variables, as noted in Table 7.1, and then looked at the increment to variance explained by adding the media indices to his predictor equation.

Both reading American newspapers and watching American television news added significantly to the empirical explanation of Korean immigrants' knowledge of American politicians, and of discussion of American politics. Television news alone, rather surprisingly, significantly predicted knowledge of American political issues. The newspaper index was the stronger predictor of interest, but its value is of course heavily dependent on reading skills in English. In sum, the Korean immigrants as a group might be said to utilize mass media in political socialization in the manner of an advanced adolescent American, in that they use television for this purpose about as much as the newspaper.

We also examined three indicators of resocialization: interest in and discussion of Korean politics, and knowledge of Korean political issues. For each, reading a Korean newspaper predicted a significant increment to variance beyond that accounted for by the 11 control variables. Korean television made no significant contribution, probably because there was so little Korean news available on that channel. This null finding reminds us of an important principle, however: In the absence of appropriate ethnic mass media in the host country, continual resocialization to the political system of one's origin becomes very difficult. The resocialization process is sustained by the Korean newspapers published in California; in their absence, we might expect desocialization to be the prevailing pattern.

## POLITICAL SOCIALIZATION IN NON-WESTERN NONDEMOCRACIES

The example of Korea points up the need for new conceptualizations of political socialization, models for research that are adaptable to countries where democracy is not the prevailing mode of governance. As a rule, these are also societies that have evolved from cultural traditions different from those of the West. In particular, as a number of Asian (and South American) nations are making the transition to democratic systems, we should be organizing our studies around problems of desocialization and resocialization in times of change. Our study of Korean immigrants examined change as the individual moved from a nondemocratic system to a democratic one; the next step might be to follow individuals as their system moves from nondemocratic to being more democratic, while they stay put. The research question would then become how political socialization helps or hinders the process of national democratization.

Meanwhile, though, many students from nondemocratic nations find Western conceptions of political socialization most difficult to apply to their home situations. It is not only that they do not have significant voting rights in a stable multiparty system, nor even that they lack news media that are free of government control. They also lack a tradition of such institutions, which further means that they lack a tradition of socialization to them. Political and media institutions, and institutionalized relationships between them, rely for their historical persistence on socialization.

Mass media will not necessarily be the key to these processes. Another Korean researcher (Choe, 1982) built her dissertation around generalized concepts of autonomy of the individual and accommodation to the reality of one's particular political system. She found a strong empirical association between adolescents' political identity and family communication patterns. This study was done with data from Wisconsin, but the concepts are abstract enough that she could replicate it in Korea. It could well be that institutionalized communication patterns at levels below that of the society at large are the important influences in socializing people to autonomous political identities, while mass media are more central in learning about political macrosystems.

## IMPLICATIONS FOR EDUCATION

What should those responsible for political education, who work through institutions whose mission is more explicitly educational than is the case with the family or the mass media, think or do about these communication influences? Most centrally, our conclusions suggest that the educator should strive to establish or encourage pluralistic communication environments. It is clear, for example, that pluralistic families produce the most active and knowledgeable youngsters; but many students come to school from nonpluralistic backgrounds. The school can provide the setting where their opinions are sought and respected, so that it will become more instrumental for every student to build and maintain an awareness of politics and how the political system functions.

This naturally leads one to the mass media. Again, we would argue for pluralism. Instruction should be stimulative, not didactic. If the student is given the idea that the answers to complex political issues are to be found in a textbook, or issued by a teacher, the opportunity provided by a free and competitive mass-media environment will be lost. Much learning occurs outside school, and educators need to find ways of making both newspapers and television news function as supplements and even spurs to daily — and lifelong — learning. This is not easily accomplished, particularly given that television is viewed as "the enemy" by most educators. True, TV entertainment does take time away from studies, but there is much of value on television if students are encouraged to find it. One proven method is to give students the opportunity, through activities such as open discussion or an essay task, to examine and utilize the political content of TV.

Television is a bridge between interpersonal and primary-group socialization, and socialization to the larger political system. Because most of its content is geared to attract large audiences through entertainment, educators tend to shy away from it. But students are attracted to it, and that attraction can be built upon. One of the great educational success stories in American television has been "Sesame Street," which has built its preschool instruction in reading readiness upon the format of the television advertisement. As part of the formative evaluation conducted before the show went into production, it was found that young children watch commercials more attentively than other programing. So "Sesame Street" was presented as if its sponsor were a letter of the alphabet ("Today's show is brought to you by the letter *W*. Let's see what *W* can do for you. It can make words like . . . )". The point here is not to reproduce a "Sesame Street" for adolescents, but to approach television positively and in its own terms, building upon the habits of attention and learning that it has established.

Political socialization via television alone is, in the long run, incomplete and inadequate. Use of newspapers and newsmagazines should in turn build upon the beginning provided by TV. Reading skill is, as we have noted, essential; but most young people will learn to read well once they have a strong reason to do so. Giving them occasions to use information from the politically oriented print media, and particularly to search various sources in a pluralistic approach, is likely to sharpen both their critical and technical skills.

## CONCLUSION

Our analysis of immigrants barely scratches the surface of the kind of challenge they present to political education. But, again, a pluralistic approach, in this case encouraging use of ethnic media as well as host media, seems most advisable. The ethnic heritage does not follow the immigrant across the sea and through radical change in political systems, unless there is provision for resocialization to it. Socialization to the host system seems to be strengthened if it is accompanied by continual resocialization to the system of origin. This is most evident in our Table 7.1, in the contrast between plural media users, who appear to understand the American system (and the Korean system) best, versus those who use only one of the two kinds of news media.

In a period of systemic political change within a nation, we might venture to extend this principle of pluralism, even in the absence of empirical evidence. Education to new political conditions is most likely to take root if it is contrasted clearly with the past. Simply forgetting the past (forced desocialization) is probably a weak approach. Didactic teaching (indoctrination) against the past may not be much better, especially if the person will eventually encounter that system firsthand. A pluralistic approach would be more experiential, giving students the opportunity to consider what actions might be possible under the earlier conditions, as compared to the present.

In advocating pluralistic approaches to education, we are admittedly recommending additional work for educators. It is twice as hard to provide alternative experiences as it is to instruct the student in a single political mode. It is time consuming to let young people express their opinions, especially at the developmental stage when they have little information. But we are encouraged by the example of those in our studies who have been involved in the "extra work" of pluralistic communication activities. Those Korean–Americans who read both Korean and American media, for example, understand both the Korean system and especially the American system more clearly. Children whose parents have tolerated and encouraged the expression of opinion in the home end up knowing more and being more active politically, in school and in later life, than do those whose homes provided no outlet for pluralistic expression. We are, then, suggesting that political education take a leaf from the book of those who have themselves found the way to political socialization through pluralistic communication.

## REFERENCES

Atkin, C. (1977). Effects of campaign advertising and newscasts on children. *Journalism Quarterly, 54*, 503–508.

Atkin, C. (1981). Communication and political socialization. In D. Nimmo & K. Sanders (Eds.), *Handbook of political communication* (pp. 299–328). Beverly Hills, CA: Sage.

Campbell, A., Converse, P., Miller, W., & Stokes, D. (1960). *The American voter*. New York: John Wiley.

Campbell, A., Converse, P., Miller, W., & Stokes, D. (1966). *Elections and the political order*. New York: John Wiley.

Chaffee, S., & Choe, S. Y. (1981). Newspaper reading in longitudinal perspective: Beyond structural constraints. *Journalism Quarterly, 58*, 201–211.

Chaffee, S., Jackson-Beeck, M., Durall, J., & Wilson, D. (1977). Mass communication in political socialization. In S. Renshon (Ed.), *Handbook of political socialization* (pp. 223–258). New York: Free Press.

Chaffee, S., & Lee, C. K. (1987, August). *Impact of media information on the structure of affect toward other nations*. Paper presented to the convention of the Association for Education in Journalism and Mass Communication, San Antonio, Texas.

Chaffee, S., McLeod, J., & Wackman, D. (1973). Family communication patterns and adolescent political participation. In J. Dennis (Ed.), *Socialization to politics: Selected readings* (pp. 349–64). New York: John Wiley.

Chaffee, S., & Miyo, Y. (1983). Selective exposure and the reinforcement hypothesis: An intergenerational panel study of the 1980 presidential campaign. *Communication Research, 10*, 3–36.

Chaffee, S., & Schleuder, J. (1986). Measurement and effects of attention to media news. *Human Communication Research, 13*, 76–107.

Chaffee, S., & Tims, A. (1982). News media use in adolescence: Implications for political cognitions. In M. Burgoon (Ed.), *Communication yearbook 6* (pp. 736–758). Beverly Hills, CA: Sage.

Chaffee, S., Ward, S., & Tipton, L. (1970). Mass communication and political socialization. *Journalism Quarterly, 47*, 647–659.

Choe, S. Y. (1982). *Autonomy and accommodation as dimensions of political socialization: A communication socialization perspective.* Unpublished Ph.D. dissertation, University of Wisconsin-Madison.

Cobb, C. (1986). Patterns of newspaper readership among teenagers. *Communication Research, 13*, 299–326.

Cohen, A., Adoni, H., & Drori, G. (1983). Adolescents' perceptions of social conflicts in television news and social reality. *Human Communication Research, 10*, 203–225.

Connell, R. W. (1971). *The child's construction of politics.* Melbourne, Australia: University of Melbourne Press.

Conway, M., Stevens, A. J., & Smith, R. (1975). The relation between media use and children's civic awareness. *Journalism Quarterly, 52*, 531–538.

Danowski, J., & Ruchinskas, J. (1983). Period, cohort, and aging effects: A study of television exposure in presidential election campaigns, 1952–1980. *Communication Research, 10*, 77–96.

Dawson, R., & Prewitt, K. (1969). *Political socialization.* Boston: Little, Brown.

Dennis, J. (1986). Preadult learning of political independence: Media and family communication effects. *Communication Research, 13*, 401–433.

Drew, D., & Reeves, B. (1980). Children and television news. *Journalism Quarterly, 57*, 45–54.

Gerbner, G., Gross, L., Morgan, M., & Signorielli, N. (1984). Political correlates of television viewing. *Public Opinion Quarterly, 48*, 283–300.

Hawkins, R., Pingree, S., & Roberts, D. (1975). Watergate and political socialization. *American Politics Quarterly, 3*, 406–422.

Kennamer, J. D., & Chaffee, S. (1982). Communication of political information during early presidential primaries: Cognition, affect, and uncertainty. In M. Burgoon (Ed.), *Communication yearbook 5* (pp. 627–650). New Brunswick, NJ: Transaction Books.

Kraus, S., & Davis, D. (1976). *The effects of mass communication on political behavior.* University Park: Pennsylvania State University Press.

Lazarsfeld, P., & Merton, R. (1971). Mass communication, popular taste and organized social action. In W. Schramm & D. Roberts (Eds.), *The process and effects of mass communication, Rev. ed.* (pp. 554–578). Urbana, IL: University of Illinois Press. (Original work published 1948)

McLeod, J., & Chaffee, S. (1972). The construction of social reality. In J. Tedeschi (Ed.), *The social influence processes* (pp. 50–99). Chicago: Aldine-Atherton.

McLeod, J., & McDonald, D. (1985). Beyond simple exposure: Media orientations and their impact on political processes. *Communication Research, 12*, 3–34.

Meadowcroft, J. (1986). Family communication patterns and political development: The child's role. *Communication Research, 13*, 603–24.

Messaris, P., & Kerr, D. (1983). Mothers' comments about TV: Relation to family communication patterns. *Communication Research, 10*, 175–194.

Meyer, T. (1976). The impact of "All in the Family" on children. *Journal of Broadcasting, 20*, 25–33.

Mutz, D. (1986, May). *Political alienation and the acquisition of political knowledge.* Paper presented to Political Communication Division of International Communication Association, Chicago, IL.

Perry, D. (1985). The mass media and inference about other nations. *Communication Research, 12,* 595–614.

Ranney, A. (1983). *Channels of power: The impact of television on American politics.* New York: Basic Books.

Ritchie, D., Price, V., & Roberts, D. (1987). Television, reading, and reading achievement: A reappraisal. *Communication Research, 14,* 292–315.

Roberts, D., Bachen, C., Hornby, M., & Hernandez-Ramos, P. (1984). Reading and television: Predictors of reading achievement at different age levels. *Communication Research, 11,* 9–49.

Robinson, M. (1976). Public affairs television and the growth of political malaise: The case of "The Selling of the Pentagon." *American Political Sceince Review, 70,* 409–432.

Rogers, E., Zhao, X., Pan, Z., Chen, M., & the Beijing Journalists Association. (1985). The Beijing audience study. *Communication Research, 12,* 179–208.

Rubin, A. (1976). Television in children's political socialization. *Journal of Broadcasting, 55,* 125–129.

Subervi-Velez, F. A. (1986). The mass media and ethnic assimilation and pluralism: A review and research proposal with special focus on Hispanics. *Communication Research, 13,* 71–96.

Tims, A. (1986). Family political communication and social values. *Communication Research, 13,* 5–17.

Tims, A., & Chaffee, S. (1983). *A test of the cumulative acquisition model of adolescent media use.* Paper presented to the Association for Education in Journalism, Corvallis, OR.

Tims, A., Masland, J. (1985). Measurement of family communication patterns. *Communication Research, 12,* 35–57.

Wilson, D. (1984). *Political opinion change in parent-adolescent dyads: The influence of communication activities.* Unpublished Ph.D. dissertation, University of Wisconsin-Madison.

Yang, S. M. (1988). *The role of mass media in immigrants' political socialization: A study of Korean immigrants in northern California.* Unpublished Ph.D. dissertation, Stanford University, Stanford, California.

# 8

# Political Socialization for Workplace Democracy

HENRY M. LEVIN

Societies that are democratic and capitalist require citizens who can function under both democratic and authoritarian political regimes. The democratic requirements are predicated upon the needs of the political institutions of such societies, and the authoritarian requirements on the needs of their economic institutions. On the one hand, it is necessary to shape a democratic personality so that individuals may be expected to participate politically in the governance of public institutions, in behalf of the public good. This participation is both encouraged and protected by a well-defined set of democratic rights, obligations, and protections. The democratic personality is expected to express its views freely and welcome the free expression of others, as well as to accept democratic mechanisms for resolving conflict in a variety of different situations.

On the other hand, the conventional workplace is governed by an authoritarian regime in which the rights of workers are derogated to the formal and informal rules and practices of those who own and manage the workplace. The prerogatives of private property and the law of contracts replace most of the political rights conferred by democracy. Workers must relinquish such basic rights as freedom of speech and association and the ability by the governed to select who will govern. Narrow self-interest, individualism, and individual competition to succeed in the workplace replace the quest for social movements and solidarity in behalf of the common good. In contrast to their performance as citizens in a political democracy, workers are expected to serve regimes that do not normally accommodate their participation in either selecting leaders or in making decisions that affect working life.

This dualism in demands upon adult competencies must necessarily be reflected in the socialization of the young. As one of the principal institutions for preparing the young for political citizenship and worker citizenship, the schools play a major role in creating the complex personalities that are able to navigate between and function within these contradic-

158

tory arenas. Schools must prepare students for both types of political regimes, the democratic and the authoritarian. Fully productive citizens must be able to shift their behavior proficiently from one to the other. But, the fact that the two political arenas are premised on conflictive principles means that the schools must mold students with dual personalities.

The questions I address in this chapter are (1) whether a movement to workplace democracy is possible that would integrate the formation of political development by creating a more nearly uniform set of requirements for adult competency and (2) what the role of the schools might be in political socialization for such an eventuality. This chapter will thus be divided into three parts. First, I will discuss the nature of the democratic and capitalist state and the dichotomy of demands faced by the schools. This will draw heavily upon previous work (Carnoy & Levin, 1985). Second, I will present the social, political, and economic arguments for moving democracy into the workplace. Finally, I will suggest changes in socialization that might be pertinent to this integration of purpose, with a special focus on the role of the school.

## DEMOCRACY, CAPITALISM, AND THE SCHOOLS

It has long been recognized that democracy and capitalism have very different features (e.g., Dahl & Lindblom, 1953; Hirschman, 1970; Schumpeter, 1942), ones that are reflected in public conflicts (McClosky & Zaller, 1984). In our public life we operate within a set of institutions that set out both rights and obligations of citizens to express themselves and participate in choosing governmental representatives and policies. We expect all citizens to be familiar with their legal rights and the institutions that guarantee those rights, as well as to exercise these rights through democratic discourse and participation. Moreover, the underlying principles of democracy are those of equality of rights under the law, the right to vote, and the right to organize with others to create political change.

In contrast, the workplace is organized under very different principles of hierarchy, inequality, and restriction of political rights. Authority is vested in the ownership of productive property, which provides leverage to capitalists and their managers to define the overall conditions of work. Individual workers do not have inalienable rights, but only contractual ones. In general, such contracts are premised on a highly uniform organizational regimen of hierarchy, close supervision, rules and regulations, and proscription of most of the democratic rights that are guaranteed outside of the workplace (Alchian & Demsetz, 1972; Ellerman, 1984; Stiglitz, 1975). Bosses are not elected democratically, nor are the rules, regulations, or human organization of the workplace set by worker participation.

The reproduction of institutions in a democratic capitalist state requires the formation of citizens who can function equally well in the two different environments. Citizenship, however, is not a creature of the genes; it is learned through early experience and training and reinforced through the contingencies of living. Most persons spend at least 10 of their early years in schools, so it is not surprising that schools must undertake much of the burden of political socialization for both the polity and the workplace.

Our schools are sponsored by a state that has been fashioned to serve both democratic and capitalist interests. On the one hand, the schools inculcate the values of capitalism, with its focus on individual competition, the sanctity of private property, and the legitimacy of inequality of wealth and income. The schools also prepare students for different positions in the productive hierarchy of capitalism, as well as for participating in capitalist work organizations that correspond closely to the structure and function of schools. Teachers serve as supervisors who direct the work of students according to a preplanned regimen and provide extrinsic rewards such as grades and promotions, much like the wages and promotions of the workplace.

On the other hand, our schools inculcate the values of democracy and democratic participation. In the United States, students have the right to freedom of expression, as long as they do not disrupt the schooling process (Kemerer & Deutsch, 1979). The U.S. Constitution protects the right of students to participate in schools, and substantial obstacles are placed in the way of removing the student from the schooling process during the compulsory schooling years (Kemerer & Deutsch, 1979). Students are taught about the values of democracy and the executive, judicial, and legislative institutions of government that serve as checks and balances in the democratic system. The universal franchise is especially celebrated in the curriculum. Finally, although inequalities exist in schooling processes and outcomes, they pale in comparison to those in the workplace (Carnoy & Levin, 1985).

Our schools thus have features of both democracy and capitalism, and this is not a surprise when one considers that they are sponsored by a democratic and capitalist state. Schools are neither capitalist workplaces nor democratic institutions, although they have features of both. That suggests a dilemma for both schools and their participants, for many aspects of capitalism and democracy are in conflict with each other. The momentum of participation, equality, and protection of rights of the state is in conflict with the individual servitude, inequality, arbitrariness, and lack of protections in the workplace.

Historically, the schools have been sites for struggle between the principles of democratic/egalitarian forces and those working to reproduce and expand capitalist relations and capital accumulation (Carnoy & Levin, 1985). We expect schools to provide an education that expands social opportunities, mobility, equality, various forms of democratic participation, and the knowledge of rights and protections. We also expect schools to provide appropriately trained workers with the required skills, attitudes, and behavior for capitalist production and accumulation. The history of schooling in the United States has been a history of struggle between these two dynamics.

The period from 1880 to 1920 saw a structural transformation of the schools which followed similar changes in the industrial system, with regard to a movement toward centralization and bureaucracy under professional control and the adoption of testing and tracking practices akin to those for the selection and allocation of workers in industry. Curriculum and school practices were also standardized, as in the industrial model (Bowles & Gintis, 1976; Tyack, 1974). Consolidation of this movement continued until World War II. The three decades following the end of the war were a period of unprecedented moves toward equality of participation and treatment. Social and legal movements during this period worked to achieve racial desegregation of schools and gender equality, and established compensatory programs for educationally disadvantaged and bilingual students and the right to an appropriate education for the handicapped. In addition, teachers and students won the rights to constitutional protections from dismissal or suspension for airing their opinions.

The period of the 1980s has been one in which the capitalist dynamic has asserted itself once again. Educational reforms have focused on education for economic competition, with a rising concern for standards, increased time in the school year, more required courses, and more use of examinations to sort out students for graduation and other purposes. The struggle between the democratic and capitalist forces for hegemony in schools continues unabated. At some points, one side gains primacy; at other points, the other side does.

Carnoy and Levin (1985) view this as a dialectical process in which there are internal contradictions within both the democratic/capitalist state and the schools that are situated within the jurisdiction of the state. The same institutions must function to support opposing internal dynamics.

Historically, a struggle has ensued between the two dynamics and their antagonists. The capitalist dynamic is supported by private property and its financial support of the state, as well as its ability to permeate institutional life to shape consciousness and ideology on what is appropriate and what is possible in terms of work relations and their educational requirements. This dynamic is also buttressed by the rather important role of business in the financial support of political candidates and in lobbying efforts. The democratic or egalitarian dynamic, in contrast, is more populist in origin and is fueled by social movements of political interest groups and their coalitions. In addition to attempts to influence laws through electoral politics, this dynamic also relies on popular movements and sympathetic media to advance an egalitarian ideology. In addition, it challenges the existing rights of capital by pressing for new laws that advance its causes as well as by seeking extension of existing laws to such ends.

Thus, the two sides to the struggle use different strategies and resources to press for gains. However, the historical ambience is not neutral and varies in its ability to buttress up the strengths of one of the contenders or the other. At times of rising national income and low unemployment, the egalitarian dynamic is able to make incursions on the prerogatives of capital. At times of economic crisis, the capitalist dynamic is reinforced in its call for greater selectivity and higher standards, in order to regain competitiveness and reduce government expenditures for social reforms.

A major issue that I wish to raise is whether that struggle would change if the principles for democratic participation became more prevalent in the workplace. I have been arguing that much of the struggle between the democratic/capitalist state and its schools is traceable to their dual and conflictive roles in simultaneously reproducing both social and political equality and economic inequality, both fuller educational participation and restrictive access to the more selective institutions and levels of education, both expansion of opportunity and enrollments and structural limits to success for the vast majority of the participants. But, what if these internal contradictions were to diminish considerably through a greater emphasis on democracy in the workplace? This would be one way of creating greater compatibility between the needs of the capitalist workplace and the democratic polity. It seems that both the functioning of schools and the socialization of their students would become less conflictive. Socialization for the workplace would share many of the same key attributes as socialization for political life, so that a more uniform approach to political socialization could address the needs of both citizen and worker.

Such a vision, however, must be based upon a compelling proposal for achieving movement toward greater workplace democracy. In the next section, the elements of this proposal will be described.

## TOWARD WORKPLACE DEMOCRACY

In this section I present the case for worker democracy, which rests on moral, political, and economic principles. At the same time, I will examine some of the dynamics of the present movement in this direction.

### The Moral Imperative

The moral argument for worker participation is one that is prominent historically. In his *Economic and Philosophic Manuscripts of 1844*, Karl Marx (1964) argues that, under capitalism, labor is just another commodity to be used by the capitalist, if it brings a profit. The result is that workers can sell their labor power only if they can find a capitalist buyer. Even then, the way in which the worker's labor is used and the product of that labor are completely beyond the control of the worker. Marx refers to this condition as one of alienation, in which workers lose control over the setting, process, and product of their labor to the capitalist owner of property.

The basic component of this alienation is that labor is external to the worker and is not directly used to meet the worker's needs to be productive, creative, or useful. It is a denial of the inner self and frustrates human development. Labor is forced or coerced rather than satisfying a human need. Marx (1964) argues that this relation derogates the humanity of laborers to an animal existence in which only such elemental functions as eating, drinking, and procreation are placed under their control. Thus, the moral imperative, for Marx, is for workers to gain ownership of the means of production, in order to control for themselves the process and product of their work activities.

Other writers have revisited the Marxian concept of alienation (Blauner, 1964; Meszaros, 1970; Ollman, 1971). John Stuart Mill (1870) believed that ultimately the industrial order must be one in which worker/owners select their own managers under a system of industrial cooperatives. A century after Marx's initial foray, a large literature had arisen on economic and industrial democracy. In contrast to Marx's revolution of the proletariat, this literature focused on ways that workers could increase their participation in the workplace through collective bargaining, collective work actions outside the bargaining framework, or worker buyouts of firms and the establishment of worker cooperatives (Blumberg, 1968; Bowles, Gordon, & Weisskopf, 1983; Carnoy & Shearer, 1980; Gorz, 1964; Jackall & Levin, 1984).

For example, Blauner (1968) revisited the subject of alienation in modern industrial production. He argued for forms of production — even within the capitalist system—that increase the degree of workers in the planning, design, and evaluation of work, as opposed to just its execution. In *The Revolution of Hope*, Erich Fromm (1968) has argued eloquently for a society that

> stimulates and furthers the growth and aliveness of man rather than cripples it; that . . . activates the individual rather than making him passive and receptive; [whose] technological capacities serve man's growth. If this is to be, we must regain control over the economic and social system; man's will, guided by his reason, and by his wish for optimal aliveness, must make the decisions. [p. 101]

This solution suggests workplaces that make it possible for workers to participate in the decisions that determine the conditions of their work and their work activities—workplace democracy.

### The Political Imperative

The political imperative is best presented in the work of Carole Pateman (1970), who addresses two main themes. First, she argues that democratic theory in the postwar period has focused on the dangers of widespread citizen participation in politics and has interpreted democracy as the "choice of leaders" rather than as participation. Indeed, she stresses that the common thread among such major democratic theorists as Schumpeter, Berelson, Dahl, and Sartori is their view that widespread or mass participation will lead to anarchy, instability, and, ultimately, authoritarian control.

She asserts that such interpretations are a perversion of the earlier democratic theorists and points out the central role of participation in the works of Rousseau, Mill, and Cole. With regard to Cole (1920), she emphasizes his recognition of the "interrelationship and connection between individuals, their qualities and psychological characteristics, and types of institutions; the assertion that responsible social and political action depends largely on the sort of institutions within which the individual has, politically, to act" (Pateman, 1970, p. 29). In other words, participatory institutions have an educative function that is absent if the individual's only experiences with democracy are through representation rather than direct participation.

Pateman's (1970) second main theme addresses the possibilities of building political efficacy through workplace democracy. As evidence she builds not only on the work of Rousseau, Mill, and Cole, but also on empirical findings. For example, she notes that Almond and Verba (1963), in *The Civic Culture*, found that among nations there was a positive relation between political efficacy and opportunities to participate in workplace decisions. More recent empirical support at the level of the business firm is found in the studies of Elden (1981) and Karasek (1976). The major exception to this pattern is Greenberg's (1981) study of U.S. plywood cooperatives, which did not show such a relation. In contrast, extensive statistical studies at both the national and crossnational levels, Sobel (1986, 1987) found support for the proposition that worker participation is associated with a higher level of political participation.

After extensive discussions of the earlier empirical findings and examples of industrial participation in capitalist countries, Pateman (1970) calls for a participatory society in which an extension of participation to the workplace is at its heart. She concludes that such a transformation will increase the sense of political efficacy and democratic participation, relative to a representative or symbolic democracy.

## The Economic Imperative

Pateman (1970) is clearly aware that any move to greater worker participation in most capitalist societies must gain the approval of capital and its managers. The rights of private property in such countries as the United States and Britain largely preclude state incursions on how that property will be used for production, generally, and the employment of labor, specifically. Exceptions are found in Sweden and West Germany, where labor interests, through the social democratic parties, have exerted powerful influences on electoral politics, resulting in the creation of farreaching national legislation that requires worker participation (Pipkorn, 1980). Therefore, regardless of the moral and political imperative, there must be an economic imperative that is not only socially compelling but will motivate capital to initiate a movement toward worker democracy. The seriousness of this challenge is witnessed by the fact that the moral and political imperatives have been addressed historically in both intellectual and political discourse, without noticeable impact in most societies.

Recent decades, however, have been characterized by a productivity crisis in the U.S. economy as well as a concern with the U.S. competitive position in world trade. At the level of the individual firm, there is a long-term challenge for profitability and survival that has initiated searches for more productive approaches to the creation of goods and services. One of the major strategies that is being pursued in the industrialized countries, with their relatively well-educated labor forces, is a movement toward greater worker participation in workplace decisions, not as a moral or political initiative, but as a strategy for raising productivity.

There is considerable evidence that worker participation is associated with increased productivity in many industries and countries. Such participation can take many forms, from increased input of individual workers into decision making, to team decision making on the shop floor, to worker-owned and managed firms that include direct participation at the level of the job and representation in decisions at higher levels (Bernstein, 1976; Crouch & Heller, 1983). Virtually all of these forms of worker participation increase the domain of decision making of workers and permit them to make decisions that entail the allocation of resources, including their own work time. A substantial empirical literature has arisen that shows a positive relation between the presence and extent of worker participation and the productivity of the firm (Cable & Fitzroy, 1980; Einhorn & Logue, 1982; Estrin, Jones, & Svejnar, 1984; Gyllenhammer, 1977; Jones & Svejnar, 1982; Kelly, 1982).

One of the most dramatic examples is found in the United States, in the joint venture between Toyota and General Motors (GM) called New United Motor Manufacturing, Inc., or NUMMI (Brown & Reich, 1988; Krafcik, 1986). The NUMMI plant in Fremont, California has been manufacturing both Toyotas and the Chevrolet Nova, a car that is identical to the imported Toyota Corolla. Toyota has had responsibility for production, and GM had been responsible for marketing. The GM plant in Fremont had been closed in 1982 because of its poor product quality, low productivity, and high rates of worker absenteeism and alcohol and drug use. It was ranked at the bottom of GM plants in productivity and had absentee rates of over 20 percent and a backlog of more than a thousand grievances.

Toyota redesigned the plant completely, and, by agreement with the United Auto Workers, some 80 percent of the workers hired by NUMMI were drawn from the previously employed GM workers from the Fremont plant. Production began in December 1984, and by the spring of 1986 the plant had reached its full capacity output of 20,000 cars per month. Productivity was 50 percent higher than in the old GM plant and was equal to that of its sister plant in Takaoka City, Japan. Unexcused absences were reduced to about .5 percent, and the level of quality was found to be comparable to the imported Toyota Corolla by both consumer and industry analyses.

The NUMMI production process is built around the use of teams of five to eight members. Teams set out the work tasks and rotate them among members. They also meet periodically to discuss how to improve the work process and product quality. Whenever possible, it is expected that the teams will solve production problems rather than calling in engineering or management representatives. Workers have the right to stop the assembly line at any time to solve an assembly problem. Emphasis is on worker flexibility and involvement in the work process.

Equally dramatic results from worker participation have been noted in automobile manufacture in Sweden (Gyllenhammer, 1977; Logue, 1981). For example, Saab converted its automobile door assembly from a conventional assembly line with rigid job definitions to a team approach in which workers participated in decisions on equipment, selection, hiring, quality control, maintenance of machinery, and organization of work (Logue, 1981). Annual worker turnover declined from 50 percent to 14 percent, and quality-control problems diminished, as did the need for quality-control inspectors. Annual savings were nine times the annual costs of the change. Renault found that the movement to semiautonomous work teams resulted in increases of almost 30 percent in defect-free assemblies (Coriat, 1979).

In electronics, a major manufacturer of integrated circuits organized one of its plants according to work teams that made decisions on work processes by consensus (Gustavson & Taylor, 1982). Yields were raised by 25 percent above those of comparable but traditional facilities, and employee turnover fell.

The economic imperative for worker participation, then, is based upon the substantial evidence that such arrangements can raise productivity substantially. I believe that this rationale will become increasingly important for shifting productive enterprises in both the private and public sectors from traditional authoritarian regimes to ones based upon worker participation in decisions. The higher the education of the workforce, the greater will be the advantages of these approaches to the production of goods and services (Levin, 1987b; Tsang, 1987). In countries like Sweden and West Germany, there is already extensive worker participation on the basis of national laws (Pipkorn, 1980). But many individual firms have adopted these practices to reap the benefits of higher productivity.

## Summary

The moral, political, and economic imperatives all support a higher degree of worker participation. As the work regime becomes more democratic, the demands for political socialization for workplace participation will become more prominent, with profound consequences for schooling. At the same time, the experience of participation in the workplace will tend to reinforce democratic participation in everyday political life and should increase political efficacy. In the final section of this chapter, I wish to address some ways in which we expect that schools might change.

## CHANGES IN SOCIALIZATION: THE ROLE OF THE SCHOOLS

How might we expect schools to adapt to a more democratic work-place? Clearly, the answer to this question depends on the specific forms of change in the workplace. It also depends on the responsiveness of schools to such changes. In this section, I address some specific workplace changes, and their educational counterparts, that are consistent with the economic imperative.

### Participative Workplaces

The movements toward worker participation can take many forms (Carnoy & Levin, 1985). For example, Swedish law provides for workers to have equal rights with management on such issues as employment levels, the work process, and the use of new technologies. Management and trade unions confer and bargain over such changes at the plant level (Ministry of Labour, Sweden, 1975). West Germany requires that one-third to one-half of the places on the boards of directors of the larger firms be delegated to workers (Furstenberg, 1977). Further, all workers either belong to or elect worker councils who are responsible for dealing with management on such issues as staffing, work processes, and other major shop-floor matters.

Yugoslavian firms are worker managed in that the major decisions are made by workers' councils that hold all formal power and determine hiring and firing, salaries, investment, and other operations of the firm (Horvat, 1976). In enterprises with fewer than 30 employees, all workers are mem-bers of the council; in larger firms, the council members are elected. Managers are appointed by the elected representatives of the central board of management. Worker income is dependent both upon the overall success of the enterprise and upon the contribution of the individual toward that success.

Other versions of worker management are found in the collective enterprises in socialist countries such as China and Cuba, where all mem-bers are expected to contribute actively to the formation of the work pro-cess (Bettelheim, 1975; MacEwan, 1975). The Israeli kibbutz or collective is a completely democratic production and living community where deci-sions on both production and consumption are made by the membership (Jenkins, 1974). Worker cooperatives are firms that are both owned and managed by their worker/members (Jackall & Levin, 1984). They are found in a wide variety of industries throughout the world.

Thus it is clear that there are many potential forms of worker partici-pation, but each has been specific to a particular set of economic, political, and social conditions. The question that arises is what type of worker participation is likely to arise or has been arising in the industrialized countries that are characterized by democratic and capitalist societies? In countries with a strong tradition of support for labor, such as West Germany and those in Scandinavia, we can expect to find the state intervening on behalf of greater worker participation. But, even in those contexts, there is an incentive for employers to adopt certain forms of organizational participation on behalf of greater workplace productivity and profitability.

The particular form that seems to meet this need best in the United States is the use of semiautonomous work groups. These groups organize their own activities with respect to planning, training the members of the group for the various tasks, executing these tasks, and evaluating performance. In some cases, the focus will be on the production of a subassembly of a larger product, and in other cases the mission will correspond to the goals of a particular service department, such as sales, accounting, or credit. This approach has been the basis for large productivity improvements generally (Kelly, 1982), as well as in some of the specific cases that we cited, such as automobile manufacture (Coriat, 1979; Gyllenhammer, 1977; Krafcik, 1986; Logue, 1981).

The specific shape of the workplace participation will depend upon the nature of the enterprise and setting, varying according to the type of product or service, the internal organization for producing it, the ability to alter technology and capital to accommodate the new forms of participation, and the capacity of management to initiate the changes. The principles of these forms of worker participation have been well established in the literature (e.g., Davis & Trist, 1976; Susman, 1976; Thorsrud, 1975; Thorsrud, Sorensen, & Gustavsen, 1976). As for worker characteristics, the following are some important points. Workers will need the skills to participate in group decisions on the nature, supervision, allocation, and scheduling of work tasks, as well as in training. In addition, more decision making at an individual level will be required. Further, skills for leadership and coordination, for developing consensus, and for defining and addressing problems will be central.

## Participative Schools

The relationship between educational reform and workplace reform has long been assumed by those who would use the schools to improve economic outcomes (Carnoy & Levin, 1985). Likewise, the emphasis on democratic participation in schools to improve democratic functioning in the larger society is hardly a new one. For example, at the beginning of the nineteenth century, Joseph Neef (1807) had developed his ideas for a self-governing school, which later became the basis for education in the utopian community of Robert Owen in New Harmony, Indiana (Lockwood, 1971). Building on the child-centered foundations established by his mentor, the Swiss educator Johann Pestalozzi, Neef (1807) viewed the school as a democratic republic. Entering children would be instructed in ethics and the rights and duties of citizens in a free society. Following this preparation, the students would form their own republic by selecting a form of government and drafting laws and a constitution.

A highly participative democracy was also at the heart of the schools espoused by John Dewey (1966). To Dewey it was impossible to create a democracy in adult life through the establishment of a schooling process that taught the young how to behave in an authoritarian regime. Unless the young could interact in democratic ways to determine their own activities in the schools, it would not be possible to expect them to undertake these responsibilities in adulthood. The progressive school placed great emphasis on students selecting and formulating their own activities, both individually and collectively.

There have been more recent calls for democratic schools, as a counter to the movements of the 1980s to tighten up the school regime by reducing student and teacher choice (Beyer, 1986; Giroux & McLaren, 1986). These appeals for democracy have been buttressed by widespread calls for increasing the autonomy and participation of teachers in educational decision making, particularly at the school site. It is remarkable how closely the logic of greater teacher participation has followed that of greater participation of all workers (Levin, 1987a).

The adoption of the use of greater worker participation and especially the reliance on work groups will entail major changes in the schooling process, especially in the areas of educational and individual decision making, minimum competencies, and peer training.

Educational Decision Making.    A major shift that is required by the use of work teams is the emphasis on group decisions by those who will actually perform the work. The more traditional approach separates the planning and evaluation of work from its execution, with the former being done by managers and technical staff and the latter by operatives. Under the team approach, workers must carry out all of these functions as well as select, train, and counsel members of the group and make decisions on the selection and maintenance of equipment.

In contrast with the present educational system, where the emphasis is on functioning as an individual in competition with fellow students, a corresponding shift in education would emphasize functioning as a member of a cooperating group. Such changes would require a greater emphasis on democracy in the school, including giving students a voice in selecting personnel and curriculum, determining resource allocation, and resolving conflict. Through both representative and participatory democracy, the fuller involvement of both students and teachers would become a part of the educational process. There would also be greater emphasis on group projects and assignments and on group awards, in place of the present focus on strictly individual performance and accountability. Emphasis would be placed on integrating student teams by race, gender, and social class, for a reduction of hierarchy in production would be inconsistent with substantial student stratification and hierarchy.

Emphasis on group decision making and problem solving would also increase the use of cooperative modes of interaction in schools, both among teachers and among students. Leadership and coordination responsibilities would be rotated among members of the group, so that all teachers and students could undertake this role. Cooperative work among small groups and training in group dynamics would become appropriate (Sharan, 1980). Cooperative problem solving would become more prominent in the school curriculum as work teams were faced with particular assignments that required a collective response (Slavin, 1983).

These changes would enhance the ability of individuals to participate in making decisions and solving problems, as members of groups outside of the workplace and schools. The same attributes that will improve political efficacy in the workplace should improve political efficacy generally.

Individual Decision Making.   Under existing forms of work, most workers make few individual decisions because, to a very large extent, the work tasks and the pace of work are determined by the equipment, technology, and organization of production. With a high level of specialization of tasks, it is only necessary to master a relatively few, simple job components and perform them on cue. But under a system of worker groups, individuals will have a much wider range of potential tasks and decisions. For example, to avoid bottlenecks, coordinators will have to make decisions regarding the availability of supplies and the allocation of team members. Schools will need to shift their emphasis to a much greater extent from memorization and routinization of learning to individual decision making and problem solving. The fact that individuals will have to make more workplace decisions, both as individuals and as members of groups, will mean that they will have to be able to seek out and use information that will help them define problems and the alternatives for addressing them. It is obvious that these skills will also be pertinent to the political efficacy of the individual.

Minimum Competencies.   At every educational level, existing schools tend to produce students who reflect a wide range of competencies, which are functional to production as long as there is a substantial hierarchy of skill needs. As the organization of production shifts to team assembly and less hierarchy, however, large differences in skill levels will become dysfunctional. This is because team assembly will require that all members of the team have skills and knowledge that are more nearly equal, in order to share tasks and participate fully. This is likely to change the nature of testing and curriculum.

Testing will shift from norm-based criteria, by which students are ranked in relation to other students, to ones in which specific performance requirements are used to ascertain that students meet or exceed certain standards of knowledge and performance. Norm-based tests can only indicate who is better or worse in a particular domain, not whether one meets a particular standard of performance. Criterion-based tests are designed to measure proficiencies of students in terms of meeting performance standards (Popham, 1978). At the same time there will be an emphasis on institutional learning expectations and curriculum approaches that attempt to bring all students up to appropriate performance levels.

These changes will enhance the ability of students to enter adulthood with the level of information they need in order to participate more fully in both the altered workplace and in political roles. Political participation requires that individuals have the requisite knowledge base for making decisions or for seeking out additional information that is pertinent to decisions.

Peer Training.   The use of work groups usually entails a high degree of training by fellow workers as new members join the teams or learn to rotate to new tasks. In this sense, all workers will need to be capable of training their peers on the various tasks that the team performs. Under the more traditional forms of work, training is generally relegated to a few specialists or supervisors who are given responsibility for initiating new workers into their roles. Similarly, in existing schools the instruction is delegated to teachers and other instructional personnel.

The widespread shift to group or team production is likely to stimulate a much greater emphasis on peer tutoring in the schools. Experiments have shown that peer tutoring improves the performance and sense of efficacy of both the tutor and the tutee (Allen, 1976). Thus there appear to be significant educational payoffs in themselves from this approach. Even more important, a proliferation of peer tutoring in the schools will make every individual both a teacher and a learner. This is a central premise of the team approach, and it is also a more general feature of a democratic organization and one that can enhance the political efficacy of all its members.

## SUMMARY

This chapter began with the fact that schools and society must develop two types of political actors within the same person. Workers need to have the ability to function effectively under an authoritarian work regime. Citizens need to have the ability to function effectively in a democracy. Each of these political roles has different and even contradictory requirements. The schools, as one of the major agencies of political socialization, are beset with the same conflicts in their own practices, creating contradictions, confusion, and inefficiencies in the schooling process. The same types of conflicts are visited upon adult political roles and personalities.

I have argued that major improvements might take place in political participation and efficacy if both schools and workplaces were to become more democratic. My discussion follows the recent arguments of Pateman (1970) and Mason (1982) in making political arguments for greater workplace democracy; of Marx (1964), Blauner (1964), and Fromm (1968) in making the ethical arguments; and a wide range of literature on worker participation and productivity in making the economic arguments. Although speculative in nature, the future scenario I have set out proposes that worker participation in decision making become a predominant feature of the workplace. Educational reforms that would support the new politics of the workplace and that would increase political efficacy for a participative politics have also been set out. The unity of purpose and functioning of such changes must surely be central to a democratic society that will be characterized by higher levels of participation and responsiveness.

## REFERENCES

Alchian, A., & Demsetz, H. (1972). Production, information costs, and economic organization. *American Economic Review, 62,* 777–795.

Allen, V. L. (Ed.). (1976). *Children as teachers: Theory and research on tutoring.* New York: Academic Press.

Almond, G., & Verba, S. (1963). *The civic culture.* Princeton, NJ: Princeton University Press.

Bernstein, P. (1976). *Workplace democratization: Its internal dynamics.* Kent, OH: Kent State University Press.

Bettelheim, C. (1975). *Cultural revolution and industrial organization in China: Changes in management and the division of labor.* New York: Monthly Review Press.

Beyer, L. E. (1986). Schooling for moral and democratic communities. *Issues in Education, 4*(1), 1–18.

Blauner, R. (1964). *Alienation and freedom.* Chicago: University of Chicago Press.

Blumberg, P. (1968). *Industrial democracy: The sociology of participation.* New York: Schocken Books.

Bowles, S., & Gintis, H. (1976). *Schooling in capitalist America.* New York: Basic Books.

Bowles, S., Gordon, D. M., & Weisskopf, T. E. (1983). *Beyond the wasteland: A democratic alternative to economic decline.* New York: Anchor Press/Doubleday.

Brown, C., & Reich, M. (1988, May 6). *When does union-management cooperation work? A look at NUMMI and GM-Van Nuys.* Paper presented for conference, Can California be Competitive and Caring? University of California, Los Angeles.

Cable, J., & Fitzroy, F. (1980). Cooperation and productivity: Some evidence from West German experience. *Kyklos, 33*(1), 100–121.

Carnoy, M., & Levin, H. M. (1985). *Schooling and work in the democratic state.* Stanford, CA: Stanford University Press.

Carnoy, M., & Shearer, D. (1980). *Economic democracy: The challenge of the 1980s.* White Plains, NY: M. E. Sharpe.

Cole, G. D. H. (1920). *Social theory.* London: Methuen.

Coriat, B. (1979, January–March). La recomposition de la ligne de montage et son enjeu: Une novelle "économie" du contrôle et du temps. *Sociologie du Travail, 21,* 19–32.

Crouch, C., & Heller, F. A. (1983). *International yearbook of organizational democracy: Vol. 1. Organizational democracy and political processes.* New York: John Wiley.

Dahl, R. A., & Lindblom, C. E. (1953). *Politics, economics, and welfare.* New York: Harper and Brothers.

Davis, L. E., & Trist, E. L. (1976). Improving the quality of work life: Sociotechnical case studies. In J. O'Toole (Ed.), *Work and the quality of life* (pp. 246–280). Cambridge, MA: MIT Press.

Dewey, J. (1966). *Democracy and education.* New York: Free Press.

Einhorn, E. S., & Logue, J. (Eds.). (1982). *Democracy on the shop floor.* Kent, OH: Kent Popular Press.

Elden, J. (1981). Political efficacy at work: The connection between more autonomous forms of workplace organization and a more participatory politics. *The American Political Science Review, 75,* 43–58.

Ellerman, D. (1984). Workers' cooperatives: The question of legal structure. In R. Jackall & H. M. Levin (Eds.), *Worker cooperatives in America* (pp. 257–274). Berkeley, CA: University of California Press.

Estrin, S., Jones, D. C., & Svejnar, J. (1984, June). *The varying nature, importance and productivity effects of worker participation: Evidence for contem-*

*porary producer cooperatives in industrialized Western economies.* Mimeo, Department of Economics, Hamilton College, Clinton, NY.

Fromm, E. (1968). *The revolution of hope.* New York: Harper & Row.

Furstenberg, F. (1977, May). West German experience with industrial democracy. *The Annals,* (431), 44–53.

Giroux, H. A., & McLaren, P. (1986). Teacher education and the politics of engagement: The case for democratic schooling. *Harvard Educational Review, 56*(3), 213–238.

Gorz, A. (1968).*Strategy for labor.* Boston: Beacon Press.

Greenberg, E. S. (1981). Industrial self-management and political attitudes. *The American Political Science Review, 75,* 29–42.

Gustavson, P., & Taylor, J. C. (1982). *Socio-technical design and new forms of work organization: Integrated circuit fabrication.* Geneva: International Labor Office. Mimeo.

Gyllenhammer, P. G. (1977). *People at work.* Boston: Addison-Wesley.

Hirschman, A. O. (1970). *Exit, voice, and loyalty.* Cambridge, MA: Harvard University Press.

Horvat, B. (1976). *The Yugoslav economic system.* White Plains, NY: M. E. Sharpe.

Jackall, R., & Levin, H. M. (Eds.). (1984). *Worker cooperatives in America.* Los Angeles: University of California Press.

Jenkins, D. (1974). *Job power.* Baltimore: Penguin Books.

Jones, D. C., & Svejnar, J. (Eds.). (1982). *Participatory and self-managed firms.* Lexington, MA: Lexington Books.

Karasek, R. (1976). *The impact of the work environment on life outside the job.* Unpublished Ph.D. dissertation, Massachusetts Institute of Technology, Cambridge.

Kelly, J. E. (1982). *Scientific management, job redesign and work performance.* New York: Academic Press.

Kemerer, F. R., & Deutsch, K. L. (1979). *Constitutional rights and student life.* St. Paul, MN: West.

Krafcik, J. (1986). *Learning from NUMMI. An International Vehicle Program internal working paper.* Cambridge, MA: Massachusetts Institute of Technology.

Levin, H. M. (1987a). *Finance and governance implications of school-based decision.* Paper prepared for Work in America Institute, Scarsdale, New York.

Levin, H. M. (1987b). Improving productivity through education and technology. In G. Burke & R. Rumberger (Eds.), *The future impact of technology on work and education* (pp. 194–214). Philadelphia: Falmer Press.

Lockwood, G. B. (1971). *The new harmony movement.* New York: Dover.

Logue, J. (1981). *Saab/Trollhattan: Reforming work life on the shop floor. Working Life in Sweden* (No. 23). New York: Swedish Information Service.

MacEwan, A. (1975, April). Incentives, equality, and power in revolutionary Cuba. *Socialist Revolution, 23,* 117–130.

Marx, K. (1964). *The economic and philosophic manuscripts of 1844.* (D. Struik, Ed.). New York: International Publishers.

Mason, R. (1982). *Participatory and workplace democracy*. Carbondale and Edwardsville, IL: Southern Illinois University Press.

Meszaros, I. (1970). *Marx's theory of alienation*. New York: Harper & Row.

McClosky, H., & Zaller, J. (1984). *The American ethos: Public attitudes toward capitalism and democracy* (a Twentieth Century Fund Report). Cambridge, MA: Harvard University Press.

Neef, J. (1807). *A proper system of education for the schools of a free people*. Philadelphia: Author.

Ollman, B. (1971). *Alienation: Marx's concept of man in capitalist society*. Cambridge, England: Cambridge University Press.

Pateman, C. (1970). *Participation and democratic theory*. Cambridge, England: Cambridge University Press.

Pipkorn, J. (1980). The legal framework of employee participation methods at national and international level and particularly within the European community. *Economic and Industrial Democracy, 1*(1), 99–123.

Popham, W. J. (1978). The case for criterion-referenced measurements. *Educational Researcher, 7*(11), 6–10.

Schumpeter, J. (1942). *Capitalism, socialism and democracy*. New York: Harper & Row.

Sharan, S. (1980). Cooperative learning in small groups: Recent methods and effects on achievement, attitudes, and ethnic relations. *Review of Educational Research, 50*(2), 241–272.

Slavin, R. E. (1983). *Cooperative learning*. New York: Longman.

Sobel, R. (1986, August). *From job participation to work participation: Results from the Fall 1985 ANES Pilot Survey*. Paper presented at the annual meeting of the American Political Science Association, Washington, DC.

Sobel, R. (1987, July). *The influence of work participation on political participation: A crossnational study*. Paper presented at the meetings of the International Society of Political Psychology, San Francisco.

Stiglitz, J. (1975). Incentives, risk and information: Notes toward a theory of hierarchy. *Bell Journal of Economics, 6*, 552–579.

Susman, G. I. (1976). *Autonomy at work: A sociotechnical analysis of participative management*. New York: Praeger.

Thorsrud, E. (1975). Collaborative action research to enhance the quality of working life. In L. E. David & B. Cherns (Eds.), *The quality of working life* (pp. 193–204). New York: Free Press.

Thorsrud, E., Sorensen, B. A., & Gustavsen, B. (1976). Sociotechnical approach to industrial democracy in Norway. In R. Dubin (Ed.), *Handbook of work, organization, and society* (pp. 421–464). Chicago: Rand McNally.

Tsang, M. C. (1987). The impact of underutilization of education on productivity: A case study of the U.S. Bell Companies. *Economics of Education Review, 6*(3), 239–252.

Tyack, D. B. (1974). *The one best system*. Cambridge, MA: Harvard University Press.

# 9

# Education and the Making of the Informed Citizen: Political Literacy and the Outside World

ANDERS WESTHOLM
ARNE LINDQUIST
RICHARD G. NIEMI

Theories of democracy are known to show much variation in the requirements and hopes directed toward the citizenry. For all their diversity, however, most of them tend to conjoin in two important areas, namely, in their demand for at least a minimum level of citizen competence and in the faith placed in social institutions, especially schools, to satisfy that demand. While the threshold has been set higher by proponents of participatory democracy than by those who have argued the benefits of limited mass participation, even the most devout Schumpeterians have found it difficult to do away entirely with the notion of an informed citizenry. Moreover, whereas some theorists, such as Mill, have assigned formal education a more prominent role than have others, few have denied it a key position in achieving the proclaimed goal.

In line with these ideas, although not always motivated by them, the postwar era has witnessed a dramatic expansion of educational opportunity in almost all industrialized countries. An important part of that expansion has been the introduction of civics and other programs, with the explicit aim of preparing citizens for democracy. Many of these programs have found their way down to the early stages of the educational sequence and have often been made part of the compulsory curriculum. As a result, an increasing proportion of adolescents have been exposed to significant amounts of civics training.

Primary financial support for this research was provided by the Bank of Sweden Tercentenary Foundation and the (Swedish) Research Council for the Social Sciences and Humanities. Support for collaboration was provided by the (American) National Science Foundation (INT-8412796).

Students of political socialization were not late to realize the potential importance of this development. Their interest was a logical consequence of the prominence originally attributed to the school system, particularly the civics curriculum, as a source of political learning for the young citizen-to-be. In an era marked by extended schooling, rapid social and technological change, and allegedly weakening ties between generations and family members, there was little on the outside to dampen expectations of strong educational effects. Thus, one of the most influential American studies (Hess & Torney, 1967) even went as far as to argue that "the public school is the most important and effective instrument of political socialization in the United States" (p. 200).

However, the empirical evidence concerning school effects on the political development of children and adolescents has been anything but unequivocal. There are actually two strands of results that, when juxtaposed, amount to what is apparently a paradox. On the one hand, a mountain of studies of adult populations have demonstrated a clear relationship between level of education and a number of qualities related to the notion of the good citizen, such as democratic values, political information, and political participation (for a review, see, e.g., Hyman & Wright, 1979; Hyman, Wright, & Reed, 1975). In addition, there are several findings of significant progression in political sophistication and knowledge as adolescents advance to higher levels of schooling (Gallatin & Adelson, 1970; Hess & Torney, 1967; Merelman, 1971; Torney, Oppenheim, & Farnen, 1975).

On the other hand, it has often proved difficult to tie these observations to the effects of education per se. A number of studies assessing variations by curriculum content as well as a host of other school-related factors have reported weak or nonexistent effects (Jennings, Ehman, & Niemi, 1974; Jennings, Langton, & Niemi, 1974; Litt, 1963). On the basis of this evidence, some have gone as far as to argue that the school system, at least in America, has failed more or less completely in its mission to prepare citizens for democracy (Merelman, 1980a).[1] The purpose of this chapter is to try to go some distance toward resolving the paradox implied by these conflicting positions and results, as well as to add new evidence to the empirical foundation on which the controversy rests.

To that end, we have consciously chosen a rather narrow focus in terms of subject matter. Our attention will concentrate on a single aspect within the wide range of qualities that could be deemed important to the citizen role. By thus delimiting the scope, we will have more room to illustrate accurately the developmental processes at work and to assess the part played by education.

## POLITICAL LITERACY

The property we have chosen to examine could adequately be termed *political literacy*. What we have in mind are the basic concepts and facts that constitute a necessary condition for comprehending the contents of public debate. Obviously, political literacy in this sense comprises a wide range of skills. For the purpose of this investigation, we selected a set of items designed to tap the level of basic information with respect to international affairs. The items, which measure awareness of major international organizations and events (see Figure 9.1), are part of a larger test of political literacy included in a national panel study of Swedish adolescents aged 15 to 18.

Our choice of content area can be motivated partly on practical grounds. For a non–Swedish audience, the relevance and difficulty of the items can be more easily judged if they deal with international rather than domestic affairs. But the choice can be justified from a theoretical perspective as well. From the point of view of public policy, world events become of steadily growing importance in an era of increasing international dependence and exchange. From the point of view of political culture more generally, knowledge about conditions in other parts of the world is an important prerequisite of such democratic qualities as empathy and tolerance. Reflecting these considerations, the national guidelines for the civics curriculum in Sweden have increasingly come to stress the importance of international awareness, as have civics textbooks.[2]

A common charge brought against measures of simple factual knowledge is that they do not capture the ability to organize information into a coherent belief system. Ultimately, it is argued, it is not the command of isolated facts but the ability to comprehend and reason politically that is the hallmark of the ideal citizen. Hence, measuring simple factual knowledge is of little value.

We acknowledge the premises of this argument but not the conclusion. The point is that a certain amount of factual information is a necessary but not sufficient condition for the development of a deeper understanding (see Sigel & Hoskin, 1981). Below a certain threshold of elementary knowledge, it is highly unlikely that anyone can develop a coherent belief system. Above the threshold, some but not all will reach a higher level of comprehension. Of course, an obsession with factual information may in the end be detrimental to understanding.

In one of the pilot studies preceding our national study, we conducted a test of this argument. A local sample of some 70 adolescents aged 16 to 17 were given a comprehensive test of political literacy similar to the one used

**Figure 9.1**  Test items for measuring awareness of international
organizations and events

---

1. *What are the names of the organizations described below?*
   *(Abbreviations suffice.)*
   a. A defense organization with many Western European countries as
      members. (NATO)
   b. A branch of the United Nations with special responsibility for world
      health. (WHO)
   c. A defense organization with many Eastern European countries as
      members. (WP)
   d. An international association of oil producing countries. (OPEC)
   e. An organization for trade and economic cooperation with many
      Western European countries as members. (EC)
   f. An organization for trade and economic cooperation with many
      Eastern European countries as members. (CMEA)

2. *A set of international political events is described below. In which*
   *countries did these events take place?*
   a. This country was hit by a military coup in 1973. Its socialist
      president, Salvador Allende, was killed and a military junta took
      power. (Chile)
   b. Soviet troops entered this country in 1979 to help the government
      fight Muslim guerillas. (Afghanistan)
   c. In the end of the 1960s and the beginning of the 1970s the United
      States participated in a major war in this country. (Vietnam)
   d. Soviet arms supply—mainly missile sites—to this country caused a
      crisis in the relations between the two superpowers in 1961. (Cuba)
   e. Troops from the United States took part in a major war in this
      country in the early 1950s. (Korea)
   f. Soviet troops invaded this country in 1968. (Czechoslovakia)

---

in the final study. In addition, we conducted open-ended interviews in
which the adolescents were invited to develop their own thoughts around a
set of defined themes such as democracy, equality, and different political
ideologies. The adolescents were also given the opportunity to express freely their views about the ideal society, the future, and Swedish society at
present. The interviews were recorded and subsequently classified by the
degree to which they were coherent, well argued, and sociocentric. The
coding of the interviews was conducted by research personnel who did not
have access to the results of the literacy test. Special care was taken not to
confuse the ability to reason politically with the language of discourse (cf.
Zillén, 1981).

When cross-tabulating the results of the open-ended interviews with the literacy scores, the relationship turned out to be exactly that hypothesized: Below a threshold close to the median level of literacy, nobody had developed evidence of deeper understanding. Above that level, some (52%) but not all respondents passed the borderline.

## SOCIALIZATION, SELECTION, AND THE ORIGIN OF EDUCATIONAL DIFFERENCES

Before we begin to probe deeper into the development of adolescents' knowledge about international affairs, it is important to return once more to the theoretical notion of educational effects. Following Meyer (1977), interpretations of the seeming impact of education can be grouped under either of two headings, socialization or allocation.

In the *socialization* perspective, the amount and kind of training— formal or informal—that takes place at school will equip students with certain abilities, interests, and values. The characteristics thus formed remain visible later in life, through inherent continuity as well as through various mechanisms of reinforcement. Although a nonrelativist conception of educational effects is not a necessary consequence of this perspective, they often join hands in practice. In other words, it is often assumed that a certain level and type of education brings about fixed consequences, even when the system of educational stratification changes. Therefore, the socialization point of view has frequently been invoked in attempts at linking rising levels of education with change in the political culture.

The *allocation* perspective stresses the way in which educational institutions act as sorters or selectors. The school system is seen as a web of pipes, valves, floodgates, and watersheds, by which individuals are channeled into different life courses. The most important mechanism is that of certification. Schools endow individuals with certain formal qualifications that serve as access points for occupations, roles, statuses, and lifestyles. These in turn lead to differential abilities, interests, and values. By implication, the allocation perspective is relativist. To the extent that it embodies notions of social change, these concern primarily the ways in which selection and certification are performed.

While the causal mechanism differs, both of these interpretations focus on effects that ultimately have their origin in educational institutions. The first stresses the process, the second, the outcome; but in both cases it is a matter of change in response to events during school years.

In interpreting educational differences, however, it is important to pay attention to a third possibility. As conventionally measured in cross-sectional studies, educational effects may indeed represent the result of schooling experiences and outcomes, but they may also represent the initial differences on which these are based. It is clearly the case that schools separate individuals according to certain dimensions of intellectual ability. Selection also takes place with respect to other potentially important attributes, such as social origin. Thus differences by education in a cross-sectional sample may to some extent be spurious in the sense of being traceable to characteristics that predate variations in schooling.

This possibility raises two important questions on which we will focus in the empirical analysis. First, how important are such selection mechanisms to the total magnitude of educational differences? To the extent that the contribution is large, it may hold part of the key to the paradox of educational effects. A significant share of the relatively greater differences found in cross-sections of the adult population may be due to factors that are not educational in origin.

Second, what is the relationship between initial selection and the impact of subsequent education? In many cases, the effect of the school system may be to reinforce and widen the differences that appear through selection, but that is not the only possibility. Depending on how educational programs are configured, schools may also help to keep the balance constant or even counteract initial differences.

The impact of the school system in this regard is of particular concern with respect to citizen competence. For many other skills and talents, large variations are not only socially acceptable but also desirable. Significant gaps with respect to the ability to fill the citizen role, however, pose obvious problems to one of the central principles of democratic theory, that of political equality (cf. Dahl 1982; Lively, 1975). This is particularly true if the gaps coincide with social cleavage lines that define political conflict, for example, class or gender.

## THE SWEDISH SCHOOL SYSTEM AND THE STUDY DESIGN

In line with the overall image of Sweden as a relatively homogeneous and egalitarian country, the Swedish school system is often described as weakly differentiated. That description is certainly correct with respect to the first nine years of compulsory schooling. Prior to seventh grade, there are no elective subjects and no differentiation on the basis of ability. From seventh to ninth grade, students are offered a choice for one elective subject (usually a second foreign language after English) and between basic and advanced courses in mathematics and foreign languages. Other than that, the curriculum remains homogeneous.

Following the end of ninth grade, however, differentiation develops rapidly. Currently about 80 percent of the graduating cohort proceeds directly to secondary education within the gymnasium system. Those who enter are divided into three major kinds of programs: three-year theoretical (about 35 percent), two-year theoretical (about 15 percent), and two-year vocational (about 50 percent). The three-year track divides further into 5 different specializations, the two-year theoretical programs into 4, and the vocational into 18.[3]

While there is little room for individual variations within each program, the differences across programs are sizable. Only one subject, Swedish, is taught to all students. The amount of coursework in civics and history, which are potentially the most relevant subjects with respect to knowledge about international affairs, varies considerably. With one minor exception, neither subject is offered to students in the vocational programs. In the theoretical programs the average exposure varies between one and four hours weekly for civics and between zero and three for history (see Table 9.1).

Our research, entitled The Young in Politics Study, was designed to make initial contact with its adolescent subjects at the time when this educational differentiation sets in. A nationally representative sample of

**Table 9.1** Weekly hours of civics and history by year and type of curriculum[a]

| Curriculum | Civics by year | | | History by year | | |
|---|---|---|---|---|---|---|
| | 1 | 2 | 3 | 1 | 2 | 3 |
| 3-year social science & humanities[b] | 3 | 3 | 4.5 | 2 | 4 | 2 |
| 3-year economics | 3 | 3 | 2.5 | 2 | 2 | 0 |
| 3-year science & technology | 3 | 0 | 2 | 2 | 2 | 0 |
| 2-year social work | 3 | 3 | - | 2 | 2 | - |
| 2-year economics | 3 | 3 | - | 0 | 0 | - |
| 2-year technology | 0 | 2 | - | 0 | 0 | - |
| 2-year vocational[c] | 0 | 0 | - | 0 | 0 | - |

[a]Based on NBE (1970) with supplements as of 1981.

[b]Students in the humanities program may choose to have two, rather than four and a half, weekly hours of civics in the third year.

[c]Students in the vocational social service program have three weekly hours of civics in each year.

all adolescents resident in Sweden and born in 1965 completed written questionnaires in the fall of 1981, shortly after the end of compulsory school. They were contacted anew in the spring of 1983, when the majority were just about to finish their gymnasium studies. The age of the respondents was 15 to 16 years at the time of the first wave, and 17 to 18 at the time of the second. For convenience, we will refer to them as 16- and 18-year-olds, respectively. The time between waves is one year and five months. Obviously, this period is too short to expect dramatic change, but it is sufficiently long to uncover systematic patterns of development.[4]

Of the entire sample, 81 percent participated in both waves. Since the complete political literacy test could only be administered to gymnasium students, the analysis is based on the subset enrolled in the gymnasium on both occasions (85 percent of the respondents). Data collection for these respondents took place in the schools, under direct supervision of personnel from the research team. Teachers were not present while the questionnaires were being filled out.

## THE OVERALL LEVEL AND GROWTH OF POLITICAL LITERACY

Students were asked to identify six major international organizations and six large-scale events in world politics (refer to Figure 9.1). Organizations were drawn from the Eastern bloc, the Western bloc, the Third World, and the United Nations, and covered military, economic, as well as health-care activities. Events ranged in time from the 1950s to the present, in place from Chile to Czechoslovakia, and included events unfavorable to the United States as well as to the Soviet Union.

Initially the most striking feature of the responses to the individual questions was how few of the adolescents were able to answer the 12 questions correctly (see Table 9.2). For example, at age 16, only half of the students knew about the war in Afghanistan, only one-third were familiar with the EC, only one in six was aware of the Korean War, and just one in 100 could correctly identify the CMEA. Although the results improved over the panel years, there was a lot left to be learned at age 18 as well. Considering what it could be hoped that young citizens would know, the results were not encouraging.

Moreover, there is little to suggest that these results were particularly low by international standards. In fact, there are at least two reasons to think the opposite. First, Sweden as a small country almost necessarily has a more internationalist perspective than many larger industrialized nations. The international emphasis is likely to be reflected in media content as well as in school curricula. Second, there is no evidence that Swedish

**Table 9.2**  Percentage correctly identifying international organizations and events

|                | Age 16 | Age 18 | Growth |
|----------------|--------|--------|--------|
| *Organization* |        |        |        |
| CMEA           | 01     | 07     | 6      |
| WHO            | 22     | 28     | 6      |
| EC             | 33     | 48     | 15     |
| WP             | 41     | 53     | 12     |
| NATO           | 47     | 56     | 9      |
| OPEC           | 40     | 61     | 21     |
| *Event*        |        |        |        |
| Korea          | 15     | 23     | 8      |
| Cuba           | 16     | 27     | 11     |
| Czechoslovakia | 28     | 34     | 6      |
| Chile          | 41     | 42     | 1      |
| Vietnam        | 52     | 58     | 6      |
| Afghanistan    | 53     | 58     | 5      |
| *Average*      |        |        |        |
| Organizations  | 31     | 42     | 11     |
| Events         | 34     | 40     | 6      |

youth in general have a lower level of cognitive achievement with respect to social and political issues than do adolescents in other countries. On the contrary, the only large-scale cross-national study in this area conducted to date showed Sweden to have the highest score out of seven industrialized countries in the West (Torney et al., 1975).[5]

Beyond these general points, there are several patterns in the results. Students were clearly more able to identify Western- than Eastern-bloc organizations, and the military organization within each bloc was better known than its economic counterpart. Knowledge about events was very strongly structured by recency and not much else. The duration or magnitude of the event appeared to be of little consequence. Events that were relatively short lived by comparison, such as those in Cuba, Czechoslovakia, and Chile were as well-known as the longer-lasting wars of Korea, Vietnam, and Afghanistan, once the location in time is taken into account.

Awareness of events as well as organizations increased over the panel years; however, the growth was far from evenly distributed. On average, knowledge about organizations grew by 11 percentage points, while the increase for events stopped at 6. There was also considerable variation within each content area. With respect to events, there appeared to be a tendency for knowledge to grow more in those areas where it was initially weakest. In the case of organizations, however, the tendency was, if anything, the opposite. As will be shown later, these variations in growth rate between as well as within the two content areas are of more than passing interest. In both cases, there is a clear linkage to educational considerations.

Before we analyze the growth in greater detail, however, it is important to consider one methodological caveat. In order to make possible a direct comparison across panel years, the same test items were used on both occasions. This obviously involves risks of inflated growth rates due to repeated exposure. In order to test for that possibility, the second-wave sample included a control group that had not previously participated in the study. The results showed that effects due to repeated exposure existed but were trivial. On average, the second-wave scores were only one percentage point higher than they would have been for a fresh sample.

Growth rates aside, the items within each area are strongly related internally. Both sets were subjected to tests of unidimensional cumulativeness by means of the $H$-coefficient suggested by Mokken (1971).[6] The values at ages 16 and 18 were, respectively, .60/.68 for organizations and .66/.70 for events, which is well above Mokken's criterion (.50) for the strongest class of scales. On the basis of these results, additive indices for each year and content area were computed. These indices will replace the individual items in most subsequent analyses.

## THE BEGINNINGS OF EDUCATIONAL DIFFERENTIATION

The three major kinds of programs in the gymnasium divide students in a number of significant ways. First, they stratify by academic ability. Students entering the three-year theoretical programs in 1981 left compulsory school with a grade average of 3.95 on a scale of 1 to 5. The corresponding figures for students in the two-year theoretical and vocational programs were 3.03 and 2.95 (NCBS, 1982). Second, they have implications for the propensity to proceed to postsecondary education. Among students completing the gymnasium in 1983, 43 percent of those graduating from three-year programs began university-level education before the end of 1985. The corresponding figures for the two-year theoretical and vocational programs were 15 and 7 percent (NCBS, 1987a). Finally, they determine the exposure to civics and history courses. Students in the theoretical programs usually get a significant amount of training in these subjects. Students in the vocational programs, as a rule, do not (refer to Table 9.1).

Table 9.3 shows the level and development of the test scores within each kind of program. Initially, the most striking feature is the differences in knowledge that already exist upon entry in the gymnasium. The percentage of correct answers is about three times higher in the three-year theoretical than in the vocational programs. In other words, students destined to rank high on education in adult cross-sections differed dramatically from those destined to rank low, and they did so *before* differences in formal education had had any opportunity to have a causal impact. It is sobering to note that, immediately upon graduation from an almost completely nondifferentiated compulsory school, the $\eta$-coefficient linking gymnasium program to political literacy scores amounts to .52 for organizations and .46 for events. These figures are comparable to many observations relating education to political information level in adult cross-sections (see Jennings, 1981).

Consequently, it is likely that such observations to no small extent reflect differences that predate, rather than result from, educational differentiation. To draw that conclusion, it is not necessary to argue on the basis of an alleged carry-over of adolescent political knowledge into adulthood, although, as will become evident, the inherent autocorrelation may be stronger in this case than in many others. It is sufficient to assume that the individual differences that produced the pattern in the results coming from 16-year-olds in Table 9.3 — particularly variations in intellectual ability aside from those produced by education — will not cease to have an impact in adult years.

**Table 9.3** Percentage correctly identified organizations and events, by type of curriculum

|  | Age 16 | Age 18 | Growth | N |
|---|---|---|---|---|
| *Organizations* |  |  |  |  |
| Three-year theoretical | 49 | 64 | 15 | 281 |
| Two-year theoretical | 29 | 46 | 17 | 84 |
| Two-year vocational | 15 | 21 | 6 | 314 |
| *Events* |  |  |  |  |
| Three-year theoretical | 51 | 59 | 8 | 282 |
| Two-year theoretical | 34 | 44 | 10 | 84 |
| Two-year vocational | 19 | 22 | 3 | 315 |

On the other hand, the changes that occur over the years suggest that selection is not the only determinant of "educational" differences. Although the development during gymnasium years tends to reinforce existing differences, it is not merely an extrapolation of them. We shall venture to show that, while initial differences cannot be explained by reference to variations in the amount of civics and history training, they are important in accounting for the changes that occur during the gymnasium.

More complete evidence on this score will be given in later multivariate models, in which we will analyze change at the individual level, but some indications are provided already by the results of Table 9.3. The variations in growth rates do not fully match those in initial knowledge. Comparing the two-year theoretical and the vocational programs, which differ strongly in the amount of social science training provided, the gap increases by nearly 80 percent for organizations and nearly 50 percent for events. With respect to the two- and three-year theoretical tracks, whose social studies curricula are more similar, the initial difference is in fact somewhat reduced. Notably, this pattern occurs in spite of the fact that the two-year theoretical programs are closer to the vocational than to the three-year programs in terms of entry-level grade average as well as initial test results.

A similar indication is given by the data in Table 9.4, where we have grouped the theoretical programs by their subject orientation rather than by their level and length. This classification does not fully correspond to the amount of civics and history training given in the various programs, but nearly so. Due partly to variations in entry-level grade averages and partly to gender composition, students in the natural science and technology programs started out considerably higher than those in the social sci-

**Table 9.4** Percentage correctly identified organizations and events, by curriculum orientation

|                    | Age 16 | Age 18 | Growth | N   |
|--------------------|--------|--------|--------|-----|
| *Organizations*    |        |        |        |     |
| Social science     | 38     | 57     | 19     | 229 |
| Natural science    | 55     | 65     | 10     | 135 |
| Vocational         | 15     | 21     | 6      | 314 |
| *Events*           |        |        |        |     |
| Social science     | 41     | 49     | 8      | 231 |
| Natural science    | 57     | 67     | 10     | 136 |
| Vocational         | 19     | 22     | 3      | 314 |

ences. But over the gymnasium years, the initial gap for organizations was reduced by half, due to a considerably higher growth rate among the social science students.

Somewhat surprisingly, the same tendency is not visible for events. The major explanation for that divergence most likely rests with the timing of history courses. The importance of history, relative to civics, is likely to be greater for events than for organizations. But, since the events asked about are recent ones, they would come up late in a history sequence. Students in the three-year social sciences and humanities programs receive the most history training, but since it stretches over three years, modern history is postponed. In our sample, it thus had not occurred by the time of our fieldwork. Students who had less history were more likely to have covered the present period by the time of the second wave.

## THE GENDER GAP REVISITED

While politics may still remain more of a male than a female world, significant steps toward the erosion of traditional differences in involvement rates have occurred over the past decades. At the same time, an almost perfect alignment between the sexes with respect to political opinion has in several cases been transformed into significant conflict. In general, there is much to suggest that the old involvement gap is vanishing and that a new opinion gap is being placed in its stead.

In many areas, the results from our study yield a good deal of support for that proposition. Differences of opinion are often significant, while differences in involvement are mostly trivial or nonexistent, or even a reversal of the longstanding primacy of males. Consider dimensions of involvement that are of immediate relevance for learning about international affairs. The correlation with sex (scored as a dummy variable with males higher) was .04 for reading political news in the newspaper, $-.03$ for reading international news, .10 for watching the television news, .01 for discussing international political affairs, and zero for discussing politics more generally.

Turning to direct measures of political participation, girls actually outstripped boys in most cases. For example, they were more likely to have taken part in communal activities, signed a petition, boycotted commercial products, contacted officials, written a letter to the editor, or marched in a demonstration. The same was true with respect to voting, where— according to data from the present study as well as from others (NCBS, 1986) — females bypassed males in this cohort on their first try in 1985. In some cases, the differences were more than trivial; for instance, 26 percent of the girls had taken part in a demonstration, compared to only 14 percent for boys.

All of these results would make a female advantage as likely as a male one when it comes to knowledge about international affairs. Other evidence would rather clearly lead us to expect female superiority. For example, girls regularly had better grade averages in the compulsory school (NCBS, 1982) as well as in the gymnasium (NCBS, 1987b). In addition, they more frequently chose programs containing significant amounts of civics, history, and other courses with a social science orientation.

Yet all this evidence turned out to be anything but an infallible guide. As shown by Table 9.5, males had a considerable edge over females with respect to knowledge about international organizations as well as events. Measured as a product-moment correlation (or, equivalently, an $\eta$-coefficient), the association upon entry in the gymnasium was .22 for organizations and .35 for events. Obviously, these results are troubling to the hypothesis that the gap in political literacy would vanish with that in involvement rates.

Moreover, as Table 9.5 shows, the difference in information level did not change appreciably during the course of the panel. For organizations, the difference declined somewhat; for events, it increased slightly.[7] It might at first seem surprising that the greater amount of social science training among girls was not more clearly reflected in the growth rates. The reason, as we shall show later, was not that the training had little impact, but that there was a direct gender effect in the opposite direction. On the other hand, that effect, as well as the gap on which it built, remain puzzling.

A focus on cultural spheres of interest would seem a promising route toward a resolution. If we look at the individual questions, there was in fact one item, the World Health Organization, on which females had a net

**Table 9.5** Percentage correctly identified organizations and events, by gender

|                 | Age 16 | Age 18 | Growth | N   |
|-----------------|--------|--------|--------|-----|
| *Organizations* |        |        |        |     |
| Males           | 38     | 47     | 9      | 353 |
| Females         | 24     | 37     | 13     | 327 |
| *Events*        |        |        |        |     |
| Males           | 45     | 52     | 7      | 354 |
| Females         | 23     | 28     | 5      | 329 |

advantage. The explanation would thus be one of item content—females doing better in areas associated with social and health policy, and males having an edge on matters related to economics and military conflict. However, such an account does not appear to be sufficient. First, students in curricula oriented toward the social sciences and health care, who were mostly female, tended to do better on the WHO question. But, consistent with the overall result, boys taking such programs scored higher on this item than did girls. Second, whereas the male edge in other areas was of considerable magnitude, the female advantage with respect to the WHO was of trivial size. Hence, the origin of gender differences in this area remains a puzzle.

## INDIVIDUAL-LEVEL CHANGE

So far we have looked at change only on the aggregate level, essentially treating the two panel waves as though they were independent cross-sections. Sources of variations in initial knowledge and learning have been examined only on a one-by-one basis. Having traced the broad contours from this point of view, we are now ready to make use of the unique features of the panel design to uncover patterns of individual-level change in a multivariate framework.

We will approach the task in three steps. First, we will consider the individual-level continuity of knowledge scores and the impact of curriculum and gender. Second, we will explore variations in impact by initial level of knowledge. Finally, we will expose our primary results to further testing by examining intracurricular variations as well as extracurricular sources of learning. In order to carry out these three analyses, a series of regression models was constructed. In each case, the dependent variable is knowledge about organizations and events at age 18. The independent variables refer specifically to the particular area under scrutiny.

### Impact of the Social Science Curriculum and Gender

The independent variables of this analysis are knowledge at age 16, gender, and amount of coursework in civics and modern history. By using the lagged dependent variable on the right-hand side of the equation, we control for a variety of factors that could confound our understanding of the effects of the curriculum, including the entry-level differences by gender and curriculum.

All variables are scored from zero to one, to ease interpretation. For the knowledge scales, this means that the score corresponds to the proportion of correct answers. Civics scores represent the average amount of coursework during the first two years of the gymnasium, scaled from one (three hours weekly) to zero (no civics). History is scored one for those who have had at least some modern history during the second year (three-year natural science, technology, and economics programs; two-year social work program) and zero for all others. Gender is scored one for males and zero for females.

The results are shown in the upper half of Table 9.6. As is almost always the case in panel models, the lagged dependent variable is by far the strongest predictor, but the autoregressive linkages are in this case unusually powerful, considering that the model does not correct for remaining unreliability. Individual differences between students were certainly very stable over time.

However, the differences at the end of the second year were not mere-

**Table 9.6** Knowledge of international organizations and events as a function of previous knowledge, curriculum, and gender

|  | International organizations | | International events | |
|---|---|---|---|---|
|  | $\beta$ | SE | $\beta$ | SE |
| *Additive model* | | | | |
| Intercept | .09* | .02 | .05* | .02 |
| Lagged dependent variable | .67* | .03 | .78* | .03 |
| Gender | .04* | .02 | .07* | .02 |
| Civics | .18* | .02 | .08* | .02 |
| Modern history | .06* | .02 | .06* | .02 |
| $R/R^2$ | .788/.621 | | .809/.654 | |
| *Multiplicative model* | | | | |
| Intercept | .07* | .02 | .04* | .02 |
| Lagged dependent variable | .80* | .05 | .82* | .06 |
| Gender | .05* | .02 | .06* | .02 |
| Civics | .20* | .03 | .07* | .03 |
| Modern history | .12* | .03 | .11* | .03 |
| (Civics)(Lagged dep. var.) | -.12* | .07 | .00 | .07 |
| (Mod. hist.)(Lagged dep. var.) | -.16* | .06 | -.10* | .06 |
| $R/R^2$ | .793/.629 | | .810/.656 | |
| *Number of cases* | 678 | | 681 | |

NOTE: Entries are unstandardized regression coefficients with associated standard errors. Coefficients marked by asterisks are significant (one-tailed test) at or below the .05 level.

ly a linear function of initial variations. All three of the remaining predictors had significant effects. The interpretation of the coefficients is
straightforward. For example, the values of .04 and .07 for gender mean
that two students of different sex but identical initial scores and equal
amounts of civics and history training will, on average, differ by 4 and 7
percentage points, respectively, at the end of the second year. Similarly, the
coefficients for civics and modern history show that students with maximum and minimum amounts of training will have an expected difference
of $18+6=24$ percentage points for organizations and $8+6=14$ percentage
points for events, when gender and initial scores are held constant.

These results demonstrate that the social studies curriculum did have
a considerable effect, but it was not equally visible across regressions and
predictors. First, the impact of civics outran that of modern history, particularly for knowledge about organizations. Second, the total curricular
effect was greater for organizations than for events. The latter finding is of
particular interest in view of our earlier results. It implies that the larger
aggregate growth for organizations than for events can be accounted for on
the individual level. The higher the net increase for the sample as a whole,
the more pronounced the educational effect. This point generalizes to
variations within the two scales as well. Cutting them in halves according
to the amount of net growth for the individual items yields significantly
higher curricular effects for the subcomponents that show high aggregate-
level gains. There is nothing in the intrinsic logic of the model that forces
this correspondence between the two levels of analysis.

## Variations by Initial Level of Knowledge

Of course, the effects of civics and history classes are not likely to be
the same for everyone. Among the many questions that may be identified
in this area, one is of particular interest in view of the theoretical concerns
spelled out at the beginning: Did students who were initially relatively
knowledgeable benefit more from further education than did those who
started out at a lower level? Or did the social studies curriculum further
equalization by giving the latter a chance to catch up?

The answer to these questions is by no means self-evident, because
two opposing mechanisms are conceivably at work. On the one hand,
learning is conditioned by *aptitude*. Students who are initially knowledgeable are likely to have greater motivation, higher learning capacity, and a
flatter retention curve. On the other hand, learning is also affected by
*redundancy* or saturation. For students who start out high in knowledge,
more of whatever is offered by the curriculum will already by known,
making opportunities for further learning less frequent.

To decide which of these processes was dominant during the gymnasium years, two interaction terms were added to the initial model. These consisted of the civics and history variables multiplied by the lagged dependent variable. The overall effect of civics work was then the combination of the civics variable and the civics interaction term; the same held for history.

As shown by the results in the lower section of Table 9.6, three of the four interaction terms are significantly different from zero.[8] In all three cases, the sign is negative. This implies that the impact of the social studies curriculum was more pronounced for those whose initial knowledge level was low. Consider, for example, the effect of civics on knowledge of organizations. The expected difference between two students with minimum and maximum exposure to civics is $20-0=20$ percentage points, if their initial level is zero. From there it decreases to a minimum of $20-12=8$ percentage points when the initial score reaches maximum. Obviously, the figures are not exact. In particular, the magnitude of the interaction term for civics relative to that for history is somewhat uncertain. The important point is that there is a clearly discernible interaction effect with a negative sign.

Given that we are working with bounded scales, there is an obvious risk that results such as these may be affected by ceiling effects that have a logical rather than empirical origin. For extremely high initial levels, it may be the case that the aggregate scores at the end of the panel are so close to the maximum that they logically exclude differences as large as those visible in the lower ranges of the distribution. However, the results of Table 9.6 are not an artifact. Only a very small set of students is at all affected by logical ceiling effects, and the negative interaction terms do not come and go with these cases. Hence, we may conclude that the social studies curriculum of the gymnasium was of greater importance to students who started out on a weak level.

Our analysis in this area can be seen as a more precise test of earlier ideas and findings concerning group-level differences. For example, the high school civics curriculum in the United States was found to have greater effects on blacks than on whites (Jennings, Langton, & Niemi, 1974; Langton & Jennings, 1968). This pattern, it was argued, had little to do with race per se, but was due to variations in redundancy. The American study could not directly investigate that proposition, but the results offered here lend some support to its contentions.

It is possible, however, to carry the analysis of differential effects one step further. The effect of the two opposing mechanisms — aptitude and redundancy — is theoretically multiplicative. The impact of any given increase in one of the two quantities depends on the level of the other. Therefore, we should expect them to operate with different strength at different points of the distribution of initial scores. At the lower end, variations in aptitude should be more decisive than variations in redundancy. At the upper end, it should be the other way around. Consequently, the effect of the social studies curriculum can be expected to fit a curvilinear function with respect to initial knowledge. Starting from the lower end, the effect should increase with higher entry-level scores, reach a maximum, and then recede. It is possible to show that such was actually the case. For illustrative purposes, we concentrate on knowledge about organizations, where the overall effect of the social studies curriculum was more pronounced.

The basic pattern may be uncovered using more or less parametric techniques. The less parametric option is to run separate regressions for each initial score. As before, the dependent variable is knowledge at the end of the panel. The independent variables are gender and an index combining the civics and modern history variables. The index, which was introduced to reduce sampling error in the subgroup analyses, weights the components three to one, according to their additive impact in the sample as a whole (.18 for civics, .06 for history). To maintain a sufficient number of cases in each subgroup and to avoid problems with logical ceiling effects, we excluded the small number of respondents (1%) who had an initial score of one.

The more parametric alternative consists in specifying a unified model. In this case we included a linear, a quadratic, and a cubic term for initial scores and permitted the social studies curriculum to interact with each. The quadratic element allows the effect of the curriculum to vary nonlinearly with initial values. The cubic element allows variation in the shape of the curve. The sample and variables are the same as in the less parametric case.

The results are presented in Figure 9.2. The vertical axis shows the estimated effect of the social studies curriculum at each initial score. The effect is expressed as the expected difference between two students with maximum and minimum exposure to civics and modern history. In the less parametric case (solid line), this is equivalent to the values of the individual regression coefficients. The standard error of each observation varies between .03 and .07. For the more parametric alternative (broken line), it is equivalent to the difference between the values of the nonlinear function for individuals scoring zero and one on the social studies index.[9]

The results possess a good deal of analytical utility. The basic bow shape of the curve, and the theoretical principles on which it rests, offer a way of clarifying how and why a given educational program, or indeed any "information campaign," may serve to heighten initial differences at one point and reduce them at another. Whether and to what extent it will

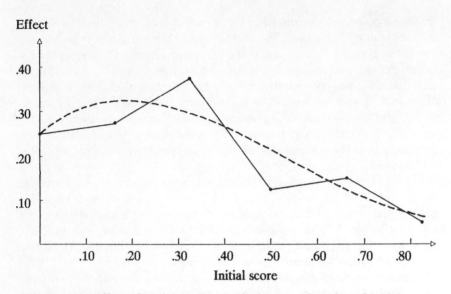

**Figure 9.2** Effect of social studies curriculum as a function of initial
             knowledge

shrink or expand the gap between any two individuals is contingent on
their initial location. By extension, the outcome for an entire population
depends on how it is distributed.

For the particular population analyzed here, the dominant negative
slope resulted from the fact that a significant share of the respondents were
located to the right of the turning point, and that the declination on that
side was sharper than the inclination on the other. Had the population
been limited to respondents with initial results of two or fewer correct
answers, the outcome would have been reversed. In other words, for a
given object of learning, the relatively more knowledgeable are likely to
benefit more from education in the early stages (i.e., compulsory school),
whereas the opposite can be expected at later points (i.e., in the gymnasium).

This analytical framework may also contribute to the understanding
of some of the contradictory results reported in the "knowledge-gap" literature. The original knowledge-gap hypothesis (Tichenor, Donohue, &
Olien, 1970) proposes that, as media publicity about any given topic increases, persons with higher education will acquire information pertaining
to that topic at a faster rate. Hence, the difference in knowledge between
more and less educated individuals will increase. This hypothesis has been
far from generally confirmed. A reduction of the gap appears to be at least

as common a consequence of increased publicity as an expansion (see Gaziano, 1983).

In a study of the campaign surrounding the Swedish referendum on nuclear power, Asp (1984) found that the knowledge gap increased in the beginning of the campaign, but decreased toward its end. The decline began well before logical ceiling effects would make their presence known. Asp suggested that the pattern uncovered may turn out to be of a rather general nature. Whether the original knowledge-gap hypothesis works or not might be contingent on the stage at which we look at the process. Our own results are eminently compatible with that perspective and provide a contribution to its individual-level underpinnings.

### Intracurricular Variations and Extracurricular Sources of Learning

As a final step in our analysis of the impact of the social studies curriculum, we will examine the importance of intracurricular variations and extracurricular sources of learning. This serves a dual purpose. On the one hand, it constitutes a means of control. The estimated impact of social science training might be confounded with the effect of associated factors. On the other hand, it provides a contrast. Those who have downplayed the effect of formal education have often underscored the importance of other sources of learning. A joint investigation provides a basis for comparison.

We consciously chose to set up the test so as to maximize the threat to our previous findings. Thus, whenever possible, we picked indicators that could be assumed to have a very intimate connection with the dependent variables. The index for exposure to printed media combines two items asking specifically about international and political news.[10] Likewise, the indicator for informal conversations is targeted to "what goes on in world politics."[11] Special mention of the subject matter is lacking only in the case of television news, where very little in the way of selective exposure is possible.[12] Several other specific as well as more general measures were tried but were found to be of little or no importance, once those just listed were taken into account.[13]

To strengthen the controls further, the measurements were taken from the second wave, rather than the first. Thus, they might themselves have been a partial outcome of the social studies curriculum, and the data indicate that such was actually the case. Consequently, their impact can to some extent be seen as an indirect curricular effect. In addition, their observed explanatory value will include any causal feedback from acquired knowledge.

Media exposure and interpersonal communication deserve to be taken into account in their capacity as contending explanations. However, a complementary control strategy is to take one step forward in the causal chain and assess the importance of those factors that allegedly mediate the curricular effect. One such factor is the attention given to international affairs in the coursework of the individual class unit. In the second wave, students were asked to recall how many lessons about "what happens in world politics" they had been offered throughout the first two years of the gymnasium. To minimize projection effects, the question was asked before the political literacy test, along with all other behavioral and attitudinal measures. To further reduce the risk, we used the mean score for each class unit, rather than the individual responses. Apart from variations due to temporary absence, the amount of instruction should be the same for all students in a class.[14]

The reported average for the entire sample corresponds approximately to three lessons. The class unit scores are highly correlated with both civics (.71) and modern history (.51). Even so, we would expect intracurricular variations to have a visible impact if indeed coursework is a decisive factor. On the other hand, we cannot expect the direct effect of civics and history to vanish altogether, once the amount of instruction about what goes on in world politics is taken into account. Obviously, the kind of training we asked about is narrowly defined. Information relevant for the knowledge items may come in under a number of other headings. For example, NATO and the WP could be brought up in the context of Swedish defense policy, and OPEC and the EC under the topic of economic geography.

The results are shown in Table 9.7. As before, all variables are scored on a scale of zero to one. To make possible a comparison in terms of standardized as well as unstandardized effects, the model is purely additive.[15] The unstandardized effect corresponds to the expected difference in knowledge between two individuals with minimum and maximum scores on the independent variable, everything else held constant. For example, the .08 value for television news in the first column means an expected second-wave difference of 8 percentage points between those who watch the news nearly every day and those who never watch it. The standardized effect (second column) takes the spread of the independent variable into account. It reflects the relative contribution of each predictor to the total variation in the dependent variable.

Nearly all coefficients are statistically significant. The single exception is the effect of civics on international events, where the mediating factor, amount of instruction, reduces the direct impact to a minimum. Considering both direct and indirect effects, there is no visible reduction of the curricular impact, compared to previous analyses. The educational factors also stand out well in comparison with the extracurricular sources of learning. In unstandardized terms, the former are at least as important

**Table 9.7** Knowledge of international organizations and events as a function of previous knowledge, curriculum, gender, and extracurricular sources of learning

|  | International organizations | | International events | |
|---|---|---|---|---|
|  | b | β | b | β |
| Intercept | -.01* | — | -.06* | — |
| Lagged dependent variable | .62* | .57 | .73* | .66 |
| Gender | .04* | .06 | .07* | .10 |
| Civics | .13* | .18 | .03 | .03 |
| Modern history | .05* | .07 | .05* | .07 |
| No. of lessons on world politics | .10* | .06 | .12* | .07 |
| Read international & political news | .08* | .06 | .10* | .06 |
| Watch TV news | .08* | .05 | .07* | .05 |
| Talk with others about world politics | .08* | .06 | .06* | .04 |
| R/R² | .796/.634 | | .817/.667 | |
| Number of cases | 663 | | 666 | |

NOTE: Entries are unstandardized (b) and standardized (ß) regression coefficients. Coefficients marked by asterisks are significant (one-tailed test) at or below the .05 level.

as the latter. In standardized currency, variations in education are more important, particularly with respect to international organizations. The presence of the controls thus strengthens our earlier inferences about educational effects.

## CONCLUSION

In contrast to several other studies, we have found that the social studies curriculum does have a considerable impact on cognitive development in mid to late adolescence. We cannot rule out that this divergent result is partly due to variations in educational settings beyond our immediate empirical reach, but we would suggest that certain other factors are also at work.

To begin with, we offer ample evidence that cross-sectional comparisons across curricula are invariably confounded by selection effects. These may be very difficult to remove by analytic means. Further, they may serve to inflate as well as to suppress the true impact. In our data, the former is illustrated in comparing programs with and without civics; the latter, in comparing curricula with a large amount of civics to those with less. If we had not had access to truly longitudinal data, it is highly uncertain what conclusions we would have reached. Here, more than in other cases, causal inference from cross-sectional evidence appears to be a perilous enterprise.

Further, the amount and kind of educational variation contained in the design is of considerable importance. In this case, that variation is fairly sizable. A large proportion of students had no social science courses at all, but a significant share also had five or more hours weekly of civics, history, and other potentially relevant subjects. Of course, less variation would not have meant less learning, but it would have made the effect less readily discernible.

Finally, what is considered to be a substantial impact depends on initial expectations. For the measures of political literacy used here, individual differences are obviously quite stable over time. We have reasons to believe that this holds for many other measures of cognitive strength as well. If variations in education do not dramatically alter those differences over one and a half years, there is no evidence that extracurricular factors are more potent in this respect. On this particular score, there are perhaps reasons for being more humble in our expectations as to what variations in schooling as well as other external factors can do.

The last two points are both highly relevant in reconciling the divergent findings of adolescent and adult studies of educational effects. First, educational differences in adult cross-sections reflect large, cumulative variations of a kind that are only caught piecemeal, if at all, by adolescent studies. Moreover, the effects created by these variations may often be reinforced by later development, whether through mechanisms suggested by the socialization or the allocation perspective. Second, effects attributed to education in adult studies may to no small extent represent differences that are not truly educational in origin. As exemplified in our results, a good deal may be attributable to individual variations that precede, rather than result from, educational differentiation.

With respect to the measures of political literacy investigated here, the overall effect of the Swedish gymnasium was to widen the initial gap between students in theoretical and vocational programs. Given the present distribution of civics training, that comes as no surprise; however, it is by no means a necessary outcome. Our results show that the social studies curriculum had a greater impact on those who started out on a low level. Had all students been exposed to the same amount of training, we might well have seen a narrowing of the gap between theoretical and vocational programs. In fact, we might go one step further. The findings suggest that the potential for social studies education to serve as an equalizer is greater in the gymnasium than at earlier stages of education. Putting it sharply, educational differentiation takes hold when equalization is ready to begin.

Of course, a cynic might always argue that this entire issue is of no real importance. Even if the knowledge gap could be kept at bay with respect to basic political literacy, we would surely see it reappear if we were to investigate facilities on a deeper or more sophisticated level. Thus, the cognitive balance of power between educational and social strata would always remain the same. The premise of this argument probably has a good deal of empirical validity, but the conclusion does not necessarily follow. On what level the gap appears is not unimportant.

The progression of the computer age may serve as a simple illustration of this point. About a decade ago, the rule of local computer experts was almost unchallenged in office environments all over the Western World. Today, that is likely to be much less true than it used to be. Both executives and rank-and-file workers have acquired a working knowledge of the basics. Although the experts may remain much more knowledgeable, they can no longer silence a concerned audience with a few bits of technical jargon. Others will know enough to insist on a sensible answer. The balance of power has been altered. So it might be with political literacy: Differences between educational strata are likely to remain, but the character of those differences might be greatly affected by the nature and depth of the social studies curriculum.

## NOTES

1. A useful review of results and theoretical positions pertaining to the issue of educational effects is found in the exchange between Merelman (1980a, 1980b, 1981) and Jennings (1980, 1981).

2. The guidelines for the two-year civics programs of the new gymnasium (NBE, 1970) put more emphasis on an international outlook than do those for the three-year programs (NBE, 1970), the latter being taken over from an older document (NBE, 1965). In a later supplement to the guidelines for the three-year curricula (NBE, 1978), the greater stress on international concerns is made explicit for these programs as well.

3. The technology program within the three-year track has an optional fourth year. In the vocational track there are, in addition to the 18 major curricula, several hundred specialized programs, some of which are shorter than two years. Despite their large number, however, these programs account for a very small portion of the students.

4. The sample is a multistage, clustered, probability sample including gymnasium students from 35 different schools all over the country, as well as adoles-

cents not currently enrolled in school. The data set used here—that is, respondents who participated in 1981 as well as 1983 and were in the gymnasium on both occasions—amounts to 1,226 individuals. To adjust for the effect of clustering, the raw $N$ was reduced on the basis of statistical estimates of actual sampling error. All tabular information is based on this reduced $N$, which allows significance statistics to be treated as though they were from a simple random sample. In addition to the data set used here, the study as a whole includes a 1985 adolescent wave, as well as data from parents and teachers. A complete description of the study design will be given in Westholm (forthcoming).

5. Sweden was third in terms of raw scores, but scored highest after adjusting for the selectivity of the school system in the various countries (Torney et al., 1975, pp. 108–109). In Sweden, the sampled population amounted to 45 percent of a cohort, roughly corresponding to the theoretical programs of the present gymnasium. In all other countries except the United States, the sample was more selective.

6. The $H$-coefficient is superior to other currently used measures for Guttman-type scales, for example, coefficients of reproducibility. Among other things, the $H$-coefficient is independent of the marginal distributions of the scale items, which is not true of most other measures.

7. The product-moment correlation actually fell slightly in both cases (to .16 and .33). This was due to an overall increase in test-score variances.

8. Both sets of interactions also yield a significant increase in $R^2$ when added to the initial model. For organizations, the increase is significant at $\alpha = .05$, for events at $\alpha = .10$.

9. In estimated form, the function is

$$K = .07 + .71I + .05G + .25S + .78SI + .31I^2 - 2.52SI^2 - .24I^3 + 1.57SI^3$$

where $K$ is knowledge at the end of the panel, $I$ is initial knowledge, $G$ is gender, and $S$ is amount of exposure to civics and modern history. Adding the quadratic terms to the equation yields a significant increase in $R^2$ at $\alpha = .05$. Subsequently adding the cubic terms improves the fit but not significantly so. Obviously, many of the individual coefficients are heavily correlated with each other and should therefore not be relied upon.

10. Following an introductory statement saying, "We should also like to know what things you usually read about in the newspapers," a list of 13 items was presented to the respondent. Of these, "politics" and "international news in general" are used here. Four response alternatives were offered, ranging from "read nothing of what is in the paper on this topic" to "read almost everything of what is in the paper about this topic."

11. The introductory statement read, "How often do you talk with somebody about the following things?" The item cited in the text was one of 12 topics subsequently presented to the respondent. Five response alternatives were offered, ranging from "never" to "almost every day."

12. The question read, "How often do you watch the news on television?" Five response alternatives were offered, ranging from "never" to "6–7 days a week."

13. These included parents' education and interest in politics (asked of the

parents), exposure to television programs dealing with social and political issues (aside from the news), frequency of political conversations in general, and frequency of conversations about peace and war issues and about Third World countries in particular.

14. The introduction read, "The amount of instruction about different things varies between different class units and programs in the gymnasium. *Approximately* how much instruction *have you received in total* about each of the following things during your time in the gymnasium *this far?*" The item cited in the text was one of 14 topics subsequently presented to the respondent. Five response alternatives were offered, ranging from "have *not received any instruction* about this" to "have had *many* (11 or more) lessons about this."

15. As shown by Allison (1977), standardized effects are not meaningful for multiplicative models.

## REFERENCES

Allison, P. D. (1977). Testing for interaction in multiple regression. *American Journal of Sociology, 83,* 144–153.

Asp, K. (1984). *Kunskapsklyftehypotesen: En kritisk granskning.* Mimeo. Department of Political Science, Göteborg University, Sweden.

Dahl, R. A. (1982). *Dilemmas of pluralist democracy.* New Haven, CT: Yale University Press.

Gallatin, J., & Adelson, J. (1970). Individual rights and the public good. A cross-national study of adolescents. *Comparative Political Studies, 3,* 98–114.

Gaziano, C. (1983). The knowledge gap: An analytical review of media effects. *Communication Research, 10,* 447–486.

Hess, R. D., & Torney, J. V. (1967). *The development of political attitudes in childhood.* Chicago: Aldine.

Hyman, H. H., & Wright, C. R. (1979). *Education's lasting influence on values.* Chicago: University of Chicago Press.

Hyman, H. H., Wright, C. R., & Reed, J. S. (1975). *The enduring effects of education.* Chicago: University of Chicago Press.

Jennings, M. K. (1980). Comments on Richard Merelman's "Democratic politics and the culture of American education." *American Political Science Review, 74,* 333–337.

Jennings, M. K. (1981). Comment on the Merelman-Jennings exchange. *American Political Science Review, 75,* 155–156.

Jennings, M. K., Ehman, L. E., & Niemi, R. G. (1974). Social studies teachers and their pupils. In M. K. Jennings & R. G. Niemi, *The political character of adolescence* (pp. 207–227). Princeton, NJ: Princeton University Press.

Jennings, M. K., Langton, K. P., & Niemi, R. G. (1974). Effects of the high school civics curriculum. In M. K. Jennings & R. G. Niemi, *The political character of adolescence* (pp. 181–206). Princeton, NJ: Princeton University Press.

Langton, K. P., & Jennings, M. K. (1968). Political socialization and the high school civics curriculum in the United States. *American Political Science Review, 62,* 862–867.

Litt, E. (1963). Civic education norms and political indoctrination. *American Sociological Review, 28,* 69–75.

Lively, J. (1975). *Democracy.* Oxford, England: Basil Blackwell.

Merelman, R. M. (1971). *Political socialization and educational climates.* New York: Holt, Rinehart & Winston.

Merelman, R. M. (1980a). Democratic politics and the culture of American education. *American Political Science Review, 74,* 319–337.

Merelman, R. M. (1980b). A reply to Jennings. *American Political Science Review, 74,* 338–341.

Merelman, R. M. (1981). Reply. *American Political Science Review, 75,* 156–158.

Meyer, J. W. (1977). The effects of education as an institution. *American Journal of Sociology, 83,* 55–77.

Mokken, R. J. (1971). *A theory and procedure of scale analysis.* The Hague: Mouton.

NBE. (1965). *Läroplan för gymnasiet.* Stockholm: National Board of Education.

NBE. (1970). *Läroplan för gymnasieskolan. Allmän del.* Stockholm: National Board of Education.

NBE. (1978). *Läroplan för gymnasieskolan. Supplement 38. Samhällskunskap för tre- och fryaåriga linjer.* Stockholm: National Board of Education.

NCBS. (1982). *Gymnasieskolan 1981/1982: Sökande och antagna hösten 1981.* (Statistiska meddelanden U1982:11). Stockholm: National Central Bureau of Statistics.

NCBS. (1986). *Valdeltagande vid riksdagsvalet 1985.* (Pressmeddelande 1986:214). Stockholm: National Central Bureau of Statistics.

NCBS. (1987a). *Övergång gymnasieskola – högskola. Studerande som avslutat en linje i gymnasieskolan 1982/1983.* (Bakgrundsmaterial om högskolan 1987:5). Stockholm: National Central Bureau of Statistics.

NCBS. (1987b). *Uppskattad utbildning.* (1987:2). Stockholm: National Central Bureau of Statistics.

Sigel, R. S., & Hoskin, M. B. (1981). *The political involvement of adolescents.* New Brunswick, NJ: Rutgers University Press.

Tichenor, P. J., Donohue, G. A., & Olien, C. N. (1970). Mass media flow and differential growth of knowledge. *Public Opinion Quarterly, 34,* 159–170.

Torney, J. V., Oppenheim, A. N., & Farnen, R. F. (1975). *Civic education in ten countries.* Stockholm: Almqvist and Wiksell.

Westholm, A. (Forthcoming). *The political heritage: Testing theories of family socialization and generational change.* Unpublished doctoral dissertation, Uppsala University.

Zillén, K. (1981). *Ungdomars politiska tänkande. (The young in politics study)* (Report No. 2). Uppsala, Sweden: Uppsala University, Department of Government.

# 10

# Citizenship Socialization in National Voluntary Youth Organizations

ABRAHAM YOGEV
RINA SHAPIRA

Most of the research concerning the effects of the educational system on the development of citizenship orientations has focused on school socialization. The role of nonformal systems of education as agents of citizenship socialization has been largely neglected. This chapter concerns citizenship socialization in one type of nonformal education — voluntary youth organizations, many of which operate on a national basis in less-developed countries.

Though voluntary youth organizations are a widespread phenomenon in many societies (Braungart, 1984a, 1984b), they have a special role in less-developed countries, where they have arisen under both democratic and totalitarian regimes. In many of these countries they emerged during periods of dynamic social change, such as rapid modernization, political revolution, or the establishment of a new state. When social change is called for, traditional socialization agents — such as schools or parents — cannot shift gears overnight to accommodate the new regime. Thus, nationally backed youth organizations come to be regarded as massive instruments of social change, capable of counteracting traditional forces.

Our primary concern is with youth associations that are organized on a national basis and operate as part of the legitimate political system. In some countries, youth associations may also take the form of local youth clubs, which operate on a restricted community basis or on a regional scale. Though these may be important in the socialization of local elites, particularly in less-developed geographical areas (Shapira, 1986), we shall limit our discussion here to youth organizations that are financed and backed either by the state itself or by national public organizations.

Our claim is that the national backing of these organizations makes them an effective agency of citizenship socialization. Various regimes use these organizations for promoting political change, such as for asserting the regime's central control or gaining legitimation, or as part of their general institution-building efforts. Though the activities these organizations pursue are quite diverse, ranging from purely recreational pastimes to semioccupational socialization and paramilitary training, their national backing turns them almost imperatively into agencies of civic and political education.

Our aim is not merely to depict the contribution that these groups make to citizenship education, but rather to distinguish between different types of national youth organizations, and on that basis to define their specific socialization roles. We thus contend that the various origins and operational patterns of these organizations have led to their different emphases in the citizenship socialization of youth.

## POLITICAL VERSUS APOLITICAL YOUTH ORGANIZATIONS

The main typology of national youth organizations (NYOs) in less-developed countries is along the axis of political characteristics. We may distinguish between political and apolitical NYOs. The political ones

1. Are sponsored and supervised directly by political powers, such as a certain political elite or political parties
2. Emphasize political and paramilitary activities

In contrast, the apolitical youth organizations

1. Are sponsored by a variety of national and public organizations
2. Emphasize vocational and agricultural training or recreational activities

We shall show that this typology, besides being meaningful for the mapping of the various organizations, is crucial in terms of socialization emphases and the potential manipulation of socialization effects. To exemplify our arguments, we shall base the discussion on several organizations for which survey research is available. On the basis of our own research and that of others, we have gathered such survey studies on NYOs in four countries: Costa Rica, Israel, the Ivory Coast, and Malawi. These studies concern a variety of NYOs with respect to operation patterns, types of activities, and the age range of members, yet they all serve well the typology just proposed.

The Young Pioneers, which is the national youth movement of Malawi, falls into the category of a political NYO, as do some of the Israeli youth movements. The Young Pioneers operate within the single-party political system of Malawi and are sponsored by the Malawi Congress party. The official aims of this youth movement are to compensate for the scarcity of secondary education, to help solve problems of youth unemployment, to teach new agricultural methods, and consequently to increase the agricultural production of the country (Malawi Government, n.d.). Members, usually between the ages of 16 to 26 and of both sexes, are volunteers recruited by local government and party officials for the basic 10-month training course, provided in several training bases throughout the country. The course consists of agricultural training, sports, educational and recreational activities, and paramilitary training. Though agricultural training is the major official aim, political and paramilitary education tend to preoccupy the trainees during the course period. Educational activities in the course emphasize the loyalty of the trainees to the party and its leader (Yogev, Shapira, & Tibon, 1982).

Most of the youth movements in Israel are politically affiliated. Several movements were established in the prestatehood years by Jewish political organizations of both the left and the right. They are now organizationally affiliated with the present political parties. In addition, there is the Scouts movement, which was established on a nonpolitical basis during the period of the British mandatory rule in Palestine (for the origins of the different youth movements, see Ichilov, 1977; Shapira, Adler, Lerner, & Peleg, 1979; Shapira & Peleg, 1984). All the youth movements operate through a national network of clubs that offer recreational activities, ideological and political education, and various community service programs. Adolescents of both sexes usually join the various movements in their early teens, and some of them retain their membership until the age of 18, when they join the army.

Though, except for the Scouts, all the movements are politically affiliated, only some of them fall into our category of political organizations. Some of the movements, especially those of the right wing, the religious movements, and a movement very far to the left, are more extreme than others in their extent of political indoctrination and the ideological commitment they require of their members. Others, namely the Scouts and the movements from the left to the center, operate as apolitical organizations, mainly emphasizing recreational activities.

Our category of apolitical NYOs thus consists of the latter type of Israeli youth movements and two additional organizations—the MNJ of Costa Rica and the Civic Service of the Ivory Coast. The Costa Rican MNJ (Movimiento Nacional de Juventudes) is the largest of several national voluntary youth organizations that exist in this small Central American democratic republic. Sponsored by the Ministry of Education, Culture and Sports, its main activity is based on a network of community youth clubs.

Club activity consists of enrichment education, recreation, and civic-service projects, either within the community or through participation in regional development projects. The majority of members are 15 to 18 years old and of both sexes. Although recruitment is conducted on a nonselective voluntary basis, most members are secondary public school students. They represent mainly the middle and lower-middle social strata (Yogev, 1980).

The Civic Service of the Ivory Coast is a voluntary wing of a nonvoluntary organization, namely, the army. Supervised by the Ministry of Armed Forces, it maintains regional training centers and a central training base. The trainees are males in their early twenties (for females there is a separate organization) and of urban and rural origins. The regional training centers recruit youth on a voluntary basis. Recruitment to the central training base is also voluntary, within the framework of military service. In addition to military training, the central base provides yearly courses in agriculture, technology, and crafts. Though the Civic Service is part of the army, its official aims are strictly economic and educational (Ivory Coast Government, n.d.). It seems that the objective need of agricultural development and the high rate of youth unemployment have created these emphases.

Though the Civic Service emphasizes vocational training, while the MNJ and the nonextreme Israeli movements emphasize recreational activities, they all represent the apolitical type of national youth organization. They may thus be contrasted with the Malawian Young Pioneers and the politically extreme Israeli youth movements. Our aim is to show that, despite the many differences among these organizations, their major typology is related to their emphases of citizenship socialization.

## OUTCOMES OF ORGANIZATIONAL SOCIALIZATION

Regarding the development of citizenship orientations among members of the NYOs, it may be argued that the socialization roles of these groups are threefold:

1. Socialization for a diffuse regime support
2. Socialization for specific ideological commitment
3. Direct and indirect socialization for participatory citizenship through influences on personal "modern" values and on career orientations

Virtually all NYOs emphasize the first socialization category. They largely differ, however, in their focus on the second versus the third roles, depending on their political nature and activities. While the political organizations emphasize the inculcation of specific ideological commitments, the apolitical ones concentrate on socialization for participatory citizenship. We shall first exemplify these different roles by presenting existing data on the various organizations. Then we shall elaborate on the implications of these roles for citizenship socialization in general.

### Socialization for a Diffuse Regime Support

Common to all NYOs is their socialization of youth for a diffuse regime support. In other words, these organizations seem to inculcate in their participants an affinity with their country and the current regime. An interesting fact is that national youth organizations promote such basic citizenship orientations regardless of their specific nature as political or apolitical. We shall demonstrate the nature of this socialization role by looking at the youth movements of Israel and Malawi.

Studies of Israeli youth movements were concerned, over the years, with the effect of membership on the identification of youth with the state, particularly with respect to "Yerida," the tendency to emigrate from Israel, which has become an acute social issue in recent years. Various studies confirm that members, regardless of the specific political affiliation of their youth movement (left- versus right-wing, or apolitical), are less prone to emigrate than nonmembers. This was found in a large-scale study (Levi & Guttman, 1976) on the values of Israeli high school students, some of whom were movement members, and in the study of Shapira et al. (1979), which compared past and present members of various youth movements with nonmembers. The latter study found that members not only oppose emigration more often than nonmembers, but that they also have a stronger identification with Israel, regardless of the specific political inclination of their youth movement.

The membership effect on identification with the state may be long lasting, as suggested by Shapira & Etzioni (1970, 1973) in their studies on Israeli university students. They found that students who grew up as movement members had a stronger affinity with Israel and opposed emigration much more than their peers who did not. A recent study (Ichilov, Hyman, & Shapira, 1988) further shows that the significant influence of youth movement membership on the opposition to emigration persists even in lower-status neighborhoods. The peripheral and disadvantaged status of adolescents in such neighborhoods does not weaken the effect of movement membership on affinity with the state.

The case of the Malawian Young Pioneers is altogether different from that of Israel. Yet, even under the constraints of imposed political socialization, the Young Pioneers succeed in transmitting basic values of citizenship and identification with the state to their members. In their study of base trainees of the Young Pioneers, Yogev et al. (1982) found that the majority agreed with the statement, "Being a citizen of my country plays an important part in my life." This agreement was lower among a control group of Malawian high school students. Furthermore, those movement trainees who had attained secondary schooling resembled, in their strong identification with the citizen role, the less-educated trainees rather than the control group of high school students. Using Cantril's (1965) symbolic numerical "ladder," which represents evaluative positions of the country, it was also found in this study that the Young Pioneers, regardless of their educational background, evaluated the position of Malawi much higher than the nonparticipating students.

### Socialization for Specific Ideological Commitment

A second activity of some — but not all — NYOs is specific ideological socialization. This is carried out as part of their focus on (1) the preparation of their members for active participation in political life or (2) their mobilization for ideological and political commitment to either the political elite or particular political parties. It is the political youth organizations that focus mainly on this particular type of socialization.

The Malawian Young Pioneers are the best representative in this category. This movement specifically aims at inculcating commitment to the president and the political elite he represents. The Young Pioneers are considered potential supporters of this elite. The political loyalty is transmitted through political indoctrination and paramilitary training in the movement's bases. As Yogev et al. (1982) note, these bases resemble total institutions, known to achieve a tremendous psychological impact on their inmates by means of their seclusion from the outside world, their separation from the socializing staff, and the creation of conditions leading to extreme dependence of the inmates on staff members (Goffman, 1961).

Considering the organizational patterns and political affiliation of the Young Pioneers, it is not surprising that this movement succeeds in inculcating values of political loyalty characteristic of a subject political culture. As Yogev et al. (1982) found in a survey of Young Pioneers, 95 percent of them agreed that if a person had to choose between a job he liked very much and a job chosen for him by the leaders of his country, he should opt for the latter. This almost total agreement persists after controlling for the educational background of the trainees, and it contrasts with the much lower agreement on this item by a control group of Malawian high school students. Furthermore, the Young Pioneers revealed a strong deference for power positions. Asked to rank a list of occupations by importance, they ranked "politician" and "army officer" much higher than did the control students, regardless of their own educational background.

Yogev and Shapira (1982) show that the Young Pioneers are strongly committed to the types of activities emphasized in their training bases. Presented with 12 photographs depicting various types of Young Pioneer activities (vocational and paramilitary training, educational activities, sports, and recreation), they selected as both most attractive and most important the photographs representing paramilitary training (i.e., obstacle course, drilling, and marching).

These selections are particularly interesting when compared to those made from the same group of photographs by the trainees of the Civic Service of the Ivory Coast. These young people ranked the paramilitary activities among the least compelling. On both dimensions of attraction and importance, the most frequently selected photographs represented strictly vocational and educational activities (i.e., technical training, class instruction, tractor cultivation, and fieldwork).

The comparison of members' choices of activities in the two organizations indicates that the operative goals of the organization are crucial for determining the extent of its ideological socialization of youth. Paradoxically, the Civic Service of the Ivory Coast, which is affiliated with the army and recruits members during their military service, emphasizes vocational rather than military and political goals. This is reflected in the apolitical orientation of its members. Judging by their choice of activities, the Civic Service cannot be regarded as an agency of socialization for specific ideological commitment, despite its affiliation with the army.

The political nature of Israeli youth movements is quite complex. As already mentioned, some of the movements are more extreme than others in their extent of political indoctrination and the ideological commitment they require of their members. In their large-scale study of past and present members of the numerous NYOs, Shapira et al. (1979) reveal some of the consequences of this political variety with respect to ideological commitment. First, they found that adolescents tended to follow their parents' footsteps in joining a youth movement. Members of right-wing, left-wing, and the apolitical movements, usually were the offspring of members of the same movements or of ideologically similar ones. Furthermore, members whose parents (especially mothers) were also movement members were more politically active. They tended to join political parties as adults, to emphasize the importance of party membership, and to develop a general interest in politics.

Besides this pattern of intergenerational continuity of youth movement membership and its impact on ideological socialization, Shapira and her colleagues (1979) show that the political and national attitudes of the members (i.e., political involvement, socialist versus capitalist ideologies, Jewish and Israeli identities) are directly influenced by the ideological orientation of their movement, rather than by the intensity of personal participation. In other words, these political attitudes are determined by the specific movement affiliation (left- versus right-wing). They are unrelated to the extent of movement involvement, such as the length of membership and participation in instruction and other special movement tasks. Similarly, the extremism of the movement predicts better than any other variable the extent to which members are satisfied with their movement and its political way. Members of the more extremist movements (mainly of the right wing and of religious movements that politically lean to the right) were more satisfied and rated their movement higher than members of the less-extreme movements (in particular, left-wing movements and the apolitical ones). Thus, the success of ideological socialization in Israeli youth movements is attributed to their structural and ideological features, rather than to the extent and intensity of members' involvement in their activities.

The cases of Malawi and Israel show that the socialization for ideological commitment is successfully carried out in NYOs that directly aim at this specific socialization goal. Members of such organizations become involved in politics due to these organizational goals and because of the ideological commitment required by their organization. It is the macroworld of politics that assures this commitment, and not the microworld of members' participation, as expressed in their variable involvement in the organization.

### Direct and Indirect Socialization for Participatory Citizenship

Contrary to the determinants of ideological socialization, education for participatory citizenship is of central concern in the apolitical NYOs. When it takes place in youth organizations of the political type, this socialization dimension will tend to be unrelated to their specific ideology. Its success will rather depend in this case on the personal characteristics of the members, such as their social background and the intensity of their involvement in the organization.

By this socialization dimension we refer to the patterns aimed at producing perceptions of an active citizen role. Members successfully socialized toward participatory citizenship will express voluntarism and interest in public affairs. In general, they will view citizenship as a participant role rather than as an inactive and subordinate one. National youth organizations may develop such citizenship orientations either directly or indirectly, by means of influencing the modernity of their members and by increasing their aspirations for status attainment. We shall discuss each of these means separately.

Socialization Toward Modernity.   The concept of individual modernity reflects personal orientations and behaviors mainly characteristic of the middle and upper strata in Western democracies. Modernity is usually portrayed as the opposite of traditional life patterns, which are slowly disappearing in many countries, including less-developed ones. Various studies have attempted an empirical investigation of individual modernity in Third World countries (for comprehensive examples, see Inkeles, 1983; Inkeles & Smith, 1974). Common to these studies is the construction of unidimensional modernity scales based on factor analysis of attitudinal and behavioral items reflecting modernity in a variety of substantive themes. These themes range from general psychosocial orientations (such as efficacy or openness to change), through family-related issues (independence from family, sex-role egalitarianism), to topics reflecting social and political attitudes (exposure to mass media, interest in public affairs, voluntary activity).

Some of these, especially interest in public affairs and voluntary activity, are directly related to participatory citizenship. The rest mainly reflect personal life spheres but may be considered indirectly related to active citizenship, since they may facilitate awareness of the participant citizen role. Though in some specific cases the "public" and "private" dimensions of modernity appear to be separate (Yogev, 1987), in most studies they were found to form a single coherent syndrome of modernity. Education toward modernity in NYOs may, therefore, serve as a means of both direct and indirect socialization toward participatory citizenship.

Socialization toward modernity mainly occurs in the organizations that are apolitical in affiliation and activity patterns. The most illuminating study on the topic investigated attitudes among members of the Costa Rican MNJ (Yogev, 1980). The survey study, which compared MNJ members with nonmember Costa Rican high school students, was based on a typical unidimensional modernity scale consisting of both "private" and "public" subdimensions of individual modernity. It was found that the MNJ members were significantly more modern than the high school students. Furthermore, while the modernity of the students was mainly determined by socioeconomic status, social origin did not affect it. Rather, modernity level was influenced more by members' involvement in club and movement activities. The more they had participated in special MNJ activities (such as particular community projects or MNJ camps), and the more they held discussions related to modernity issues in their club meetings, the more modern they were.

As noted, political youth organizations are less successful in socializing toward modern orientations, probably because of their emphasis on ideological indoctrination. Levi & Guttman's (1976) study on the values of Israeli high school students reveals that voluntary involvement in special public projects is more common among members of the apolitical youth movements (the Scouts) or the less politically extreme (left-wing rather than right-wing or religious) movements. The survey of the Malawian Young Pioneers (Yogev et al., 1982) shows that this movement is successful only in the ideological socialization of its members. When the members and the Malawian high school students were compared with regard to a list of individual modernity items (efficacy, universalism, independence from family, and receptivity to change), it was found that the students were more modern than the movement members, especially the less-educated ones.

Participation and Status Aspirations.   An additional means of indirect socialization toward participatory citizenship is the relation between organizational participation and career orientation. Participation in some national youth organizations may increase their members' aspirations for future educational and occupational attainments, and subsequently may increase their actual status attainment. Since socioeconomic status and participatory citizenship are positively related, this influence may indirectly make the members active citizens in the future. This, however, depends on the realization of the status aspirations and, therefore, on the opportunity structure of specific societies. Nonformal education programs have been criticized for having only a small impact on social mobility, relative to the school (Bock, 1976; La Belle & Verhine, 1975). However, for these NYOs mainly recruiting students of formal schools, rather than serving as alternative educational channels to the school, the possibility of influencing future status attainments of their members does exist.

Similarly to modernity socialization, we find that the organizations increasing the status aspirations of their members are usually apolitical. In the political organizations that do have such an influence, we find that members' aspirations are not determined by the specific political ideology of the organization, but rather by individual participation factors.

In the case of Costa Rica, for example, it was found by Yogev (1980) that MNJ members developed higher aspirations regarding educational and income attainments than their nonparticipating peers. This was true of all MNJ members studied, but particularly for youth club leaders, whose aspirations were higher than those of both the students and the regular movement members. Similar evidence is provided by Israeli youth

movements. As Shapira and Etzioni (1970, 1973) revealed, past membership increased the occupational aspirations of university students, especially those of the minority Oriental group (of Middle Eastern or North African ancestry). In their later study of past and present movement members, Shapira et al. (1979) showed that exmembers had achieved higher
educational and occupational status than nonmembers, and that this
was unrelated to the specific ideology of the movement (left- versus right-
wing politics). Instead, they were influenced by the intensity of participation, that is, the length of membership and the holding of leadership
positions.

## WHAT MAKES NATIONAL YOUTH ORGANIZATIONS
## EFFECTIVE AGENCIES OF CITIZENSHIP SOCIALIZATION?

Our discussion to this point shows that national youth organizations
are effective agencies of citizenship and political socialization in less-developed countries, perhaps more effective than the school. What makes them
so effective? The reasons for their success seem to be related to (1) their
societal context, (2) their operative context, and (3) the social stratification
context regarding their membership patterns.

Regarding the first, it should be realized that these organizations are
designated by their societies to serve as agencies of political or citizenship
education. Whether they are affiliated with political organizations (political parties or elites), with the state apparatus, or with apolitical organizations, they are initiated, financed, and backed by these organizations in an
attempt to reinforce the civic or political awareness of youth. The goals of
the formal school system are quite different. Citizenship education is not
the major official goal of schools, especially in less-developed countries.
Schools focus on academic achievements. To the extent that they socialize
for citizenship, it is within the framework of general knowledge transmission. In some countries — Malawi, for instance — teachers are forbidden to
discuss political issues. In other countries, such as Israel, the division of
labor between the school and the voluntary youth movements was officially enforced during certain periods of early statehood. The youth movements were forbidden to enter schools and recruit members during school
hours.

Regarding their operational context, the ways in which NYOs function as informal education frameworks also facilitate their citizenship socialization role. Kahane (1975; see also Kahane & Rapoport, Chapter 11 of
this volume) has outlined a general model that specifies the particular

patterns of NYO operation. He argues that these organizations differ from formal schools by the following eight operative dimensions:

1. Voluntarism
2. Multiplexity (maintaining different activity spheres of equivalent importance)
3. Moratorium (the delay of obligations and decisions, allowing and encouraging trial-and-error experiences)
4. Symmetry (balanced reciprocal relations among participants)
5. Modularity (arrangement of social activities according to changing circumstances and interests)
6. Pragmatic symbolism (the ability to convert symbols into deeds and vice versa)
7. Expressive instrumentalism (activity performance for its own sake and as a means for achieving future goals, thus linking immediate satisfaction with the ability to postpone gratification)
8. Structural dualism (the ability to support two or more sometimes contradictory orientations)

Obviously, this is an ideal model of informal youth organizations. Yet, even if only part of these patterns are revealed in the real operation of specific youth organizations, they should facilitate their socialization roles regarding citizenship, especially in comparison to the more formal school structure.

Finally, we should also consider the relations between NYOs and the wider context of social stratification in society. Frequently we find that NYOs attract adolescents of the middle and upper social strata. This facilitates their socialization, since by virtue of their social origin such adolescents are receptive to citizenship and partisan roles. Israeli youth movements, for example, are known to attract adolescents whose parents attained higher education and prestigious occupations. For years they have fulfilled the role of reproducers of social elites in Israel (Shapira et al., 1979; Shapira & Peleg, 1984). Even today, while the importance of this role is diminishing, its traces are found in the lower-status development towns. In these relatively new towns, built by Oriental immigrants, the movements mainly attract children of the local elites (Shapira, 1986). Similarly, the Young Pioneers of Malawi have concentrated their recruitment efforts among the tribes affiliated with the political elite. The Costa Rican MNJ, as already noted, mainly attracts the selective sector of high school students.

Yet, national youth organizations also attract marginal social groups, which strive for social mobility and are therefore receptive to organizational socialization. Eisenstadt (1956) considered youth organizations to provide an answer to status anxiety during adolescence. Following this notion, Ben David (1954) found that membership in Israeli youth movements was related to inconsistencies in the components of parents' status. It has also been found that the offspring of ethnic intermarriages in Israel (children whose parents are of Ashkenazi and Oriental origins) show a high tendency of joining youth movements, probably because of their unclear ethnic status (Yogev & Jamshy, 1983). Similarly, members of the Costa Rican MNJ were found to have an inconsistent status of origin more often than the nonparticipating students, while intercorrelations among the status components of their parents (education, income, and occupational prestige) were much lower (Yogev, 1980). All these findings coincide with the thesis of status anxiety, which causes adolescents of marginal or uncrystallized status to seek an alternative or a compensatory status framework in the youth organization.

It is, therefore, a combination of factors that enhances the functioning of national youth organizations in less-developed countries with respect to citizenship socialization. By virtue of these, we can explain how separate organizations, which differ in their specific operational patterns, are all successful in inculcating citizenship orientations of one form or another.

## CONCLUSION

At the end of his review of the literature on youth groups, La Belle (1981) stated,

> We know very little, for example, about the kinds of things that we take for granted when we talk about school, like who are the actors, what is the scope of their relationship and on what does the nonformal education process focus. We also know little about how nonformal education contributes to child development, its relationship to family socialization, or its effects on values. [p. 23]

This chapter has attempted to shed some light on one socialization dimension of national youth organizations. We have shown that practically all these organizations inculcate a diffuse regime support, but they differ in their emphasis on ideological commitment versus the socialization toward active citizenship. This difference enables us, first, to distinguish between types of NYOs, mainly the political and the apolitical ones. Examining the social determinants of each of the two types of socialization patterns may also enable reaching some conclusions regarding the manipulation of these processes.

In general, the socialization for ideological commitment is determined by general organizational variables, that is, the political affiliation of the organization, its specific ideology or political extremism, and the types of activities it sponsors. The more particular internal processes regarding the participants — such as the extent of their activity involvement, their length of membership, and whether they attain leadership positions — are irrelevant to their consequent political and ideological commitments. In contrast, the success of socialization toward participatory citizenship, in the organizations that emphasize it, largely depends on these microsociological participation variables.

Hence, we may conclude that specific ideological socialization is, in a way, an easier task than socialization toward participatory citizenship, since its ultimate success rests on the manipulation of the organizational structure, rather than the individual members. The larger world of politics and the commitment invariably required of the participants will do the rest. On the other hand, in order to succeed with citizenship socialization, the organization must invest in its members. It must develop attractive activities that may intensify their involvement and lengthen their membership period, as well as create opportunities for the advancement of capable members to leadership positions in their local clubs and higher up in the organizational hierarchy. The need to pay attention to individual members makes the socialization for participatory citizenship a difficult task, even for these informal organizations.

National youth organizations, as well as other systems of informal education, have been viewed as potential agents of social change. While the school system of various less-developed countries has been criticized for being too selective, rigidly structured, and meritocratic, programs of informal education have been praised for their flexibility and responsiveness to clientele needs (Coombs, 1976; Grandstaff, 1976). Though NYOs reach only some segments of the adolescent population, certainly more limited sectors than those attending school, it is the nature of the population they reach that matters. Adolescents of established social origins or those striving for social mobility are attracted to these organizations. It is perhaps for this reason that the role of NYOs in citizenship socialization is important, and their potential impact on future citizenship perceptions in less-developed countries may be significant.

## REFERENCES

Ben David, J. (1954). Membership in youth movements and social status [in Hebrew]. *Megamot, 5*, 227–247.

Bock, J. C. (1976). The institutionalization of nonformal education: A response to conflicting needs. *Comparative Education Review, 20*, 346–367.

Braungart, R. G. (1984a). Historical generations and generation units: A global pattern of youth movements. *Journal of Political and Military Sociology, 12*, 113–135.

Braungart, R. G. (1984b). Historical generations and youth movements: A theoretical perspective. In R. E. Ratcliff (Ed.), *Research in social movements: Conflict and change* (pp. 95–141). Greenwich, CT: JAI Press.

Cantril, H. (1965). *The pattern of human concerns.* New Brunswick, NJ: Rutgers University Press.

Coombs, P. H. (1976). Nonformal education: Myths, realities and opportunities. *Comparative Education Review, 20*, 281–293.

Eisenstadt, S. N. (1956). *From generation to generation.* New York: Free Press.

Goffman, E. (1961). On the characteristics of total institutions. In A. Etzioni (Ed.), *Complex organizations: A sociological reader* (pp. 312–340). New York: Holt, Rinehart and Winston.

Grandstaff, M. (1976). Nonformal education: Some implications for use. *Comparative Education Review, 20*, 294–304.

Ichilov, O. (1977). Youth movements in Israel as agents for transition to adulthood. *The Jewish Journal of Sociology, 19*, 21–32.

Ichilov, O., Hyman, F., & Shapira, R. (1988). Social and moral integration of adolescents in an urban neighborhood and their attitudes toward emigration from Israel [in Hebrew]. *Studies in Education, 48*, 69–82.

Inkeles, A. (1983). *Exploring individual modernity.* New York: Columbia University Press.

Inkeles, A., & Smith, D. H. (1974). *Becoming modern: Individual change in six developing countries.* Cambridge, MA: Harvard University Press.

Ivory Coast Government. (no date). *Le Service Civique Ivoirien.* Abidjan: Ministère des Forces Armées du Service Civique.

Kahane, R. (1975). Informal youth organizations: A general model. *Sociological Inquiry, 45*, 17–28.

La Belle, T. J. (1981). An introduction to the nonformal education of children and youth. *Comparative Education Review, 25*, 313–329.

La Belle, T. J., & Verhine, R. E. (1975). Nonformal education and occupational stratification: Implications for Latin America. *Harvard Educational Review, 45*, 160–190.

Levi, S., & Guttman, L. (1976). *Values and attitudes of Israeli high school youth.* Jerusalem: The Institute of Applied Social Research.

Malawi Government. (no date). *Youth in Malawi.* Blantyre: Department of Information and Malawi Young Pioneers' Headquarters.

Shapira, R. (1986). Role of youth movement, community center and IDF workshop as integrating and differentiating factors in a development town [in Hebrew]. *Studies in Education, 43–44*, 119–135.

Shapira, R., Adler, C., Lerner, M., & Peleg, R. (1979). *Blue shirt and white collar* [in Hebrew]. Tel Aviv: Am Oved.

Shapira, R., & Etzioni, E. (1970). "Individual" and "collective" values of Israeli students: The impact of youth movements. *The Jewish Journal of Sociology, 12*, 165–179.

Shapira, R., & Etzioni, E. (1973). *Who is the Israeli student?* [in Hebrew]. Tel Aviv: Am Oved.

Shapira, R., & Peleg, R. (1984). From blue shirt to white collar. *Youth and Society, 16,* 195–216.

Yogev, A. (1980). Modernity and aspirations: Youth organizations in the Third World. *Comparative Education Review, 24,* 353–370.

Yogev, A. (1987). Modernity and ethnic affiliation in Israeli schools: A dependence approach. *Ethnic and Racial Studies, 10,* 203–223.

Yogev, A., & Jamshy, H. (1983). Children of ethnic intermarriage in Israeli schools: Are they marginal? *Journal of Marriage and the Family, 45,* 965–974.

Yogev, A., & Shapira, R. (1982). African rural youth organizations: Goal assessment by photographic survey. *International Journal of Comparative Sociology, 23,* 242–249.

Yogev, A., Shapira, R., & Tibon, S. (1982). Political socialization in an African national youth movement. *International Journal of Political Education, 5,* 211–223.

# 11

## Informal Youth Movements and the Generation of Democratic Experience: An Israeli Example

REUVEN KAHANE
TAMAR RAPOPORT

Despite unstable security conditions, a wide variety of political sub-cultures (some of which lack a democratic tradition), and a polarization of attitudes over basic societal issues, Israeli society has been able to maintain its democratic system over its 40 years of existence. Both decision-making and electoral processes have remained faithful to democratic ideals. Even highly controversial decisions (such as those made in the wake of the Camp David agreement between Egypt and Israel) have not shaken the democratic culture. The support expressed by Israelis for democratic principles has been rooted in a social structure composed of many competing voluntary associations and informal agencies representing a wide variety of interests; even new immigrants and the non–Jewish sector of the population have gradually received greater political representation and have demonstrated active participation (Arian, 1985).

Against this background of strong democratic commitment, there has been a noticeable deterioration in democratic values and behavior in recent years. In the last decade Israeli society has witnessed a proliferation of signs indicating a degree of withdrawal from democratic ideas and a partial rejection of democratic institutions, by certain marginal population sectors. This has been expressed, for example, by the rise of social movements that officially advocate antidemocratic orientations (e.g., the extremist Kach movement led by Rabbi Kahane). There has been a tendency to hold the democratic system responsible for the inefficiency, mediocrity, and corruption that have recently become salient in the country's major

The authors wish to thank the National Council of Jewish Women's Research Institute for Innovation in Education, the Hebrew University of Jerusalem, for its support. We also express our gratitude to Eyal Ben-Ari and Israelit Rubinstein for their comments on an earlier version of this paper and to Helene Hogri for her outstanding editorial assistance.

political and economic institutions (Kahane, 1985). Furthermore, members of nationalist and of fundamentalist religious sectors have exhibited an increasing inclination to believe blindly in "supernatural" powers (Aran, 1986) or in prominent religious, military, and nationalistic figures as substitutes for democratic political institutions.

Most recent surveys on the political values of Jewish Israeli youth have revealed a diverging pattern of attitudes. On the one hand, there is still strong support (about 80%) for the priority of democratic values and their importance to Israeli society, and the large majority of youth express a personal commitment to these values. On the other hand, youth tend to apply democracy differentially to Jews and Arabs (Ichilov, Bar-Tal, & Mazawi, in press), as they consider the latter a threat to the very existence of the State of Israel (Zemach & Zin, 1984). This is a typical example of an objective condition that brings people to accept nondemocratic ideas as unavoidable; in essence, this places the whole issue of commitment to democracy on trial.

It is also important to note that the minority of youth who hold antidemocratic views is growing. In a relatively recent attitudinal survey of high school students, Zemach and Zin (1984) found that about 25 percent expressed antidemocratic opinions, while another 40 percent expressed inconsistent views; only one-third of the students interviewed consistently espoused democratic viewpoints. Research on the political values of elementary and high school students (Ichilov et al., in press) obtained similar results; one-quarter of the subjects did not see democracy as an adequate pattern of regime in Israel. More recent surveys indicate that about one-third of Israel's youth support Kahanism and other nondemocratic movements (*Davar*, November 15, 1987) and that one-quarter would like to see a strong, charismatic figure leading the government (*Davar*, December 7, 1987).

This partial alienation of some Israeli youth from democratic principles and ground rules has generally been attributed to broad sociopolitical conditions, such as the continuous security threat, slow economic development, and widespread governmental and bureaucratic rigidity, as well as to the political background of Israel's largely immigrant population, many of whom are originally from Eastern European and Arab countries lacking in a civic democratic tradition. In addition, the traumatic history of the Jewish people in the Diaspora, particularly their experiences under Nazi Germany, together with a lifetime of terrorism and recurrent wars in Israel, have evoked individual and collective anxieties that may have fostered nondemocratic trends and a longing for a dominant leader and a strong regime (Adler & Kahane, 1984).

Without denying the explanatory power of the foregoing factors, which have been said to contribute to antidemocratic trends, we nevertheless claim that they are insufficient to explain Israel's recent weakening of support for democracy. The mere aggregation and accentuation of sociopolitical and economic strains, some of which have existed since the beginning of Zionist settlement almost a century ago (Horowitz & Lissak, 1978), and most of which have been present since the establishment of the state, cannot in itself explain the differential intensification of antidemocratic orientations among certain sectors of Israeli society and certain groups of Israeli youth over the past decade. Indeed, these very conditions can be seen as the results of antidemocratic trends rather than their cause. Furthermore, it seems more to the point to question how the strong democratic culture characteristic of the society since prestate times has survived despite these very strains.

It is our contention that part of the answer can be found in the voluntary nature of the society and in the structure of social mechanisms designed to counter or institutionalize these tensions and anxieties. More specifically, it may be suggested that, alongside the social conditions that foster the weakening of democratic commitment, there has been a diminishing of the impact of socialization agencies that once nurtured democratic values and countered antidemocratic trends. Along these lines, we present the case of the Israeli youth movement, an informal voluntary youth association which, to greater and lesser degrees, has fostered democratic commitment and has offset antidemocratic orientations. There is evidence, for example, that until the end of the 1960s members of youth movements demonstrated stronger commitments to an open political culture and democracy than nonmembers (e.g., Adler, 1962; Ichilov, 1977). This trend is revealed in both their official literature and their daily activities, including a propensity to participate in protest movements, demonstrations, and public debates. Members also exhibited a greater sensitivity to issues of justice and fairness, especially under conditions of war. This is expressed, for example, in the arguments raised by veteran youth movement members in *Siah Lohamim* (Discourse of Warriors, 1968), one of the postwar books (published after the 1967 war) that discusses the problems of maintaining humanitarian and democratic values under battle conditions. (For an analysis of the impact of war situations on democratic ideals and behavior, see Creighton & Shaw, 1987; Kimmerling, 1985; Sorokin, 1928.) In recent years, however, the differences in such attitudes between youth movement members and nonmembers have diminished (Shapira, Adler, Lerner, & Peleg, 1979).

While most research has implicitly or explicitly assumed that democratic values are embodied in the youth movement, it has not specified the precise characteristics of this socialization agency which explain the intensity of its impact upon democratic values and behaviors. What is it, then, about the structure of youth movements (and other informal associations) in pre- and poststate Israel which renders them capable of generating commitment to democratic values, and which conversely has engendered their declining impact in recent years? The following discussion of the informal principles that characterize these movements attempts to provide some answers. First, however, we anchor this discussion within the broader context of political socialization.

## THE POLITICAL SOCIALIZATION OF YOUTH

The centrality of adolescence in shaping political values and behavior has long been recognized. Scholars have shown that moral, egalitarian, pluralistic, and universalistic values and orientations are acquired and consolidated during this period (Adelson & O'Neil, 1966; Danis, 1973; Inhelder & Piaget, 1958; Kohlberg, 1969). There is also research indicating that sociopolitical and educational settings affect the growth of political attitudes and activism among youth (Easton & Dennis, 1969; Ichilov, 1984; Jennings & Niemi, 1974; Sigel & Hoskin, 1981; Stevens, 1982). Though based on different and sometimes contradictory theoretical frameworks, these approaches share the assumption that democratic behavior can be either discouraged or fostered in a given socialization agency.

According to Merelman (1986), who recently elaborated upon a wealth of theories on political socialization, most scholars agree that differential experiences in different socialization agencies largely affect the political behavior, culture, and attitudes of youth, fostering either authoritarian or democratic orientations. For example, several studies seem to imply that socialization agencies based on peer relationships are more likely to enhance a sense of universal justice, morality, and commitment to democracy (Baumrind, 1968; Enright et al., 1984; Silbiger, 1977; Youniss, 1980), while agencies based on formal, strict discipline discourage and hinder the development of democratic ideas and a commitment to universal values (Adorno, Frenkel-Brunswik, Levinson, & Sanford, 1950; Danis, 1973; Renshon, 1977; Rokeach, 1960). In contrast, Charles Merriam, in *The Making of Citizens* (1931), assumed that the school is a "major instrument in the shaping of civic education" (quoted in Prewitt, 1971, p. x). He argued that, unlike the tribe or the family, the school commands individual attention for long hours over many years; hence, it may raise or extend a universal sense of citizenship. Merriam (1931), as well as newer research (e.g., Hess, 1968) do not, however, specify the kind of school that has such an impact or the factors underlying its ability to develop concepts of citizenship.

From a different vantage point, Gutmann (1987) defines democratic education as a "virtue" consisting of "the ability to deliberate and hence to participate in conscious social reproduction" and suggests that the principles of such a virtue "are compatible with our commitment to share the rights and obligations of citizenship with people who do not share our complete conception of the good life" (pp. 46–47). We suggest that only socialization agencies that enable children to participate in decision-making processes can promote a democratic "virtue." Furthermore, Gutmann views "protective discrimination" for youth (i.e., preferential treatment beyond their official rights aimed at compensating youth for their disadvantage) as a necessary condition for their democratic participation (p. 213). It is our view, however, that this kind of artificial equalization can hardly generate democratic "virtue" in the long run. Rather, the treatment of nonequals as equals can emerge only within institutionalized informal settings.

On the macrosocietal level, while there is wide research on democratic political culture and regimes (see Alford & Friedland, 1985; Almond & Verba, 1963), little is known about the precise characteristics of the agencies that generate such systems. Furthermore, many of the classical studies mentioned earlier are often tautological in that they argue that democratic agencies generate democratic attitudes (White & Lippitt, 1960). New research in the same direction has hardly corrected this bias (Smith, 1975; Smith & Berg, 1987).

It is our contention that it is not the agencies per se (e.g., family or school) that determine the experience, but rather their structure, a concept that incorporates three interdependent senses: (1) a pattern of relations between units of the same universe, (2) conditions influencing the boundaries and direction of human action, and (3) a symbolic framework ascribing social or individual significance to an action or relationship (see Boudon, 1971). In other words, the peer group, family, school, and university may all have different structural patterns generating different political experiences, and it is useful to analyze them in terms of their endogenous structure. More specifically, we argue that democratic values have a greater tendency to develop in socialization agencies characterized by an informal structure or code.

## CONCEPTUAL FRAMEWORK: THE INFORMAL CODE

The experience gained in a given socialization agency can be largely explained by its *code*, which has been defined as "a system of explicit social conventions" by which "an assimilation of the unknown to the known is made" (Guirond, 1975, pp. 41, 61). Parsons (1967) referred to the concept of code as an elementary set of rules that constitute concrete norms and behavior in three senses: by giving them meaning, by providing a measure of value, and as a medium of exchange (see also Rossi, 1983). Bernstein (1975), emphasizing the constitutive interactive uses of *code*, conceives it as a principle embodying a transformation of signals (i.e., their encoding, decoding, and integration) and views different codes as dictating different kinds of behavioral regulations. In this chapter, we will use the term *code* to mean a set of generalized principles that constitute the meaning or patterning of activity and can be converted or articulated in different contexts and modifications. The advantage of this concept of code lies in its providing a flexible tool by which different kinds of social phenomena gain equivalency and can be related theoretically to one another.

The informal code, which underlies informal organizations, can be said to encompass the following eight basic components, derived from research on youth associations (see Adler, 1962; Eisenstadt, 1971; Ichilov, 1977; Kahane, 1975).

1. *Voluntarism* refers to a relatively constraint-free choice of goals, means, and affiliations by participants based on (1) the existence of several alternatives from which to choose, (2) the possibility of freely revising choices in accordance with new desires or interests, and (3) the attachment of minimal cost or risk to any shift in choice or change in desires. The greater the voluntarism, the stronger the participants' bargaining power and sense of freedom, and, in turn, the greater the value commitment.

2. *Multiplexity* denotes a wide range of available activities that are different in substance yet equivalent in social value or importance (e.g., studies, dance, sports, camping, games, parties). Such an opportunity structure underlies a pattern of division of labor by which individual actors have the opportunity to express their interests and talents differentially and to aggregate power and prestige. Thus, multiplexity fosters a sense of self-worth and tolerance to pluralism, enhancing the likelihood that an "organic" pattern of exchange will develop (see Durkheim, 1949).

3. *Symmetrical* relationships are based on participants possessing fairly equivalent resources and consequently tending to accommodate mutually their expectations and criteria of evaluation. Because persons in such a relationship cannot impose their own terms on others — as opposed to a nonsymmetrical relationship, where the weaker party accepts the terms of the stronger one, for lack of a better choice — consensus can only be reached through the assumption of universalistic principles of behavior. In other words, under conditions of symmetry the terms of social exchange

will be agreed upon only when there is mutual consent as to the equivalency values of the commodities exchanged and mutual benefits accruing to the parties involved. This equivalency is possible when there are universal values in Kantian terms. As he put it, "Act as if the maxim of your action were to become through your will a universal law of nature" (Kant, 1785/1964, p. 89). These universal values underlie the development of the personal trust or noncontractual elements needed for any social relationship (Durkheim, 1949).

4. *Dualism* refers to the coexistence of different and even contradictory orientations, such as ascription and achievement, collectivism and individualism. It often emerges under conditions of liminality, when actors are between or within the subsystems or stages of life. A dual structure provides a legitimate setting in which actors experience different and sometimes contradictory norms; in turn, this teaches them to consider and tolerate opposing viewpoints.

5. *Moratorium* refers to an arrangement in which ordinary social obligations are delayed and a temporary deviation from commonly accepted norms is considered legitimate (Erikson, 1955). Under such conditions, experimentation with a variety of rules and roles takes place within a peer-supervised setting which ensures the minimalization of sanctions. Moratorium provides legitimate opportunities to try out different kinds of norms before any enduring commitment is made. Paradoxically, by widening the scope of behavior to include deviation, moratorium creates conditions for learning normative behavior. It is the move from nonnormative to normative that underlies the formation of personal and responsible civic identity.

6. *Modularity* denotes an ad hoc organizational pattern in which social units are flexibly arranged in clusters according to changing circumstances and interests. A framework is modular in the sense that it is composed of a number of units (i.e., activities), with varying degrees of autonomy, which are interchangeable and can be clustered in many ways (in different proportions and profiles). Each activity can be performed independently or in relation to others, in different orders, simultaneously or consecutively, in different locations, and under different circumstances. Modularity enables actors to learn to adjust their expectations to reality and to reach a compromise between their own interests and those of different groups.

7. *Expressive instrumentalism* refers to a framework of activities performed both for their own sake and as a means of achieving future ends. In other words, activities are oriented simultaneously toward immediate rewards and future gains. This combination links instantaneous satisfaction

with postponement of gratification, and it increases the ability to cope with situations involving frustration and to pursue long-range tasks. It also enhances the attractiveness of activities and diminishes role differentiation (Bales, 1950). Consequently, the authority structure tends to be diffuse — that is, based on a wide variety of principles — and relatively egalitarian.

8. *Pragmatic symbolism* is a frame of reference in which symbols are converted into deeds or deeds are ascribed a symbolic significance. This extends the meaning of activities and makes them objects for identification. Because young actors in informal socialization agencies and activities do not need to assume full responsibility for their deeds, they can afford to reduce the gap between reality and symbols. As a result, the whole concept of legitimacy gains pragmatic significance.

The impact of these eight elements lies mainly in their grouping together within the informal context. They complement and supplement one another, together enhancing democratic principles of equality, tolerance, and pluralism. Thus, symmetry encourages consideration of the interests and expectations of others and generates balanced reciprocal patterns of relations. Multiplexity and modularity enhance symmetry and offer a context for the provision of equal opportunities, pluralism, and tolerance. Moratorium provides a context in which youngsters can test their beliefs, while dualism allows them to experience norms characterizing different sectors and groups. Finally, pragmatic symbolism ensures that values will be translated into actual roles and participatory citizenship. More generally, informal agencies of socialization provide young people with an open arena in which they can examine their beliefs and interests and can compete and negotiate with one another freely. In this lies their potential to generate democratic values.

Yet, at the same time, the informal agency contains the potential to be transformed into an anarchistic, sect-like, or formal "oligarchic" organization. In other words, its very structural looseness makes it a setting in which contradictory values and patterns of regime can be experienced. Whether or not such a transformation will take place depends on both the intensity of the informal code in a given agency and the severity of societal strains and social problems, a topic which is beyond the scope of the present discussion. Of pertinence to our argument is that such a transformation into less-informal organizations changes their meaning and impact, reducing their ability to generate democratic values and to function as mediatory bodies among the individual, the society, and the state. We shall return to this point after considering the case study of the Israeli youth movement.

## THE CASE OF THE ISRAELI YOUTH MOVEMENT

### The Informal Code in Operation

Youth movements in Israel developed out of the Scouts movement in Britain, the Wanderfogel in Germany, and the Zionist movements established in the Diaspora at the turn of the century. They emerged within a prestate society that, from its very beginnings, was organized into voluntary associations, most of which were based on informal relationships (Eisenstadt, 1967; Horowitz & Lissak, 1978). Socialization agencies at that time, including the family and the school, were largely based on the informal code; as such, they provided the prestate Jewish community with a sense of order, on the one hand, and a sense of freedom, on the other. The former was necessary in order for the community to cope efficiently with heavy economic and security pressures, while the latter was needed to mobilize the commitments of members and to acquire legitimation for the agency.

Of the socialization agencies in prestate Israel, the youth movement was perhaps the most central and influential one (Adler, 1962). Indeed, veterans of most of them, who were members prior to the 1970s, have been characterized by a deep commitment to the concepts of freedom and democracy and a sense of public responsibility and justice based on egalitarian and equity approaches (Lotan, 1974). While these qualities have generally been at least partially attributed to their socialization experiences in the youth movement, little study has been devoted to an explanation of the process through which such democratic values were acquired.

We attempt to explain this process by relating the informal code just outlined to the structure of Israeli youth movements, focusing on their basic institutions, activities, roles, networks, and curricula. It should be kept in mind that this description is of a general nature, covering the common traits of Israel's seven major youth movements until the 1960s (divided into left-wing, right-wing, religious, and neutral, nonaffiliated blocs), which today include about 35 percent of Israeli youth between the ages of 11 and 18. To avoid confusion, the description is worded in the present tense, although it should be kept in mind that many of the features of these movements have eroded in recent years.

Israeli youth movements have been semiautonomous agencies which have dealt mainly with noninstrumental spheres of life (Adler, 1962; Eisenstadt, 1971; Ichilov, 1977; Shapira et al., 1979). They have been constructed as minisocietal systems in which youth can experiment with both immature and mature behavioral patterns and roles in a relatively constraint-free, voluntary setting. This system has operated through three basic kinds of institutions. First is the movement's general assembly, which is based on the full participation of local branch members or their elected representatives; it generally operates as a decision-making body regarding both collective and personal issues. Second are the local functional committees, such as the secretariat or cultural committee, which are responsible for promoting or accomplishing a particular task or activity. Third is the local quasijudiciary committee, which is involved in conflict resolution and deals with ongoing disciplinary issues. All of these bodies are based on the principle of election and of member rotation between and within them. This rotation has largely prevented crystallization of vested interests and has contributed to the flexibility of these institutions.

Each age group and cohort has virtually equal representation in these three institutions, but the older members (most of whom serve as youth leaders of the younger members) and the few young adults who supervise the older members have a senior status and a greater say in the management of the system. Because of the negotiable power of all members, however, leaders must employ persuasion (rather than coercion) to gain the right to intervene and guide other members and must couch their decisions in universalistic (rather than particularistic) terms. Furthermore, the legitimacy of any authority in the movement is perpetually subject to doubt and reexamination and has to be repeatedly affirmed. Under these conditions, authority is rarely taken for granted, either by those holding it or by those who are subject to it.

Whereas the youth movement's institutions are based on a structure that approximates symmetry and equality, their activities may be said to be multiplex. Thus, there is little difference in social value and prestige ascribed to the different activities (e.g., political discussions, partying, cultural activities, sports) that take place, and participation in each is of a similar importance. Consequently, stratification of members is rather weak and uncrystallized. Just as they rotate among positions in movement committees, members alternate among activities, thereby leading to rotation in status and to the trying of different types of roles (e.g., between those based on gamelike behaviors and those involving responsible, serious decision making). Thus, in one context, a member may act as a patron and sometimes as a leader, while in another she or he may serve as a client or follower. In this way, members experience both superior and inferior statuses.

The movement's social networks are intricately composed of three overlapping layers of relationships: those among members, generally of the same age or grade; those between young members and their youth leader; and those between all members and adult figures of authority (including young adult leaders aged 18 to 23, who serve as leaders of the senior members and as advisors of the youth leaders). The interaction among these networks, which sometimes runs to antagonism, increases the negotiating power of participants, thereby enhancing their sense of freedom.

The first network is primarily based on symmetrical peer relationships among equals and on a combination of spontaneity and rigid norms, both of which are articulated within the institutional framework of the committees described earlier. In this network, authority is minimized and thus relationships within it can easily fall prey to anomie or arbitrary group pressures and compulsions.

The network of relations between members and youth leaders is somewhat less symmetrical than that among members and incorporates both equality and inequality. In this respect, it should be noted that a large proportion of members become youth leaders at one time or another and for varying periods of time. Essentially, the youth leader operates as an intermediary between members and adults (including the young adult leaders). Owing to the complex nature of this network, we treat it in some detail.

The youth leader undergoes special "soft" training, combining improvisational and semiprofessional elements. This training, which takes place both before and after assumption of the leadership position, teaches "instant" psychology and various ideologies in an eclectic and vague way. It aims at maintaining spontaneity, or at least at not suppressing it. Most of the training is based on trial and error and is geared toward a participatory ethos, which is aptly described in the following translation of a song that was composed spontaneously one evening by a group of Scout youth leaders:

> To sleep last, to wake first,
> And to every member who comes to talk a little nonsense,
> To say, "Come in."
> To maintain the morale, to raise one's head high,
> To always be polite.
> We can't complain, because the kids are listening.
>
> To answer every query,
> To be a superior being,
> To tolerate the member who errs for the millionth time.
> To sing when you want to cry,
> To keep on running when you've had enough,
> To give an explanation instead of a beating,
> To let them fool around.
>
> To check that each member's uniform is in order,
> To always be pure,
> To be just, to be honest,

Even if the heart is black.
When there is room for improvement
To say, "Don't be disrespectful,"
Instead of, "You've made a mess of it, kids— go to hell."

Owing to the voluntaristic participation of members, youth leaders cannot impose desired behavior, but rather have to persuade their charges that such behavior is in accordance with the best public interest. Thus, their moral authority is not based on resources of exchange such as arbitrary power, but rather on influence and value commitment, to use Parsons's (1967, 1968) terminology. In that sense, they are on equal footing with members and act as friends rather than as patrons or parental figures; they serve as exemplary models, doing things first and asking members to follow. In short, the youth leaders learn to minimize intervention and to act as arbitrators rather than commanders.

Not only are influence and value commitment the media of exchange, but youth leaders also rarely base their leadership solely on their charismatic appeal. Rather, they combine personal charisma with the authority of their office and with the movement's "great" universal values. Thus, the relationships with members are crystallized in an implicit quasicontractual agreement based on both a power balance between the two parties and on universal moral laws. This agreement emerges through a dialectical process. In the first stage, both parties exert their power over the other; in the second, a degree of equilibrium is established; finally, a state of balanced reciprocity, based on universal laws, is reached (after Sahlins, 1972; also see Aguilar, 1984; Laumann, 1979). Such a balance is arranged in "package deals" in which goods are exchanged in sets rather than as separate entities.

In both of the networks just described, there are transactions, negotiations, and even struggles that operate as mechanisms shaping a specific pattern of behavior and exchange. While the exchange relationship is characterized by division along age lines— older members, by virtue of their seniority, having greater power than younger ones— there is no such clearcut division in terms of prestige. Status is gained mainly by the performance of "extra" obligations and services and on the basis of fair and honest behavior rather than through popularity, achievement, or official position. Thus, authority is often defined in terms of extra duties rather than privileges. Furthermore, it is not merely the assumption of duties that generates status, but also the manner in which duty is assumed. Thus, the would-be youth leader first has to manifest disinterest in gaining authority and must refuse outright the offered position several times before being "persuaded" to accept. Such a ritual of refusal substantiates the existence of both a symmetrical and authoritative relationship between members and youth leaders. It gives youth leaders authority and simultaneously makes them highly dependent on member support. In this way, the ritual of refusal enhances status dualism and ambiguous orientations. This dualism, though creating tensions, also increases the ability of members to respond flexibly to changing values and circumstances.

The youth movement also incorporates a social network among members, youth leaders, and adults. This three-way system both enhances and institutionalizes conflicts, as it encompasses a conflict between adult intervention, reflecting societal control of the behavior of youth, and the autonomy of youth inherent to the symmetrical framework of the movement. Consequently, it fosters experiences involving both rebellion and obedience.

The curricula of the youth movement combine values and deeds. The values are often universal and generalizable in the sense that they rest on the basic maxim of doing for your friends what you would wish them to do for you (Kahane & Rapoport, 1984). Equally important, members are required to put ideas into practice. Thus, abstract values of justice, freedom, and equality are realized in the movement's daily activities and in voluntary work on the kibbutz.

The movement's socialization process involves a value-added pattern of training. Initially junior members (about 11 years old) are exposed, in various ways, to the movement's basic social ideas, which are related to such universal values as justice, equality, and freedom. Having begun to internalize these values, more experienced members are then involved in simulations in which they test and realize their commitments within a group setting, either in the local branch meetings or while in an external setting, such as work on a kibbutz. Only after such experiences are members allowed to participate in actual tasks. This gradual exposure to social responsibilities serves as a training ground for the undertaking of civic obligations.

In general, the networks, institutions, roles, and curricula of the Israeli youth movements have been based on the informal code. Consequently, they have enabled members and youth leaders of different ages to experience a balanced mutual relationship, to take the interests of others into account, and, in general, to act in a nonarbitrary, institutional way in accordance with legitimate rules. This very structure has served to mitigate anxieties on the individual and collective levels and has allowed the youth movement to function as a framework in which the interests of youth are expressed. More pertinent to the present topic of discussion, the informal

qualities of the youth movements (and, indeed, all other voluntary associations) in Israel have enabled the promotion of democratic values and behavior; at least, such was the case up to the early 1960s, when a significant
change in the youth movement structure—and, soon after, in the democratic orientation of Israeli youth—first became noticeable.

## The Transformation and Decline of Informality

In recent years, Israel has witnessed a degree of structural change and
deterioration of the informal code in both youth movements and other
voluntary associations. The following discussion refers specifically to our
case of the youth movement, but it can be extended to the other voluntary
associations as well.

Owing to a lack of hard data, one may tentatively distinguish three
basic patterns of transformation in the structure of Israeli youth movements. First, at the local level, there is a decline in the intensity and
meaning of the informal code. For example, during such activities as ex-
cursions or dances, there is evidence of routinization and increased adult
and professional intervention. In other words, moratorium is lessened in
order to minimize the risks involved. The reduced intensity of the informal
code diminishes the impact of the youth movement in general and of those
spheres of learning that have been idiosyncratic to it—democratic experience, in particular—and has probably increased the inclination of members to rely on formal legality.

A second pattern of transformation is evident in certain branches of
religious youth movements. This entails their shift toward sectlike organizations, involving not only reduced informality but also selective replacement by near-total obedience, exclusivity, self-identification, segregation,
and commitment to transcendental symbols (Wallis, 1975; Wilson, 1970).
Such youth movements emphasize primary relationships and employ group
pressures to enforce their ideologies and patterns of behavior. As a result of
the decline of informal experience, members are more likely to express
commitment to authoritarian figures and regimes.

Finally, certain youth movements have exhibited a tendency to transform informality into a nihilistic framework. Thus, moratorium, for example, has been transformed into permissiveness (i.e., boundless behavior);
oversymmetry has destroyed the authority structure; and multiplexity has
been transformed into endless choice opportunities with little preference
assigned to any given choice. Consequently, veterans often identify democracy with anarchy.

Regardless of the direction of change in the youth movements, the
weakening of informality has created a situation that not only greatly

reduces their unique impact, including their tendency to foster democratic values and behavior, but also makes one question their usefulness to youth and to society. For the loss of some of their unique characteristics has made youth movements relatively similar to schools in some respects and to entertainment agencies in others. In either case, this resemblance has greatly reduced their attractiveness and impact. In general terms, the overall decline in informality and in the idiosyncracy of the volunteer sector seems to have partially diminished the capacity of Israeli society to cope with its problems and strains and to develop its democratic institutions.

While the causes underlying the decline in informality and in voluntary associations are beyond the scope of this chapter, three basic factors can be briefly outlined. First, the resources controlled by the Israeli political elites have enabled them to strengthen bureaucratic bodies at the expense of voluntary associations, which threaten the elites' monopoly. Second, increasing social complexity and the growing demand for scientific knowledge have increased the importance of the school system, which over the last two decades has become increasingly professionalized and has adopted a narrower curriculum oriented more toward particularistic elements of the Jewish tradition (Kahane, 1988). This has reduced the attractiveness of informal socialization agencies. Third, in a narrower sense, the transformation of the youth movements in Israel may be related to an increasing tendency of adults to control children. This has not only reduced informality but has also often created overconformity or a counterresponse among youth that sometimes borders on anomie and deviancy, trends that are essentially two sides of the same coin.

In sum, the structural transformation of the Israeli youth movement has changed its potential to promote democratic commitment and to counter individual and societal strains that enhance nondemocratic trends. It should be noted that the extent to which these changes occur on the local level of youth movements is unknown and in need of investigation.


## CONCLUSION

It has been our contention that it is the very informal structure of Israeli youth movements that has generated civic democratic experience among members; moreover, it has been their transformation into less-informal or formal structures that has reduced such impact. This thesis is supported in a brief historical comparison with other youth movements (see Braungart, 1984). For example, the German Wanderfogel was constructed according to a loose informal code combined with strong sentimental and romantic principles, such as a pantheistic love of nature, a mystical love for the fatherland, a perception of the movement as existing for its own sake, an integration of all spheres of life, and rhetoric of oversymbolization (Gay, 1968). This combination of code and principles probably accounts for its failure to develop democratic beliefs and permitted its easy transformation into the fascist Hitler Youth (Satachura, 1975). In contrast, the Soviet Komsomol has been based on informal principles of weak intensity combined with formal and primary pressures, and this, too, has failed to generate democratic experience (Kassof, 1965). Finally, the British Scouts movement has been based on consistent informal principles of a strong intensity and has thereby been able to foster a civic democratic experience (Springhall, 1976).

As mentioned earlier, the youth movements are but an example and may be said to represent other voluntary associations and socialization agencies constructed according to the informal code. Indeed, the connection between voluntary bodies and democracy has long been acknowledged: A century and a half ago, Alexis de Tocqueville (1835/1954) demonstrated that such associations are an essential component for maintaining democracy and countering authoritarian orientations, as they allow people to experience a sense of freedom, provide a channel for the expression of private and public interests, and enable participants to learn the basic universal laws of mutuality.

There are indications that societies lacking informal agencies of socialization and other voluntary associations are less likely to preserve a democratic order, especially under conditions of crisis and rapid change. Such societies have often witnessed waves of fundamentalism and fascism, manifested in growing extremist, antidemocratic, right- and left-wing attitudes and behavior or, conversely, apathy and anomie. (For the German case, see Gay, 1968; Mosse, 1966; Stern, 1974). Indeed, a democratic social order holds within it the potential for the development of anarchy on the one hand and totalitarianism on the other (Lipset, 1959; Mannheim, 1951; Schumpeter, 1943), and thus requires ongoing socialization mechanisms capable of countering antidemocratic beliefs and behavior. It seems that socialization agencies and other voluntary associations, constructed according to the informal code, provide such mechanisms (inferred from Smith 1975; Tocqueville, 1835/1954; Wolfenden Committee, 1978). Indeed, there are indications that boarding schools that are based on informal principles also provide a useful background for democratic experience (Cookson & Persell, 1985; Kahane, 1988; Walford, 1986). Along these lines, a fuller understanding of the fostering and decline of democratic beliefs and behavior requires a broader cross-cultural perspective (Prewitt, 1971), which takes into consideration the structure of educational institutions, the mass media, age-group and family relationships, and the internal framework of voluntary associations.

## REFERENCES

Adelson, J., & O'Neil, R. (1966). The development of political thought in adolescence: A sense of community. *Journal of Personality and Social Psychology, 4*, 295–308.

Adler, C. (1962). *The youth movement in Israeli society* [in Hebrew]. Jerusalem: Szold Institute.

Adler, C., & Kahane, R. (1984). Introduction to youth in Israel. *Youth and Society, 16*(2), 115–128.

Adorno, T. W., Frenkel-Brunswick, E., Levinson, D. J., & Sanford, R. N. (1950). *The authoritarian personality.* New York: Harper & Row.

Aguilar, J. L. (1984). Trust and exchange. *Ethos, 12*(1), 3–29.

Alford, R. R., & Friedland, R. (1985). *Powers of theory: Capitalism, the state and democracy.* Cambridge, England: Cambridge University Press.

Almond, G. A., & Verba, S. (1963). *The civic culture: Attitudes and democracy in five nations.* Princeton, NJ: Princeton University Press.

Aran, G. (1986). From religious Zionism to Zionist religion: The roots of Gush Emunim. In P. V. Medding (Ed.), *Studies in contemporary Jewry* (pp. 116–143). Bloomington: Indiana University Press.

Arian, A. (1985). *Politics in Israel: The second generation.* Chatham, NJ: Chatham House.

Bales, R. F. (1950). *Interaction process analysis.* Cambridge, MA: Addison-Wesley.

Baumrind, D. (1968). Authoritarian vs. authoritative parental control. *Adolescence, 3*, 255–272.

Bernstein, B. (1975). *Class codes and control* (Vol. 1). London: Routledge & Kegan Paul.

Boudon, R. (1971). *The uses of structuralism.* London: Heinemann.

Braungart, R. G. (1984). Historical generations and youth movements: A theoretical perspective. In R. Ratcliff (Ed.), *Research in social movements: Conflicts and change, Vol. 6* (pp. 95–142). Greenwich, CT: Jai Press.

Cookson, P. W., & Persell, C. H. (1985). *Preparing for power: American elite in boarding schools.* New York: Basic Books.

Creighton, C., & Shaw, M. (Eds.). (1987). *The sociology of war and peace.* London: Macmillan.

Danis, J. (Ed.). (1973). *Socialization to politics.* New York: John Wiley.

Durkheim, E. (1949). *The division of labor in society* (G. Simpson, trans.). Glencoe, IL: Free Press.

Easton, D., & Dennis, J. (1969). *Children in the political system.* New York: McGraw-Hill.

Eisenstadt, S. N. (1967). *Israeli society: Background, development and problems* [in Hebrew]. Jerusalem: Magnes Press.

Eisenstadt, S. N. (1971). *From generation to generation*. New York: Free Press.

Enright, D. R., Bjerstedt, A., Enright, F. W., Levy, M. V., Lapsky, D. K., Buss, R. R., Harwell, M., & Zindler, M. (1984). Distributive justice development: Cross-cultural, contextual, and longitudinal evaluations. *Child Development, 55*, 1737–1751.

Erikson, E. H. (1955). Ego identity and the psychosocial moratorium. In H. L. Witner & R. Kotinsky (Eds.), *New perspectives for research in juvenile delinquency*. Washington, DC: U.S. Department of Health, Education and Welfare.

Gay, P. (1968). *Weimar culture: The outsider as insider*. New York: Harper & Row.

Guirond, P. (1975). *Semiology* (G. Gross, trans.). London: Routledge & Kegan Paul.

Gutmann, A. (1987). *Democratic education*. Princeton, NJ: Princeton University Press.

Hess, R. D. (1968). Political socialization in the schools. *Harvard Educational Review, 38*, 528–535.

Horowitz, D., & Lissak, M. (1978). *Origins of Israeli polity: Palestine under the mandate*. Chicago: University of Chicago Press.

Ichilov, O. (1977). Youth movements in Israel as agents for transition to adulthood. *Jewish Journal of Sociology, 19*(1), 21–33.

Ichilov, O. (1984). *The political world of children and adolescents* [in Hebrew]. Tel Aviv: Yachdav.

Ichilov, O., Bar-Tal, D., & Mazawi, A. (in press). Israeli adolescents' comprehension and evaluation of democracy. *Youth and Society*.

Inhelder, B., & Piaget, J. (1958). *The growth of logical thinking from childhood to adolescence*. New York: Basic Books.

Jennings, M. K., & Niemi, R. C. (1974). *The political character of adolescence*. Princeton, NJ: Princeton University Press.

Kahane, R. (1975). Informal youth organizations: A general model. *Sociological Inquiry, 45*(4), 17–28.

Kahane, R. (Ed.). (1985). *Pattern of corruption in Israel* [in Hebrew]. Jerusalem: Academon.

Kahane, R. (1988). Multi-paradigm institutions: A conceptual framework for the analysis of boarding schools. *Sociology of Education, 61*(4), 211–226.

Kahane, R., & Rapoport, T. (1984). *The Zionist pioneering youth movements: Their rise and transformation* (Preliminary research report submitted to the Konrad Adenauer Foundation). Jerusalem: The Hebrew University.

Kant, I. (1964). *Groundwork for the metaphysics of morals* (H. J. Paton, trans.). New York: Harper Torchbooks. (Original work published 1785)

Kassof, A. (1965). *The Soviet youth program: Regimentation and rebellion*. Cambridge, MA: Harvard University Press.

Kimmerling, B. (1985). *The interrupted system: Israeli civilians in war and routine*. New Brunswick, NJ: Transaction Books.

Kohlberg, L. (1969). Stage and sequence: The cognitive-developmental approach to socialization. In D. A. Goslin (Ed.), *Handbook of socialization theory and research* (pp. 347–480). Chicago: Rand McNally.

Laumann, N. (1979). *Trust and power*. New York: John Wiley.

Lipset, S. M. (1959). Some social requisites of democracy: Economic development and political legitimacy. *American Political Science Review, 53*, 69–105.

Lotan, M. (1974). *The youth movement* [in Hebrew]. Ramat Gan, Israel: Association for Sociological Service.

Mannheim, K. (1951). *Freedom, power and democratic planning*. London: Routledge & Kegan Paul.

Merelman, R. M. (1986). Revitalizing political socialization. In M. G. Hermann (Ed.), *Political psychology* (pp. 279–319). San Francisco: Jossey-Bass.

Merriam, C. E. (1931). *The making of citizens*. Chicago: University of Chicago Press.

Mosse, G. L. (1966). *Nazi culture*. New York: Grossett & Dunlap.

Parsons, T. (1967). *Sociological theory and modern society*. New York: Free Press.

Parsons, T. (1968). On the concept of value commitments. *Sociological Inquiry, 38*, 135–160.

Prewitt, K. (Ed.). (1971). *Education and political values: An East African case study*. Nairobi, Kenya: East African Publishing House.

Renshon, S. A. (Ed.). (1977). *Handbook of political socialization*. New York: Free Press.

Rokeach, M. (1960). *The open and closed mind*. New York: Basic Books.

Rossi, I. (1983). *From the sociology of symbols to the sociology of signs*. New York: Columbia University Press.

Sahlins, M. (1972). *Stone Age economics*. London: Tavistock.

Satachura, P. D. (1975). *Nazi youth in the Weimar Republic*. Santa Barbara, CA: Clio Books.

Schumpeter, J. (1943). *Capitalism, socialism and democracy*. New York: Harper.

Shapira, R., Adler, C., Lerner, M., & Peleg, R. (1979). *Blue shirt and white collar: The social world of youth movement graduates in Israel* [in Hebrew]. Tel Aviv: Am Oved.

*Siah Lohamim* [Discourse of warriors]. (1968). Tel Aviv: privately published.

Sigel, R. S., & Hoskin, M. B. (1981). *The political involvement of adolescents*. New Brunswick, NJ: Rutgers University Press.

Silbiger, S. L. (1977). Peers and political socialization. In S. A. Renshon (Ed.), *Handbook of political socialization* (pp. 172–190). New York: Free Press.

Smith, D. H. (1975). Voluntary action and voluntary groups. *Annual Review of Sociology, 1*, 247–278.

Smith, K. K., & Berg, D. N. (1987). A paradoxical conception of group dynamics. *Human Relations, 40*, 633–658.

Sorokin, P. (1928). Sociological interpretation of the struggle for existence and the sociology of war. In *Contemporary Sociological Theories* (pp. 309–356). New York: Harper.

Springhall, J. (1976). *Youth, empire and society: British youth movements 1883–1940*. London: Croom Helm.

Stern, F. (1974). *The politics of cultural despair: A study in the rise of Germanic ideology*. Berkeley: University of California Press.

Stevens, O. (1982). *Children talking politics*. Oxford, England: Martin Robertson.

Tocqueville, A. de (1954). *Democracy in America* (Vol. 2). New York: Alfred A. Knopf. (Original work published 1835)

Walford, B. (1986). *Life in public schools*. London: Methuen.

Wallis, R. (Ed.). (1975). *Sectarianism: Analyses of religious and non-religious sects*. New York: John Wiley.

White, R., & Lippitt, R. (1960). Leader behavior and member reaction in three social climates. In D. Cartwright & A. Zander (Eds.), *Group dynamics* (pp. 527–553). Evanston, IL: Row, Peterson.

Wilson, B. (1970). *Religious sects*. London: Weidenfeld & Nicolson.

Wolfenden Committee. (1978). *The future of voluntary organizations*. London: Croom Helm.

Youniss, J. (1980). *Parents and peers in social development*. Chicago: University of Chicago Press.

Zemach, M., & Zin, R. (1984). *Attitudes towards democratic values* [in Hebrew]. Jerusalem: Van Leer.

# PART IV

# Social Movements and Political Socialization in Democracy

# 12

# The Case for Educating for Gender Equality

## ROBERTA S. SIGEL

Gender relations in the United States present us with a curiously complex and paradoxical picture. On the one hand we notice a trend in the direction of greater equality on both the attitudinal and the behavioral level. Public opinion surveys as well as more scholarly publications give evidence that support for the equality of the sexes has grown steadily — some would say dramatically — over the past two or three decades (Mason, Czajak, & Albert, 1976; Tolleson Rinehart & Perkins, 1986). Mason et al. (1976), reviewing changes in women's sex-role attitudes between 1964 and 1974, noted that the "sex-role attitude changes . . . for the 1970–1973 period are, in many instances, as large as those observed between 1964 and 1970, even though the time period is half as long" (p. 587). While she found "a continuing tendency in this period for women to shift toward a more egalitarian sex-role stance" (p. 587–588), she also noticed that this tendency was domain-specific (such as advocating pay equality) but did not extend to all domains of life, especially not the more private ones. Other indications of a general trend in the direction of greater equality can be deduced from changes in women's socioeconomic status, with more women having entered the workforce (including types of work from which they previously had been excluded), having been elected or appointed to public office, and generally having assumed somewhat more of a presence in the "male" world.

These findings, however, must be balanced against counterindicative evidence that suggests that the changes in material conditions as well as poll responses are not nearly as extensive or intensive as frequently claimed and are accompanied by a good deal more ambivalence — if not outright

I wish to express my thanks to the School of Education of Tel Aviv University, which hosted the conference at which an earlier version of this chapter was presented. I especially would like to thank Dr. Orit Ichilov, who organized the conference. Thanks also are due to the workshop participants for their helpful comments. Partial support for the study reported in this chapter came from a grant of the National Science Foundation.

vestiges of traditionalism — than egalitarian responses to sample surveys would lead one to believe. Equally informative is the finding that both men and women, but particularly women, express the opinion that sex-based discrimination continues to be pervasive in society, in spite of superficial appearances to the contrary. Men and women are in agreement that men continue to occupy most of the crucial power positions, to enjoy more prestige than women, and to control most of the nation's major resources. In short, women, more often than not, continue to be in the subordinate position. Given the state of affairs, feminists and others writing about current gender relations often ask the question, Are women angry about their second-class status, and, if they are not angry, *why not?* This is the question this chapter will seek to answer.

## THEORETICAL FRAMEWORK

The thesis I wish to propose is the notion that gender equality evokes a great deal of ambivalence in women as well as men, although not necessarily for the same reasons. In the case of men, the ambivalence represents the conflict between their beliefs in equality and their preference for the traditional pattern of male hegemony. Women, on the other hand, are conflicted because they may desire change in their own status, but they are also apprehensive of what such change would entail, if not for women as a group, then at least for them personally. Ambivalence of this kind is apt to diffuse and/or repress overt anger. Women's ambivalence, as I shall explain in more detail later, stems from a variety of factors. The one on which I will focus here is related to women's self-concept or what it means to be a woman. This is by no means independent of their perception of males' view of what real women are like; in fact, it is shaped by it. It is thus a curiously split or fractured self-image.

Spence (1985) holds that "it is unarguable . . . that gender is one of the earliest and most certain components of the self-concept and serves as an organizing principle through which many experiences and perceptions of self and others are filtered. What is equally unarguable is that such self-schema are highly dependent on the widely accepted gender stereotypes that prevail in a given society" (p. 64).[1] Gender stereotypes include beliefs about male/female "natures" and how they allegedly differ from each other, and notions of how they differ or ought to differ in the way they behave (i.e., in their roles). Such stereotypes are taken as truth statements which contain prescriptive as well as descriptive elements.

What is particularly noteworthy about gender stereotypes is the widespread, even ubiquitous agreement that exists with regard to the attributes that are considered to be feminine or masculine (Broverman, Vogel, Broverman, Clarkson, & Rosenkrantz, 1972; Spence & Helmreich, 1978). Social psychologists have designed a great variety of different methods for assessing the presence of sex stereotypes in subjects. Among such measures are adjective checklists, rating scales, and open-ended descriptions, as well as experimental studies. The results have always been the same. Men as well as women think about each sex in categorical and stereotypical ways. What is even more significant is that the image of the typical male or female does not vary greatly, if at all, by gender. Men and women share the same image of what "women in general" are like, and they also hold similar views of the typical man. Many studies, moreover, have shown that the traits generally ascribed to men are considered to be more desirable than those attributed to women (Broverman et al., 1972; Goldberg, 1968), although Ashmore, Del Boca, and Wohlers (1986) consider the evidence with respect to desirability to be quite inconclusive. Whether men are seen as better and/or superior to women or merely as different from them, most people "think that women and men ought to differ in many of the ways in which they are perceived to differ" (Eagly, 1987, p. 13). As Eagly further points out, this leads people to have normative expectations, concerning characteristics and behaviors, that are in consonance with this consensus.

Deaux and associates (Deaux, 1977, 1984; Deaux & Major, 1987) have developed a model, based on expectancy theory, that I find particularly persuasive in that it permits us to anticipate the consequences such shared stereotypes are likely to have, both for women's self-concept and for the behavior they are prone to adopt. Beginning with the assumption (Deaux & Major, 1987) that "the enactment of gender primarily takes place within the context of social interaction, either explicitly or implicitly" (p. 370), they then proceed to describe the interaction that is apt to ensue as follows: Both men and women enter the interaction with specific expectations of the image each has of the opposite sex and the behaviors he or she expects from the other.[2] Inasmuch as men in many situations occcupy the superordinate position, it is the men's (the "perceiver's," to use her terminology) expectation that exerts considerable influence on the woman's (the "target's") behavior. Because women believe that men will judge them negatively if they fail to live up to the expectation of appropriate female behavior, they are likely to engage in the proper behavior whether they find it congenial or not, because "people strive to disconfirm negative labels" (Deaux & Major, 1987, p. 378). The desire to live up to (in this case, male) expectations, these authors hold, is dependent on the degree to which the individual woman is more concerned with self-presentation or self-verification.[3]

A second major factor in predicting whether the target's behavior will confirm or disconfirm a perceiver's expectancy . . . is the degree to which self-
presentation or self-verification concerns are aroused in the target. . . . Specifically, to the extent that the target's concerns with self-presentation are
aroused, the behavior of men and women is most apt to be shaped by the
expectancies of the perceiver. . . . In contrast, when the target's concerns
with self-verification are enhanced, it is more likely that his or her behavior
will conform to self-beliefs. Under these circumstances, women's and men's
behavior should best be predicted by the content of their individual gender-
linked self-schemata. [Deaux & Major, 1987, p. 379]

These authors, as well as others (e.g., von Baeyer, Sherk, & Zanna,
1981), hold that it is the concern with self-presentation, rather than differences in male/female potentials, that accounts for many of the observed
gender-based behavioral differences in these interactions.

A classical illustration of this phenomenon is furnished by Horner's
(1968, 1972) pioneering study of women's aspirations. She noticed a phenomenon that she labeled "fear of success," by which she sought to desig-
nate the "extent to which women have incorporated society's attitudes
which stress the idea that competition, success, competence, and intellectual achievement are basically inconsistent with femininity" (Horner,
1972, p. 65). This would suggest, then, that the traditional, stereotypical
image of femininity has become so internalized by these women as to have
become part of their image of what women should be like and perhaps, by
inference, of who they themselves should be. This dynamic persists because
"the gender system insists on and rewards difference, and men and women
are created who have an interest in presenting themselves as 'real' men and
'real' women, that is, without the elements socially defined as belonging to
the other category" (Ferree & Hess, 1987, p. 16).

The analysis that follows builds on the foregoing analysis and takes as
its point of departure the assumption that women's gender schema continue to bear the imprint of society's gender stereotype, which, after all, is
also the male stereotype of femininity. In addition, I propose that internal-
izing the cultural gender stereotypes probably helps shape a person's self-
concept. Inasmuch as our gender stereotypes tell us that women are by
nature tender, nurturant, emotional, dependent, and so on (Ashmore, et
al., 1986), I find it persuasive to assume that women not only would
behave in that way but would *want* to think of themselves in these terms,
in order to authenticate their gender identity. This should hold particularly for those women who grew into adulthood before the women's movement's consciousness-raising efforts. To sum so far, the assumption that
guides this chapter is that cultural stereotypes exert powerful pressures on
women's behavior and the formation of their self-concepts.

It would be misleading, however, to overdraw the extent to which such pressures succeed in shaping the self-concept. In two early studies on the topic, Sheriffs and McKee (1957; McKee & Sheriffs, 1959) found that women's *ideal* self-image varied considerably from their *actual* self-description and from the role they chose to play. McKee and Sheriffs (1959) found that differences by gender in *ideal personal self-concept* were not large, in that women showed considerable preference for traits generally characterized as "masculine." The same women (all college students), however, professed that they did not behave or play their role in accord with their ideal self-concept, but rather played it in accord with the restrictions they believed men wished to impose on women's behavior. Men, on the other hand, refrained from electing "feminine" traits for their ideal male self-concept. This led the authors to conclude that "if one's *ideal* be taken as the criterion of one's conformance to a social norm, then, rather surprisingly, it is men who conform to a social norm more than the other way around. . . . But if one's self-description be the criterion, then women are the conformers" (p. 360). This points to one type of conflict which, as we shall show presently, lies at the root of the postulated female ambivalence, namely, the discontinuity between the self one would like to be and the self one feels one has to present to society.

With the advent of the Women's Liberation Movement, the notion of male/female differences in competencies, temperament, and level of aspiration began to be questioned. The instant popularity of *The Feminine Mystique* (Friedan, 1963) attests to the fact that the liberation message had great appeal, at least for large segments of the female population. And yet, in spite of resonating to the message, we find little overt anger expressed by women over the persistence of male dominance and even less evidence of a willingness to go about actively seeking redress (Gurin, 1985). What is the explanation for this phenomenon?

## THE ROLE-AMBIVALENCE THESIS

The answer I wish to propose is that women experience a good deal of ambivalence when contemplating full equality with men. By ambivalence I mean the state of simultaneously experiencing conflicting attitudes and feelings concerning one's role and role-related behaviors. In the case of women, these conflicting attitudes and feelings involve (1) the desire to attain positions of equality and greater respect than was heretofore accorded them and (2) the natural anxiety of what such change would involve for themselves and for their relations with the male world, in general, and the significant men in their lives, in particular. They neither know how they would feel about the "changed self" nor how it would be accepted by others. Many women, I wish to propose, feel this conflict very keenly and seek to reduce it by accommodating societal expectations rather than resisting them. Even those who do resist really are not totally free of our age-old definitions of "natural" gender relations. What ensues, therefore, is that women find themselves in a state of ambivalence about their own dispositions and behaviors, on the one hand, and societal expectations, on the other. Frequently they also are not quite certain whether the "new-woman" ideal really accords with their own idea of what it means to be a woman. The conflicts that exist are thus not only between self and society but intrapsychic as well. In short, *all ambivalence, regardless of its source, reflects the continued presence of culturally accepted stereotypes.*

Let us have a look at several important sources of role ambivalence and how each impacts on women's identity. The first source relates to the previously discussed all-too-human fear of change, or of the unknown. This should apply especially to those women who experience considerable sex-based discrimination but, having been socialized prior to the women's movement, dread the consequences of insisting on equal treatment and might even consider certain aspects of it unacceptable and nonfeminine (Sigel & Reynolds, 1979). After all, it must be remembered that gender identification occurs very early in childhood (Maccoby, 1966) and receives persistent reinforcement through sex-role socialization during the young person's development (Kagan, 1964).

The second source of role ambivalence must be sought in the reality of the current situation, or at least the reality as women perceive it. In their daily lives, modern American women — whether at work, at home, or in other situations — too often receive the message, "Don't rock the boat." Women note that other women who want to alter the status quo frequently do not succeed or, worse yet, are seen as troublemakers. Thus, even women who do not subscribe fully to the prevailing gender stereotypes (i.e., have not internalized them) are likely to experience a good deal of role ambivalence, especially when they choose to be passive rather than fight. "People often conform to gender-role norms that are *not* internalized, because of the considerable power that groups and individuals supportive of these norms have to influence others' behaviors through rewards and punishments of both subtle . . . and more obvious varieties" (Eagly, 1987, p. 19). The conflict thus is between the costs society exacts and the willingness of the individual to pay the price.

The third source of role ambivalence is related to the second. Its roots lie in the proverbial public/private dichotomy (public men and private women). Here the ambivalence is activated by women's construction of men's construction of them. Women who aspire to both a public and a private life hold to the conviction, rightly or wrongly, that men are resentful or uncomfortable when women hold such aspirations. As women see it, men have fused for themselves the private role of husband/father with the public one of breadwinner. The two roles are one, as men see it, so there is no duality or potential conflict in the two roles; they are two sides of the same coin. Equally important, men — according to women — assume that women subscribe to the same version of the male role. But when contemplating the proper role for women, so women assume, men do not readily entertain the notion that women want the same, that it is as natural for a woman as it is for a man to play both roles simultaneously. Women believe that in the minds of men it is the private role that defines women, that this is what most women aspire to or ought to aspire to, if not for their own good then for that of society, especially the children. Women believe that men continue to think of women's public role as an add-on, rather than an intrinsic part of being a woman much in the same way that it is for men (Giele, 1982).

While the number of men who consider the private role to be the only appropriate or natural one for women no doubt has decreased sharply — if we are to give credence to their views voiced on repeated public opinion polls — what matters for our analysis is not the reality but that many women believe men would prefer to see them, if not barefoot and pregnant, at least in more privatized and "feminine" spheres. To be sure, the overt situation has changed, women concede, with ever-increasing numbers of women entering the public sphere and working alongside men, but women think that this phenomenon has not greatly changed men's gender-related belief structure.

Why, we may ask, should women be so sensitive to the pictures in men's heads? Why not forge ahead and devote energies to making further progress toward equality? I would suggest that women's attitudes and actions are never completely free of these constructions that they attribute to men. It may be an erroneous attribution, but it has reality for them. Why? Precisely because of the wide consensus that prevails with respect to gender stereotypes. Not only, as we have seen, do men subscribe to it, but so do women. After all, "the traditional gender roles have long been deeply etched in social consciousness, [and] perceptions of egalitarian roles are fraught with confusion" (Komarovsky, 1985, p. 227). There is no reason to assume that women do not share in this deeply etched social consciousness. Consequently, wanting to reject males' definition outright by engaging in "masculine" behaviors and ambitions may cause in women some doubt as to their intrinsic femininity. While more and more women today subscribe to egalitarian role definitions, it is conceivable that prior sex-role socialization is still strong enough for them not to be able to dismiss men's gender perceptions entirely. As a result, their gender beliefs remain ambiguous and greatly shaped by what they perceive to be male perspectives.

## SUMMARY OF GENDER-ROLE ISSUES

To check into these far-reaching speculations (to say "to test them" would be rather presumptious), focus group observations were video-recorded prior to the conducting of a telephone survey of 600 randomly selected New Jersey residents; 400 women and 200 men. Since the main object of this chapter will be to speculate on and explore the plausibility of the female role-ambivalence thesis, most of the data analysis will be devoted to the women, although occasional references will be made to findings from the male sample. In addition to the 400 women interviewed by phone, 50 women were observed during the focus groups. The women in these groups ranged in age from the early twenties to mid-sixties and represented a good cross-section (although, of course, not a random sample) of the adult female population of the state. The ideas I have already sketched did not drive this research, so, unfortunately, many questions that could have tested the validity of the role-ambivalence thesis directly, especially those focusing on definitions of womanhood and life goals, were not asked. Nonetheless, the results are sufficiently suggestive to permit speculating along the lines I have just indicated.

By way of introduction, let me briefly refer to some relevant earlier findings from these data, before focusing more specifically on the role-ambivalence thesis. The hypothesis the survey sought to test was that women looked upon themselves as being part of a relatively deprived, disadvantaged group, analogous to other disadvantaged (generally minority) groups. I labeled that construct — probably not too felicitously — "minority consciousness" (MC). MC consisted of two major components: awareness of sex-based discrimination (DA) and resentment over its practice (AI, for "affective involvement"). The results clearly indicate that most women would readily acknowledge that such discrimination is prevalent in today's society; moreover, they blame men for this state of affairs (Sigel & Whelchel, 1986a, 1986b). Those women in this survey who scored high in *both* DA and AI were characterized as exhibiting a high degree of MC (for methodological details of index construction, see Sigel & Whelchel, 1986b).

Not unexpectedly, women high in MC also saw the need for major and swift change in an egalitarian direction (Sigel & Whelchel, 1986a). What was less expected and, in fact, came as a surprise was the observation that relatively few women (38%) scored high in MC. To put it another way, although women had reached a high level of agreement that they were discriminated against just because they were women and considered this to be unfair, many did not seem to be very angry, or at least did not permit themselves to admit to anger. Given their belief in the unfairness of this arrangement, how can we explain their relative equanimity? Would the concept of ambivalent gender perspectives help us explain it?

## Women's Beliefs About Male Gender-Role Expectations

Results from our telephone survey offer strong evidence that women's seeming lack of resentment over discrimination is, as suggested earlier, greatly dependent of their perceptions of males' definition of gender roles. These women firmly believed that men essentially prefer the traditional role definitions. Men, so women think, may concede—from a sense of fairness or necessity—that women should enjoy greater equality than used to prevail, but they are not yet as ready to relinquish customary male prerogatives. The women we interviewed gave the impression that men were more likely to inhibit than to advance women's move toward equality. One example shall suffice: In these women's opinion, men are not upset by sex discrimination (66% thought men are not bothered or hardly at all); on the other hand, women as a group are much bothered by it (84% thought so). In other words, our respondents held that the sympathy that exists for women's relatively deprived status comes from other women rather than from men. Interestingly, men shared with women the impression that "most other men" face women's inequality with equanimity; 66% felt other men are not bothered by sex discrimination, and only 7% were themselves much bothered.

As these women saw it, then, this is still a man's world where women continue to be treated as second-class citizens and men reap most of the benefits in public and private life. This state of affairs is reflected in many different ways, among them the lack of cooperation they receive from men, either at work or at home, and—particularly vexing—the lack of respect with which their opinions are treated on the job and in other settings. Their reactions to these practices tells us much about women's coping techniques. Although many[4] are bothered by the practices, a roughly equal proportion accepts them as a given and either refuses to think about it or to get angry. Throughout the survey I found innumerable instances where women professed to "letting it pass" because "that is just the way life is." Such acceptance must be interpreted, if not as ambivalence, then at least as a sign of resignation. Alternately, we could also infer that women have internalized what they believe to be society's definition of the normal life and seek to integrate it with their own needs, thus leading to a split or fractured self-concept.

My observations of the focus groups showed me just how convinced women were that men really didn't want to see the status quo changed.[5] Let me quote a few typical comments. An Army sergeant in her late thirties who was the mother of a boy had this to say: "It's supposed to be the Pepsi generation; the generation that's supposed to be thinking so much more liberal, and yet the males that are coming, growing up, they've got very old-fashioned ideas. . . . They only see us in the kitchen and in front of the stove. I mean, you could come in with your briefcase . . . " Another woman commented, "The double standard, it's still there." Another talked about meetings she attended with male co-workers: "Every time I started to say something or even ask a question, it was like I was the invisible person, . . . I would start to say something, and he would start talking about something else. And, like I said, it was just as if I wasn't there. If any of the men in the group said something, then they got listened to. . . . But I couldn't even say anything." A middle-aged secretary said, "At work I have done things for the man . . . and he has taken all the credit. I would like some of the credit, too." There were many similar comments, all attesting to women's conviction that men would prefer to continue with the traditional gender relations.

The men we surveyed, however, did not see themselves the same way; that is, they did not think they were old-fashioned patriarchs. When asked during the telephone survey if they would prefer the traditional role for women, men didn't appear to be significantly more traditionalist than women. Only 10% of the women preferred traditional role definitions for women, with an additional 10% leaning in that direction; for men, the respective distributions were 6% and 13%. Nor did our observations of the male focus groups convince us that these men were staunch "male chauvinists," although, not unexpectedly, they did express some nostalgia for "the good old days." The overall picture, however, was not nearly as one-sided as women were wont to assert, notwithstanding the fact that some male focus-group members certainly did live up to women's negative expectations. On the whole, however, men, too, reflected a good deal of ambivalence about the changes that were occurring around them, although the dynamics of this change were of a very different nature. Inasmuch as this chapter focuses primarily on women, I shall not dwell any longer on male reactions, but it is important that we take cognizance of the possibility that a discrepancy exists between women's and men's views of men's preference.[6] Such misinterpretations of men's motivations, in turn, may partly explain the role-conforming behavior observed among women. Examples of this are the woman who resented but did not protest about not being heard in meetings, or the one who let the male colleague get all the credit.[7] It also would explain why women's self-concepts so frequently incorporate the previously mentioned two images of self — the societal, male-prescribed one and one that responds to the liberation message.

## Women's Accommodation to Male Expectations

Just how much men's expectations and decisions figure in women's lives was illustrated by the frequency with which they asserted that it is men who have "held women back." Most women (85%) agreed that, if a woman wants "to get ahead in the world, she would have to be much better at what she does than a man." We asked a whole array of questions and always got a similar answer — men or society (a pseudonym for men) were felt to be to blame if women got treated worse at work, in public life (including contacts with institutions such as banks and courts), and even at home. There was no doubt in these women's minds that, if a woman wanted to make it, she would have to do it on her own.

Here, again, the women of the focus groups offered more detailed insights than I could glean from the replies to highly structured telephone queries. After listening to example after example of discrimination on the job, of men deliberately not helping women and even obstructing their progress, one woman asked, "Why do we sit for that, though?" This was among the answers she received: "See one thing . . . if I went to my boss and said, 'Hey, these guys are picking on me,' then I'm a crybaby girl and 'Aw, you can't take it.' So you don't do that. I have never cried on the job, no matter what they did to me." Another said, "It doesn't pay to see how men got there. . . . If you're serious about your career, don't waste time looking back. Yeah, just keep going." Another woman, reflecting on the many and varied ways in which men tried to keep her down at work, compared it to being Jewish (although she was not) and added, "You can't abdicate." Many women agreed that "men just wait for a woman to stumble and then they push you down." This, then, is the way these women looked at their position vis-à-vis men in the new world of women's liberation. It is immaterial in this context whether the attributions they made are correct or not. What is important is that they are the motives women attribute to men and that these attributions exert a good deal of influence on women's behavior. As the examples show, women will adapt their behaviors to the reactions they anticipate of the men with whom they interact. The woman who would never cry in front of a male colleague, for instance, said she got rid of her frustrations by chopping wood when returning home.

## Women's Coping Strategies

What we see here are women who neither cry, complain, nor fight,[8] but who do not abdicate either. Instead they adopt strategies that they believe get them what they want.

*What do women want?* The answer is quite simple. They want from life what, in their opinion, men want and have always considered their due, namely respect and recognition from the other sex; a certain amount of control over their own lives (i.e., power); and, above all, a public life (i.e., an existence beyond the confines of the home, mostly in the form of desirable work) without having to give up a fulfilling family life. Two examples from the focus groups illustrated this rather touchingly: "I think the ideal situation would be being able to work alongside of a man and have an intelligent conversation, not have him look at you and say [with surprise], 'Oh, you have thoughts on that subject; oh, that sounds logical.' [But I also] like old-fashioned swings on the frontporch, go to church on Sundays . . . but that's dreamland." Another said this in describing her ideal life: "There are so many things I would probably change. I think mostly it is just that I would like to [have him share] maybe a little bit more, my housework. . . . I would like him to appreciate that I work a hard day, too." She continued by illustrating how most men refused to interact with her on any other terms than that of housekeeper and cook for her young husband: "And it's not just from my husband, it's . . . from other people that I would like, you know, just the respect, I worked a hard day today, and I deserve to sit down, too."

These same observations and complaints were echoed in the telephone survey. Women deplored the lack of respect accorded them, felt they were not offered enough assistance at home, and rejected the idea that a woman's role should be confined to that of housekeeper and mother.

How do women cope with the fact that they fail to obtain the treatment they desire and feel they deserve? Generally they adopt two strategies. I'll call one the "doing double-duty" strategy and the other the "not me" strategy. Let us begin with the point of doing double duty. As we have already seen, most women surveyed felt they had to work much harder than a man to get the same rewards in the outside world. So they kept trying harder. Much the same held for the home. Most felt that, if both a man and a woman worked, it would only be fair that domestic chores should be shared, but only 10% believed that this condition prevailed in many households. But these women continued to do most of the work at home and still worked hard on the job, that is, they did double duty. No wonder that 60% thought that women today have a tougher life because too much is expected of them (an assessment not shared by men).

The plethora of studies that have been conducted over the past few decades corroborate these women's assessment. A recent *New York Times* (1988) article summarized a poll with the headline, "Women: Out of the House But Not Out of the Kitchen." Even studies of supposedly modern two-career families, with both adults holding important jobs, far from reflecting more egalitarian perspectives, present a similar picture. The wife continues to play the traditional role of care-providing housekeeper and mother, frequently assuming all or most of these responsibilities (Haw, 1982). Husbands in such families, though supportive of their wives' careers, continue to give higher priorities to their own careers than to their domestic obligations or their wives' careers (Gilbert, 1985; Kahn, 1984; Lott, 1981; Rapoport & Rapoport, 1976). There is apparently an "imbalance in women's lives between demands to care for others and opportunities to care for themselves" (Giele, 1982, pp. 20–21). By living up to society's role expectations (with some modifications, to be sure) and bearing as well the major brunt of domestic duties, women consequently confirm men's perception of domesticity as a typically female sphere of activity. Women's domestic behavior thus is likely to strengthen rather than to disconfirm men's initial expectations.

The second or "not me" strategy is another way of coping with the situation. Women who use this tactic readily concede that most women are treated poorly but that they personally receive fair treatment. This is much the same phenomenon that Crosby (1982) observed in her study of working women. "The typical working woman may, in short, see herself as the lucky exception to the discriminatory rule because at some level she knows that to do otherwise simply courts further problems" (p. 164). Not only that, but, I venture to guess, the "not me" strategy is also a mechanism by which she can maintain her self-respect. Answers to the telephone survey indicated how often women adopted this strategy. They thought of themselves as exceptions. Thus, though others have been discriminated against at the workplace, she has not; though others have not been hired or promoted because they are women, she has not had that experience; though others' opinions are ignored, her own opinion is given equal weight with that of men.

The focus groups, by contrast, gave a very different picture. During these sessions, as we have seen, women were quite ready to admit that at times their personal treatment left much to be desired. I have no evidence with which to account for this discrepancy. It is entirely possible that a certain amount of group contagion took place; that is, when one woman began by mentioning an incidence of personal discrimination, others became more inclined to admit the frequency of similar experiences. The potential for group contagion constitutes one of the drawbacks of the focus-group technique. On the other hand, it is equally plausible to assume that in this instance focus groups were useful because they permitted respondents to open up to feelings they otherwise might have felt obligated not to mention, just because they did not know if such feelings would be shared by others and hence be "correct." This should hold particularly for research on women, in view of the frequently documented tendency of women to conform to attitudes expected of them (Eagly, 1987; Tuthill & Forsyth, 1982). It is a proposition that really calls for very careful and systematic testing, should focus groups remain as popular in research as they have been over the past few years.

Even if the focus groups did have such a contagion effect, the presence of an initial malady cannot be denied. All the women, whether in focus groups or interviewed over the phone, saw a great deal of sex-based discrimination around them and didn't like it. They said they would welcome change, for the most part major change in an egalitarian direction. Yet only one-third permitted themselves to feel angry about it (those scoring high in MC). Moreover, neither that minority nor the majority was willing to fight the system, including the men in their lives, outright. Instead they sought a modicum of self-fulfillment by steering midway between compliance and meeting their own needs.

To conclude, these young and older women preferred accommodation rather than resistance or militancy in reaching their goals. At home they were still the mainstay of the household, and at work they strove for excellence rather than make any protest. Though they no longer dismissed the possibility of protest and other means (court actions and appeals to government agencies), this was not the preferred strategy for many women. Instead they opted for accommodation. Under no circumstances, however, should we permit ourselves to confuse this tactic with genuine submissiveness. To make this point, I shall conclude with a quotation from a middle-aged woman holding a job in a predominantly male setting:

> Women can never admit being hurt or not able to do something like lifting heavy boxes which was not part of my job. But I did. I got stronger. And I work for some pretty tough men that pushed you to the edge where they waited for you to say it. And I used to hold it in. I didn't scream back. They would try to press a button and get a reaction, and I would just do what I had to do. Okay, fine. And that night I'd go home, and I'm a great person for weeding. . . . I learned what game they were playing. . . . *So it made me very strong.*

Gaining personal strength, however, is not the same as gaining political strength. Maybe the reason the so-called gender gap has not yet been translated effectively into political clout can be attributed to the fact that most women — with the exception of those affiliated with the women's movement — have chosen the path of individual meritocracy rather than actively supporting the women's agenda. The New Jersey women we interviewed are a perfect example. Their advocacy of so-called women's issues was pronounced and differed significantly from that of men (Sigel & Whelchel, 1986a, 1986b), but their involvement, let alone actions, on behalf of such an agenda was virtually nill. We can label as progress that women today seem to have gained personal strength, but one should not permit oneself to ignore that as yet they have not channelled their energies into translating *personal* strength into *group* power.

## Discussion

The 1985 survey of New Jersey women gave strong evidence that they rejected the traditional version of the ideal role for women, which defines them mostly in terms of wife and mother. They did not object to assuming these roles; in fact, they strongly desired them, but they also desired a public life, and to the same degree as did men. Yet they were also keenly aware of the persistence of sex-based discrimination in all spheres of life and attributed it to the fact that men do not welcome the "new woman" and prefer the status quo.

Although these women may have wanted to reject the old definition, many were aware that they could not yet free themselves completely of it. They had trouble doing it precisely because it was so tied into the national gender perspective, to which they were socialized and which is reflected in so many different phases of daily life. As Sexton (1980) wrote, "Young women are caught between two worlds, the feminine mystique of their mothers and the feminist mystiques of their own generation. Young women want both career success and family intimacy. The issue is how to get it" (p. 121). So far, society has not offered them an unambiguous script for getting it. Consequently they experience confusion and ambivalence in their gender perspectives. But, we have also seen that such ambivalence has, for the most part, not led them to abandon the goals just referred to. What they have done instead is to adjust their tactics for achieving them, so they avoid challenging male expectations too directly and do not permit themselves the luxury of feeling rage.

Accommodation takes two forms. First, women work extraordinarily hard to succeed at work and also continue to carry the major weight of household responsibilities. Second, in interaction with males, whether in private or public life, they tend to behave in a manner that conforms to the expectations they believe that men have formed of what constitutes appropriate female behavior. To the extent that they do conform, men find their assumptions or expectations confirmed, and the cycle repeats itself. Even when women (or men, for that matter) do not engage in stereotypical behavior, however, the other person in the interaction (in this case the man) does not process that information to disconfirm his initial expectations, as we have seen in the reports from the focus groups. Gender stereotypes simply have become so firmly ingrained in most of us that both men and women find it hard to abandon them, even when the evidence disconfirms their appropriateness. As Ferree and Hess (1987) state,

> Because the gender system is not a reflection of natural differences, creating gender is a struggle. We all bear "the traces of conscription" into a system that represses part of our potential and no one ever fully conforms to it. On the other hand, even those individuals who deliberately refuse to take their allotted place in the system cannot escape from knowing what it is.[p. 16]

Democracy, however, so its advocates claim, seeks to actualize rather than repress human potential. Stereotypes of the kind just described consequently must be seen as dysfunctional. What, one may ask, are the schools supposed to do about that? That is the question to which I now would like to turn.

## SOCIALIZATION FOR DEMOCRACY

Educating young people for democracy is one mission with which public schools in the United States are charged. Inasmuch as democracy rests on the twin pillars of equality and liberty, socialization for gender equality must be an integral part of public education. A genuine challenge for the schools, therefore, is how to educate young people in such a fashion that they internalize gender equality as a component of their value system. Given the fact that gender stereotypes are deeply ingrained in most of us and meet with cultural approval, this is indeed a formidable task. In a way, it charges the schools, which themselves are part of the mainstream culture, to become vanguards on behalf of cultural change.

Some schools nonetheless have accepted the charge. For example, over the past decades, textbooks in many school systems have been revised to give more credit to the achievement of women and to present a less sex-segregated view of society. While such revisions have to be welcomed, they have at best been quite sporadic and selective. In fact, during a recent observance of the bicentennial of the American Constitution, a group of prominent women (among them some very conservative ones) gathered in Atlanta in order to insist that textbooks and curricula be revised to give women's contributions to Early American life recognition on a par with that of men (*New York Times*, 1988). The jury is still out on just how successful such efforts and similar others will be. No empirical data exist as yet, although they are badly needed to guide future efforts. One also may be permitted to wonder whether a purely didactic approach is likely to combat deeply ingrained values and emotions. This is not to say that such attempts should be discouraged; on the contrary, they should be insisted upon, but it would be naive to rely exclusively on them in the hope of promoting major resocialization.

Insufficient attention to women's contributions to the American polity is but one of the many reasons why young people continue to subscribe to prevailing gender stereotypes. Inadequate instruction in democratic theory and practice is probably another. Teaching democracy and how its principles can guide us in solving problems of governance apparently is not done very well in our schools, or at least is not very successful. Students generally are lacking in full understanding of basic democratic principles, such as liberty and equality. To be sure, they are familiar with the terms and associate them with the "American way of life," but they frequently are incapable of applying such principles to actual problems and practices, including the practice of gender equality. "At times one cannot help but think that these principles are only slogans to the students" (Sigel & Hoskin, 1981, p. 117). The principles possess name recognition for the young but not much else (Sigel, 1979). Better instruction into the meaning and dimensions of democratic citizenship would, one might hope, enhance the likelihood that young people will learn to develop more egalitarian attitudes and to apply them when appropriate.

A related issue is the need to instruct young people in the many different ways of *exercising* democratic citizenship. Judging from the behavior of American adults as well as the survey responses of pupils, it would not seem that the schools have done a particularly effective job in training them for active citizenship, especially not for citizenship that is exercised in order to influence government and not merely to support it and be allegiant to it. A study of 1,000 high school seniors during the turbulent Vietnam era found them to be singularly unacquainted with participatory modes beyond voting and letter writing (Sigel & Hoskin, 1981). Likewise, as we well know, most teachers do not like to engage pupils in the discussion of controversial issues, especially as they relate to pending policies (Ziegler, 1967). Yet, how can the schools hope to fulfill the mission of resocializing for gender equality if they do not (1) illuminate how current political arrangements are an obstacle to it, (2) discuss what policy innovations might be conducive to attaining equality, and (3) instill in young men and women the conviction that becoming active on behalf of policies one desires is the way to proceed as a democratic citizen? So long as the schools put more emphasis on obeying the law[9] rather than urging students to help shape it in the interest of the common good, it is not likely that textbook biographies of famous and strong women will do a great deal to combat gender stereotypes.

Other attempts to combat gender stereotyping among the young are less overtly didactic. Just two that have been introduced in school systems shall be cited. One centers on acquainting young people with role models who function in gender-atypical occupations and/or pursuits. To that end, some schools have invited visits from prominent women and men who operate successfully in realms not generally associated with their gender. Inviting female judges as commencement speakers and asking female athletes to address gym classes are among the strategies adopted now and then by a specific school. As far as I know, here, too, empirical studies assessing the impact of this approach are lacking. One problem with bringing such successful individuals into the school in the hope that they can function as role models is that students at times have trouble relating these persons to their own career goals. As I once heard a female student say of a prominent woman, "But she has all the feathers. Not everyone can be a chief. What is in it for us ordinary Indians?"

Another way to promote gender equality in the schools has been the attempt to combat the notion that some topics are meant for girls only and some for boys. To that end, some school systems have sought to eliminate as much as possible sex-segregated instruction in certain subject matters, such as athletics, home economics, shop, and related activities. If reports from the United States and other countries are any indication, these efforts have had very limited success. By and large boys tend to avoid "girls' subjects" and to resent girls' efforts to participate with them on teams and intramural sports. Girls, on the other hand, often are fearful of enrolling in subjects that are alleged to be hard for girls, such as mathematics and the sciences. (These, of course never have been officially sex-segregated in the way in which sports used to be and still are in some schools.)

The very fact that students tend to resist enrolling in such subjects would suggest that by adolescence gender stereotypes have already become deeply embedded. What is less clear is just how much teachers and coaches, deliberately or inadvertently, contribute to the firming up of the stereotypes by not being vigorous enough to resist student efforts to persist in traditional gender patterns. It must be remembered that many teachers are themselves from a generation that subscribes to many of the traditional cultural stereotypes. Some of them may be dubious about the desirability of changing traditional arrangements and may lack enthusiasm for urging pupils to choose courses or careers that are atypical for their gender. After all, it is one thing to offer previously sex-typed courses on a unisex basis; it is quite another for a faculty member actively to recruit girls for classes in shop and boys for cooking classes (Klein, 1985). Yet it is essential that sufficiently large numbers of both sexes be coaxed or even mandated into such enterprises. Two boys who take a cooking class, perhaps because they want to become gourmet chefs, and one girl taking shop won't do. Kanter (1977) has demonstrated how important balanced gender representation is in industry. It is equally important in school, and maybe more so, because young people can be introduced to new ideas and practices before the old ones become entrenched.

## CONCLUSION

While all the foregoing "reforms" are meritorious and should be either initiated or continued, it is doubtful that they alone could bring about fundamental changes in value and belief patterns. Such practices can only be considered as a first step toward resocialization for gender equality. Precisely because many adolescent boys and girls are likely to operate from a traditional gender-role belief system, it is necessary that schools provide youngsters with meaningful experiences designed to disconfirm old constructs. Providing visits from appropriate role models may be a fine first step; but this alone will not do it. Such visits must be followed by sensitive, open explorations of the feelings and anxieties such role models evoke in some young people. Students need to address the question of why they feel startled or even threatened by a woman in a "man's" job. Teachers and counselors need to help students address these issues and to guide the explorations in such a way that the deconfirming evidence, far from becoming disorienting or even threatening, can become liberating.

Sponsoring consciousness-raising groups might be one way of accomplishing this. We have seen that women of all ages are ambivalent and anxious about challenging the sex-role status quo. Female adolescents, as we have also seen, are not exempt from such conflicts. Neither are adolescent boys, who are entering the stage where they have to begin to develop their own identity. How threatening it must be for them to question whether the traditional definition of the male might be outmoded! It is here where sensitively conducted consciousness-raising encounters might be more effective than all the textbook materials and classroom visits.

To be sure, introducing such innovations into the curriculum might meet with considerable resistance from parents and teachers alike, but, if the women's movement is any indication, it might well be the most appropriate and effective way of proceeding. To ignore young people's ambivalence and confusion certainly is counterproductive. To seek to cope with it, even if it should meet with only partial success, is an experiment worth trying. Failure to address such feelings will make it next to impossible to help young people to develop a personal construct system in which men and women enjoy equal status. As more women enter the workforce, head households, and so forth, there is more and more disconfirming evidence all around us. It tells us that men and women can indeed function equally competently in many contexts. Yet, as the data I presented in this chapter show, we frequently are so bounded in the constructs we learned while still young that we tend to reject or avoid evidence that challenges our assumptions.

Young people of school age are not exempt from this. They are coming of age in a transitional era where new values arise while old ones persist. Consequently, boys and girls receive many conflicting messages these days. One message for girls is, "Go play ball; girls can do anything boys can do." Another says, "If you play as fast and tough as a boy, the boys may not like you." The girl is thus subject to role ambiguity. Within our society it is not yet sufficiently clear what women's roles should be. As far as women can see, what they want and what they feel capable of doing may conflict with the norms society has evolved for them, or what they believe society has evolved for them. Boys with a vested interest in the more traditional perspectives also are ambivalent and confused and may need even more assistance in comfortably reaching an androgynous construct. As it now stands, society, the schools included, sends too many inconsistent, even contradictory messages to young people to accomplish its alleged goal of promoting an egalitarian, democratic polity.

## NOTES

1.  Some intercultural differences in sexual stereotypes notwithstanding, Williams and Best (1982) found more overlap than differences in the 30 nations they studied.

2.  Deaux and Major (1987) do not maintain that this phenomenon extends across all situations, but they hold that gender-related behaviors are likely to become activated in situations where gender schema are very salient.

3.  Deaux and Major (1987) define some ways of engaging in the process of self-verification, as follows: "Concern with self-verification is enhanced by focusing a person's attention on private aspects of the self such as privately held attitudes, beliefs, and dispositions" (p. 379). As the name suggests, concern with self-verification centers on a person's aim to stay consonant with his or her sense of self, attitudinally as well as behaviorally. Self-presentation focuses on concern with the impression one makes on others — how one wishes to be perceived.

4.  All told, 18 questions inquiring into various phases of discrimination were

posed to respondents. The percentage who professed to being bothered versus those who accepted society's ways varied slightly from question to question. In most instances the division was fairly even.

5. Members of focus groups represented a cross-section of New Jersey women, having been initially contacted by random-number phone calls. Assignment to specific focus groups, however, was determined by specific research considerations.

6. It is, of course, also possible that men's self-concepts in the year 1985 did not permit them to look upon themselves as lacking in egalitarian dispositions; hence their verbal disavowals.

7. Social psychological studies have shown this to be a fairly typical tendency among women. For some of the more recent studies, see Gould and Slone (1982), who document women's tendency to let men take credit for tasks performed by women (the "feminine modesty" effect). Golub and Canty (1982) offer yet one more confirmatory study of women's willingness to let men assume leadership positions, regardless of the women's own talents and dominance traits.

8. Responses to the telephone survey question asking what women thought they should do if they felt discriminated against found a majority opting for doing nothing or very little. This finding held even for women scoring high in MC, although they were twice as likely as women low in MC to entertain the possibility of some form of political action (31% and 16% respectively).

9. Even during the allegedly rebellious decade of the 1960s, students tended to equate good citizenship with obedience to law and order (see Sigel & Hoskin, 1981).

## REFERENCES

Ashmore, R. D., Del Boca, F. K., & Wohlers, A. J. (1986). Gender stereotypes. In R. D. Ashmore & F. K. Del Boca (Eds.), *The social psychology of female-male relations: A critical analysis of central concepts.* New York: Academic Press.

Ashmore, R. D., & Del Boca, F. K. (Eds.). (1986). *The social psychology of female-male relations: A critical analysis of central concepts.* New York: Academic Press.

Broverman, I. K., Vogel, S. R., Broverman, D. M., Clarkson, F. E., & Rosenkrantz, P. S. (1972). Sex-role stereotypes: A current appraisal. *Journal of Social Issues, 28*(2), 59-78.

Crosby, F. J. (1982). *Relative deprivation and working women.* New York: Oxford University Press.

Deaux, K. (1977). Sex differences. In I. Blass (Ed.), *Personality variables in social behavior* (pp. 357-377). Hillsdale, NJ: Lawrence Erlbaum.

Deaux, K. (1984). From individual differences to social categories — Analysis of a decade's research on gender. *American Psychologist, 39,* 105-116.

Deaux, K., & Major, B. (1987). Putting gender into context: An interactive model of gender-related behavior. *Psychological Review, 94,* 369-389.

Eagly, A. H. (1987). *Sex differences in social behavior: A social role interpretation*. Hillsdale, NJ: Lawrence Erlbaum.

Ferree, M. M., & Hess, B. H. (1987). Introduction. In B. H. Hess & M. M. Ferree (Eds.), *Analyzing gender: A handbook of social science research* (pp. 9–30). Newbury Park, CA: Sage.

Friedan, B. (1963). *The feminine mystique*. New York: Dell.

Giele, J. Z. (1982). Women's work and family roles. In J. Z. Giele (Ed.), *Women in the middle years — Current knowledge and directions for research and policy* (pp. 115–150). New York: John Wiley.

Gilbert, L. A. (1985). *Men in dual-career families: Current realities and future prospects*. Hillsdale, NJ: Lawrence Erlbaum.

Goldberg, P. (1968). Are women prejudiced against women? *Trans-action, 5*(5), 28–30.

Golub, S., & Canty, E. M. (1982). Sex-role expectations and the assumption of leadership by college women. *Journal of Social Psychology, 116,* 83–90.

Gould, R. J., & Slone, C. G. (1982). The feminine modesty effect: A self-presentational interpretation of sex differences in causal attribution. *Personality and Social Psychology Bulletin, 8,* 477–485.

Gurin, P. (1985). Women's gender consciousness. *Public Opinion Quarterly, 49,* 143–163.

Haw, M. (1982). Women, work and stress: A review and agenda for the future. *Journal of Health and Social Behavior, 23,* 132–144.

Horner, M. S. (1968). *Sex differences in achievement motivation and performance in competitive and non-competitive situations*. Unpublished doctoral dissertation, University of Michigan.

Horner, M. S. (1972). Toward an understanding of achievement related conflicts in women. *Journal of Social Issues, 28,* 157–197.

Kagan, J. (1964). Acquisition and significance of sex typing and sex role identity. In M. L. Hoffman & L. W. Hoffman (Eds.), *Review of child development research* (pp. 137–168). New York: Russell Sage.

Kahn, A. (1984). The power of war: Male response to power loss under equality. *Psychology of Women Quarterly, 8,* 234–237.

Kanter, R. M. (1977). *Men and women of the corporation*. New York: Basic Books.

Klein, S. (Ed.). (1985). *Handbook for achieving sex equity through education*. Baltimore: Johns Hopkins University Press.

Komarovsky, M. (1985). *Women in college: Shaping new feminine identities*. New York: Basic Books.

Lott, B. (1981). *Becoming a woman: The socialization of gender*. Springfield, IL: C. C. Thomas.

Maccoby, E. E. (Ed.). (1966). *The development of sex differences*. Stanford, CA: Stanford University Press.

Mason, K. O., Czajak, J. L., & Albert, S. (1976). Change in U.S. women's sex-role attitudes. *American Sociological Review, 41,* 573–596.

McKee, J. P., & Sheriffs, A. C. (1959). Men's and women's beliefs, ideals, and self-concepts. *American Journal of Sociology, 64,* 356–363.

Rapoport, R., & Rapoport, R. N. (1976). *Dual career families re-examined*. New York: Harper & Row.

Sexton, L. (1980). Between two worlds. *Radcliffe Quarterly, 66*, 5–14.

Sheriffs, A. C., & McKee, J. P. (1957). Qualitative aspects of beliefs about men and women. *Journal of Personality, 25*, 451–464.

Sigel, R. S. (1979). Students' comprehension of democracy and its application to conflict situations. *International Journal of Political Education, 2*, 47–65.

Sigel, R. S., & Hoskin, M. (1981). *The Political Involvement of Adolescents*. New Brunswick, NJ: Rutgers University Press.

Sigel, R. S., & Reynolds, J. V. (1979). Generational differences and the women's movement. *Political Science Quarterly, 94*, 635–648.

Sigel, R. S., & Whelchel, N. L. (1986a, July). *Changing gender roles: Male and female reactions*. Paper presented at the meeting of the International Society for Political Psychology, Amsterdam.

Sigel, R. S., & Whelchel, N. L. (1986b, September). *Assessing the past and looking toward the future: Perceptions of "Change in the Status of Women."* Paper presented at the meeting of the American Political Science Association, Washington, DC.

Spence, J. T. (1985). Gender identity and its implications for concepts of masculinity and femininity. In T. Sondregger (Ed.), *Nebraska Symposium on Motivation* (pp. 59–95). Lincoln, NE: University of Nebraska Press.

Spence, J. T., & Helmreich, R. L. (1978). *Masculinity and femininity: Their psychological dimensions, correlates, and antecedents*. Austin: University of Texas Press.

Tolleson Rinehart, S., & Perkins, J. (1986, September). *Change and stability in feminist attitudes: 1972-1984*. Paper presented at the meeting of the American Political Science Association.

Tuthill, D. M., & Forsyth, D. R. (1982). Sex differences in opinion conformity and dissent. *Journal of Social Psychology, 116*, 205–210.

von Baeyer, C. L., Sherk, D. L., & Zanna, M. P. (1981). Impression management in the job interview: When the female applicant meets the male (chauvinist) interviewer. *Personality and Social Psychology Bulletin, 7*, 45–51.

Williams, J. E., & Best, D. L. (1982). *Measuring sex stereotypes: A thirty nation study*. Beverly Hills, CA: Sage.

Women: Out of the house but not out of the kitchen. (1988, December 8). *New York Times*, p. A28.

Ziegler, L. H. (1967). The political life of American teachers. Englewood Cliffs, NJ: Prentice-Hall.

# 13

## The Women's Movement and the Creation of Gender Consciousness: Social Movements As Socialization Agents

VIRGINIA SAPIRO

How can we expect to develop independent, self-reliant, *democratic* traits, when children see that one member of the family has her whole life centered on performing intimate and personal services for others? [Amelie Oksenberg Rorty, quoted in Ruddick & Daniels, 1977, p. 44]

The past century and a half has witnessed the rise of numerous national and international women's movements oriented toward expanding the range of public and private roles women play, and devoted especially to the proposition that women should exert increasing amounts of influence over their own destinies and the choices made by the societies. At least some sectors of each of these movements have argued explicitly that their goal was not simply to improve the conditions in which women live, but also to advance the cause of democracy.

Women's movements are examples of political mobilization of and by a social group that is both economically and politically subordinate. Even in nations in which women have the same formal political rights and privileges of men, in no country do women wield nearly as much political influence as men. In no country in which systematic studies have been undertaken is political participation and influence considered as important or normal for women as for men. Women's movements are aimed at eliminating the subordination of women and at releasing the female half of the population for participation in political decision making. Part of this task depends on redefining *democracy* itself: convincing women (at least) that a political system cannot be termed democratic if they systematically occupy only a secondary political role.

This chapter addresses the problem of socialization for democracy by considering the contemporary women's movement as an agent of socialization with effects on both participants and the wider political culture. It will focus primarily on one outcome of socialization: development of gender consciousness, a politicized form of social identity.

Students of political socialization have paid curiously little attention to social movements. There are many reasons for this. Social movements are populated by adults, and only recently have socialization scholars turned their attention in any serious way to adult socialization. Moreover, and probably more important, political behavior or participation in political organizations is generally conceived of as a dependent rather than independent variable. Socialization research has been aimed at understanding why individuals do or don't participate in politics, not at revealing the effects of political activity. We have rarely studied the socialization effects of explicitly political organizations as compared with others such as families or schools. Much of the work on the political psychology of social movements, therefore, has focused on who joins and, to some degree and usually by implication, why they join, but not on the effects of social movements on long-term patterns of political behavior and orientation.

In order to assess the impact of a social movement, including the women's movement, it is necessary to view it as an agent of socialization. We may then evaluate the degree to which it transforms individual patterns of political thinking and behavior and outline the ways in which it does so. In order to accomplish this task, we must look at the impact both on social movement participants and on individuals in the wider society. Above all, we must consider what role social movements might play in the *process* of political socialization, by integrating them, as agents, into our theories of this process.

## THE DEVELOPMENT OF GENDER CONSCIOUSNESS

One of the most intriguing recent developments in the study of political psychology is research on group identification and consciousness (Billig, 1976; Conover, 1984, 1988; Gurin, Miller, & Gurin, 1980; Tajfel, 1981, 1982). Those interested in women and politics quickly followed through to consider the development and impact of gender consciousness, especially among women (Conover, 1987, 1988; Fowlkes, 1986, 1987; Gurin, 1985; Kalmuss, Gurin, & Townsend, 1981; Klein, 1984; Miller, Gurin, Gurin, & Malanchuk, 1981; Sigel & Whelchel, 1986).

Group consciousness is based on a foundation of group identification, or a feeling of membership in or belonging to a social group. As Gurin et al. (1980) put it, "Identification refers to the awareness of having ideas, feelings, and interests similar to others who share the same stratum characteristics. Consciousness refers to a set of political beliefs and action orientations arising out of this awareness of similarity" (p. 30). Group consciousness, then, is intended to refer to a *politicized* form of social identification, a more complex structure that includes the subjective political significance of social identification. If social or group identity connotes a sense of membership in or attachment to the group, group consciousness incorporates an awareness of the group's relationship to the larger sociopolitical context.

The precise definition of group consciousness, and certainly of gender consciousness, has provoked controversy, but we can draw an outline that includes shared components. In addition to group identification, group consciousness on the part of subordinate groups involves a recognition of intergroup disparity in resources, power, or status; beliefs about the legitimacy of this disparity; attributions of social rather than merely individual causes for the relative standing of these groups; and a belief that collective rather than merely individual action is necessary to affect the future fortunes of the group.

Most of the empirical attention to group consciousness has focused on subordinate social groups, especially women. Thus, for women, gender consciousness can be defined loosely as identifying with women as a social group, having an awareness of gender inequality and believing this inequality to be illegitimate, locating the reasons for inequality in social causes (e.g., discrimination), and assuming a need for collective as opposed to individual solutions. Not surprisingly, gender consciousness thus defined may equally be labeled "feminist consciousness." Gender consciousness, clearly, does not refer to attitudes toward specific issues on a "feminist agenda," although we should expect gender consciousness to lend some structure to one's configuration of attitudes toward these issues.

A number of studies have demonstrated links between group consciousness, including gender consciousness, and other political orientations and behavior (Conover, 1987, 1988; Miller et al., 1981; Shingles, 1981). For many subordinate social groups, including women, group consciousness appears to boost political participation. We will turn more directly to these links in the final section of this chapter. For now, let us consider the nature of the development of gender consciousness.

By all accounts, gender consciousness is a complex structure, encompassing a number of different elements. Although it would be wrong to analyze any psychological structure as though it were a Lego set of discrete pieces, we can consider the timing and process of the development of the components of gender consciousness in order to arrive at some hypotheses about the development of gender consciousness itself. Some of these elements clearly develop relatively early in life. Gender identity is one of the earliest aspects of social identity to develop. Most children can label themselves and others as females and males consistently and correctly by the age of three or four. At the same time, children begin to understand the social significance of gender; that is, they begin to learn the pattern of characteristics and roles assigned to females and males in their culture.

Most individuals, then, develop fairly early in life a stable identification of themselves as members of one or the other sex, and a clear sense of social differences and divisions of labor between the sexes (Block, 1984). But gender may be the best example of how group identity may remain devoid of explicit political content, in other words, not become a part of group consciousness. While possessing a clear sense of gender identity, most women never develop a sense of gender consciousness.

At what stage, if at all, is gender consciousness likely to develop in individuals? Here I will argue that, although there are other elements of consciousness present early in childhood, a number of conditions make it unlikely that gender consciousness could develop in most individuals until late in adolescence at the earliest.

Any form of group consciousness must involve some moderately demanding cognitive skills. Group consciousness implies a recognition of social difference and inequality; that is, the ability to compare and evaluate different groups. It also involves questions of legitimacy of difference and frameworks for solution and therefore, it can be argued, an ability to reason through problems of social causation. Group consciousness among members of subordinate groups implies a critique of the social relations one observes in the surrounding society.

This notion of critique suggests that, while we may be able to analyze gender consciousness as an example of the more general phenomenon of group consciousness, it is also likely to be very different in its genesis from other forms of group consciousness, particularly when we are talking about individuals shifting toward feminism within an androcentric or patriarchal environment. In brief, this shift, which is implied by gender consciousness, requires a greater degree of autonomy from and critical orientation toward individuals to whom one's very identity is bound, than is likely to be required of other forms of group consciousness.

A considerable amount of research in social psychology on group identity and comparison and its political implications suggests how the process of developing gender consciousness might pose particular problems (Billig, 1976; Tajfel, 1981, 1982). This body of research emphasizes the process of developing awareness of groups and group differences, the integration of individual and group identity, and the formation of the elements of what we are calling group consciousness through "us-versus-them" comparisons.

One can see how the process might work for class, race, or ethnic

consciousness, for example, because of the particular structure of segregation in the child's institutional world. The child's family and also, for the
most part, the child's peers and playmates are from the "us" group, providing a strong motivational basis for "in"-group identification and perhaps
for fairly consistent stories (stereotypes) about the nature of the relatively
unknown "them" or "out" group. We can also see powerful examples of this
process in Robert Coles's companion volumes, *The Moral Life of Children*
(1986a) and *The Political Life of Children* (1986b). Both reveal very sharply the process by which social boundaries both flow from and recreate
political conflict among groups.

The institutionalization of gender and gender relations is very different from that of class, race, or ethnicity. The intimate and social world of
most children is relatively unsegregated on the basis of gender. The intense
emotional bonds with mother and father are likely to inhibit the development of social categorization, which might otherwise support gender consciousness. The child knows and loves individuals of both sexes, which
makes perception of a basic conflict between the sexes difficult and anxiety
producing. But also, through the child's relationship to the division of
labor between mother and father (and, indeed, gender-based divisions of
labor among other significant people in the child's environment), the child
comes to depend upon and respect the institutionalization of gender itself.
Where the social scientist might see the "institutionalization of gender" or
the "division of labor," the child in the family will see "what Mommy and
Daddy do" or "how we are as a family." It is precisely a cognitive autonomy
from and critique of institutionalized gender relations that must form the
basis of gender consciousness; this autonomy cannot be easy to achieve.

This latter point, the peculiar dependence of children upon the institutionalization of social difference and inequality by gender, is very important to understanding how different is the task of developing gender consciousness as compared with most other forms of group consciousness. For
example, although children who are poor or part of racial, ethnic, or other
minorities may be exposed to ideologies that justify their subordinate position in society, they are not so consciously and carefully taught to cherish
and reproduce these forms of social difference and inequality as they are
those based on gender. It is true that children of subordinate social groups
have often been taught by their own kin to perform the subordinate roles
expected within the dominant culture. Recently scholarly work on social
domination, however, emphasizes the degree to which the acceptance of
subordination is often, in reality, a strategy reserved for public performance.

Studies of wife battering show how, even in extreme (although all too
common) examples of the domination of women within family structures
that have become most explicitly brutal, victims are often unable to place

blame on others or on the institution in which they find themselves. Rather, victims of spouse abuse or, for that matter, child abuse and incest, tend to define their situations as normal and, if they recognize their pain, blame themselves. The inability to criticize systems of violent domination is enhanced by female economic dependence in adulthood (Kalmuss & Strauss, 1982; Strube & Barbour, 1983). It is difficult to develop the autonomy within familial and intimate relationships that appears necessary to enable a person to object to even the most obviously painful forms of subordination. Research shows that male violence against women and tolerance of such violence is related to their ideologies of female subordination (Breines & Gordon, 1983; Burt, 1980).

There are a number of reasons, then, to expect gender consciousness to be unlikely to emerge until late in adolescence or early in adulthood. First, its structure appears complex; it is a relatively sophisticated edifice constructed upon identity. Second, because the family is the centerpiece of the institutionalization of gender inequality, in order to develop gender consciousness, an individual has to be in a position to be able to criticize family structures and processes without necessarily feeling one is attacking one's own loved ones. This would seem to require both cognitive skills and emotional complexity unlikely to appear at an early age.

Finally, we can suppose that in order to develop gender consciousness a woman must be able to imagine herself as being harmed by the sex/gender system around her. (On the history, meanings, and applications of the concept "sex/gender system," see Sapiro, 1986.) This requires understanding that Sleeping Beauty may not necessarily live happily ever after just because the prince has kissed her, and that her education or training will not buy her the same job and salary as it would buy a man. The experiences that lead to these types of awareness, again, are unlikely to occur until early adulthood.

What might happen in adulthood to spark as profound a change in sociopolitical identity as the development of gender consciousness in women? Here we can turn to some of the empirical evidence that probes the correlates of gender consciousness and its key elements. These correlates appear to be of two types. One has to do with demographic characteristics: Women of higher education, those who enter the labor force, and those who are not married are more likely to show signs of gender consciousness. Women in each of these circumstances are more able to be independent of men and are more apt to be in positions that enable direct comparison of their treatment as women with the treatment of men.

We cannot argue, however, that these circumstances really have the power to "cause" gender consciousness. Although survey research in recent years clearly reveals these relationships, we know that in other historical eras we probably would not see the same connection between education,

employment status, or marital status on the one hand and gender consciousness on the other. Rather, we can make a more convincing case that
these life situations can put women in a better position to develop gender
consciousness, but without the simultaneous existence of a women's movement, these personal life experiences would probably have little bearing on
the development of gender consciousness. Few individuals would, on their
own, construct a new social theory of gender and society just because they
are relatively educated; or because they are employed; or because they
experience a divorce. But if there is a women's movement, and the new
ideas are being circulated by word of mouth or press, women who are
relatively educated or employed or not married may either have more
access to the ideas or be more receptive to them than are other women.
This point is related to a more general question in the study of political
socialization: the relationships among life course and period effects.

A second condition for the development of gender consciousness seems
to be interaction among women in the absence of men. Research suggests
that women who belong to all-female organizations, whether politically
oriented or not, show more signs of developing gender consciousness than
do other women (Chapman, 1987). The effects of consciousness-raising
groups, discussed more later, also suggest that, again, if feminist ideas are
"in the air," it is not difficult for women discussing their own situations
with each other to develop at least a basic political understanding of gender relations. It certainly seems plausible to suggest that, in order to develop a form of group consciousness, members of a subordinate group would
usually have to interact with each other, and in a setting where they are
free from the supervision of the dominant group and thus able to negotiate
their own group identity and consciousness. (For more on the negotiation
of social identity, see du Preez, 1980.)

## THE WOMEN'S MOVEMENT AND GENDER CONSCIOUSNESS

I have argued that the presence of a women's movement is a necessary
condition for the development of gender consciousness on a large scale. But
this point raises a question: Did a rise in gender consciousness among
women give rise to the women's movement, or does the women's movement
effect a rise in gender consciousness? The answer must be both. As Ethel
Klein (1984) argues persuasively,

The emergence of a mass movement depends on the development of group
consciousness. People need to reject old group images for new roles to understand that the roots of their problems cannot be solved by their individual

efforts, before they will look to political remedies. This consciousness is learned. It usually arises out of changed social conditions and economic circumstances, which alter people's understanding of themselves and their lives. [p. 81]

Klein demonstrates that the interaction of changes in women's labor-force participation, fertility, and marriage "led to the growth of a feminist consciousness which in turn promoted the emergence of the women's movement" (p. 81).

It is difficult to imagine a voluntarily organized women's movement arising in the absence of gender consciousness on the part of the founders. Histories of the formation of women's movements, and especially the letters and autobiographies of the women most responsible for the initiation of movements, often point out the key role of specific precipitating events in stimulating a change of consciousness that served as the motivation for political action. It is important to remember, however, that, no matter how large many women's movements have grown over time, they usually begin with intense organizing efforts on the part of relatively few people.

Once the formation of a movement has begun, we must also consider the impact of the movement on gender consciousness. Historically, the women's movement, not just in the United States but in other nations as well, has served as an active and purposeful agent of socialization in developing and mobilizing such consciousness. It must be emphasized that women's movements are not simply aggregates of lobbyists or interest groups that attempt to influence the development of public policy. Indeed, some wings of feminist movements eschew the very idea of becoming entangled with politics, as conventionally defined, for what they regard as political reasons. Rather, one of the most central goals of women's movements, regardless of their specific construction of political practice, is to change women's understanding of themselves, that is, to develop a sense of gender consciousness among women.

The most well-known and obvious strategy for such development is the consciousness-raising (CR) group, which emerged in women's movements around the world (see, e.g., Dahlerup, 1986). The formation of CR groups was encouraged by sectors of the women's movement, and, no matter how informally and spontaneously organized, they came to be defined as a part of the women's movement. Sara Evans (1979) discusses the rise and function of CR groups in the early days of the contemporary women's movement:

The experiences of the first few women's liberation groups were repeated hundreds of times over. Young women's instinctive sharing of their personal experiences soon became a political instrument called "consciousness-raising." The models for consciousness-raising ranged from the earliest SNCC meetings, to SDS's "Guatemala Guerilla" organizing approach, to the practice of "speaking bitterness" in the Chinese revolution. It evolved into a kind of phenomenological approach to women's liberation. [p. 219]

The ties among personal development, social identity, and political ideology and strategy are further underscored by the relationship between the political strategy of consciousness raising and some forms of group therapy, especially feminist therapy, which also grew out of the context of the women's movement.

Although CR groups differ, the basic process and outcome are widely shared. Small groups of women meet informally and with as nonhierarchical a group structure as possible (i.e., no designated "leader" or "expert") and discuss their personal situations and problems. The rejection of hierarchy is an important clue to how carefully activists in the women's movement have emphasized not just the goal of value change or resocialization, but also the significance of the *process* of resocialization. It is important to note that, when feminists use the terms *nonhierarchical* or *rejection of hierarchy*, they are not usually referring to practices of rotating leaders, elections, or majority rule, which are usually the cornerstones of liberal democratic political theory on structure and process. Rather, CR groups, as well as a wide range of other feminist groups, are structured in a more radically egalitarian way. Feminist theorists tend to argue that their radical egalitarianism is both a means (in part through its socialization effects) and an end.

Women in CR groups took the first step in development of gender consciousness as they came to realize that many of their problems were shared and located in their situations as women, and as they recognized an understanding of themselves that they had not gained from men. This step marked the transition to acquiring a social identity as women. Almost invariably, women also began to identify the source of their difficulties not in their private choices, but in the social forces acting on women as a group. This stage led to an identification of collective rather than (or in addition to) individual action as a necessary step for achieving change. This step would indicate the development of gender consciousness.

Although the term *consciousness-raising group* is not heard as often now as it was a few years ago, these groups continue to serve as models for political practice within the women's movement. Examples include women's political groups of all kinds, such as feminist rape crisis centers and shelters for battered wives, women's arts collectives, and some feminist commercial collectives. Even where the practice is difficult to maintain, as in the cases of women's suborganizations or caucuses within larger, bureaucratic, and male-dominated institutions, the notion of nonhierarchical, mutually negotiated definitions of social identity and practices of problem solving in a "women's space" still tend to be regarded as ideal within the women's movement.

CR groups were perhaps the most explicit but not the only means by which the women's movement effected changes in social and political identity. Women's movements usually engage in a wide range of activities designed to change women's understanding of the social and political significance of gender. Many of these activities are aimed at explicitly educational institutions. "Women's studies" at institutions of higher education began in most countries as informal study groups and voluntarily offered courses on the heels of the founding of the wider social movement. Among the earliest efforts of the Women's Liberation Movement was the attempt to alter curricula and introduce nonstereotypic material on women into textbooks. Indeed, feminists have also argued that pedagogical *practices* (as well as content) must change in order for women to achieve an understanding of themselves that is not based on subordination. The point, once again, is the belief that social practices have socializing effects, and effects with significance for political consciousness at that (See Culley & Portuges, 1985; Hanmer & Saunders, 1984).

The women's movement also directed attention to the mass media, both by trying to alter the coverage of women and women's issues in the mainstream media and by founding their own media of mass communication. Indeed, the women's movement took socialization theory to heart and systematically identified agents of socialization that would need to change their gender-laden messages in order for women to become more aware of their situation as women.

While it is true that feminists focus on institutions of education and the mass media in order to widen women's *access*, they are also clearly concerned with the role these institutions play in the socialization process. Indeed, a considerable amount of feminist argument and policy debate regarding most major social institutions — not just the mass media and schools, but also the family, workplace, and health care delivery systems — is focused on what senses of social and self-identity women develop as a result of their experiences with these institutions, and how these socialization effects might change if the institutions were less partriarchally or androcentrically structured. Although Betty Friedan's (1963) *The Feminine Mystique* is often (questionably) cited as the book that created the dramatic change in consciousness necessary to spark the development of a *mass* movement among women, one could as easily argue that the Boston Women's Health Book Collective's (1971) *Our Bodies, Ourselves*, ostensibly a manual to help women become healthier, did at least as much, especially among younger women.

Finally, social movements' engagement in demonstrations and symbolic political acts must be understood as consciousness-raising efforts. In the women's movement, demonstrations such as marches, "Freedom Trashcans," and "Take Back the Night" events serve not just to call attention to the existence of the movement or to influence or threaten opponents, but, even more, to trigger a changed awareness of women's situation among women themselves. Indeed, the women's movement has consciously engaged in the politics of symbolism in diverse ways, pressing for events such as "Women's History Month" in the United States, for example.

The women's movement, then, acts in a number of ways as an agent of socialization, through its effects on gender consciousness. It has attempted to bombard the public, including women who do not identify themselves with the women's movement, with critical questions about women's situation and new information about women. It has provided a "social space" in which women can consider and negotiate their social identity as women and its relationship to politics (Evans & Boyte, 1986).

The type of change engendered by the women's movement and the process by which this change occurs are exemplified in the life stories of women writers, artists, scientists, and scholars, collected by Sara Ruddick and Pamela Daniels in *Working It Out* (1977). At the time of its publication, the book's authors wrote,

> Almost all of us are near forty. Educated in the 1950's, at the height of the feminine mystique, we are a pivotal generation. [We] encountered the women's movement late, usually in our thirties. . . . [As a result of that contact], all of us have had to relearn our pasts. We have had to reevaluate our purposes in working and re-view our commitments to our work and to those we love. Raised consciousness, whatever its ultimate value, has brought vulnerability and has invited risk. It has insisted on change. Our stories are the evidence that significant changes can and do occur in adult lives — after we are supposed to be "grown up" and "settled down." [pp. xxviii, xxix]

These words constitute only an anecdote, not systematic evidence of the type that is usually demanded in socialization research, but they represent a story that has been told, independently and repeatedly, by many women through their writing and speaking about the women's movement.

## GENDER CONSCIOUSNESS AND DEMOCRACY

The political significance and impact of women's movements are all too often assessed according to the degree to which governments adopt specific policy proposals offered by the movements, and especially particular pieces of equal-pay or work-opportunities legislation, divorce or marital property reform, or expansion of the power of women over their fertility through birth control or abortion policy. It is true that most women's movements do have lists of policy proposals of this sort that are the subject of considerable political activity. But the political writings of most women's movements also indicate a widespread belief that, without a fundamental change in the way women understand themselves as a social group in a political context, the effects of success in creating these specific policy changes on the status of women will be limited.

It is clear that a social movement such as the women's movement can have profound and widespread socialization effects on individuals in society, by transforming their sense of identity and politicizing the resulting social identification. As we have seen, the women's movement has been acutely aware of this transformational potential.

The well-known slogan, "the personal is political," has been used by feminists to refer to the belief that much of what is regarded in liberal democracies as "personal" and "private" is properly the subject of political discussion and also has long been the object of state regulation. More than this, acknowledging that "the personal is political" points out that personal identity is inextricably linked to social and political identity, and that private and public practices are not as distinct as some would hold. The subordination of women within families or to domestic duties is not merely a private practice that can exist within a larger framework of "democracy." The subordination of women, feminists argue, decreases the measure of democracy itself. Feminist practice tends to be extraordinarily self-reflective, embedding within itself the habit of asking at each turn not just whether a decision is consistent with feminist principles, but whether the decision-making process is as well.

Women's movements organized by women are important arenas for the development of democracy in a number of respects. They engage in many different types of programs aimed at generating new orientations toward women that would support ending social, economic, and political practices and policies that subordinate women. They help to give women a political consciousness that outfits them to be citizens who can take up political action on their own behalf instead of remaining subjects whose lives are governed by others. In these senses women's movements can be schools for democracy. But insofar as women's movements offer a space in which an otherwise subordinated social group can negotiate its own sense of political identity and consciousness, and particularly in those widespread parts of the movement that strive toward radically egalitarian and democratic practices of such negotiation, women's movements are not just schools *for* democracy, they are democratic institutions themselves that are established and structured by their participants.

## RESEARCH IMPLICATIONS

This chapter is obviously not the result of a particular, systematic empirical investigation of the socialization impact of women's movements; rather, it represents an attempt to synthesize disparate studies of social identity and group consciousness, social movements, and the study of political socialization. Serious scholarly study of women and politics has been going on for the past 15 years, but there has been little empirical work on the political psychology of women's movements; indeed, as I argued at the beginning, there has been little work on the relationship of social movements of any sort to individual political learning and development.

One major problem is that investigation of the kinds of transformations discussed here is not likely to be best achieved through large-scale sample survey designs. Rather, more appropriate designs would involve observational and in-depth clinical techniques. These have not been the favored techniques within the field of political socialization, but the field itself has been remarkably little concerned with the process of political socialization (Cook, 1985), particularly if it involves willful self-transformation, nor has it been very interested in identity.

The question of the participation of individuals in their own political socialization merges questions of theory, substance, and method. In accepting, at least by implication, the substance of social learning theory as the basis for political socialization, scholars in this field have painted the subject of socialization in most respects as a passive canvas. Perhaps the growing interest in developmental theories will correct this image and give us back a picture of human beings who play active roles in their own lives (Cook, 1985; Gibbs & Schnell, 1985). Surely this is one of the effects of social movements: motivating or helping people to develop their own political ideal types and also to pursue them.

If we accept the notion that individuals can play key roles in their own political development and, indeed, that democratic politics places positive value on at least some degree of self-determination, it would be reasonable also to accept the idea that research strategies for investigating the course of development can involve more attention to subjects' own understanding of their development (e.g., de Monteflores & Schultz, 1978).

It is true that there are serious drawbacks to relying only on self-reflection and recall (e.g., Markus, 1986). On the other hand, clinical techniques have been designed and refined in order to overcome some of the deficiencies in self-perception and barriers of self-presentation that are likely to arise in the context of lengthy but relatively superficial survey instruments. Moreover, when the subjects being studied are individuals such as those in the women's movement, who have gained considerable experience in political self-analysis, it is incumbent upon the researcher to listen.

## REFERENCES

Billig, M. (1976). *Social psychology and intergroup relations.* New York: Academic Press.

Block, J. H. (1984). *Sex role identity and ego development.* San Francisco: Jossey-Bass.

Boston Women's Health Book Collective. (1971). *Our bodies, ourselves.* New York: Simon & Schuster.

Breines, W., & Gordon, L. (1983). The new scholarship on family violence. *Signs, 8,* 490–531.

Burt, M. R. (1980). Cultural myths and supports for rape. *Journal of Personality and Social Psychology, 38,* 217–230.

Chapman, J. (1987). Adult socialization and out-group politicization: An empirical study of consciousness-raising. *British Journal of Political Science, 17,* 315–340.

Coles, R. (1986a). *The moral life of children.* Boston: Atlantic Monthly Press.

Coles, R. (1986b). *The political life of children.* Boston: Atlantic Monthly Press.

Conover, P. (1984). The influence of group identification on political perceptions and evaluations. *American Journal of Political Science, 46,* 760–785.

Conover, P. (1987, April). *Gender identities and basic political orientations.* Paper presented at the annual meeting of the Midwest Political Science Association, Chicago.

Conover, P. J. (1988). The role of social groups in political thinking. *British Journal of Political Science, 18,* 51–76.

Cook, T. E. (1985). The bear market in political socialization and the costs of misunderstood psychological theories. *American Political Science Review, 79,* 1079–1093.

Culley, M., & Portuges, C. (Eds.). (1985). *Gendered subjects: The dynamics of feminist teaching.* Boston: Routledge and Kegan Paul.

Dahlerup, D. (Ed.). (1986). *The new women's movement: Feminism and political power in Europe and the USA.* Beverly Hills, CA: Sage.

de Monteflores, C., & Schultz, S. (1978). Coming out: Similarities and differences for lesbians and gay men. *Journal of Social Issues, 34,* 59–72.

du Preez, P. (1980). *The politics of identity.* New York: St. Martin's.

Evans, S. (1979). *Personal politics: The roots of women's liberation in the Civil Rights Movement and the New Left.* New York: Vintage.

Evans, S. M., & Boyte, H. C. (1986, November). *Free spaces: The sources of democratic change in America.* New York: Harper & Row.

Fowlkes, D. (1986). *Feminism or feminine-ism? Forms of political consciousness of white female activists.* Paper presented at the annual meeting of the Southern Political Science Association, Atlanta.

Fowlkes, D. (1987, September). *Feminist consciousness of Englishwomen: "Women's sphere" and "women's culture."* Paper presented at the annual meeting of the American Political Science Association, Chicago.

Friedan, B. (1963). *The feminine mystique.* New York: Dell.

Gibbs, J. C., & Schnell, S. V. (1985). Moral development "versus" socialization: A critique. *American Psychologist, 40,* 1071–1080.

Gurin, P. (1985). Women's gender consciousness. *Public Opinion Quarterly, 49,* 143–163.

Gurin, P., Miller, A., & Gurin, G. (1980). Stratum identification and consciousness. *Social Psychology Quarterly, 43,* 30–47.

Hanmer, J., & Saunders, S. (1984). *Well-founded fear: A community study of violence to women.* London: Hutchinson.

Kalmuss, D. S., Gurin, P., & Townsend, A. (1981). Feminist and sympathetic feminist consciousness. *European Journal of Social Psychology, 11,* 131–147.

Kalmuss, D. S., & Strauss, M. A. (1982). Wife's marital dependency and wife abuse. *Journal of Marriage and the Family, 44,* 277–286.

Klein, E. (1984). *Gender politics.* Cambridge, MA: Harvard University Press.

Markus, G. B. (1986). Stability and change in political attitudes: Observed, recalled, and "explained." *Political Behavior, 8,* 21–44.

Miller, A., Gurin, P., Gurin, G., & Malanchuk, O. (1981). Group consciousness and political participation. *American Journal of Political Science, 25,* 494–511.

Ruddick, S., & Daniels, P. (Eds.). (1977). *Working it out: Twenty-three women writers, artists, scientists, and scholars talk about their lives and work.* New York: Pantheon.

Sapiro, V. (1986). *Women in American society: An introduction to women's studies.* Palo Alto, CA: Mayfield.

Shingles, R. D. (1981). Black consciousness and political participation: The missing link. *American Political Science Review, 75,* 76–91.

Sigel, R., & Whelchel, N. (1986, April). *Minority consciousness and sense of group power among women.* Paper presented at the annual meeting of the Midwest Political Science Association, Chicago.

Strube, M. J., & Barbour, L. S. (1983). The decision to leave an abusive relationship: Economic dependence and psychological commitment. *Journal of Marriage and the Family, 45,* 785–793.

Tajfel, H. (1981). *Human groups and social categories.* New York: Cambridge University Press.

Tajfel, H. (Ed.). (1982). *Social identity and intergroup relations.* New York: Cambridge University Press.

# 14

# Environmental Understanding: A New Concern for Political Socialization

## LESTER W. MILBRATH

Almost every modern society makes a concerted effort to train its young people to participate in the society and its political affairs. Why do we not also train our young people to participate as good citizens in their ecosystem? This is a strange and disconcerting oversight, as nearly all primitive societies emphasized environmental understanding as a central feature of helping their young people to live a good life. In the industrial era we seem to have adopted the idea that science and technology will give us such complete control of the environment that we do not need to be concerned about the good functioning of ecosystems or about the possible damage we may be inflicting on them.

Our perspective has been changing in recent decades, and once more the human family is rediscovering its need to live harmoniously with all other creatures in a viable ecosystem and to ensure the good functioning of our biosphere. Why has this happened, and what does it mean for political socialization?

In answering that overarching question in this chapter, I will speak to the following particulars:

1. Why did the environmental movement arise?
2. What kind of movement is it?
3. What are its main concerns?
4. What kinds of people support it?
5. Why do governmental and political leaders try to ignore the environment?
6. Why has social science mainly ignored environmental problems?
7. Why have schools mainly ignored environmental education?
8. Should environmental understanding become a concern for political socialization?

9. What would be the main features of adequate environmental education?

## ORIGINS OF THE ENVIRONMENTAL MOVEMENT

As I have studied the history of the relationship between humans and Nature, I have been astonished at the sweeping change in perspective that accompanied the early stages of the Industrial Revolution. Instead of the long-standing traditional perspective that humans should live harmoniously with Nature, we shifted to a perspective of being master, even rapist, of Nature. This was especially true of the "pioneers" who lead the European invasion and exploitation of such undeveloped continents as North and South America, Africa, Australia, and New Zealand. They displaced indigenous humans, slashed down forests, mined for resources, transformed ecosystems, dumped their wastes everywhere, and squandered natural wealth. In the process, they inadvertently changed climates.

The belief system of the early industrial era, which still dominates much thinking today, emphasizes the following:

1. It is right and proper for humans to dominate and control Nature.
2. Science and technology are humans' means for doing this, and their development should be emphasized.
3. Acquiring material goods is the key to a good life.
4. There are plenty of resources, so we need not be concerned about running out.
5. Nature will absorb our wastes.

Dunlap (1983) has called this the "human exemptionalist paradigm," because it assumes that humans are not bound by the laws of Nature that restrain the behavior of all other creatures.

In the latter half of the nineteenth century, especially in England, Germany, and North America, some observers of the human raping of the landscape became alarmed at its wasteful destruction and began the conservation movement. The first national parks were set aside at this time. Those in the movement wished to preserve Nature for enjoyment and to stretch out utilization of resources to meet the needs of future generations. They also launched the first efforts to control pollution. People believing in this movement called themselves "progressives" and the period became known as the Progressive Era. The progressive conservation movement restored some valuation to Nature, but it was a very human-oriented movement, in which Nature was seen as valuable for humans to enjoy and use.

Wild animals were protected and propagated for humans to "harvest." Fish were hatched and nurtured for humans to catch and consume. Natural habitat was preserved for wild creatures, but the motivation was human needs. Those active in the movement believed in the values and structure of modern industrial society. They saw no reason to doubt the basic soundness of modern civilization; their main desire was to make it more efficient (Hays, 1958).

By the middle of the twentieth century, the conservation movement began to transform into the environmental movement (Hays, 1987). The most immediate stimulus was the increasingly serious pollution of the air, water, and soil, to the point where human health was at risk. As a matter of fact, many people today still perceive the environmental movement mainly as an antipollution movement. Those studying environmental problems closely, however, came to see them as a complex nested set of interrelated issues. World population had doubled from 1.2 billion to 2.5 billion from 1875 to 1950, and it doubled again to 5 billion by 1986. (It will probably double again to 10 billion before 2050.) This larger population became wealthier, consumed more, and cast an increasingly greater volume of wastes into the biosphere. Many of these wastes also were more toxic than ever before. Natural ecosystems became increasingly crippled in their ability to support life. Health problems of humans and other creatures were traced again and again to environmental degradation. Mineral and natural resources became scarcer, and reserves were drawn down swiftly. Those in the new environmental movement also came to see that these problems could not be solved simply by passing stronger legislation and developing better technology; rather, the very thrust and structure of modern society would have to change. Many environmentalists now call for a new society that can live harmoniously in a long-run, sustainable relationship with Nature.

Hays (1987) sums up the transition from conservationism to environmentalism as follows:

> The conservation movement was an effort on the part of leaders in science, technology, and government to bring about more efficient development of physical resources. The environmental movement, on the other hand, was far more widespread and popular, involving public values that stressed quality of human experience and hence of the human environment. Conservation was an aspect of the history of production that stressed efficiency, whereas environment was a part of the history of consumption that stressed new aspects of the American standard of living. [p. 13]

The new environmental movement mainly resulted from social learning. Nature was our most powerful teacher. Our own health problems convinced us that pollution injured us as well as other creatures. Increased crowding and scarcity of resources convinced us that human population must be controlled. Wastes seeping into our soil and water convinced us that we must find better ways of disposal. Lack of space to put our wastes convinced us that we must reduce waste generation, which, in effect, meant reducing consumption. The hollowness of material consumption persuaded us that quality of life was nurtured as much, or more, by beautiful Nature as by consuming material things — that the goal of life is not wealth but quality in living. Our experience with these problems gave us better insight into our deepest values. Of course, our learning also was aided by scientific research that helped us to understand better the sources of our problems and the consequences of our actions. We also are constantly learning more about how ecosystems and the biosphere function.

## CHARACTERISTICS OF THE MOVEMENT

The environmental movement is most fundamentally a citizen's movement. It developed its own indigenous leaders. Elites in other sectors such as politics or science have played little role in the environmental movement. In modern industrial countries like England, Germany, and the United States, 20 to 30 percent of the adult population share the beliefs and values of the environmental movement and perceive themselves as environmentalists (Milbrath, 1984). An even larger proportion — in the 60- to 80-percent range — approve of the environmental movement. Of course, the activists in the movement are a much smaller group, probably less than 1 percent of adults.

It is a worldwide movement and growing rapidly in less-developed countries (LDCs). It began in developed countries (DCs) and is strongest there, but Nature has been teaching people in LDCs that they, too, must give high priority to environmental protection. If anything, environmental problems are greater in LDCs than in DCs, because population growth in LDCs is faster and their resource base is smaller and more fragile. Poverty is the greatest environmental problem in LDCs. Poor people tend to injure their ecosystem, literally stripping the land of food and fuel in order to stay alive (World Commission on Environment and Development, 1987).

The environmental movement most visibly finds expression in environmental organizations, some of which have members in many nations. The organizational structure grew out of the conservation movement, but the organizations currently have a broader range of concerns and many new organizations have been formed. In the United States there are 10 large national environmental organizations, the largest having 4.5 million members, but there are many thousands of additional groups. Some of these are national in scope, but most are purely local. Many of these local groups grew from the grass roots, in response to a specific environmental threat. At Love Canal in Niagara Falls, New York, for example, the home-owners who saw their community threatened by a toxic dump formed a vigorous political action group that eventually changed public policy at the local, state, and national level with respect to toxic waste handling and disposal.

A conservative estimate is that there are 20 million members of environmental organizations in the United States. Some of these groups espouse the belief that modern society is fundamentally sound and that stronger and better-enforced legislation, combined with better technology, will adequately handle our environmental problems. Let us call these the "Nature conservationists." Others believe that we must transform society to accept new values, new lifestyles, new policies, and a new direction that orients society to living harmoniously with Nature. Let us call these the "greens." In several countries, persons foreseeing the need for a new society have formed Green political parties. None has yet formed a government, but they are well established and growing in several European countries, especially West Germany (Capra & Spretnak, 1984).

## MAIN CONCERNS OF THE MOVEMENT

Within the environmental movement, then, there are *greens* who want to transform society so that it takes a new direction with new values and new lifestyles, and there are *conservationists* who want our present society to take better care of the environment but do not want it to take a new direction with new goals. Both of these perspectives must be taken into consideration in summarizing the concerns of the movement.

Both groups agree that society must take greater care to protect the environment from being damaged by our activities. Stricter laws forbidding damaging activities must be better enforced. They also agree that we need better technologies to prevent damage and to clean up the damage that has already occurred. Both sides agree further that we should restore and protect natural habitats so that other creatures can flourish and Nature can be beautiful and enjoyable. Both agree that we should foster research to help us better understand the functioning of natural ecosystems, so that we can be more effective in our attempts to protect, nourish, and restore them.

The main point of disagreement is over the means to these ends. The greens believe humans must limit growth in human population, in economic activity, and in consumption of material goods. The conservationists believe limits to growth are not necessary. They have strong faith that we will develop new technology, find more resources, and develop better ways to prevent and/or clean up environmental damage. The greens would also have us draw back from our attempts to dominate Nature and urge us to find simpler ways to live lightly on the Earth. The conservationists believe humans should continue to dominate and manage Nature. The greens typically press for citizen participation and grass-roots democracy as the best process for setting the direction for society and for making policies, while the conservationists are more inclined to call on experts and managers to make and execute policy. Greens are inclined to be gentle and pacifist, while conservationists are more inclined to accept the use of violence and are accustomed to using guns. A strong sense of compassion leads greens to support policies of social responsibility; nature conservationists would not renounce that goal, but would be more inclined to let people look out for themselves.

Over the last 15 years these two kinds of environmental groups seem to have drawn closer together, at least in the United States. The Nature conservationists seem to be discovering that beliefs about the goals of society as well as personal lifestyles must be transformed in a "green" direction, whereas the greens are recognizing that societal transformation will have to come in incremental steps that are akin to those supported by the conservationists.

## REASONS WHY PEOPLE SUPPORT THE ENVIRONMENTAL MOVEMENT

Love of Nature draws people to environmentalism. Those who had strongly rewarding experiences with Nature as children seem to have been "imprinted" with a predisposition to seek similar experiences throughout life and to express this desire as adults by supporting actions and policies that protect Nature.

Another way people come to value environmental quality is to suffer an injury or deprivation due to environmental deficiency or damage. People who suffer ill health due to a nearby toxic dump, for example, are quickly mobilized for political action demanding changes in policies. Some of those people have their consciousness so aroused and their values so clarified that they become environmental activists for life (e.g., Gibbs, 1982).

Given a high valuation on environmental quality, developing an understanding of the way ecosystems and social systems function fosters a deeper determination to work for a better environment in most people. Those who can imagine the long-run consequences of present actions are more environmentally protective. People who can see the connection between a healthily functioning ecosystem and a healthily functioning social system are more likely to work for social change to get a better environment. People who can imagine the suffering of humans and other creatures if their environment fails to nourish them will want to work to prevent that failure.

Level of education is positively correlated with increasing environmentalism (Milbrath, 1984). The difference is most striking when we compare those with four years of college education to those with postgraduate training, as those who study beyond college are significantly more environmentally oriented. This means that most secondary schools and colleges seriously fail in environmental education. This "failure" is more like an abdication than a shortcoming, since most schools simply do not even try to provide environmental education. (Later in this chapter, I outline my views on a satisfactory environmental education.)

Whether or not a person becomes an environmentalist also depends on what other values that person holds highly. The old aphorism that where one stands depends on where one sits holds here as well. People working for business corporations, which typically emphasize production and acquiring wealth, uphold values that conflict with environmentalism. People working in the service sector of society experience less internal conflict if they press for the realization of environmental goals, since protection measures usually do not entail an economic loss for them (Cotgrove, 1982; Milbrath, 1984). As another example, people who are desperately poor are likely to focus their attention on getting the next meal or finding shelter and have little reserve psychological energy to devote to something as long-range as environmental protection.

Women are more likely to support environmentalism than men; one study (Milbrath, 1984) shows that typically about 15 percent more women than men will support a protection policy. This difference highlights the disparity between women's and men's psychosocial cultures. Environmentalism involves compassion for other creatures and for future generations, which is part of the role to which women are socialized. In contrast, men in most societies are socialized to be aggressive, competitive, and dominating, and one easy target is Nature. The macho man sees himself as conquering Nature. If one examines environmental groups that arose because people experienced some environmental injury or threat, one finds that most indigenous leaders are women. Men are socialized to express their manhood by denying the importance of the threat.

## POLITICIANS AND THE ENVIRONMENT

Almost every initiative for a new or more protective environmental policy that I am familiar with had its origin in the grass roots. Citizen activists have placed nearly all environmental questions on the public agenda in nearly all countries. China is one exception where the political leadership has been ahead of the public in calling for more environmentally protective actions. Why have political leaders been so slow in recognizing the need for environmental protection?

The world view that dominates thinking and public discourse in most countries holds that humans should control and exploit Nature, to produce more material goods that will bring a better life to people. Quality of life typically is equated with standard of living. Political leaders are drawn from the dominant elements of society that hold this world view. Furthermore, candidates hoping to be elected believe that they must urge economic growth as a central policy. Only when the public clamors for environmental protection will candidates also push for it. Typically, they try to finesse the conflict between the two values by claiming that economic growth does not conflict with environmental protection.

Another consideration is that political leaders in most countries believe they must take a dominator posture to be successful. Political leadership of a society is won in a competitive contest among several candidates, most of whom seek a top position in order to wield power. Most leaders desire to expand their power, since the cost of not doing so often is the loss of their position. Those who succeed best in this game are those who can most effectively dominate others, or have power over them. This posture of domination is easily and legitimately expressed in domination of Nature. It is little wonder that men more than women are attracted to politics and governance and play the key roles there. Their typical approach to environmental problems is to manage and dominate the situation through laws and powerful technology.

A third consideration behind the reluctance of public officials to recognize environmental problems is that to acknowledge them is to admit the deficiency or failure of one's policies. If left to its own management, Nature would not be likely to fail. To make the point another way, if there were no humans in an ecosystem, the system would get along just fine. Even though humans are not essential for the good functioning of an ecosystem, a good ecosystem is essential for our ability to lead a good life. If we think about this, we will recognize that protection of ecosystem integrity must have the highest public priority. Most officials do not think this way, however, and choose to maximize growth and wealth instead.

Because of these strong forces driving officials to ignore environmental problems, environmentalists have learned that rational arguments are of little help in getting environmental problems on the political agenda. The only tactic that seems to be effective is to raise a clamor among the public. When officials perceive that they might lose votes if they do not respond, they do respond. Using these tactics, environmentalists have won some striking public policy victories, even though they are "swimming against the stream" of most policy-making forces.

## SOCIAL SCIENCE AND ENVIRONMENTAL PROBLEMS

Social scientists are not as strongly subject to public opinion and pressure from dominant institutions as are public officials. Most social scientists are free to choose their subject and mode of inquiry; yet, most have not chosen to focus on environmental questions. Why have they not studied the relationship between environment and society? It probably is fair to say that most are insufficiently aware of the possibility for meaningful social science inquiry concerning the environment to be able to have considered it. This is partly due to the emphasis on specialization and on defense of one's disciplinary turf, which dominates so much of modern university life. Selecting an environmental emphasis in graduate work, be it in education, political science, sociology, economics, psychology, or history, simply does not occur to most graduate students.

Another consideration is that most social scientists share in the popular perception that humans are exceptional creatures. Because humans can dominate Nature, we easily slip into the notion that we are exempt from the natural laws that restrain other species. Social scientists seem to believe that human society is a unique creation on the planet and in order to understand it one need only look to its internal dynamics. For example, one can search through the entire history of political sociology and find hardly any mention of the impact of ecosystems, biospheric elements, or technological development on the way that politics is conducted (Wasburn, 1982). In contrast, my own analysis suggests that knowledge of ecosystemic and technological influences is requisite to understanding social systems and that environmental and technological considerations will be the predominant influences on the politics of the twenty-first century.

One would expect that economists, of all the social scientists, would be most sensitive to the impact of environmental and technological considerations on the phenomena they study. Yet their theoretical presuppositions that the environment is a given and technology will turn up whatever resources are needed lead them to define these influences as external to their inquiry.

Urging social scientists to give deep and sustained attention to the relationship between environment and society is probably a waste of time;

most of them simply are not listening. Instead, Nature will once more have to be our most influential teacher. When Nature's restraints are insistently obvious, even social scientists will be roused.

## SCHOOLS AND ENVIRONMENTAL EDUCATION

Primary and secondary schools mainly attend to three kinds of signals as they set their priorities: traditional societal values, the concerns developed in higher education, and the job market. Even though environmental education was always prominent in traditional (primitive) societies whose members lived close to Nature, none of the three signals currently guiding priorities in schools in modern industrial society encourage them to teach students about environmental problems. Such education is underplayed or ignored in schools in nearly all countries. Of course, information about plants and animals has traditionally been taught in biology classes, but little attempt is made there to link the health of biosystems to human activities. Students are seldom urged to reflect on the impact of their own behavior and of society's activities on the functioning of ecosystems. Soon we must learn that it is important and urgent to help all students to understand this relationship.

Students in social science classes are seldom instructed on the ways social systems are impacted by physical systems, nor are they urged to reflect on the way human activities impact the biosphere. This is due at least in part to the fact that such content was not part of the training of social science teachers in college. Furthermore, administrators who decide on degree requirements and hire teachers seldom bring environmental knowledge into their consideration. It would seem that to correct this deficiency the environmental awareness of the entire school system must be raised.

Since modern industrial society is developing jobs that require environmental training, one could imagine that schools would respond to that need. Regrettably, those jobs tend to be cast in such traditional categories as engineer, biologist, or geologist. The schools do not perceive them as environmental jobs, nor do they provide broad integrative environmental training for those jobs. Firms and governments that find they must be concerned about environmental policy mainly hire technical specialists in their entry-level positions. Many of these people go on to make environmental policy but without the benefit of appropriate training. Students who decide to focus their study on the relationship between environment and society or on environmental policy find that they must hurdle system barriers as they seek a position in the present job market.

## ENVIRONMENTAL UNDERSTANDING
## AS A CONCERN FOR POLITICAL SOCIALIZATION

It is my belief that environmental understanding should be a concern for political socialization, a position that should be obvious from the foregoing discussions in this chapter. Let me summarize my reasons. First, modern industrial society cannot continue on its present trajectory; there simply are not sufficient resources, or sufficient capacity in the ecosystem to absorb our wastes, for us to be able to continue our present rates of growth in population and economic activity. Growth of both kinds must be limited, perhaps stopped altogether. The environmental problems of modern society cannot be fixed by better technology and/or better laws. Limiting our growth and learning to live harmoniously with Nature will require us to transform modern society.

This means that we all must pay much more attention to the relationship between environment and society. We must constantly ask how societal activities impact the environment and how environmental realities shape what society can or must do. This is the most urgent problem facing society today (Milbrath, 1989). Teachers and students must learn much more about that relationship. Even though it is an urgent priority, most schools currently fail miserably in addressing it. It is an equally urgent concern for politics; that is why it must become a central task for political socialization.

## PRINCIPAL FEATURES OF ENVIRONMENTAL EDUCATION

An adequate environmental education must begin with learning about the basic physical "media" of the biosphere (soils, water, and air) and the way these media are related in a biospheric system. Students also must develop a basic knowledge of the living creatures that inhabit the ecosphere, especially the way the living and nonliving elements are systemically related. Schools do teach in these areas presently, but usually not well, and this knowledge is not required of all students. It is especially important that environmental education not end at this basic level.

As noted earlier, ecosystems function just fine without humans, but humans cannot function at all without a viable ecosystem. Environmental problems have their origins in modern society, and we will solve them only by studying much more closely the relationship between society and environment. Environmental understanding must become an integral part of the social science curriculum. Students must learn how our production activities, consumption, lifestyles, and politics impact the environment.

Reciprocally, they must learn how environmental realities and our degradation of the environment impact our production, consumption, lifestyles, and politics. Ecosystems and social systems are integrally connected, and we all must learn how to think about them as such. Impact or injury in one sector reverberates and generates consequences in other sectors. A central axiom of environmentalism is, We can never do merely one thing. We must learn to ask, for every action, And then what?

Almost everyone who has taught environmental studies comes to recognize that ethics are an integral part of the inquiry. As with learning about democracy, an appreciation of such central values as life, health, ecosystem viability, compassion, justice, security, and quality of life must be a central component of the environmental socialization process. In the summer of 1987 the United Nations Environment Programme and the United Nations Educational, Scientific and Cultural Organization called a world conference on "Environmental Education and Training." Every one of the three commissions and five symposia at the conference emphasized learning environmental ethics (UNESCO-UNEP, 1987).

## CONCLUSION

Learning about the relationship between society and environment is just as urgent a task for political socialization as learning about democracy. Environmentalism is a product of democracy and is becoming an integral part of political thinking. How do we encourage greater attention to developing environmental understanding? Teaching about environmental problems in schools needs to become a political priority. Students and other informed citizens need to demand that their polity become more environmentally sensitive and protective. Which comes first? Action must get under way on both fronts. Since neither the government nor the schools currently perceive this as a priority, the environmental movement itself must be the main socializing agent. Its consciousness-raising efforts must target people of all ages, people in all walks of life, and people in all parts of the world. The movement's fundamental role is that of interpreter of the meaning of the unfolding drama of the relations between humans and Nature.

## REFERENCES

Capra, F., & Spretnak, C. (1984). *Green politics*. New York: Dutton.
Cotgrove, S. F. (1982).*Catastrophe or cornucopia: The environment, politics and the future*. Chichester/New York: John Wiley.

*Connect: UNESCO-UNEP Environmental Education Newsletter.* (1987, September). *12*(3), entire issue.

Dunlap, R. E. (1983). Ecologist vs exemptionalist: The Ehrlich–Simon debate. *Social Science Quarterly, 64,* 200–203.

Gibbs, L. M. (1982). *Love Canal: My story.* Albany: SUNY Press.

Hays, S. P. (1958). *Conservation and the gospel of efficiency: The progressive conservation movement.* Cambridge, MA: Harvard University Press.

Hays, S. P. (1987). *Beauty, health, and permanence: Environmental politics in the United States, 1955–1985.* New York: Cambridge University Press.

Milbrath, L. W. (1984). *Environmentalists: Vanguard for a new society.* Albany: SUNY Press.

Milbrath, L. W. (1989). *Envisioning a sustainable society: Learning our way out.* Albany: SUNY Press.

Wasburn, P. (1982). *Political Sociology.* New York: Prentice-Hall.

World Commission on Environment and Development. (1987). *Our common future.* London and New York: Oxford University Press.

**PART V**

# Socialization for Democracy: A Lifelong Process

# 15

# Fostering Group-Based Political Participation

## M. MARGARET CONWAY

A common axiom in democratic theory is that the good citizen participates in the political life of the community. While political participation
may be viewed as largely symbolic (Edelman, 1964), an alternative view is
that participation is instrumental. The goals sought through participation
may be external to the citizen, such as preferred sets of leaders and policies,
or they may be internal, leading to self-actualization.

Can citizens attain instrumental ends through political participation?
Is political participation rational? If it is, how can people be convinced
that participation is worthwhile?

These questions are particularly relevant to civic education. Certainly
one of the major goals of civic education is to convince young people that it
is rational to become involved in politics, yet the immediate concerns of
young people are much more likely to focus on social integration and
school or work tasks. Youth subcultures may be politically apathetic or
even antiestablishment, resentful of authorities and of the social institutions that empower them and, in young people's perceptions, restrict their
social choices.

This chapter examines the rationality of political participation and
the implications of arguments made by Anthony Downs (1957) and Mancur Olson (1965) that under many conditions such participation is irrational. Alternative views about the role of groups in the political process, the
rationality of a group-based approach to political participation, and the
implications for democratic citizenship education are then considered. The
argument is made that education for democratic citizenship could promote
higher levels of effective participation if the mechanisms for participation
through group activity and the utility of group-based participation received more emphasis. However, the implications for governing which
stem from high levels of effective participation in the political system by
groups must be considered. The process of governing may become more
complex as the number and effectiveness of politically active groups increases.

## PATTERNS OF POLITICAL PARTICIPATION

Regardless of the perspective provided by various formulations of democratic theory, some degree of political participation is expected and required. It may consist only of joining in selecting those who govern, or it may require more active forms of expression and commitment to a democratic system of government.

Trends in the level of political participation in the United States between 1960 and 1984 vary with the type of political participation being considered. Bureau of the Census surveys suggest that voting turnout substantially declined from 1960 through 1980. Analyses of the University of Michigan's American National Election Studies (NES) data (Conway, 1985; Miller, Miller, & Schneider, 1980) indicate that approximately the same proportion of respondents reported trying to influence the votes of others, attending political meetings or rallies, and working for candidates or the political parties, from 1960 through 1984. The proportion who reported giving money to a party or candidate increased slightly from 1960 to 1976, then declined to the 1960 level in 1980. Displaying campaign signs or wearing campaign buttons declined significantly between 1960 and 1984, which may be attributable to a change in campaign finance laws and to greater knowledge about the relative effects of different methods of communicating the campaign message to the potential electorate.

Participation in nonconventional forms of political action appears to have increased, but that type of activity is stimulus related. Perceptions of higher levels of protest participation, however, may be more a function of greater visibility given such events by television and the print media than any significant trends in protest participation patterns.

The increased number of organizations operating at the national level (Berry, 1984; Schlozman & Tierney, 1986; Walker, 1983) and within the states could be interpreted as reflecting increased levels of citizen participation in organizations. Similar patterns of increased organizational activity are also perceived in other developed democracies; however, the evidence necessary to support such trend analyses is generally lacking. While more issue, cause, and advocacy organizations exist and the proliferation of economic interest organizations continues, technological changes permit the appearance of active organizations without active, or even extensive, membership. An organizational entrepreneur who secures adequate funding can create the appearance and, in terms of lobbying and giving campaign contributions, the reality of an active organization, without an active membership (Cigler, 1986).

The role of groups in the political process has been a central focus of theorizing throughout the history of political science as a discipline (Garson, 1978). Even before the discipline evolved, those concerned with the creation and operation of democratic governments examined the actual and potential role of interests and factions in politics. For example, fear of an unrestrained role of groups in the political process stimulated James Madison's proposals for the then radical structure of the American federal government (Fairfield, 1981). While concern with the political roles of groups remains a recurrent theme in theories of democratic political systems (Garson, 1978), the inadequacies of purely group theories of politics have motivated scholars to search for other, more viable theories (Bachrach & Baratz, 1962; Rothman, 1960; Walker, 1966). Nonetheless, the role of groups as vehicles for the articulation of citizen demands and in monitoring policy-making and -implementation processes and politically mobilizing group members continues to be a research focus.

Evidence that democratic political systems grant both tacit and explicit support for the role of groups is provided by the formal, institutionalized processes created in order to consult with group representatives at multiple stages of the policy-making process. Evidence of that support is also presented by the informal, issue-related networks that evolve in policy arenas.

While support for the role of groups is provided by political systems, both the types of groups that serve as vehicles for political action and the forms of participation in which individuals engage can be expected to vary significantly with the political culture (or cultures) and the types and intensity of political cleavages that are present in the society. Thus, ideological groups may be more relevant in one society, while in another economic and social interest groups predominate.

Political socialization of young people to political activism through group involvement can occur through participation in various types of youth group activity. Participating in religious youth groups, school clubs, voluntary organizations, or student government activities provides an apprenticeship form of political socialization. Skills, attitudes, and values are developed that can then be transferred to political participation through more politically relevant groups. (See Yogev & Shapira, Chapter 10 of this volume.) Politically relevant learning in nonpolitical settings also occurs in adulthood (Almond & Verba, 1963.)

While politically relevant attitudes, values, and skills may be acquired through apprenticeship experiences, several facets of the citizenship concept conveyed by these experiences may not be conducive to political activism (see Ichilov, Chapter 1 of this volume). Participation may come to be viewed as voluntary, not obligatory; experiences within youth groups may foster inactivity or passivism rather than political activity; and the action perspectives developed may be diffuse.

## AGE-RELATED DIFFERENCES IN PARTICIPATION

Are various forms of individual political participation age-related phenomena, with participation increasing with age? Are there generational differences in participation patterns, with younger cohorts not attaining levels equivalent to those of older cohorts?

Young adults tend to participate less than older citizens in almost all forms of political activity. In the United States, although younger voters tend not to turn out at the same rate as their elders, voting turnout rates increase as the younger cohorts age, approximating the level attained by the older cohorts (U.S. Dept. of Commerce, 1971, 1973, 1976, 1978a, b, 1981, 1983, 1985, 1987).

While younger persons may appear to be less politically active than their parents' generation, this is in part a function of the political environment. A comparison study (Jennings & Niemi, 1981) of two high school senior cohorts, one interviewed in 1965 and the other in 1973, indicates that significant differences existed between these two groups, with the 1973 group participating less. Members of the 1973 group were more cynical and skeptical about institutions, placed less value on political participation, and gave less centrality to politics in their lives. The 1973 seniors were also significantly lower in political trust and political efficacy, but only slightly lower in interest in public affairs than the 1965 group (Jennings & Niemi, 1981).

In contrast to other forms of participation, the high school student sample first interviewed in 1965 reported in 1973 levels of protest participation that were much higher than those of their parents. Furthermore, levels of participation in most forms of campaign activity equaled or exceeded that of the parental group. An examination of participation patterns among equivalent age groups using the 1956 through 1976 American NES data sets (Beck & Jennings, 1979) shows that the pattern found in the high school senior and parent samples was also present among the 1968 and 1972 samples of the national electorate, but not in the other years. Comparing the 21-to-29-year-old group with those in the 44-to-64 age group, younger citizens had higher mean rates of participation.

Another study (Delli Carpini, 1986), using American NES data from 1952 to 1980, concluded that trends varied by type of political activity, with electoral participation increasing with age. Most other, more costly types of participation did not vary with age, although trying to influence others how to vote and displaying campaign materials evidenced a slight negative relationship with age. Those individuals classified as members of the 1960s generation, in contrast to older generations, were less likely to engage in political activities of any kind.

While differences in age and generational patterns of participation are suggested by these studies, inferences should be drawn from these patterns with considerable caution. As Dennis (1986) has pointed out, age-related differences may reflect such other factors as differences in strength and stability of community ties; rates of geographic mobility; perceived stake in the community; group memberships; and the learning of attitudes, habits, skills, and information.

Differences in educational attainment complicate evaluation of the political environment's effects on participation. By 1973, the younger generation in the high school seniors panel study (Beck & Jennings, 1979) had significantly more years of education than did the parental group, and those individuals with higher levels of educational attainment are more likely to have the skills, knowledge, motivation, and opportunity to engage in various forms of political participation.

## ATTITUDES, INTEREST, AND INVOLVEMENT

Social psychological theories of political participation emphasize attitudes, beliefs, and values as the crucial explanatory elements in accounting for patterns of political participation. While socialization through the family, peer groups, mass media, and direct experiences with political authorities has a significant impact on political attitudes, the educational process can also significantly affect these attitudes. Although Jennings and Niemi (1974) suggest that the impact of the civics curriculum is largely redundant for majority-race students in the United States, the curriculum did have a small but significant effect on the political attitudes of minority-race children. The limited effects may have been a consequence of the nature of the curriculum content and how the material was presented in most classrooms.

Other research, using experimental methods, suggests that civics courses can significantly affect relevant political attitudes (e.g., Button, 1974; Conway, Ahern, & Feldbaum, 1977; Conway, Wyckoff, Feldbaum, & Ahern, 1982; Gillespie & Mehlinger, 1972; Patrick, 1971). Some studies also suggest that the civics curriculum may have an impact on political knowledge and attitudes (e.g., Torney, Oppenheim, & Farnen, 1975; also see Chapter 9 of this volume). The failure to find significant effects in some studies may be a consequence of either the student's prior predispositions or the civics curriculum content. The material presented in the curriculum may be new to disadvantaged students and not easily learned; for more sophisticated students, the material may be repetitious and contribute little to their understanding of political institutions and processes.

Certain attitudes appear to be related to patterns of participation, and declines in levels of these attitudes would be expected to reduce participation. While aggregate levels of a sense of *internal* political efficacy have not changed substantially over time in the United States, fewer citizens express high levels of *external* political efficacy — the perception that individuals similar to oneself have a say about what the government does and that public officials care about what such people think (Conway, 1985). Perceptions of government attentiveness and the perceived utility of congressional elections, elections in general, and political parties to serve as instruments of citizen influence on government decision making have declined. A social psychological explanation of participation would lead us to emphasize the need for curriculum content that would enhance students' perceptions of citizens' abilities to influence government officials.

Several social-psychological variables relevant to political involvement through participation in organized groups could be significantly affected by civics education. Among these are interest in political processes and an increased understanding of how political institutions affect the individual's own interests. One crucial product of the civics curriculum could be increased knowledge of the mechanisms through which the citizen can influence the decisions made and the actions taken by political institutions (Button, 1974). Students could acquire an enhanced understanding of the mechanisms for collective action that can be used to produce preferred changes in government policies, and of which ones have been used successfully. The impact that individual participation, channelled through groups, can have on governmental decisions should be one focus of the civics curriculum, with several examples of the effectiveness of group efforts being presented. The variables that contribute to group effectiveness in the political arena should be thoroughly examined.

Of course, this assumes that political participation is rational, that collective action is an effective mechanism for the attainment of political goals, and that engaging in collective action to attain goals is a rational form of political activity. These are the issues to which I now turn.

## THE RATIONALITY OF POLITICAL PARTICIPATION

### The Meaning of Rationality

Economic theories of politics have challenged the rationality of political participation, but, before that can be addressed, the meaning of rationality must be considered. Anthony Downs (1957) defines a rational person as one who "moves towards his goals in a way which, to the best of his knowledge, uses the least possible input of scarce resources per unit of valued output" (p. 5). Thus, according to Downs, rationality equates with maximizing efficiency in the production of valued outcomes. The rational person seeks to maximize expected utility.

An alternative formulation of rationality provides a more elaborate definition. Rationality is perceived to be a process by which individuals evaluate alternatives on the basis of personal preferences that are consistent and transitive, with the preferred alternative always being chosen (Frohlich, Oppenheimer, & Young, 1971). Individuals do not, in this formulation, take into account the impact of their choices on the happiness of others; that is, "the individual does not value the utility of others as an end in itself" (p. 27). This view of rationality also assumes that individuals operate in terms of a set of roles, with one role within the set being paramount; implicit in this notion is the view that role conflict does not present a problem in rational decision making. Furthermore, the costs and benefits derived from actions related to one role are differentiated from those associated with other roles. Lastly, individuals must make decisions with less than perfect information available to them; some degree of uncertainty exists in the decision-making process.

## Voting

Using the criteria of rationality just described, is political participation rational? Examining participation in elections through voting behavior, Downs (1957) concluded that, taking into account the costs of acquiring information necessary to make a rational decision and the benefits to be derived from one electoral outcome as opposed to another, weighted by the probability that one's vote would make a difference in the outcome, voting is irrational. Downs then added another term to the equation—the long-run participation value, that is, the value of the system's survival, which requires that some people participate. Some people respond to this incentive, because they value the survival of the system.

Other scholars have added alternative variables to the basic cost/benefit calculations, to increase the benefit value. These include the pleasure and satisfaction derived from supporting the system, expressing partisan preferences, carrying out one's civic duty through participation, and deciding how to vote (Riker & Ordeshook, 1973); minimizing one's maximum regret (Ferejohn & Fiorina, 1974); and meeting one's ethical obligations (Goodin & Roberts, 1975). Although weighing these alternatives can be seen as an attempt to make participation a rational act within the context of the traditional model of rational choice theory, these additions to the basic cost/benefit analysis can be viewed as going beyond traditional notions of rationality (Berry, 1977).

## Collective Action to Attain Collective Goods

The rationality of other forms of political activity has also been questioned. Of central interest here is the rationality of contributing to attaining collective goods. Collective goods are characterized by indivisibility of the benefit conveyed by the good (available for use by all citizens, even if they have not contributed to its attainment) and jointness of supply (one person's use does not reduce the amount available to others). Collective goods may be subject to crowding, as evidenced by highway traffic jams, or they may be optional, with individuals excluding themselves from using the good, as in placing one's children in a private rather than public school.

Mancur Olson (1965) developed a model of collective action in which joining in the efforts to obtain collective goods would under many circumstances be irrational. Contributing resources to obtain a public good would be rational only if the benefit exceeded the cost and if the individual's contribution was crucial for obtaining the good. Furthermore, Olson emphasized the impossibility of excluding those individuals who have not contributed to obtaining the collective good, which creates the "free-rider" problem. Contributions can, however, be induced through coercion, such as with the imposition of taxes, or through the provision of special incentives in the form of side payments to those who contribute.

Both experimental and field studies indicate that Olson's (1965) theory does not adequately explain the nature of collective action (Hastie, 1984; Schoemaker, 1982). Studies of interest-group activity indicate that citizens contribute to collective action without being stimulated by various types of side payments or by coercion. Many individuals may be motivated by altruism in making decisions about their contributions to collective action activities (Frohlich & Oppenheimer, 1984; Marwell & Ames, 1979, 1980). Furthermore, the number and activity of interest groups whose goal is influencing the creation and distribution of collective goods has increased significantly (Schlozman & Tierney, 1986; Walker, 1983).

Several explanations have been suggested for why individuals contribute to obtaining collective goods. One emphasizes the entrepreneur's role in generating organizational formation and maintaining the organization through offering valued goods and services to those who join the organization (Frohlich et al., 1971; Moe, 1980). These valued goods and services may be side payments, such as lower-cost health insurance, or there may be other kinds of incentives involved, both tangible and intangible. These may include the enactment and effective implementation of a preferred policy or the rewards derived from political action itself. Rewards from the act of participation may be material or social (Clark & Wilson, 1961).

## Self-Interest Versus Group Interest

Another explanation for why individuals contribute to the attainment of collective goals is provided by Howard Margolis's "fair share" model (1984). Defining rationality as "consistency of choice," Margolis assumes that individuals see utility in pursuing both narrow personal self-interest and outcomes that contribute to the welfare of others. Two types of motivation stimulate actions that enhance the welfare of others: "participation altruism" and "goods altruism." Participation altruism means that individuals gain utility from the act of using their resources to benefit others, while goods altruism means that the individual derives a personal benefit from an increase in the goods available to others.

According to this theory, an individual distributes resources between narrow self-interest and group interest. The weights given to self-interest and to group interest vary over time, depending both on current personal circumstances and the weight given in the past to these two interests. Margolis (1984) describes the thought process involved in such allocation decisions as follows:

> The larger the share of my resources I have spent unselfishly, the more weight I give to my selfish interests in allocating marginal resources. On the other hand, the larger the benefit I can confer on the group compared with the benefit from spending marginal resources on myself, the more I will tend to act unselfishly. [p. 36]

The weight also varies among individuals and between different cultures. However, allocating scarce resources to group interest is a superior good, and those who have higher incomes would be expected to allocate a greater share of their resources to group interests.

Several types of group interest could stimulate this type of allocation of resources. Family membership could be the basis for resource allocation, and its primacy varies among different cultures (Banfield, 1958). Cooperative activity may be generated and become the basis of resource allocation to group interests. In particular, Margolis (1984) highlights "group-focused altruism," in which the allocation of resources is not based on the expectation of personal benefit. If the aim is to increase group-oriented altruism, this can be done by strengthening the importance of future considerations in current decision making; increasing the payoffs to those who allocate resources to the group; and inculcating the skills, values, attitudes, and knowledge that promote cooperative behavior (Axelrod, 1984). Because the allocation of resources to group interests as compared with individual interests is quite small, decision making with respect to this type of allocative problem would be based on limited information and a minimal search for new information. Designating the citizen as "Smith" and the resources allocated to group interests as "G," Margolis (1984) states,

> In a large society, both Smith's spending and the benefits from that spending will be microscopically small from a social point of view. It will often be hard, therefore, for Smith to "see" the ratio of benefit to cost directly in terms of his own act. However, it may be quite easy to estimate this ratio (in particular to compare this ratio across alternative ways of using G resources) in terms of a judgment about the ratio of aggregate benefits and costs of everyone in Smith's position behaving in a certain way. [p. 51]

G resources are not, according to Margolis, considered to benefit personally the individual providing the resources.

Another view of individuals' relationships to groups is that individuals naturally tend to be group oriented, with narrow self-interest being a learned behavior (Gilligan, 1982; Uhlaner, 1986a). If narrow self-interest is learned behavior, considerable variation would be expected in the extent to which it guides or limits contributions to collective action. Group leaders, through their manipulation of symbols and incentives, can foster and increase individuals' sense of reference-group membership. Members' awareness of the importance of particular political outcomes can be enhanced, and their willingness to contribute to obtaining those political results may be increased, thus turning a reference group into a political interest group. Group leaders can bargain with political leaders on behalf of members, promising the leaders political support from the group in return for political leaders' providing preferred political outcomes. Thus, both normative commitments and more tangible incentives fuel members' actions, enhancing the probability of attaining collective goods. Both policy benefits and "consumption" (participation) benefits can stimulate group members' activities. Uhlaner (1986a) summarizes this model as follows:

> Group elites provide their members or identifiers with incentives to vote in order to capture a collective benefit for the group through shifts in candidate positions. Leaders jockey for position in turnout space as candidates move in policy space; the leaders' payoffs consist of policies, while the candidates' payoffs consist of votes. The individual voters' payoffs consist of a small policy term and a large consumption benefit. [pp. 561–562]

Uhlaner in effect argues that the policy payoff from collective action need not be large for those engaging in it to perceive it as a benefit.

In another work, Uhlaner (1986b) argues that individuals may participate to obtain relational goods, which grow out of the relationship between two or more individuals. Benefits of this type include approval conferred by the individual's primary group, meeting others through engaging in political action, and reinforcement of a sense of belongingness or approval. The instrumental type of relational benefit depends on the actions of both the individual and at least one other, with the benefit conferred depending on the actions of both actors. An example provided by Uhlaner is the situation where "action by one's group bolsters the group's political identity and individual participation is necessary as an entry ticket to claim group identity" (p. 9). Protest marches by civil rights, environmental, or antinuclear groups and the mobilization of the Christian New Right in elections during the 1980s could be examples of political activities that would generate instrumental relational goods. The benefits obtained through participation in such politically oriented group activity include both increased identity with the group and increased influence over public policies and their implementation.

To summarize, several alternative types of benefits to be derived from collective action can be formulated, establishing the rationality of collective action. The perceived efficacy of individually based political action through more traditional mechanisms such as political parties and elections has declined; group-based political action can be fostered as a rational alternative mechanism for the expression and achievement of citizen demands.

## THE ROLE OF EDUCATION

An increased emphasis, in the educational system, on political socialization for political action through organized interest groups could foster increased levels of effective citizen participation. For example, as noted earlier, research indicates that one's sense of personal political effectiveness in influencing government officials (external political efficacy) is an important stimulus to participation. A social psychological explanation of participation, therefore, would suggest more emphasis on curriculum content that would enhance students' perceptions of citizens' abilities to influence government officials. The impact that individual participation channeled through groups can have on governmental decisions should be one focus, with several examples of such action being presented. The factors that contribute to group effectiveness in the political arena should be thoroughly examined.

The impact of interest groups on such aspects of the political process as agenda setting; the making of policy decisions (whether through the executive, legislative, or judicial branches of government); the writing and revising of regulations to carry out policies; and the implementation, enforcement, evaluation, and revision of policies should receive more emphasis in social studies and civics education. Acquisition of an understanding of how groups can affect policy outcomes and development of the skills and attitudes necessary for effective participation should be products of education for democratic citizenship. This can be done both through the content of school curricula and through the methods by which curriculum materials are presented in the classroom.

One of the distinguishing characteristics of modern industrial or industrializing democracies is the plethora of groups that are active in the public arena. A second feature is the diversity of these groups, whose interests promote a variety of points of view. A third characteristic is the relative ease with which such groups can be formed, given modern methods of mass communication and the constitutional guarantees of the right to organize and of freedom of speech. While adolescents are prone to flaunt their individuality and uniqueness, this is usually done by making contrast with peer groups or an older generation. The diversity of groups in a society, including those whose members are opposed to the processes or policies of dominant groups, provides evidence of how group participation can promote opportunities for the expression of different points of view.

Educators must emphasize, however, that group participation cannot replace individual participation. First, a group's effectiveness is usually related to the extent that *individuals* participate through formal membership and by making contributions of time, effort, and money. Groups provide an efficient mechanism for participation because an organization can convey to those making government decisions a sense of shared saliency and intensity of concern which may not register with decision makers if a set of individuals expresses the same views, each acting separately. Second, some forms of political action, such as voting and personally contacting public officials, are individual acts. While citizens may be mobilized by a group, they must perform these political acts as individuals. In effect, acting through groups adds to the participatory repertoire available to the individual and may increase the attention paid to the individual's concerns and the impact of those concerns on policy outcomes.

The utility of participation, both as an individual and through groups, can best be demonstrated by examining particular policies that have been created, modified, or completely revised as a function, at least in part, of political action by individuals or groups. The policies selected for examination should be either currently or recently in the news or so major that the average student would either be aware of them or could easily become acquainted with them. Also, the impact of these policies on the individual student's life should be quickly comprehensible by the student.

An example of the policy impact of participation through an organized group is provided by Mothers Against Drunk Driving (MADD). Angered by her daughter being killed by a drunken driver, one woman organized a group to lobby for stronger drunk driving laws in California. Her efforts to change that state's laws received national publicity and stimulated the organization of MADD chapters in other states. These groups have had significant success in stiffening state laws against drunk driving, thus demonstrating the effectiveness of working through organized groups, as opposed to working as a single individual acting alone, to bring about preferred policy changes.

## IMPLICATIONS OF HIGH LEVELS OF ORGANIZATIONAL ACTIVISM

High levels of political participation through special-interest groups are not an unmixed blessing. Olson (1982) has argued that, "on balance, special interest organizations and collusions reduce efficiency and aggregate income in societies in which they operate and make political life more devisive" (p. 47). Focusing on the activities of interest groups in redistributing income and thus their role as distributional coalitions, Olson asserts that "the accumulation of distributional coalitions increases the complexity of regulation, the role of government, and the complexity of understandings, and changes the direction of social evolution" (p. 74). He concludes that widespread activity by such organizations, which through lobbying and other political efforts limit governability and economic efficiency, has reduced economic growth and its social benefits among democracies that have not recently experienced a major shock that could destroy the power of these organizations. In a period of resource scarcity, the limiting effects of extensive and intensive political organization become even more corrosive, resulting in what Uslaner (1987) has referred to as the politics of destructive coalitions of minorities.

Public perceptions of institutionalized forms of political participation (e.g., partisan activity and elections) as relatively ineffective in influencing political decision making have increased. If we encourage participation through group activity that focuses on narrow economic interests or value-laden social issues whose advocates abjure negotiation, we contribute to the difficulties in achieving the political compromises usually necessary in a democratic society composed of many diverse interests and groups.

**REFERENCES**

Almond, G., & Verba, S. (1963). *The civic culture*. Princeton, NJ: Princeton University Press.

Axelrod, R. (1984). *The evolution of cooperation*. New York: Basic Books.

Axelrod, R. (1986). An evolutionary approach to norms. *American Political Science Review, 80*, 1095–1112.

Bachrach, P., & Baratz, M. (1962). Two faces of power. *American Political Science Review, 56*, 947–952.

Banfield, E. C. (1958). *The moral basis of a backward society*. Glencoe, IL: Free Press.

Barry, B. (1978). *Sociologists, economists, and democracy*. Chicago: University of Chicago Press.

Beck, P. A., & Jennings, M. K. (1979). Political periods and political participation. *American Political Science Review, 73*, 737–750.

Berry, J. (1977). *Lobbying for the people*. Princeton, NJ: Princeton University Press.

Berry, J. (1984). *The interest group society*. Boston: Little, Brown.

Button, C. B. (1974). Political education for minority groups. In R. Niemi and Associates (Eds.), *The politics of future citizens* (pp. 167–198). San Francisco: Jossey-Bass.

Cigler, A. J. (1986). From protest group to interest group: The making of the American agricultural movement. In A. J. Cigler & B. A. Loomis (Eds.), *Interest group politics* (pp. 46–69). Washington, DC: Congressional Quarterly Press.

Clark, P. B., & Wilson, J. Q. (1961). Incentive systems: A theory of organizations. *Administrative Science Quarterly, 6*, 219–266.

Conway, M. M. (1985). *Political participation in the United States*. Washington, DC: Congressional Quarterly Press.

Conway, M. M., Ahern, D., & Feldbaum, E. (1977). Instructional method, social characteristics, and children's support for the political regime. *Simulation and Games, 8*, 233–254.

Conway, M. M., Wyckoff, M. L., Feldbaum, E., & Ahern, D. (1982). The news media in children's political socialization. *Public Opinion Quarterly, 45*, 164–175.

Delli Carpini, M. X. (1986). *Stability and change in American politics*. New York: New York University Press.

Dennis, J. (1986). *Theories of turnout: An empirical comparison of alienationist and rationalist perspectives*. Paper presented at the meeting of the Midwest Political Science Association.

Downs, A. (1957). *An economic theory of democracy*. New York: Harper & Row.

Edelman, M. (1964). *The symbolic uses of politics*. Urbana, IL: University of Illinois Press.

Ferejohn, J. A., & Fiorina, M. P. (1974). The paradox of not voting: A decision theoretic analysis. *American Political Science Review, 68*, 525–536.

Frohlich, N., & Oppenheimer, J. A. (1984). Beyond economic man: Altruism, egalitarianism, and difference maximizing. *Journal of Conflict Resolution*, *28*, 3–24.

Frohlich, N., Oppenheimer, J. A., & Young, O. (1971). *Political leadership and collective goods*. Princeton, NJ: Princeton University Press.

Garson, G. D. (1978). *Group theories of politics* (Sage Library of Social Research, Vol. 61). Beverly Hills, CA: Sage Publications.

Gillespie, J., & Mehlinger, H. D. (1972). Teach about politics in the "real" world — the school. *Social Education, 36,* 598–603, 644.

Gilligan, C. (1982). *In a different voice*. Cambridge, MA: Harvard University Press.

Goodin, R., & Roberts, K. W. S. (1975). The ethical voter. *American Political Science Review, 69,* 525–536.

Hamilton, A., Jay, J., & Madison, J. (1981). *Federalist papers* (R. P. Fairfield, Ed.; 2nd ed.). Baltimore: Johns Hopkins University Press.

Hastie, R. (1984). A primer of information-processing theory for the political scientist. In R. R. Lau & D. O. Sears (Eds.), *Political cognition*. Hillsdale, NJ: Lawrence Erlbaum.

Jennings, M. K., & Niemi, R. (1974). *The political character of adolescence*. Princeton, NJ: Princeton University Press.

Jennings, M. K., & Niemi, R. (1981). *Generations and politics*. Princeton, NJ: Princeton University Press.

Margolis, H. (1984). *Selfishness, altruism, and rationality*. Cambridge, England: University of Cambridge Press.

Marwell, G., & Ames, R. E. (1979). Experiments on the provision of public goods: Part 1. Resources, interest, group size and the free rider problem. *American Journal of Sociology, 84,* 1335–1360.

Marwell, G., & Ames, R. E. (1980). Experiments on the provision of public goods: Part 2. Provision points, experiences, and the free rider problem. *American Journal of Sociology, 85,* 927–937.

Miller, W. E., Miller, A. H., & Schneider, E. J. (1980). *American National Election Studies data sourcebook, 1952–1978*. Cambridge, MA: Harvard University Press.

Moe, T. M. (1980). *The organization of interests*. Chicago: University of Chicago Press.

Mueller, D. C. (1983). *The political economy of growth*. New Haven, CT: Yale University Press.

Olson, M. (1965). *The logic of collective action*. Cambridge, MA: Harvard University Press.

Olson, M. (1982). *The rise and decline of nations*. New Haven, CT: Yale University Press.

Patrick, J. (1971). The impact of an experimental course, "American Political Behavior," on the knowledge, skills, and attitudes of secondary school students. *Social Education, 36,* 168–179.

Riker, W. H., & Ordeshook, P. S. (1973). *An introduction to positive political theory*. Englewood Cliffs, NJ: Prentice-Hall.

Rothman, S. (1960). Systematic political theory: Observations on the group approach. *American Political Science Review, 54,* 15–33.

Schlozman, K. L., & Tierney, J. T. (1986). *Organized interests in American democracy*. New York: Harper & Row.

Schoemaker, P. J. H. (1982). The expected utility model: Its variants, purposes, evidence, and limitations. *Journal of Economic Literature, 20*, 529–563.

Torney, J., Oppenheim, A. N., & Farnen, R. F. (1975). *Civic education in ten countries*. New York: John Wiley.

Uhlaner, C. J. (1986a). The impact of rational participation models on voting attitudes. *Political Psychology, 7*, 551–573.

Uhlaner, C. J. (1986b). *Relational goods and participation: Incorporating sociability into a theory of rational action.* Paper presented at the meeting of the International Society for Political Psychology, Amsterdam, The Netherlands.

U.S. Department of Commerce, Bureau of the Census. (1971, December). *Registration and voting in the election of 1970* (Current Population Reports, Series P-20, Vol. 228). Washington, DC: U.S. Government Printing Office.

U.S. Department of Commerce, Bureau of the Census. (1973, October). *Registration and voting in the election of 1972* (Current Population Reports, Series P-20, Vol. 253). Washington, DC: U.S. Government Printing Office.

U.S. Department of Commerce, Bureau of the Census. (1976, April). *Registration and voting in the election of 1974* (Current Population Reports, Series P-20, Vol. 293). Washington, DC: U.S. Government Printing Office.

U.S. Department of Commerce, Bureau of the Census. (1978a, March). *Registration and voting in the election of 1976* (Current Population Reports, Series P-20, Vol. 322). Washington, DC: U.S. Government Printing Office.

U.S. Department of Commerce, Bureau of the Census. (1978b, December). *Registration and voting in the election of 1978* (Current Population Reports, Series P-20, Vol. 332). Washington, DC: U.S. Government Printing Office.

U.S. Department of Commerce, Bureau of the Census. (1981, January). *Registration and voting in the election of 1980* (Current Population Reports, Series P-20, Vol. 359). Washington, DC: U.S. Government Printing Office.

U.S. Department of Commerce, Bureau of the Census. (1983, November). *Registration and voting in the election of 1982* (Current Population Reports, Series P-20, Vol. 383). Washington, DC: U.S. Government Printing Office.

U.S. Department of Commerce, Bureau of the Census. (1985, January). *Registration and voting in the election of 1984* (Current Population Reports, Series P-20, Vol. 397). Washington, DC: U.S. Government Printing Office.

U.S. Department of Commerce, Bureau of the Census. (1987, September). *Registration and voting in the election of 1986* (Current Population Reports, Series P-20, Vol. 414). Washington, DC: U.S. Government Printing Office.

Uslaner, E. M. (1987). *The decline of comity*. Paper presented at the meeting of the Midwest Political Science Association.

Walker, J. (1966). A critique of the elite theory of democracy. *American Political Science Review, 60*, 285–295.

Walker, J. L. (1983). The origins and maintenance of interest groups in America. *American Political Science Review, 77*, 390–406.

Wilson, G. K. (1981). *Interest groups in the United States*. Oxford, England: Clarendon Press.

# 16
## Educating Political Leaders in a Democracy

STANLEY A. RENSHON

The major contributions of political socialization theory and research have been in the area of citizenship development. It is now widely accepted that citizenship is as much a psychological/developmental concept as it is a legal/philosophical one. Moreover, the research of the last two decades has resulted in a genuine increase in our knowledge of the processes by which citizens learn about their political world, and the same holds true for the development of the attitudes, beliefs, and information that underlie the enactment of citizens' roles.

The attention paid to citizenship development is solidly anchored within the traditional concerns of democratic political theory, which has viewed informed, active citizens as the core ingredient of democratic process. This chapter, however, takes a somewhat different approach to the question of maintaining and developing democratic processes. I argue that political leadership is also a key — but neglected — element of democratic functioning, and that the traditional emphasis on citizenship development has overlooked the equally important opportunities and responsibilities for preparing political leaders for the exercise of power in a democracy.

Any discussion of leadership education must face two major barriers at the outset. First, the field of political leadership is in the early stages of its development (Paige, 1977). Therefore, the amount of conventional wisdom, which evolves in most fields as the by-product of several decades of systematic thinking and research, in this area is rather small. Second, the

This chapter was supported in part by grants to the author from the City University Faculty Research Award Program, the Earhart Foundation, and Tel Aviv University, which helped to support the conference at which an earlier version of this chapter was given. I wish to express my appreciation for that support and to the conference participants for their comments. Professor Barbara Kellerman provided a close reading, and her comments are also appreciated. Certain observations on decision making training are drawn from my role as long-term consultant to the New York City Department of Personnel's Top 40 program, a two-year training program for top-level public officials. That agency bears no responsibility for the views expressed in this chapter.

313

amount of theory and research linking political leadership studies with models and theories of political socialization is smaller still. Dennis (1968), in an early article on the major problems of political socialization theory, called elite socialization "one of the least developed areas of political social-ization" (p. 112). A recent review of political leadership and socialization studies (Renshon, 1989) reached similar conclusions.

One result of this is that a number of important theoretical questions, whose answers could anchor discussions of leadership education, have not yet been adequately addressed. For example, the concept of education implies the existence of a set of goals, but in leadership education the nature of these goals is far from clear. Do we aim for more technical competence, more commitment to democratic values, or better leadership skills? A skeptic might even ask whether it is possible to educate political leaders. This is not a cynical question. Individuals become political leaders well after they reach adulthood. By this time, many deeply rooted ways of doing things may have developed. It follows from these people's achieve-ment of leadership roles that at least some of their ways have proved successful. Given this situation, how much change could education, what-ever its goals, be reasonably expected to produce? From the standpoint of developmental theory and personal history, the question then arises as to whether leadership education isn't an oxymoron.

The difficulties go beyond these issues. Even if discussions of leader-ship education could draw on a longer research tradition and could affirm that leaders can, in fact, learn, the question of desirability would remain. The idea of preparing political leaders for the exercise of political power has deep historical roots in both Eastern and Western cultures (e.g., Kahn, 1967; Sonnino, 1970) and is widely practiced in contemporary political systems (Wilkenson, 1969). Nevertheless, the idea presents two major diffi-culties from the standpoint of traditional democratic theory. The first is the concern that leadership education is inherently "elitist" and therefore sus-pect. The second is that such education would result in an increase in the psychological and political distance between leaders and citizens and tend to encourage citizen passivity and erode accountability. Let us take a closer look at these issues.

## SOURCES OF AMBIVALENCE TOWARD LEADERSHIP PREPARATION

### Equality and Accountability Versus Elitism and Alienation

Preparation for political leadership today consists primarily of on-the-job training. This is somewhat of a paradox in a country in which the personal qualities and skills of leaders have become increasingly important to citizens in making electoral choices (Miller, Wattenberg, & Malanchuk, 1986). How, then, can we account for the high expectations with which citizens approach the evaluation of their leaders, and the lack of attention given to their development?

One set of answers is to be found in the nature of American political culture, which is ambivalent about the exercise of political power. Americans in general agree with Lord Action ("Power tends to corrupt and absolute power corrupts absolutely") and our constitutional system of checks and balances reflects this. We can also see evidence of this ambivalence in our frequently oppositional but nonetheless firmly held expectations for political leaders. On the one hand, we expect leaders to be strong, effective, and even combative. We cheer when our presidents "stand up" to the Russians, our allies, or others in general, and we dislike leaders who give the impression of weakness or, worse, irresoluteness. On the other hand, we expect our leaders to be above the fray, while at the same time keenly tracking the results of their efforts (or lack thereof) and apportioning our support accordingly. Given this situation, it is not surprising that the idea of systematic preparation for exercising political power has not made great inroads in our tradition. After all, one hardly wants to devote resources to making people more proficient at what the political culture views as problematic in the first place.

Another theme of American political culture relevant to our concerns here is that of equality. Our political culture is egalitarian in premise, if not fully so in fact. Central to this set of beliefs is the view that there should be no great distinctions between leaders and ordinary citizens. In a country where "every kid can be president," it is somewhat problematic to stress the "professionalization of politics." By doing so, one implies, if not directly states, that exercising political power is a specialized occupational skill. It further follows that every citizen (including those already in such positions) may not be temperamentally, psychologically, cognitively, or otherwise suitable for those roles. From this perspective, any specialized preparation is suspect on the grounds of real or potential elitism.

This argument reflects the concern that specialized preparation may increase the psychological distance already built into leader/citizen relations, with damaging results for the leader's identification with and ties to ordinary citizens. Leaders ordinarily have more contact with each other than with the average citizen, and as a result may be more likely to develop feelings of group solidarity with their peers. Fostering such differences in experience, perspective, or psychology, it is feared, may lead those in power to become less responsive. It is at this point that the wish to have more able, competent leaders runs up against the fear of making them more so.

These concerns are not baseless. The possession of special qualities, information, perspectives, and so forth is frequently used to justify leadership. On the other hand, claims of special knowledge by leaders must ultimately be understandable and make sense to those who are going to pass final electoral judgment on them. Being serious about preparing leaders for power does not preclude them from trying to justify their decisions on these grounds, but neither does it preclude citizens from registering their concluding assessment of the results.

## Fatalism and Distrust

Concern with problems stemming from issues of equality and accountability are not the only aspects of American political culture that inhibit leadership preparation. Among the characteristics that run pervasively throughout our political culture in the present period are a sense of fatalism, coupled with a diminished feeling of trust in institutions and leaders. The sense of fatalism is evident in some of our political aphorisms, such as, "You can't fight city hall" or, "There are only two things in life that are certain — death and taxes." As our society grows larger and more differentiated, the relationship between individual and institutional efforts and their effects grows more attenuated. Moreover, as our social problems become more complex, there is less confidence that real solutions can or will be found. Given these feelings, leadership preparation may be seen more as futile than dangerous.

As noted, ambivalence about political power and those who exercise it has deep roots in American political culture. The decline in overt political trust within the American electorate in the period between 1964 and 1970 has been well documented (Miller, 1974), and it has shown only marginal improvement in the decade since, in spite of Ronald Reagan, who retained a substantial measure of public support during most of his presidency. These two aspects (fatalism and distrust) of our relationship with those in power have led to an emphasis in our democracy on getting rid of leaders whom we perceive as inadequate in some way (Miller & Wattenberg, 1985). The problem with this process, however, is that it is *post hoc* and thus requires painful political experience as a precondition for activation.

This has led to renewed attention to the importance of political campaigns, and especially the focus on character and leadership, as a method of protecting citizens from inadequate leaders. There are many reasons why this is a less-than-satisfactory method of insuring that those who are most suitable are selected. Among the problems are

1. The relatively short time in campaigns during which attention is acutely focused on the candidates
2. The increasing skill of candidates and their advisors in shaping what is known of leaders

3. The question of whether the skills displayed during the campaign are relevant to performing well in the role
4. The fact that discussions of a candidate's general stands on the issues may not be good predictors of how she or he might handle an issue in a particular context (novel issues/situations may also arise)
5. The number of candidates in many primary contests and the resulting shortness of time available to assess the final candidates
6. The attention, interest, and ability of the public in sorting through all of the preceding factors

Because of these factors, the use of elections for assessing skills, capacities, and functioning relevant to leadership roles is imperfect at best.

## THE VALUE OF EXPERIENCE AND SUCCESS

The importance of electoral success in our system leads to some difficult issues in leadership development. There is a presumption of competence in success, especially when repeated. Isn't there good reason to believe that political success indicates that political learning has and will take place? Certainly it is a fact of political life that leaders who do not master their roles to some degree will not acquire much on-the-job experience. But there is also something to be said for this position from a more theoretical view. Political leaders are called upon to perform in ways that can be only slightly anticipated by earlier socialization. Most leadership skills are developed or refined within the context of adulthood, not childhood, which makes learning by experience, rather than by instruction, a more important and legitimate source of leadership development.

There are, however, limitations to experience as the sole source of preparation for leaders. First, experience more often is a variable than a constant. Leaders differ with regard to the kind and range of experience they have, of course, but, equally important, they differ in how they understand it. One source of difficulty here is that decision contexts are frequently complex and ambiguous (Dror, 1986; George, 1980). This may lead, as Neustadt and May (1986) have argued, to decision makers drawing on inappropriate analogies because they have either misunderstood the "lessons" of past events or else failed to see that other equally plausible lessons might be extracted.

Other aspects of leadership life that tend to undercut the usefulness of experience are time pressures and workloads. Powerful political roles are time- and effort-intensive. Even if a leader's characteristic approach to governing is more passive than active (cf., Barber, 1985),[1] political reality exerts a certain pressure toward at least moderate investments of time and effort. Leadership culture frequently emphasizes "getting things done," and indeed there is much to do. Allies must be consulted, enemies considered, strategy planned, decisions made, and so on. These pressures provide little time for reflective thinking, even if the leader is so inclined.[2] Thus, one recent study of upper-level political officials in Washington, D.C. (Adams, 1978/79) found that one of their chief complaints was that they had very little time to think!

It is not to be expected that reflection alone will necessarily result in adequate policies. For some problems, there are no "good" solutions (Calabresi & Bobbitt, 1979). Even when there are, it must be emphasized that thorough thinking is an aspect of, but not synonymous with, good policy judgment. Furthermore, the quality of policy thinking must also be considered in the context of leadership skills. Good policy judgment is one thing; effective leadership, another; and good political judgment, yet another. Still, sustained, thoughtful attention to policy issues would seem to be one ingredient of improving policy judgments, and the lack of time for such activities is a cause for concern.

One paradox of good personal, political, and policy judgment is that, while all are crucial to leadership performance, our present campaign system does not adequately examine such matters. Only in extreme cases of poor judgment (e.g., Gary Hart's midcampaign challenge to reporters to follow him at the same time he was carrying on an affair) do such matters come to the fore. We are much more likely to ask for a candidate's policy positions than detailed information about their processes of policy thinking. In part, this misplaced focus reflects a lack of conventional wisdom regarding the factors associated with principled, thoughtful, and effective leadership, which could be more widely disseminated as a basis for public judgments. But it also reflects a current emphasis in public relations for showing the leader "in action." It is a rare political commercial that shows a candidate thinking, rather than doing. One reason for this is that action is frequently associated in the public imagery with being "on top of things." Furthermore, activity is equated with the leader both having a direction and taking it. These are powerful psychological statements in a society where there is no consensus regarding direction and where there are pervasive public fears about the loss of ability to influence events.

It is worth noting here that emphasis on action in leadership may influence recruitment processes in ways that downplay the importance of other leadership characteristics, in favor of aspiring leaders who appear energetic. Yet energy itself can be derived from very different sources, not all of them equally suitable as the foundation of leadership performance in a democracy. One source of political energy is a personal commitment to policy agendas. Leaders motivated by this commitment will invest enormous time and energy to push their policy initiatives. As an alternative, consider the leader whose enormous investments of time and energy come primarily from personal ambition, and for whom policy issues are secondary. In reality, most political leaders combine both personal and policy ambitions, but not in equal amounts. Focusing on activity without distinguishing between the two misses an important point.

At present, drawing such distinctions in evaluating leadership continues to be secondary to an emphasis on electoral success. As already noted, electoral success cannot be wholly dismissed as an indicator of previous and continuing learning of political skills. Still, some cautionary considerations are in order. Many political successes are the result of narrow but effective forms of political learning, in which the aspiring leader has become adept at "playing the system." One illustration of this can be found in the rise of campaign advisors, who set the general strategies of a campaign in terms of specific policies designed to send messages to distinct demographic groups and psychological types. Another illustration is the tendency of these political managers to micro-manage the candidate's presentation of self, and for candidates, with varying degrees of reservation, to allow it. One result is that, while citizens are given the impression they are seeing more of a candidate, they are in reality learning less. The gap between the real skills necessary to be an effective, productive leader and the information that modern campaigns increasingly present is widening.

There is another source of narrow political learning that is very highly associated with electoral and general political success, and that is powerful ambition. The functioning of personal ambition in political leaders is complex. The dilemma of political ambition is that it is both necessary and dangerous for political leaders. Without ambition, the long hours, great uncertainties, high risks, and mixed rewards in political life would hardly seem worthwhile. On the other hand, the very great degree of effort necessary to obtain powerful political positions almost guarantees that persons of small or more balanced levels of ambition will not make the attempt. There is nothing necessarily sinister about political leaders satisfying their needs for accomplishment and recognition through their political activities. The problem emerges when a leader's ambition is, to a substantial degree, a compensation for poor self-development, such that policy accomplishments are secondary to the main object of success, which is to make up for the leader's psychological deficits.

How is strong, compensation-based ambition related to leadership learning? One plausible answer is that high ambition will be associated with substantial political learning. Lasswell (1930), in his discussion of "political man," who is primarily oriented toward power, notes two basic characteristics of such persons which are relevant to our discussion here.

First, the expectations of such political persons will be focused on the historic and future possibilities regarding power, which is to say they will be alert to the environment of power, a precondition for learning. Second, Lasswell says, they will be sufficiently capable to acquire and supply the skills appropriate to their demands, which is to say that they will develop skills needed to obtain power. In short, the motivated pursuit of power leads to a similarly motivated effort to learn about it.

While we can suggest that compensatory ambition is coupled with political learning, it is also useful to consider its nature and scope. Strongly ambitious leaders who successfully develop political skills can rise to the top of our political order, but they often do not display flexibility and resourcefulness in exercising power (Barber, 1985; George & George, 1956). One problem is that compensatory ambition leads to disruptions of the cognitive processes, which in turn make the leader vulnerable to making faulty judgments. Richard Nixon's view, expressed clearly on the Watergate tapes, that "we have no friends," in spite of just having won a landslide election, suggests a frame of mind and feeling consistent with the actions that led to his resignation.

An important question, therefore, is not only whether a leader is successful, but how he or she has become so. The power of leadership in a democracy, as Neustadt (1960) points out, rests on the ability to persuade. This ability in turn reflects a capacity to develop and maintain relationships that are mutual (Erikson, 1956), not exploitative. This suggests that leadership development and education require more than politically strategic learning.

## DEVELOPMENTAL LINES AND POLITICAL CAREERS: CAN LEADERS LEARN?

This discussion regarding the preparation of adult leaders for positions of political responsibility is based on two premises. The first is that it is necessary; the second that it is possible. In this section, the focus is on the latter. In pursuing this discussion, I would like to distinguish among three related aspects of leadership functioning, each of which is relevant to adult political learning: (1) character, (2) cognitive frames (including personal/political belief systems) and operations, and (3) personal and political self-identity. In the discussion that follows I will trace the developmental lines of each of these layers, as well as their interrelationships.

I will not deal in this section with the more concrete, informational aspects of leadership role learning. Rather, given our interest in leadership preparation, I will be interested in the degree of accessibility of these more basic levels of psychological functioning. In order to link this discussion more directly to questions of leadership education, we must also distinguish between development and learning. The latter is reserved to note the relatively context-specific acquisition of information and approaches to political action. An example would be the appropriate time for a junior United States Senator to make a maiden speech. Development, on the other hand, refers to the integration of understandings that significantly alter the leader's ways of thinking and acting. These may take the form of either reversal or elaboration. The first can occur when a leader's non-confirming critical experience leads to a substantial change in the direction of a characteristic—for example, a leader who starts out political life as a liberal but, because of a related set of critical experiences, reverses belief system and becomes a conservative. A second example of development occurs when the leader's understanding of the interpersonal and political world deepens and becomes more highly elaborated, differentiated, and integrated.

Each aspect of psychological functioning noted above would also be linked with learning and development in different ways. For example, concrete information would seem to be the most tied to immediate experience and learning, cognitive frames and processes less so, and character least of all. On the other hand, immediate experience can play an important role in developmental processes. In the section that follows, I would like to distinguish these aspects of psychological functioning and briefly trace their development with specific reference to issues of continuity and change during political careers. We would then be in a better position to address more realistically the question of leadership education.

## Character

The nature of character and its relationship to political leadership has become an increasingly important theoretical and public question. Barber's prescient book, *Presidential Character*, first published in 1972, formulated some of the linkages whose consequences have increasingly become a matter of public concern. In the past decade, for example, "character issues" have emerged as a powerful force in American presidential campaigns (Miller et al., 1986; Renshon, 1989b).

Interestingly, the emergence of character as an important political concern has been paralleled by an increasing appreciation of its importance in clinical and psychoanalytic analysis. Freud discussed character briefly in three early papers written in 1916. In these papers, character difficulties were considered as one aspect of the more general problem of neurosis and were given no special role in his models of psychological functioning. Freud did distinguish several "character types," among them those who claimed special privileges as compensation for childhood deprivation, those "wrecked by success," and those whose oedipal intentions produce enormous guilt. Somewhat later, two of Freud's disciples, Karl Abraham and Otto Fenichel, added to this list the "obsessive-compulsive" character, and another analyst, Wilhelm Reich, investigated the nature of character as a completely defensive structure whose purpose was to check unconscious impulses. More recent analytic theorizing on character has expanded knowledge of the range of character types (e.g., borderline and narcissistic character disorders), but the focus has not necessarily been on the concept of character itself nor on character functioning in the non-disordered range.

Most clinical and political discussions still define character as a pattern of behavior that persists across time and situations. While accurate to a degree, this formulation does not adequately distinguish character from other psychological characteristics or processes, such as beliefs or even attitudes. Moreover, it defines character in terms of (some of) its operational properties, not its content. Theories of character and political leadership must be concerned with both, especially if we wish to draw any educational implications.

One way in which character differs from other psychological characteristics (e.g., beliefs and attitudes) is that it is not only enduring through time and across situations, but pervasive in impact on the psychological functioning of the individual. Beliefs, attitudes, and even neuroses typically represent only small parts of the total personality system. Character, on the other hand, stands at the center and core of the personality system and is the basic foundation on which other psychological structures and processes develop. It is deeply embedded in the most basic areas of psychological functioning, including the development of personality traits, interpersonal styles, and the content and operation of cognitive frames.

While these introductory comments tell us something about the nature of character, they do not precisely suggest the elements of which it consists. In my view, the foundation of character rests on two sets of fundamental elements. The first and most basic set of elements consists of the sense of effective capacity and the sense of self-esteem. The former develops from the experience of successfully applying self to circumstances. It reflects, when consolidated, a capacity to accomplish one's goals. The sense of self-esteem on the other hand, reflects one's fundamental experience of oneself — both on one's own and as reflected in the perceptions of others—as basically authentic and honorable. At issue here is not only *what* the person is able to accomplish, but *how* it is done. Most accomplishments are embedded in an interpersonal context, and one's sense of self-esteem is tied not only to personal achievements but to the relationships that were part of the process. The development of both the sense of effective capacity and self-esteem therefore are not only a matter of competence, but relatedness.

At the same time that these character elements are developing in relation to experience, a parallel set of cognitive frameworks is also evolving. These basic frameworks of assumption I term "character beliefs." The sense of effective capacity, for example, is part of several such beliefs, among them the assumption that initiatives are worth taking because experience confirms that success is a product of effort. Among the character beliefs that arise from the sense of self-esteem are assumptions regarding relatedness to others—for example, whether they can be trusted or will respond to overtures. At some point, these beliefs and the character elements that accompany them will coalesce into a personal and interpersonal style of dealing with the external world. This style becomes part of the leader's personal and political self.

The clinical literature on personality change that is most relevant to this level of psychological functioning suggests that it is neither quickly or easily achieved. But these findings need to be considered in the context of at least three caveats. First, the clinical literature almost always reports on patients with varying degrees of deficiency or disturbance in these areas. It is therefore not clear how persons who have fewer or less substantial deficiencies would behave. Second, even those who, to some degree, have not adequately consolidated these character elements can, nonetheless, become more elaborated, differentiated, and integrated. If this were not true, psychoanalysis and its many therapeutic variations would be unable to justify their clinical existence.

Third, it seems clear that changes in external circumstances can bring about changes at this level of functioning. Psychoanalytic work, for example, makes strong use of the disconfirming experience (for example, the analyst does not act according to the patient's transferential expectations) in facilitating change. We will present some evidence shortly from the second layer of psychological functioning (political beliefs and values) that reversals of political belief systems are possible in response to disconfirming political experiences.

Last, there is some evidence that political leaders can become aware of their own damaging patterns of behavior, even those that originate in the operation of character elements. For example, in discussing Wilson's reoccurring political difficulties, George and George (1956) note that "Wilson sensed the dangers implicit in his compulsive ambition" and made some "rudimentary effort of finding a means of protecting himself" (p. 321). Mazlish (1972), assessing the development of Richard Nixon over the proceeding decade, did note some changes:

> He has turned his problems and weaknesses into strengths. Racked by indecision, he has learned how to plan and contrive ahead of time. Faced with the constant need to test himself, he has shown real courage on a number of occasions. [p. 125]

One has to consider whether these changes constitute development, given what is now known about his post-election behavior. Still, both the Nixon and the Wilson examples suggest that leaders can become aware, perhaps with the help of trusted others (Colonel House in Wilson's case), of patterns of personally or politically damaging behavior.

Overall our analysis suggests that while development and even change are difficult at this level of psychological functioning, they cannot be ruled out. This in turn suggests that some context in which to systematically consider patterns of personally and politically damaging behavior might not only be useful, but possible. We will examine some implications of this in a later section.

## Cognitive Frames

The second layer of psychological organization and functioning contains primarily cognitive elements and processes. Cognitive frames include beliefs, values, schemas, and attitudes. For the most part cognitive frames are accessible to oneself (and others). Some parts of these frames, however, are more latent than manifest and therefore somewhat less accessible to the leader (although not necessarily to the professional observer).

There are several ways to analyze cognitive frames. One important focus of analysis is content. Obviously, what a leader believes will influence his or her political behavior. How to specifically conceptualize cognitive frames is a more open question. A number of frameworks of analyzing political belief systems are available (see, e.g., Inglehart, 1988; Lane, 1969; Putnam, 1973), but among the most useful is the "operational code" framework first developed by Leites (1951), revised and systematized by George (1969), and further developed by Holsti (1982) as the basis of a typology of leaders' cognitive frames.

Do the belief systems of political leaders develop in either of the two senses in which we have used that term? Evidence suggests the answer is yes. Johnson (1977) examined the operational code of former U.S. Senator

Frank Church at the time of his emergence in politics (1956) and again at mid-career (1972) and found evidence both of continuity and development. The latter was strongly related to changes in the international system, including the Vietnam conflict and a thaw in the cold war that brought about deep changes in his views on Russia and China.

The importance of disconfirming political experience in the development of belief systems is also illustrated by the case of Richard Nixon; after graduating from law school, Nixon went to Washington and briefly worked for the Office of Price Administration (OPA). Here is how he describes the changes:

> I came out of college more liberal than I am today. I became more conservative after my experience at OPA. I also became greatly disillusioned about the bureaucracy and about what the government could do because I saw the terrible paperwork that people had to go through. For the first time when I was in OPA, I saw that there were people in government who were not satisfied with merely interpreting the regulations, enforcing the law that Congress passed, but who actually had a passion to get into business and used their government jobs to that end. That set me to think a lot. [quoted in Mazlish, 1972, p. 58]

This is, of course, Nixon's view of what prompted him to change. It is instructive because it shows how old lessons and assumptions ran up against disconfirming experience and as a result were revised and replaced with new beliefs more consistent with that experience. A similar reevaluation may be seen in Ronald Reagan's political transformation. He went from being a founding member of Americans for Democratic Action to a conservative anti-communist at least in part because of his experience while president of the Screen Actors Guild during a time when an attempt was made by communist sympathizers to infiltrate it.

While content is clearly important, cognitive frames are not passive filing systems. In discussing character beliefs, we noted that cognitive frames develop from accumulated experience, which provides one possible avenue of development and change. However, the dynamic quality of cognitive frames is not only a function of their relationship to experience, but also to the affect that accompanies that experience. Cognitive frames therefore, will be selective in their screening functions not only because of their content, but because they are to some degree motivated.

The motivational relationship between cognitive frames and character elements is only one part of the operational side of the former. In addition to the perceptual screening of content, cognitive operations also reflect individual perceptual style. Some persons, for example, tend to see more details than whole configurations in viewing the world (Exner, 1986); in some persons perception is more heavily weighted toward stimulus properties, while other persons afford more weight to their own intrapsychic constructions (Witkin, Goodenough, & Karp, 1967), and so on. To these operational factors a third must be added, that of judgment heuristics. Judgment heuristics refer to the actual process of calculation that accompanies decisions. It includes cognitive content and the frame's related dynamic perceptual operations, but also involves the weighing of this information in relation to the problem at hand.

The amount of research on these aspects of leadership decision making is small but interesting. Glad (1983) reviewed Ronald Reagan's style of cognitive operations and suggested the important role that a few basic values, coupled with a tendency to see the world in somewhat global terms, played in his policy decisions. Neustadt and May (1986) have focused on the appropriateness of the analogies that political decision makers use in their policy thinking and have found many instances in which their use is questionable. Finally, Tversky and Kahneman (1981) have shown that the way a political problem is presented will lead to a change in a person's calculation and decision, even when the alternatives presented have exact numerical equivalence! Taken together, these studies suggest that judgment heuristics have an independent effect on political and policy decisions that goes beyond the content of the particular cognitive frame.

The role that these or other cognitive operations play in producing *better* political decisions is not always clear. One reason is that because specific definitions of improved outcomes are rare and difficult to formulate, research in political decision making (George, 1980; Janis, 1989; Janis & Mann, 1977) has focused on improving process, and inferred (to some degree correctly) that in doing so the decision outcome would be improved. A second reason is that the "best" decision for a particular issue must also be in harmony with several other requirements for being an effective political leader and decision maker, namely, building consensus and accommodating time/resource constraints (George, 1980). Still, it is hard to argue that (for example) using inappropriate analogies, failing to see patterns, or inadequately distinguishing what is known from what is unclear or presumed (Neustadt & May, 1986) will lead to better decisions.

Assuming for a moment that some form of examination by leaders of the cognitive operations they use in political and policy decision making would, on balance, be beneficial, the question arises as to how much can be accomplished in this area. Neustadt and May (1986) felt that the course they taught at the Kennedy School to mid- and upper-level government officials did effectively challenge how their students approached decision making. On the other hand, some aspects of cognitive routines are firmly anchored in the operation of character elements, and not so easily changed (Renshon, 1989a). It may prove easier to change *what* leaders think than it is to change *how* they think.

## Personal and Political Self-Identity

*Self-identity* is a term coined by Erikson (1968) to denote the successful integration of two aspects of the self, one's ego ideals and the unfolding sense of one's actual self within social reality. Ego ideals provide a set of internalized goals toward which the person strives and may be more or less conscious. The person's sense of himself or herself in the world is in turn dependent on both personal skills and traits and the repertoire of social roles available.

Successful self-identity requires the integration of a number of psychological structures and processes, including several we have discussed to this point. For example, self-identity would clearly be built in part on character elements and on cognitive frames (beliefs, values, etc.) and processing. But it would also include other aspects of psychological functioning we have not discussed here, such as the person's skills (intellectual, interpersonal, etc.) or character (personal and interpersonal) style.

However well it is psychologically integrated, self-identity must still operate in a real social world. This important point is often lost in discussions of the term. Personal skills become instrumental in relation to their effective impact on accomplishment. Or to put it another way, available social roles make differential use of personal skills.

The individual's selection from among the role domains available will have an impact that goes beyond the differential usefulness of skills. In selecting a particular role domain — political leadership, for example — one must also to some degree deal with that role's historical and contemporary ideals, norms of action, and role prescriptions. These are, like the individual, not fixed, but to some degree evolving.

If we look at the development of self-identity from the standpoint of our concern with preparing political leaders for power in a democracy, several points stand out. First, personal and political self-identity would seem to have separate developmental lines, at least initially, with the former preceding the latter. Second, the sense of political self-identity would become over time a substantial, even crucial, part of a political leader's overall self-identity. Third, an important part of the leader's political self-identity will evolve in relation to *contemporaneous* ideals, actions, and prescriptions, which means that effective leaders will to some degree be responsive to external circumstances. Let us briefly examine each of these points.

While both personal and political self-identity will develop in part out of character elements and cognitive operations and frames, it seems obvious that aspects of directly political (as opposed to politically relevant) self-identity will emerge somewhat later in the individual's life history. Merelman (1971) found, for example, that policy thinking tended to emerge in adolescence. For the political leader, the movement into politics as a career occurs even later. Barber (1985) defines this as the leader's first independent political success, which occurs when "the person moves from contemplation to responsible action and adopts a style. In most biographical accounts, this period stands out in stark clarity" (p. 7).

Not all aspects of the leader's political self-identity need emerge in early adulthood. Woodrow Wilson saw himself very early in his youth as a giver of laws and great political leader, and followed that ideal into the White House. In general, though, we would expect political self-identity to evolve more substantially during adulthood than childhood.

We can assume that leaders who have invested great personal and interpersonal resources in obtaining political leadership will substantially define their self-identity in relation to their professional identity. Practically speaking, this means that leaders with strong ambitions, having invested enormous resources in obtaining and practicing their roles, are likely to be intensely aware of and responsive to changes in the environment that affect their performance and tenure. At worst, this can lead to an emphasis on the skills of deception and the presentation of a "false self," which may nonetheless be politically expedient. On the other hand, an honest attempt to grapple with the dilemmas of leadership will lead to search for role and performance solutions that maintain a leader's sense of self-esteem and the integrity of his or her personal/political self-identity.

Finally, the fact that political self-identity develops in part out of the needs and situations of contemporaneous circumstances almost insures that it will evolve to some degree over time. Certainly, as a political leader rises through the layers of power and responsibility and enacts different roles, we can expect to see development and consolidation throughout mid adulthood and even beyond. A leader's response to these changing circumstances and their implications for self-identity and political performance would seem to be a useful topic for collective self-reflection.

## ISSUES IN THE EXERCISE OF POLITICAL POWER

A major difficulty with preparing persons for holding political power in the United States is simply that it isn't systematically done. For a variety of reasons noted in a previous section, in the United States, unlike in other Western democracies such as France and England, developing leaders and leadership skills is not viewed as an important issue for which a comprehensive, integrated policy approach must be developed. In the sections that follow I will suggest some preliminary considerations for developing such an approach.

## Concepts of Leadership

A crucial question we need to ask is, What do we want to prepare leaders for in a democracy? This is not answered easily. Hermann (1986) has described four views of the political leader, as a "pied piper," as a salesperson, as a puppet tossed on the winds of fate, and as a fire fighter. Each of these views of leaders presents us with quite different directions for leadership preparation. If we assume the first, our objective may be to desocialize any antidemocratic tendencies on the leader's part. If we assume the second, we may wish to concentrate our energies on educating citizens to be more intelligent "consumers" of leadership. If we assume the third, there will be little point in educating leaders, except perhaps to be more accepting of their fate. If we assume the last, we will want to equip our leaders with all the skills necessary to put out the many fires they will have to face. At some point, we will need to ask whether the purpose of leadership education is to prepare trained technicians, develop supportive authority figures, train policy experts, or perhaps something else altogether. We will have to ask not only what leaders do, if we are to think seriously about preparation, but what special capacities or talents political leadership in a democracy requires.

At present there is considerable disagreement about what political leadership entails. In a recent paper, Kellerman (1984) has noted at least 10 possibilities:

1. A focus on group process
2. Personality and its effects
3. The ability to induce compliance
4. The exercise of influence
5. Behavior
6. A form of persuasion
7. A power relationship
8. An instrument of goal achievement
9. A differentiated role
10. The initiation of structure

Burns (1987), meanwhile, distinguishes between two types of leaders: transactional and transformational. The former exchange policy rewards

for support (similar to the Easton & Dennis, 1969, notion of specific support), while the latter educate and transform both their followers and
themselves.

To these characterizations of leadership in democratic societies we can
add that leadership roles can be differentiated along formal structural
lines, as well as functional ones. We can distinguish executive, legislative,
and judicial roles, and we can further differentiate more specific role
constellations within these larger categories. Barber (1965), for example,
in studying state legislators, found four different legislative types who
combined particular motivations with particular styles of performance.
These were the advertiser, the spectator, the reluctant leader, and the
lawmaker. The various ways in which leadership can be viewed underscores some dilemmas of preparation. Do we prepare persons only for
formal roles, and, if so, how do we engender a variety of within-role
possibilities?

## Elements of the Leadership Process

A beginning in sorting through these difficulties can be made by
attempting to extract some basic elements of the leadership process from
various conceptualizations already advanced. Almost all definitions of political leadership include the premise that leaders exercise power, but they
leave unclear exactly what that means and, more particularly, how it is
done. Here I would like to propose two basic ingredients of the leadership
role in democracies. The first focuses on the *making of decisions* as a key
element in the exercise of political power, while the second emphasizes the
crucial importance of *relationships* in carrying them through. Before discussing each aspect in detail, I would like to make some general observations.

The emphasis on making decisions as a key ingredient of political
power is implied in many definitions of politics. Easton (1965) defined the
field as concerned with the authoritative allocation of scarce resources,
implying that decisions about these allocations are crucial. Even earlier,
Lasswell (1930) proposed that politics be defined as dealing with the questions of who gets what, again implying that decisions about these matters
are central to the understanding of the field. The modest contribution
advanced here is that making decisions is a fundamental element which
rests on both formal and functional grounds. It is elemental in a formal
sense because the right to decide on institutionalized leadership roles is
derived from statutory authority as well as historical precedent. It is elemental in a functional sense because every leadership role also contains

zones of decision discretion that are implied by the necessity of carrying out the leader's "formal" responsibilities.

Emphasizing relationships as a crucial element in the exercise of political power in democracies may seem somewhat odd at first. We think of relationships as belonging to the personal sphere of life, and the exercise of power as belonging to the more formal, public sphere. The argument advanced here is that the exercise of power is as much an interpersonal as it is a political process.

The importance of a leader's relationships has been recognized to some degree in previous research. Neustadt's (1960) argument that the essence of presidential power lies in persuasion underscores the importance of interpersonal processes. Similarly, recent analyses of President Reagan's political success (Greenstein, 1983; Jones, 1988) suggest that it was related to his administration's ability to develop and maintain good working relationships with key Washington power centers. The failure to accomplish this, incidentally, is frequently suggested as one reason why the Carter presidency floundered (Buchanan, 1987).

The psychological processes involved in relationships are complex (Greenberg & Mitchell, 1983), and those involved in exercise of political power are equally subject to them. Being in such a position guarantees that a leader will have numerous and varied functional relationships, including those with colleagues, protégés, opponents, supporters, and so on. Depending on the particular role constellation we are examining, these individuals may be above, below, or equal in formal status and power to the leader. It will also be true that each relationship (or set of relationships) will be characterized by differences in the degree of intimacy and trust, as well as in shared views and history.

Do these provisional statements regarding two essential features of leadership roles have implications for preparing individuals to exercise political power? To some extent, they do. In pointing out two basic components of leadership skill and performance, they identify areas that would benefit from consideration throughout the leader's career. Focusing on decision making as a key function of leadership points directly to the need to increase our knowledge about it, while at the same time improving the skills associated with it. Focusing on interpersonal relationships points to the need to have some mechanism by which those who exercise power can consider and reflect on the dilemmas involved in their varied and complex relationships. Let us now take a closer look at each element.

Making Decisions.    There is in the decision-making literature a gap between the general models we use and the actual processes they are meant to describe. As Allison (1971) has pointed out, there has been some utility over the years in viewing decision makers as "rational actors," able to make sophisticated inferences and calculations from complex and ambiguous data. On the other hand, in a classic article some years ago, Lindbloom (1959) described this model as the perfect description of what no one does.

In the process of reforming the comprehensive rationality model, researchers on political and other forms of decision making have developed more realistic descriptions of this process (George, 1980; Janis & Mann, 1977). They have also identified some personal, group, and structural factors that either inhibit or facilitate effective decision making. Among these are the role of defensive avoidance (Janis & Mann, 1977), the advantages and disadvantages of different ways of organizing staff functions relevant for decision making (George, 1975), and the problems involved in decision making by small groups (Janis, 1984). Important work would also include appreciation of the social attribution process (Nisbett & Ross, 1980) and the framing of decision questions and heuristics (Tversky & Kahneman, 1981).

Familiarizing political leaders with the results of this research would certainly be helpful in preparing leaders for their work, especially those in executive positions. Merely acquainting political leaders with these materials, however, is not likely to be enough. Educating leaders to make better decisions by exposing them solely to didactic courses or seminars is like trying to develop good psychoanalysts solely by having them read Freud.

What, then, do we want? Decision makers need periodic in-depth experiences that allow them not only to confront the dilemmas of their responsibilities, but to reflect on how they have approached them. This means gaining further appreciation of how they think, how and why they tended to weigh information as they do, and how their own values and motivations influence their decision-making processes. The need for this kind of self-knowledge among decision makers is well captured in the following comments of Saul Alinsky, who spent many years organizing radical reform. Here he is discussing political activists, but his point is equally applicable to other kinds of leaders:

> The one problem that the revolutionary cannot cope with by himself is that he must now and then have the opportunity to reflect and synthesize his thoughts. To gain that privacy in which to figure out what he is doing, why he is doing it, where he is going, what has been wrong with what he has done, and above all to see the relationships of all the episodes and acts as they tie into a general pattern [is extremely difficult]. [quoted in Paige, 1977, p. 201]

Alinsky suggests that, for most radicals, the most convenient and accessible time to begin this process is while the activist is in jail. One would hope that this undertaking could be accomplished in more congenial surroundings for those who would govern.

I suggest the term *guided self-reflection* for this process, to distinguish it from its psychotherapeutic counterparts, on the one hand, and more didactic methods, on the other. It would not be a psychotherapeutic process per se, since its direct purpose would not be to alleviate or resolve psychological conflict (although this might be a by-product). Even so, it would make use, in a modified way, of some analytic techniques that have developed over the past 60 years, to encourage the reflective process. It would not be purely didactic, since one focus would be to allow the decision maker to look inward, and not only to master a set of strategic skills taught directly by teacher to student. The process would be aimed at developing self-insight and knowledge connected with making public decisions, as well as increasing leaders' knowledge of the process itself.

This is not to say that decision making can ever be a totally transparent activity. Allison (1971) began his classic book on the Cuban missile crisis by quoting John F. Kennedy's observation that "the essence of ultimate decision remains impenetrable to the observer—often, indeed, to the decider himself. . . . There will always be the dark and tangled stretches in the decision-making process—mysterious even to those who may be most intimately involved" (p. i).

The purpose of guided self-reflection would not (indeed, could not) be the impossible task of eliminating those stretches, but rather uncovering and tracing the connections within the leaders' policy thinking. This will require attention to at least two levels. The first would include how leaders gather and organize information relevant to solving particular problems. The second would look more closely at leaders' beliefs, assumptions, and inferences as they proceed through the process of reaching a decision.

Developing Relationships.    Exercising political power in a democracy is not only a matter of making the right choices, or even of designing and implementing policies that effectively carry them out. Attention also must be given to the political context, in which interpersonal relations play a crucial role. The basic currency of power is compliance, and its ultimate weapon is force. The basic ingredients of democratic political power are earned legitimacy and authority, which reflect certain kinds of relationships between leaders and others involved in the democratic process.

Why emphasize the interpersonal nature of political power? One reason is that it focuses attention on the processes that underlie the outcomes of leadership initiatives. Another is that it underscores the important point that psychological processes relevant to leadership (and politics more generally) are interpersonal as well as intrapsychic. But, equally important, given our concerns, is that it focuses attention on an area of conflict and dilemma for leaders that has not received adequate attention.

The interpersonal world of the leader, as noted, is complex because of developmental and institutional reasons. By the time a leader has reached adulthood, patterns of relating to people have developed. In broad terms, among other elements, the leader has developed views of whether people can be trusted or whether the world is a hospitable or hostile place. These character beliefs operate at the level of global assumptions, but they alone do not determine the nature of a leader's contemporaneous relationships. One reason is that relationships, like other aspects of individual functioning, generally become more differentiated throughout adulthood. So, while relationships reflect a person's basic assumptions, they frequently can include a more differentiated set of expectations as well as relationship-specific behavior. For example, a leader may not trust people in general, but may develop an expectation that certain classes of persons (e.g., large or small) are different. If this does not occur, the leader may still be able to develop trust with particular individuals, perhaps those who have devotedly served the leader over time.

Trust, of course, is only one element of relationships. Whatever the level of basic trust, the leader must still deal with a variety of people important to her or his personal, political, and policy needs. These people, in turn, will have their own personal, political, and policy motives, which will tend to increase the complexity of the leader's relationships as she or he gains in stature, visibility, and power. At the same time, the leader's own public and private sets of responsibilities and obligations will be developing. Martin Luther King and Jesse Jackson provide two among many illustrations of leaders who had to confront the dilemmas of continuing to speak for groups that had provided them with early support, even as they reached to expand the scope of their support.

### Role Conflicts and Ethical Dilemmas

The interpersonal complexities of leadership in a mass society are enormous. Public officials and political leaders must distinguish among their loyalties, obligations, and responsibilities to, among others, themselves, their superiors, their agencies, their professions (if they come from backgrounds that claim independent professional status and norms), "the public interest," and of course other relevant elected and appointed leaders. One result is "role strain" and "role conflict," but at base these dilemmas raise intense and difficult questions of character, values, policy goals, and, ultimately, personal and political ethics.

Political leaders are frequently required to make policy choices that affect themselves and others, often without time to reflect on all the values and considerations that went into them. One result may be that the process by which conflicting values, claims, and preferences have been weighed and decided will remain to some degree unresolved within the decision maker. The danger of this is that the full force of the conflictual elements may not be adequately addressed and will spill over, inappropriately, into other decisions.

Even if the political decision maker recognizes these problems, there may not be an adequate context in which they can be worked through. In working with groups of high-level city officials in a management development program, I found that many had faced similar dilemmas but had had no place to discuss and share their experience. For example, one participant, a black man, relayed a story of being asked by his superior to represent his agency's position at a public hearing for a policy to which he was intensely opposed and which he felt, on both policy and personal grounds, was detrimental to the community involved. That community was black and also this official's community of origin. Furthermore, the official felt that he was being asked to perform this role in part because of his race and his policy credentials. This conflict raised intense dilemmas for him, and he was at a loss as to where to turn for help. As he soon discovered, his predicament was not unusual, and once his story was on the table, many others in the class were able to discuss similar experiences. What had heretofore been private was transformed into a shared experience, with corresponding increases in consideration of the complex issues involved.

This story is meant to be both representative of a class of problems and illustrative of the benefits of having contexts where these issues can be raised and considered. Early socialization is not much help here. Political life is not easily lived by the Golden Rule, nor is any list of moral virtues likely to be helpful to leaders facing complex, frequently agonizing value trade-offs.

How can leadership education help to address these problems? One obvious way is to provide a role-distant forum in which leaders can grapple with these and related issues. Many of the dilemmas surrounding the exercise of power, where the leader must balance conflicting motives, values, information, and feelings, are recurring. These issues have a basis not only in ongoing responsibilities, but in developmental history. Both could profitably be explored in a neutral context.

Why would leaders be willing to undertake this somewhat difficult form of personal and political education? One reason is that their roles and their work are likely to be key elements in their sense of self and their developing political identity. Obtaining positions of policy or political leadership is labor-intensive work, to which leaders commit tremendous personal resources, not infrequently at the expense of other interests. Any-thing that improves their capacity in an area of significant personal invest-ment and importance is likely to gain at least a sympathetic hearing.

It is true that the higher one goes in policy or political hierarchies, the more one is likely to encounter strong ambition. But ambition is rarely the sole motivation of persons in those positions, and, even where it predomi-nates, it is frequently in the service of other needs. Like other roles, politi-cal or policy leadership positions reflect many motivations. One of these will be the need for accomplishment, not only in the sense of having obtained a position, but in doing something with it. These motivations are likely to be allies in the process of examining these personal, interpersonal, policy, and leadership dilemmas.

## FORMAL EDUCATION FOR LEADERSHIP DEVELOPMENT

Political socialization theory has not seriously addressed the issue of leadership development, for several reasons. First, the field began with, and to some degree retains, a focus on childhood processes. Second, the systematic examination of adulthood itself is a relatively recent phenome-non, and it is not entirely clear what aspects of adult theories and analyses are relevant to leadership development. Up to this point, I have offered some suggestions on elements of leadership development that it would appear useful to consider, but I have not yet discussed the scope of such education or what its infrastructure might be. It is to these two issues that I turn in this final section of the chapter.

### Scope

When we discuss leadership education, we must of necessity consider its possible scope. Is it meant only for the very highest levels of policy makers or political leaders, or are there other clientele to be found else-where? Since there has been so little discussion of systematic preparation for leadership positions in the United States, it is not surprising that our thinking has not progressed very far beyond the mention of Plato's philoso-pher king.

For Plato, the key to enlightened rule was knowledge, in particular a knowledge of philosophy. It is unlikely that Plato meant this in the narrow sense of acquiring a philosophy, but rather in a larger sense consistent with our foregoing discussion regarding a leader's self-knowledge. Plato's discus-sion of this important concept is, however, somewhat limited in its applicability to present circumstances, for several reasons. First, the development of psychoanalytic and cognitive psychology has given us new tools with which to understand both psychological functioning and leadership performance. Second, while Plato's concept of philosopher kings is an intellectual antecedent of this discussion, he was concerned with the circumstances of a relatively small, relatively homogeneous society; our concern is with large, complex, heterogeneous societies. Third, Plato's discussion is focused on those who exercise power at the very pinnacle of society. We, on the other hand, must ask whether leadership development should properly be so limited.

One of the rare contemporary discussions of these issues is found in Paige (1977). He suggests that leadership development training would be particularly appropriate for "all successful candidates for national public office and to other leaders and citizens of national political prominence or promise" (p. 205). This suggestion goes some distance beyond Plato's idea; in considerably opening up access to the process, it tends to decrease the element of elitism involved in the undertaking. Several questions remain, however. Paige's suggestions appear to emphasize the national level. At the time of his discussion, he could not have anticipated the increasing importance of state governments in policy making (Osborne, 1988). Therefore, it would seem prudent to include the state level in any discussions of leadership development, and one might add here as a caution that local policy makers and leaders should not be automatically excluded, either. In many cases even local decisions can have large-scale impact.

Paige's (1977) suggestions for training seem to emphasize the importance of elected leaders, and this, too, raises several issues. The first is a functional one: Is it useful to focus solely on elected leaders? The only U.S. leaders who are elected at the national level are the president and members of Congress. Is leadership development to be limited primarily to legislators? In my view, this would be a mistake. Leadership development would of course include legislative roles, but there is a substantial degree of discretionary, independent policy and political power in many other roles. Certainly, we would not wish to exclude from consideration other functional policy-making roles in the federal, state, and perhaps local bureaucracies. Nor would we wish to exclude, on an a priori basis, judicial roles.

A second issue in Paige's (1977) emphasis on elected national officials is that of timing. Paige's discussion leaves the impression that leadership development is best undertaken *after* the leader has successfully been elected at the national level. In my view, the time to begin such education is not at the culmination of a political career, but at its beginning.

The ideal view of education for leadership development is that it is a learning process that continues throughout one's career. To be sure, we can speak of the general preparation of political leaders as taking place over the entire life cycle, beginning in childhood and progressing through primary, secondary, and college experiences, and so on. This is a broadly accurate reflection of the socialization histories of many (but not all) who rise to positions of policy making and political importance. But it is a debatable question whether, beyond the most general educational experiences, there should be comprehensive, special programs for leaders prior to the completion of undergraduate education.

There are several reasons for this concern. First, the further back one begins comprehensive leadership education, however that is defined, the more likely it will be that a gap will develop between leaders and citizens. Second, such a policy would have to confront the importance of having a wide-ranging general education as a basis for later, more specialized training. This dilemma can be seen most clearly in medical schools, which to date have required very specialized undergraduate training in the sciences, to the exclusion of other subjects. As sources of broadened judgment, these subjects are receiving increasing attention in the medical profession. Third, there is strong reason to believe that, while general anticipatory socialization to leadership roles may be valuable, it can not substitute for attention to leadership development once the person is actually attempting to gain or is in such a position.

Anticipatory socialization can provide a general approach to the dilemmas of exercising policy or political power, but many of the dilemmas that leaders face arise from the concrete circumstances of making decisions. It is, for example, one thing to favor policy values in the abstract, but it is quite another to have to decide among competing values. Moreover, one can never fully anticipate all the factors that might bear on any decision, or the ways in which circumstances may change over time. This is why political gaming, used as a learning exercise for leaders, can have important but only limited impact on how a leader might really decide, given a complex array of real circumstances. For these reasons, anticipatory socialization, however thorough, can never fully address the issues of exercising policy-making or political power.

These thoughts indicate that education for leadership development, in its specific sense, is the legitimate province of adult, role-related learning. But where in adulthood should such efforts be focused? Should they occur throughout adulthood? If so, how are they to be reconciled with the enormous demands on the leader's time and the equally strong pressures for accomplishment that underlie leadership culture?

One suggestion regarding timing comes from the work of adult development theorists, especially Levinson (1978). Levinson found in his research on adult men that the adult life cycle could be characterized by attempts to build stable life structures, in which the person's aspirations and skills would find a place within the range of possibilities extant in society. Since no single life structure could contain all of these aspirations and skills simultaneously, and since the nature of these elements themselves underwent change, Levinson discovered that each stable life structure was the product of changes, in some cases changes involving the transformation of previous life structures. These transitions occurred to some degree in all of Levinson's subjects, in their twenties, thirties, forties, and fifties. The common thread was that the individual, to a greater or lesser degree, began to question aspects of the life structure already established. This suggests the possibility that education for leadership development should attempt to take advantage of these apparently natural (within our culture, at least) developmental periods of questioning and consolidation.

The point of focus should obviously be the individual's entry into policy-making or leadership roles. Among the many important questions that could be raised at this stage of development are, What values and ambitions does this individual begin with? How do these first experiences in the role affect him or her? As the policy maker moves upward in the organizational hierarchy, the focus would include the consideration of lessons learned and changes in values and beliefs as a result of experience, as well as a contemporaneous focus on specific role-related skills appropriate to new levels of expectation and performance.

## Infrastructure

Under whose auspices would such programs be developed? Several possibilities are available. Paige (1977) has suggested a national institute for developing and training political leaders, which would offer "research, seminars, tutorials, lectures and travel-study" (p. 205). Until such time as an institute can be created, he suggests that departments of political science and other university-based entities take the lead in developing such programs.

To some degree a university-based infrastructure has already begun to emerge. Schools of public policy or administration have developed training components in their curricula for those who exercise policy-making power. In addition, research institutions such as the Rand Corporation and universities such as Harvard, MIT, and the University of Chicago have run or are currently operating a variety of in-service or preservice programs.

These vary in their content, but a number generally stress the development of analytic skills for the policy maker. Unfortunately (from my perspective), such training emphasizes "management science," or the specific methods of cost/benefit analysis. This highlights the so-called objective tools of analyzing "out there," without giving sufficient attention to the development and integration of decision makers' understanding of the psychological processes, beliefs, and values that underlie the stands they take in the policy-making or political process.

Universities are not the only institutions plausibly concerned with and potentially able to provide education for leadership development. Schmidt (1960) reports the results of a collaboration between the state Democratic and Republican political parties and the University of California, in this area. Topics included "Leadership and the Discussion Process" and "Parliamentary Procedures and Political Parties," which are somewhat far afield from the areas developed in this chapter. Nonetheless, the experience did leave Schmidt with the impression that such an undertaking was both possible and worthwhile. It is unfortunate that this experiment remains the exception and not the rule.

Political parties have also provided programs of campaign and issue development for candidates, as well as orientation sessions for newly elected officials. In general, though, the contributions of the political parties to education for leadership development are short term and strategic. Political parties could undertake more effective, professional rather than partisan socialization of their leadership. To do so, they would have to look beyond winning the next election and move instead toward a comprehensive, long-term approach. To some degree, given the public's concern with issues of competence and character, this would seem to have potential for long-lasting strategic benefit for the political parties, but whether such an attitude can be established remains an open question.

Another set of institutional prospects for developing programs of leadership education are the various professional associations whose members exercise policy-making or political power. An example of this would be the National Governor's Association (NGA), which provides a number of policy and other support services to the nation's governors. There is no doubt that a substantial amount of informal socialization goes on at the various regional and national meetings of the association, which are attended by the nation's governors, and the NGA is also instrumental in sponsoring policy debates among the governors. Further, the association has taken some preliminary steps in the directions discussed in this chapter, through the publication of a handbook for new governors (NGA, 1978) and of a book of reflections of former governors on holding that position (NGA, 1981). It is not an enormous conceptual step to move from the concerns that these publications represent to providing the kinds of leadership development issues we have been discussing.

## CONCLUSION

I asked at one point in this chapter why leaders should be willing to undertake the kind of professional education we have been discussing. A similar question could be asked of us as citizens: Why should we support programs for developing leadership skills? The answer is that public support for leadership development is a matter of citizen self-interest. In a complex, interdependent world, where difficult policy problems cannot always be solved, much less anticipated, we are increasingly dependent on the character, good judgment, and competence of our leaders. Our current laissez-faire approach to leadership development is consistent with our democratic mythology, for example, the assumption that "every child can become president." As an expression of our idealistic aspirations for equality of leadership opportunity and access, this aphorism has considerable ethical and substantive weight. But, as a comment on the universal availability of the complex cognitive, emotional, and character traits essential to effective policy making and political leadership in a democratic society, it is certainly not the case.

The fact that political leaders or policy makers require special skills and capacities does not lend itself well to equal-opportunity arguments, but this does not necessarily make their pursuit antidemocratic. There is research to suggest that leaders tend to be more supportive of democratic values than are citizens in general (Sniderman, 1975), but of course one could argue that these commitments in principle may not hold in practice. Regardless, those who express concerns about elitism must also address the crucial issues of competence and capacity.

Above all, we need to look at the development of policy makers and political leaders as a *policy issue*, that is, as an important national problem that requires a comprehensive, integrated approach. We need to think through the problems of leadership development in a way that takes into account the skills and capacities necessary for service in a wide range of important roles in our society, where discretion and judgment are key ingredients. In addition, while placing our efforts into developing policy, we also need to invest resources in developing the people who will be responsible for them. None of this will happen easily or quickly, but the present patchwork of leadership development programs insures gaps between what is needed and obtained. Democracies not only deserve better, they require it.

## NOTES

1. There is a paradox in Barber's (1985) passive-positive presidential type, whom Barber asserts does not invest enormous energy in exercising political power. It lies in the fact that, while such a person may not invest a lot of emotional energy in exercising power, the nature of the contemporary American presidency almost guarantees that such a person must invest heavily in order to obtain it. Thus, Ronald Reagan, whom Barber characterizes as a passive investor in exercising power in the presidency (and this would appear to be borne out by the Tower Commission report on the Iran-Contra Affair), nonetheless undertook a grueling campaign for the office, which required enormous investment.

2. The problem of busy lives raises a practical issue for leadership development, namely, when there will be time for it. The higher in office decision makers go, the more demands there are on their time. Many efforts to provide systematic, developmental experience, therefore, must contend with continuing operational responsibilities. The problem is most likely to be acute with the higher-level decision makers and less so as one goes down the operational hierarchy. For these and other reasons, entry-level and mid-career developmental efforts are likely to have some advantages. Having said this, it is important to keep in mind that treating the issue of leadership development seriously, as it deserves to be, will require more attention to very senior decision makers, too.

## REFERENCES

Adams, B. (1978/1979). The limits of muddling through: Does anyone in Washington really think anymore? *Public Administration Review, 22,* 35–43.

Allison, G. T. (1971). *Essence of decision: Explaining the Cuban missile crisis.* Boston: Little, Brown.

Barber, J. D. (1965). *The lawmakers.* New Haven, CT: Yale University Press.

Barber, J. D. (1985). *Presidential character* (3rd ed.). Englewood Cliffs, NJ: Prentice-Hall.

Browning, R. P., & Jacob, H. E. (1964). Power motivation and the political personality. *Public Opinion Quarterly, 28,* 75–90.

Buchanan, B. (1987). *The citizen's presidency.* Washington, DC: Congressional Quarterly Press.

Burns, J. M. (1978). *Leadership.* New York: Harper & Row.

Calabresi, G., & Bobbitt, P. (1979). *Tragic choices.* New York: Norton.

Dennis, J. (1968). Major problems of political socialization research. *Midwest Journal of Political Science, 12,* 85–114.

Dror, Y. (1967). The improvement of leadership in developing countries. *Civilisations, 112,* 72–79.

Dror, Y. (1986). *Policymaking under adversity.* New Brunswick, NJ: Transaction Books.

Easton, D. (1965). *A systems analysis of political life.* New York: John Wiley.

Easton, D., & Dennis, J. (1969). *Children and the political system*. New York: McGraw-Hill.

Erikson, E. (1956). The problem of ego identity. *Journal of the American Psychoanalytic Association, 4*, 56–121.

Erikson, E. (1958). *Young man Luther*. New York: Norton.

Erikson, E. (1969). *Gandhi's truth*. New York: Norton.

Exner, J. E. (1986). *The Rorschach: A comprehensive system. Volume I: Basic foundations* (2nd ed.). New York: John Wiley.

George, A. (1969). The "operational code" approach: A neglected approach to the study of political leaders and decision making. *International Studies Quarterly, 13*, 190–222.

George, A. (1975). *Towards a more soundly based foreign policy: Making better use of information* (Report to the Commission on the Organization of Government for the Conduct of Foreign Policy). Washington, DC: U.S. Government Printing Office.

George, A. (1980). *Presidential decision making in foreign policy: The effective use of information and advice*. Boulder, CO: Westview.

George, A., & George, J. (1956). *Woodrow Wilson and Colonel House: A personality study*. New York: John Day.

Glad, B. (1983). Black-and-white thinking: Ronald Reagan's approach to foreign policy. *Political Psychology, 4*, 33–76.

Greenberg, J. R., & Mitchell, S. A. (1983). *Object relations in psychoanalytic theory*. Cambridge, MA: Harvard University Press.

Greenstein, F. (1969). *Personality and politics*. Chicago: Markham.

Greenstein, F. (Ed.). (1983). *The Reagan presidency: An early assessment*. Baltimore, MD: Johns Hopkins University Press.

Hermann, M. G. (1986). Ingredients of leadership. In M. G. Hermann (Ed.), *Political psychology* (pp. 167–192). San Francisco: Jossey-Bass.

Holsti, O. R. (1982). The operational code approach: Problems and some solutions. In C. Jonsson (Ed.), *Cognitive dynamics and international politics* (pp. 75–90). New York: St. Martin's Press.

Hook, S. (1955). *The hero in history*. Boston: Beacon.

Inglehart, R. (1988). The renaissance of political culture. *American Political Science Review, 82*, 1203–1230.

Janis, I. (1984). *Victims of groupthink*. Boston: Houghton Mifflin.

Janis, I. (1989). *Crucial decisions: Leadership in policy making and crisis management*. New York: Free Press.

Janis, I., & Mann, L. (1977). *Decision making*. New York: Free Press.

Johnson, L. (1977). Operational codes and the prediction of leadership behavior: Frank Church at mid-career. In M. G. Hermann (Ed.), *A psychological examination of political leaders* (pp. 80–119). New York: Free Press.

Jones, C. O. (Ed.). (1988). *The Reagan legacy*. New York: Chatham.

Kahn, H. L. (1967). The education of a prince: The emperor learns his role. In A. Feuerwerker (Ed.), *Approaches to modern Chinese history* (pp. 15–44). Berkeley: University of California Press.

Kellerman, B. (1984). Leadership as a political act. In B. Kellerman (Ed.), *Political leadership: Multidisciplinary perspectives* (pp. 63–89). Englewood Cliffs, NJ: Prentice-Hall.

Lane, R. E. (1969). *Political thinking and consciousness*. New York: Markham.

Lasswell, H. D. (1930). *Psychopathology and politics*. Chicago: University of Chicago Press.

Leites, N. (1951). *The operational code of the Politburo*. New York: McGraw-Hill.

Levinson, D. J. (1978). *The seasons of a man's life*. New York: Knopf.

Lindblom, C. (1959). The science of muddling through. *Public Administration Review, 9*, 79–99.

March, J. G. (1978). Bounded rationality, ambiguity, and the engineering of choice. *Bell Journal of Economics, 9*, 587–608.

Markus, G. B. (1982). Political attitudes during an election year: A report on the 1980 NES panel study. *American Political Science Review, 76*, 538–560.

Mazlish, B. (1972). *In search of Nixon*. New York: Basic Books.

Merelman, R. M. (1971). The development of policy thinking in adolescence. *American Political Science Review, 65*, 1033–1047.

Miller, A. H. (1974). Trust in government 1964–70. *American Political Science Review, 68*, 951–972.

Miller, A. H., & Wattenberg, M. P. (1985). Throwing the rascals out: Policy and performance evaluations of presidential candidates 1952–1980. *American Political Science Review, 79*, 359–372.

Miller, A. H., Wattenberg, M. P., & Malanchuk, O. (1986). Schematic assessment of presidential candidates. *American Political Science Review, 80*, 521–540.

National Governors Asociation. (1978). *Governing the American states: A handbook for new governors*. Washington, DC: Center for Policy Research, National Governors Association.

National Governors Association. (1981). *Reflections on being governor*. Washington, DC: Center for Policy Research, National Governors Association.

Neustadt, R. (1960). *Presidential power: The politics of leadership from FDR to Carter*. New York: John Wiley.

Neustadt, R., & May, E. R. (1986). *Thinking in time: The uses of history for decision makers*. New York: Free Press.

Nisbett, R. E., & Ross, L. (1980). *Human inference: Strategies and shortcomings in social judgment*. Englewood Cliffs, NJ: Prentice-Hall.

Osborne, T. (1988). *Laboratories of democracy*. Cambridge, MA: MIT Press.

Paige, G. D. (1977). *The scientific study of political leadership*. New York: Free Press.

Patrick, J. J. (1977). Political socialization and political education in schools. In S. Renshon (Ed.), *Handbook of political socialization: Theory and research* (pp. 190–222). New York: Free Press.

Putnam, R. (1973). *The beliefs of politicians*. New Haven, CT: Yale University Press.

Renshon, S. A. (1989a). Psychological perspectives on adult development theory and the political socialization of leaders. In R. Sigel (Ed.), *Political learning in adulthood: A sourcebook of theory and research* (pp. 203–264). Chicago: University of Chicago Press.

Renshon, S. A. (1989b). Beneath the mask: The character issue in presidential campaigns. *Thesis, 1,* 22–35.

Schmidt, W. H. (1960). Developing a university bi-partisan political program. *Journal of Social Issues, 16,* 48–52.

Sniderman, P. M. (1975). *Personality and democratic politics.* Berkeley: University of California Press.

Sonnino, P. (Trans.). (1970). *Louis XIV: Memoires for the instruction of the Dauphin.* New York: Free Press.

Tversky, A., & Kahneman, D. (1981). The framing of decisions and the psychology of choice. *Science, 211,* 453–458.

Wilkenson, R. (Ed.). (1969). *Governing elites: Studies in training and selection.* New York: Oxford University Press.

Witkin, H., Goodenough, D. R., & Karp, S. A. (1967). Stability of cognitive style from childhood to young adulthood. *Journal of Personality and Social Psychology, 7,* 291–300.

**About the Contributors**

**Index**

# About the Contributors

DANIEL BAR-TAL received his Ph.D. in social psychology from the University of Pittsburgh in 1974. He is currently an Associate Professor at the School of Education, Tel Aviv University, where his major area of interest is the acquisition and change of political knowledge. Bar-Tal is the author of *Group Beliefs* (Springer-Verlag, 1989) and coeditor of *Social Psychology of Knowledge* (Cambridge University Press, 1988), *The Social Psychology of Intergroup Conflict* (Springer-Verlag, 1988), and *Stereotyping and Prejudice* (Springer-Verlag, 1989). He also has written numerous articles and chapters on the formation and change of political beliefs.

STEVEN H. CHAFFEE is Janet M. Peck Professor of International Communication at Stanford University. He was formerly a Vilas Research Professor of Journalism and Mass Communication at the University of Wisconsin — Madison. He has served as editor of the journal *Communication Research: An International Quarterly*. His books include *Political Communication: Issues and Strategies for Research* (Sage, 1975), *Television and Human Behavior* (coauthored with George Comstock and others; Columbia University Press, 1978), and *Handbook of Communication Science* (coedited with Charles Berger; Sage, 1987). He is a past president and Fellow of the International Communication Association.

M. MARGARET CONWAY is a Professor in the Department of Political Science at the University of Florida. She received her Ph.D. in political science from Indiana University in 1965. Her research focuses on mass political behavior, including participation and electoral behavior. Her most recent book is *Political Participation in the United States* (CQ Press, 1985). Professor Conway has also published extensively on the role of various agents of political socialization.

GORDON J. DIRENZO is Professor of Sociology at the University of Delaware in Newark. A certified social psychologist, he specializes in the fields of personality, social psychology, and social psychiatry. DiRenzo received his Ph.D. in sociology from the University of Notre Dame in 1963 and has done graduate and postgraduate work at Harvard, Columbia, and the University of Colorado. Among his publications of relevance to political socialization are *Personality and Society* (Ginn, 1986), "Socialization,

Personality, and Social Systems" in *The Annual Review of Sociology* (1977), and *Personality and Politics* (Doubleday, 1974).

ORIT ICHILOV is a Senior Lecturer of Sociology of Education at the School of Education, Tel Aviv University. She received her Ph.D. in sociology from the Graduate Center of the City University of New York in 1972. Her research has focused on political socialization, citizenship education, and youth subcultures in Israel. Ichilov is the author of *The Political World of Children and Adolescents* (1984, in Hebrew) and of many works that have been published in Israeli and international scientific journals.

REUVEN KAHANE is an Associate Professor in the Department of Sociology and Social Anthropology and the School of Education, Hebrew University in Jerusalem. He received his Ph.D. in sociology from the University of California, Berkeley in 1968. His research interests include the structural analysis of informal patterns of socialization, technological education, and the role of universities in the formation of elites in developing countries. He has published articles and books in these areas in Israel and in international scientific journals.

HENRY M. LEVIN is a Professor of Education, Affiliated Professor of Economics, and Director of the Center for Educational Research (CERAS) at Stanford University. He received his Ph.D. in economics from Rutgers University in 1966. Prior to his arrival at Stanford in 1968, he was on the economic research staff of the Brookings Institution in Washington, DC. Levin is a specialist in the economics of education and educational policy. His most recent publications address issues of worker participation and workplace democracy, as well as skill and educational requirements for changing work situations. These include *Schooling and Work in the Democratic State* (coauthored with Martin Conroy; Stanford University Press, 1985) and *Worker Cooperatives in America* (coedited with Robert Jackall; University of California Press, 1984).

ARNE LINDQUIST is a Senior Lecturer in the School of Education, Uppsala University, Sweden. He received his M.A. in education from Uppsala University in 1963. Lindquist is currently engaged in the study of the effects of secondary education upon the political socialization of Swedish adolescents.

RICHARD M. MERELMAN is a Professor of Political Science at the University of Wisconsin—Madison. He received his Ph.D. from Yale University in 1966. His recent publications on political socialization include "The Development of Political Activists" (coauthored with Gary King; *Social Science Quarterly*, 1986); "Role and Personality among Adolescent Political Activists" (*Youth and Society*, 1985); "Revitalizing Political Socialization," in Margaret Herman (Ed.), *Political Psychology* (Jossey-Bass, 1986); "Domination, Self-justification, and Self-doubt: Some Social-Psychological Considerations" (*Journal of Politics*, 1986); *Making Something of Our-selves: On Culture and Politics in the United States* (University of Califor-nia Press, 1984); and "On Culture and Politics in the United States: A Perspective from Structural Anthropology" (*British Journal of Political Sci-ence*, 1989).

LESTER W. MILBRATH is the Director of the Research Program in Envi-ronment and Society and Professor of both Political Science and Sociology at the State University of New York at Buffalo. Prior to coming to SUNY/ Buffalo in 1966, he served on the faculties of Northwestern University, Duke University, and the University of Tennessee. He was twice a Fulbright Scholar to Norway, in 1961–1962 and in 1972–1973. He has also been a visiting professor at Aarhus University in Denmark, and a visiting scholar at the Center for Resource and Environmental Studies at the Aus-tralian National University in Canberra. He was a visiting Fulbright Pro-fessor at National Taiwan University in Taipei in 1988. Milbrath's research has focused on lobbying, political and citizen participation in environmen-tal policy decisions, political beliefs, and environmental beliefs and values. He is the author of *The Washington Lobbyists* (1963), *Political Participa-tion* (Rand McNally, 1965, 1977), *The Politics of Environmental Policy* (Sage, 1975), *Environmentalists: Vanguard for a New Society* (SUNY Press, 1984), and *Envisioning a Sustainable Society: Learning Our Way Out* (SUNY Press, 1989).

RICHARD G. NIEMI is a Professor of Political Science, Distinguished Professor of Graduate Teaching, and Associate Dean for Graduate Studies at the University of Rochester. He received his Ph.D. from the University of Michigan in 1967. Niemi is the author of *How Family Members Perceive Each Other* (Yale University Press, 1974), coauthor (with M. Kent Jen-nings) of *Generations and Politics: A Panel Study of Young Adults and Their Parents* (Princeton University Press, 1981), and editor of and con-tributor to *The Politics of Future Citizens* (Jossey-Bass, 1974).

TAMAR RAPOPORT received her Ph.D. in the sociology of education from the Hebrew University in Jerusalem, where she is currently a Lectur-er at the School of Education and the School of Social Work. She is also a Research Associate at the National Council of Jewish Women's Research Institute for Innovation in Education. Her research interests include infor-mal educational organizations, the sociology of youth, and political and gender socialization. Her most recent articles in these areas were published in *Sociological Inquiry* (1988) and *Youth and Society* (1988). She is also the editor of *Patterns of Transition to Adulthood: The Israeli Case* (in Hebrew; Academon, 1988).

STANLEY A. RENSHON is an Associate Professor of Political Science at Lehman College and the Graduate School and University Center of the

City University of New York. At the Graduate Center he serves as coordinator of the interdisciplinary specialization in the psychology of political behavior, and as newly elected editor of the journal *Political Psychology*. He received his Ph.D. from the University of Pennsylvania, was an NIMH postdoctoral Fellow in Psychology and Politics, and has also had advanced training in clinical psychology. He is the author of *Psychological Needs and Political Behavior* (Free Press, 1974), editor of the *Handbook of Political Socialization: Theory and Research* (Free Press, 1977), and author of a forthcoming book entitled *The Psychological Assessment of Political Leaders*.

VIRGINIA SAPIRO is a Professor of Political Science and Women's Studies at the University of Wisconsin — Madison. She received her Ph.D. from the University of Michigan in 1976. Her research interests include the areas of political socialization, gender and politics, and the application of political psychology to policy questions. Sapiro is the author of *Women in American Society* (Mayfield, 1986), and *The Political Integration of Women: Roles, Socialization, and Politics* (University of Illinois Press, 1983).

LEONARD SAXE is a social psychologist and Co-director of Boston University's Center for Applied Social Science. He has served as a Fellow for the U.S. Congress Office of Technology Assessment and was a Fulbright lecturer at the University of Haifa in Israel. His work focuses on the use of scientific analysis in public policy making and the application of psychology to real life problems. Saxe is the author of several monographs for the U.S. Congress on the effectiveness and cost-benefit ratio of mental health interventions. He is also the coauthor (with Michael Fine) of *Social Experiments: Method for Design and Evaluation* (Sage, 1981) and has written numerous journal articles on social science methodology and problems.

DAVID O. SEARS is Professor of Psychology and Political Science, and Dean of the Social Sciences, at the University of California, Los Angeles. A graduate of Stanford University, he received his Ph.D. from Yale University in 1962 and has taught at UCLA since then. He has been a Visiting Professor at Harvard University and the University of California, Berkeley, a Guest Scholar at the Brookings Institute, a Guggenheim Fellow, and a Fellow at the Center for Advanced Study in the Behavioral Sciences. He has served on the review panel on social psychology for the National Science Foundation, on the Council of Representatives for the American Psychological Association, and on the Board of Overseers of the National Election Studies. His books include *Public Opinion* (with Robert E. Lane), *The Politics of Violence: The New Urban Blacks and the Watts Riots* (with Jack Citrin), *Tax Revolt: Something for Nothing in California, Political Cognition: The 19th Annual Carnegie Symposium on Cognition* (edited with Richard R. Lau), and *Social Psychology* (with various coauthors). He has published articles and book chapters on a wide variety of topics in social and political psychology, including attitude change, mass communications, ghetto riots, political socialization, voting behavior, and racism.

RINA SHAPIRA is a Professor of Sociology of Education at the School of Education and the Department of Sociology and Social Anthropology at Tel Aviv University. She is the Chairperson of the Unit of Sociology of Education and the Community at the School of Education. She received her Ph.D. from Columbia University in 1965. Shapira's research has focused on political culture, youth movements, and students' subcultures in Israel, as well as various aspects of education and the community. She is coauthor of *Political Culture in Israel* (with E. Etzioni-Halevey; Praeger, 1977), *Blue Shirt and White Collar* (with C. Adler, M. Lerner, and R. Peleg; 1979, in Hebrew), and *Who Is the Israeli Student?* (with E. Etzioni-Halevey; 1973, in Hebrew).

ROBERTA S. SIGEL is Professor of Political Science at Rutgers University. She received her Ph.D. in history and international relations from Clark University. Her research interests include political change and political behavior, with a special interest in political socialization of youth and adults. She is the author of *Adult Socialization to Politics: Constancy and Change* (University of Chicago Press, 1989), coauthor (with Marilyn Hoskin) of *The Political Involvement of Adolescents* (Rutgers University Press, 1981), and editor of *Learning About Politics* (Random House, 1970).

JUDITH TORNEY-PURTA is Professor of Human Development in the College of Education at the University of Maryland in College Park. A graduate of Stanford University, where she majored in psychology, she received her Ph.D. in Human Development from the University of Chicago. She is the coauthor (with Robert Hess) of *The Development of Political Attitudes in Children* (Aldine, 1967), an early book on political socialization. In 1975 she published a major cross-national survey on this topic, *Civic Education in Ten Countries: An Empirical Study* (Wiley). In her current research she is moving away from large-scale surveys to study political cognition in adolescents. Her chapters appear in collections on child development and education, and her research articles in periodicals such as *Human Development*.

ANDERS WESTHOLM is a Senior Research Associate for the Study of Power and Democracy in Sweden at Uppsala University, Sweden. He received his M.A. in political science from the University of Michigan in 1979. His recent publications on political socialization and political sociology more generally include "Measurement Errors in Causal Analysis of Panel Data: Attenuated Versus Inflated Relationships," in *Quality and Quantity* (1987) and two works coauthored with R. G. Niemi: "Youth Unemployment and Political Alienation," in *Youth and Society* (1986), and

"Issues, Parties, and Attitudinal Stability: A Comparative Study of Sweden and the United States," in *Electoral Studies* (1984). He is also coauthor of *Medborgarnas makt* [Citizen Power] (Carlssons, 1989).

SEUNG-MOCK YANG completed his Ph.D. in communication at Stanford University in 1988. He is a graduate of Seoul National University, where he also received an M.A. in communication, and holds an additional M.A. in communication from the State University of New York at Albany. He has coauthored articles, with William Gudykunst and Tsukasa Nishida, on cross-cultural comparisons of communication in *Communication Research* and *Human Communication Research*.

ABRAHAM YOGEV is an Associate Professor in the School of Education and the Department of Sociology and Anthropology at Tel Aviv University, and Chairman of the Department of Educational Sciences. He received his Ph.D. in sociology from the University of Wisconsin—Madison in 1976. His research has focused on the interrelationships among education, social stratification, and social change, especially in the less-developed countries. His recent publications are "Modernity and Ethnic Affiliations in Israeli Schools: A Dependence Approach" (*Ethnic and Racial Studies*, 1987); with coauthor Rina Shapira, "Ethnicity, Meritocracy, and Credentialism in Israel: Elaborating the Credential Society Thesis" (*Research in Social Stratification and Mobility*, 1987); and with coauthor H. Ayalon, "High School Attendance in a Sponsored Multi-ethnic System: The Case of Israel" (*Research in Sociology of Education and Socialization*, 1986).

# Index